"It is essential that as the World moves through the vario[us stages of the] pandemic that we do not lose sight of the intransigent prob[lems that beset so]ciety. *Contemporary Social Problems in the UK* returns our a[ttention to issues] that intersect communities with traumatic consequences. ... .g Dr Stanley has brought together several respected academics and practitioners who draw our attention to the theories, models and research that underpin debates concerning social problems. It also highlights the way these issues transcend political and administrative boundaries across health, social care, social security, housing, employment and criminal justice. *Contemporary Social Problems in the UK* provides essential reading for students and practitioners involved in social care, health, and criminal justice. As well as providing examples of 'real world' applications for students of Sociology, Psychology, and behavioural sciences."

Dr. Tony Gilbert, Associate Professor in the School of Health Professions, University of Plymouth, UK

"This text approaches a range of contemporary social issues and considers these within a number of frameworks where their differing manifestations are articulated, debated and contextualised against the backdrop of extant theoretical approaches and practice-based interventions. The text will be of value to both students and professionals across a range of disciplines."

Dr. Steve J. Hothersall, Head of Social Work, Mental Health and Learning Disability Education and Practice, Edge Hill University, UK

"Social Problems in the UK are of growing concern not only for academics, policy makers and social practitioners but also the general population. This new edited book from Selwyn Stanley takes the reader through contemporary social issues and illustrates a range of debates and theoretical concepts. For the social sciences, this is a must read for students of all levels, academics and researchers."

Dr. Martin Partridge, Senior Lecturer and Programme Lead for BA Social Care and Health, University of Wolverhampton, UK

"This book provides a comprehensive overview of contemporary social problems in areas that can often be overlooked in compact curricula, for example, substance misuse and homelessness. As such, this book is useful for modules in undergraduate and post graduate studies that explore sociology, criminology, applied social work practice and contemporary society. A useful text for the student on a range of important topics."

Dr. Karen D. Roscoe, Assistant Professor in Social Work, Coventry University, UK

Contemporary Social Problems in the UK

Social problems are endemic to all societies. The UK is no exception and is grappling with a plethora of issues including poverty, family breakdown, domestic violence, teenage pregnancy, child abuse and neglect, youth offending, alcohol and drug misuse, mental health issues, homelessness, and ethnic and religious discrimination. These problems have huge implications for the individual, the family unit and society at large, and take their toll on health, well-being, and community resources. They place an enormous amount of strain on government finances and the welfare state, and add to the burden on social institutions such as the National Health Service and the social work and criminal justice systems.

Contemporary Social Problems in the UK explores a wide range of social problems in the UK. Each social problem has been explored using a range of psychosocial theories to generate an understanding of various causal factors and to examine the linkages between different social problems. Government policy and legislation, remedial measures, preventive approaches, and strategies of intervention are also considered for each social problem that has been dealt with. Each chapter deals with a particular social problem and has been penned by an expert in that topic. The endeavour has been to provide a multi-dimensional overview of the social problem in a manner that is engaging and easy to read. The end-of-chapter content includes supplementary reading, useful topic related websites besides a quiz and individual/group activities to generate discussion and stimulate learning.

This informative yet accessible textbook will be an invaluable resource for instructors and students in the social sciences as well as professionals who work with people who experience some of these problems.

Selwyn Stanley is Senior Lecturer in Social Work at Edge Hill University, UK. He has published extensively in the areas of mental health, alcohol misuse, informal caregiving in chronic illness, and family life dynamics. He is the editor of *Social Problems in India: Perspectives for Intervention* (Allied Publishers, 2004) and *Social Work Education in Countries of the East: Issues & Challenges* (Nova Science, 2011). His research orientation is in quantitative methods and areas of research interest include stress, resilience, coping, well-being, and quality of life issues in different populations. His recent publications have explored occupational stress and its correlates in social work practitioners and students in India. He is currently involved in studies that look at family caregiving issues for people with cancer and children with learning disabilities.

Contemporary Social Problems in the UK

A Comprehensive Overview

Edited by Selwyn Stanley

Routledge
Taylor & Francis Group
LONDON AND NEW YORK

First published 2023
by Routledge
4 Park Square, Milton Park, Abingdon, Oxon OX14 4RN

and by Routledge
605 Third Avenue, New York, NY 10158

Routledge is an imprint of the Taylor & Francis Group, an Informa business

© 2023 selection and editorial matter, Selwyn Stanley; individual chapters, the contributors

The right of Selwyn Stanley to be identified as author of the editorial material, and of the authors for their individual chapters, has been asserted in accordance with sections 77 and 78 of the Copyright, Designs and Patents Act 1988.

All rights reserved. No part of this book may be reprinted or reproduced or utilised in any form or by any electronic, mechanical, or other means, now known or hereafter invented, including photocopying and recording, or in any information storage or retrieval system, without permission in writing from the publishers.

Trademark notice: Product or corporate names may be trademarks or registered trademarks, and are used only for identification and explanation without intent to infringe.

British Library Cataloguing-in-Publication Data
A catalogue record for this book is available from the British Library

Library of Congress Cataloging-in-Publication Data
Names: Stanley, Selwyn, 1961– editor.
Title: Contemporary social problems in the UK:
a comprehensive overview / edited by Selwyn Stanley.
Description: Abingdon, Oxon; New York, NY: Routledge, 2022. |
Includes bibliographical references and index.
Identifiers: LCCN 2022021204 (print) | LCCN 2022021205 (ebook) |
ISBN 9780367764203 (hardback) | ISBN 9780367764227 (paperback) |
ISBN 9781003166887 (ebook)
Subjects: LCSH: Great Britain—Social conditions—21st century. |
Social problems—Great Britain—History—21st century.
Classification: LCC HN390 .C66 2022 (print) |
LCC HN390 (ebook) | DDC 361.10941—dc23/eng/20220518
LC record available at https://lccn.loc.gov/2022021204
LC ebook record available at https://lccn.loc.gov/2022021205

ISBN: 978-0-367-76420-3 (hbk)
ISBN: 978-0-367-76422-7 (pbk)
ISBN: 978-1-003-16688-7 (ebk)

DOI: 10.4324/9781003166887

Typeset in Bembo
by codeMantra

Contents

List of figures	ix
List of tables	x
Notes on contributors	xi
Foreword	xv
Acknowledgements	xvii

1 **Social Problems: Exploring the Landscape**   1
SELWYN STANLEY

2 **Understanding and Making Sense of Social Problems**   15
WILL HAY

3 **Poverty: *the* social problem of all time?**   33
ELIZABETH RICHARDS

4 **Fractured families: causes and consequences of family breakdown**   58
AYOMIDE OLUSEYE AND AARON F. MVULA

5 **A domestic violence pandemic: outlining victim and perpetrator perspectives**   82
HELEN HOLMES

6 **Teenage pregnancy – a social problem or public health issue?**   101
RAJEEB KUMAR SAH AND RITU MAHENDRU

7 **Child abuse, child neglect and safeguarding children: an overview**   123
PENELOPE WELBOURNE

8 **Youth offending: nature, causes and implications**   147
SALLY-ANN ASHTON AND ANNA BUSSU

9 **Alcohol misuse: one too many?**   168
SELWYN STANLEY

10 **A Bitter Pill to Swallow: Exploring and Understanding Drug Misuse in the UK** 196
DARREN HILL AND PETRA SALISBURY

11 **Constructing and conceptualising suicide and self-harm** 217
STEVEN JONES AND RAJAN (TAJ) NATHAN

12 **Exploring Homelessness** 233
WILL HAY AND MIKE TAYLOR

13 **Multicultural societies: diversity, discrimination and social inclusion** 255
BERKELEY WILDE

Index 279

Figures

3.1	Trussell Trust emergency three-day food parcels 2008–2021	51
4.1	Percentage distribution of family structures in the UK	59
4.2	Key factors causing family breakdown	64
4.3	Family breakdown and lifecycle	68
6.1	Under-18 conception rates per 1,000 women, 1969–2018, England and Wales	103
6.2	Ten key factors of effective local strategies in addressing teenage pregnancy	114
9.1	The addiction cycle	170
9.2	Low-risk drinking guidelines	171
9.3	Conceptual causal model of alcohol consumption and health outcomes	173
9.4	Alcohol and the body	179
9.5	Alcohol impacts on a range of priorities	181
9.6	Estimated alcohol-related hospital admissions	182
9.7	Parental alcohol misuse	183
9.8	Evidence-based policy	187
10.1	Drug misuse in England and Wales: year ending March 2020 (ONS, 2021)	197
10.2	The stages of change (Prochaska & DiClemente, 1983)	208
13.1	Protected characteristics under the Equality Act	271

Tables

1.1	Potential social impacts of Brexit on women	8
1.2	Potential social impacts of Brexit on people with disabilities	8
1.3	Potential social impacts of Brexit on black and minority ethnic people	9
9.1	Alcohol attributed deaths in the UK	182
10.1	Positive and negative factors of stimulants, depressants, and hallucinogens	198
10.2	Legal classification of various drugs in the UK	199
10.3	Drug strategies in the UK	211

Contributors

Sally-Ann Ashton is a Chartered Psychologist (British Psychological Society) and a Research Scientist in the Texas Juvenile Crime Prevention Center. Her doctoral thesis (University of Huddersfield) explored the psychological and social risk factors associated with gang membership and group offending, with particular reference to desistance from crime. She is a two-time recipient of the National Gang Crime Research Center's Frederic Milton Thrasher Award for *Superior Accomplishments in Gang Research* (2017) and *Superior Accomplishments in Gang Training* (2020). Her research interests include violent youth offending, co-offending, gangs, child criminal exploitation, policing of vulnerable communities, psychopathy, and the development of psychologically informed interventions for justice-involved youth.

Anna Bussu is a Senior Lecturer and Programme Leader of Psychosocial Analysis of Offending Behaviour in the Department of Law and Criminology at Edge Hill University. During her *postdocs* (2009–2012) and assistant professorship at the University of Sassari (2012–2015), she collaborated on several international research projects. From 2015 to 2016, she worked at the Faculty of Psychology (University of Guayaquil, Ecuador) to implement her project on life skills and restorative practices. She is a Chartered Psychologist with the British Psychological Society (BPS). Anna's research interests include offending behaviour, risk and protective factors, restorative justice, and restorative practices.

Will Hay is a former probation officer and youth justice worker. He has worked on two major research projects: one conducted by Cambridge University into the maintenance of order in maximum security prisons; and the other a study of the work of family court advisors conducted by Hull University. He has published in both areas. Over the years, he has been active within the voluntary sector including spells as a trustee with Citizens Advice and the Devon Law Centre. He left Plymouth University in 2018, having taught social work there for over 20 years, with specialisation in criminal justice.

Darren Hill is a Reader in Social Work at Leeds Beckett University. Darren is a qualitative researcher who uses an ethnographic case study method; he favours direct observation, focus groups and interviews as data collection methods. Darren also contributes to Youth Work, Nursing and Mental Health awards through the inclusion of substance use-related teaching. Darren's professional background includes community social care experience within housing support, mental health, family support, and community drug treatment services.

Helen Holmes is a London-based, trained, and qualified psychoanalytic, forensic psychodynamic, family practitioner and integrative psychotherapist. Helen works in private practice alongside South London and Maudsley NHS Trust in the Eating Disorder Unit, and in a Psychosis unit as an individual and group therapist. In 2020, Helen's innovative book was published by Routledge, exploring pre- and perinatal foundations of religious development. Helen's other specialism is in adolescent self-harm and suicidality. She has led on a popular clinical research project at IOPPN in London and has written and taught psychology-related courses at LSE and Birkbeck colleges.

Steven Jones is a Professor of Mental Health and Director of International Health at Chester Medical School. He is an experienced clinician, educator and widely published researcher focusing on substance misuse, self-harm, suicide, and cognitive disorders including dementia. He has worked clinically with complex high-risk patients (and families) throughout his mental health career. In UK and India, he has worked with individuals following suicide attempts. Steve has been a consultant adviser/educator on many NHS Trust projects. His external roles include working as Adjunct Professor, Department of Clinical Psychology, MCHP, Manipal Academy of Higher Education, India; and Consultant Adviser of Youth Mental Health for World Awareness for Children in Trauma (WACIT).

Ritu Mahendru is a seasoned professional with 20 years of experience in promoting women's rights and preventing gender-based violence. She is a Research Associate at Canterbury Christ Church University. She has worked with UN agencies, INGOs, and government agencies providing policy and evaluation advise in Africa, Asia, and Europe. Her work has been published in peer-reviewed journals, book chapters, and project reports. She authored the book *Young People's Perceptions of Gender, Risk and AIDS: A Comparative Analysis of India and the UK*. Ritu is currently writing a book *Young Sikh Women and the Fundamentalist Project of Purity* to be published in 2023.

Aaron F. Mvula is a PhD scholar in the Faculty of Wellbeing, Education, and Language Studies (WELS) at The Open University Milton Keynes, UK. His dissertation explores the lived experiences of unmarried young fathers in rural Zambia. He is interested in children, young people, and families; violence against women and children; adolescent and sexual reproductive health; fatherhood and qualitative methods. Previously, Aaron worked as a part-time lecturer in social work: children and families at the University of Zambia. He also worked as a senior social worker under the University Teaching Hospital HIV and AIDS Programme (UTH-HAP) in Zambia.

Rajan (Taj) Nathan is a Consultant Forensic Psychiatrist and Director of Research at Cheshire and Wirral Partnership NHS Foundation Trust, Senior Research Fellow at University of Liverpool, Visiting Professor at University of Chester, Adjunct Professor at Liverpool John Moores University, and CRN-NWC Clinical Lead and Mental Health Specialty Lead at National Institute for Health Research. He has extensive experience of working in a wide variety of forensic and non-forensic mental health settings and as a medico-legal expert. Professor Nathan has undertaken extensive research including in the fields of risk, suicidal behaviour, and violence.

Ayomide Oluseye is a research expert in Sexual and Reproductive Health (SRH) topics, with a focus on low- and middle-income contexts. Her research interests include adolescent sexual and reproductive health, teenage pregnancy and motherhood, and gender analysis. She currently holds a postdoctoral fellowship position at the United Nations University, International Institute of Global Health in Malaysia. Prior to this, she worked as a consultant for The Open University and partnered with notable institutions such as The Royal College of Obstetricians and Gynaecologists (RCOG) and The Wellcome Trust Foundation on projects to improve women's health.

Elizabeth Richards is a Senior Lecturer in Social Sciences at Edge Hill University. Her research and teaching interests include the relationship between childhood, family, and the state in law and policy; child poverty; promoting equality for marginalised children and families; children and young peoples' rights; and children's health and well-being. She has published in the areas of childhood and migration and behaviour management of young children. She is currently researching changes to sex-education law and policy for primary aged children and collaborative methods of assessment for childhood studies students.

Rajeeb Kumar Sah is a Senior Lecturer in Public Health at the University of Huddersfield within the School of Human and Health Sciences. He is trained as a Medical Doctor and is an interdisciplinary researcher with particular interest in international aspects of health and education. His PhD study was about an ethnographic exploration of social and cultural factors affecting sexual lifestyles and relationships of Nepalese young people in the UK. His research interests include global public health, young people and social changes, sexual and reproductive health, social justice and inclusion, mental health and COVID-19 and health inequalities.

Petra Salisbury is a qualified Youth and Community Worker and later qualified in Social Work. Petra has 20 years practice experience in the substance use field, earlier working with young people and later within adult services. The latter part of her career was managing Harm Reduction and Needle Exchange services. Petra is currently a Lecturer at Leeds Beckett University primarily lecturing Youth and Community development students, both BA and MA. Petra also contributes to teaching across various degrees within the School of Health. Petra is currently working on her PhD, focussing on qualitative research around women and their drug use.

Mike Taylor is the Director (CEO) of a homelessness charity in a large city in the Southwest. The role involves him working with a board of trustees, managers, and staff to continue and develop its services. This includes developing partnerships with statutory and voluntary agencies, tendering for services, supporting work with landlords, Rough Sleeper strategies and housing support for refugees and other marginalised groups, along with developing its role as a provider of accommodation.

Penelope Welbourne is an Associate Professor of Social Work at Plymouth University. She has been an academic since 1999 and prior to this was a practitioner and manager in children's social care services in North and East London. Her research interests include children and families and adults who lack capacity. She is currently involved in research and publication concerning the use of research in social work and social care services, and co-production of research with experts by experience.

Berkeley Wilde has been working as an Equality, Diversity and Inclusion Researcher and Educator for three decades. A long-term human rights campaigner, his interests are in the social construction of gender and sexual orientation, identity, and politics. He has led national research projects into health inequalities, through the Department of Health. Berkeley has worked internationally, with non-governmental organisations based in Brussels including the European Union and European Parliament. He won the Ann Wood Award for making an outstanding contribution to Tackling Domestic Abuse (2016), and an Outstanding Contribution Award in the Bristol Diversity Awards (2020). He is the Founder and Executive Director of the Diversity Trust CIC.

Foreword

The Second World War revealed significant problems in British society. Deep wounds were found at home while the fight to combat the Nazi threat continued abroad. In 1942, Sir William Beveridge set out a plan to declare war on what he referred to as want, disease, ignorance, squalor, and idleness. The welfare state was thus born to tackle poverty, illness, poor education, poor housing, and unemployment.

In the early 2020s, the global COVID-19 pandemic similarly exposed the depth of social problems in the UK following successive attacks on the welfare state which has eroded the safety net it set out to provide. A new set of problems may have replaced the original five evils that Beveridge set out to combat, though recent evidence suggests that they have not disappeared entirely.

A decade of austerity since 2010 has had tragic social consequences. The increase in the number of people accessing food banks has been a visible sign of the resurgence of poverty; about 40% of children in the UK are living in poverty. In 2019, the United Nations Special Rapporteur on extreme poverty and human rights, Professor Philip Alston, reported on his visit to the UK, that government policies had resulted in the 'systemic immiseration' of a significant part of the UK population. In the world's fifth largest economy, income inequality has grown inexorably in the last decade and the gap between the richest and poorest in society has widened.

Inequalities in health have grown alongside the rise in income inequality. Life expectancy is more than 18 years lower for those living in the most deprived communities in contrast to the richest. COVID-19 has widened health inequalities by disproportionately affecting those in the most-deprived areas and people from ethnic minority backgrounds. As a result of the COVID-19 pandemic, life expectancy in England fell in 2020 for the first time since 2000. In 2021, the number of people on waiting lists for NHS treatment in England hit a record high. Sustained under-investment in the NHS is now visibly harming the nation's health.

While access to free education has significantly improved in the last 80 years, recent studies have found that literacy and numeracy levels among young people in England are among the lowest in developed economies. Pre-dating the pandemic, a squeeze on the budget for education has led many schools to face difficulties in providing even basic equipment. COVID-19 has now significantly disrupted education for many young people, with many still to return to school at the time of writing in early 2022. Our education system has a long way to go to produce critical thinkers who can see beyond social media influencers and can appreciate nuanced arguments. Such skills are urgently required in debates about social and other issues, which are becoming increasingly polarised.

Slum clearance programmes from the 1950s to 1970s improved post-war housing conditions, though the building of affordable council homes slowed and was reversed through the right-to-buy scheme in the 1980s. The building of new social housing has not kept pace with the demand for it and, with Housing Benefit now covering the rent of only the cheapest 30% of homes, there is a crisis in the availability of affordable housing. With rising rents, food, fuel, and other living costs, homelessness is becoming a growing problem again.

Although sustained low levels of unemployment suggest that the evil of 'idleness' has been banished, the reality for many people is precarious, low pay and temporary employment. The withdrawal of cheap EU labour following Brexit has led to shortages in key industries and has been accompanied by the rhetoric of creating a high-wage economy. The reality, though, is one of insecurity and poverty for many.

While it is clear that 20th-century evils remain, albeit in altered form, new ones have emerged in the 21st century. Climate change is perhaps the most significant concern for communities and populations across the globe at present. While it is having an immediate impact on some communities, forcing people out of their homes and creating mass migration in some parts of the world, others remain in a state of denial. The resulting reluctance of governments to take radical action to halt global warming is likely to exacerbate the crisis and create more fundamental problems for many years to come.

In the UK, we are experiencing an increasing prevalence of mental health problems; growing numbers of children and young people in need of safeguarding, care, and support; and an ageing population with an understaffed social care workforce to meet their needs. Social workers are faced with an increasing array of challenges, often caused by a complex interplay of social problems, though they often lack the resources they need to tackle them. Political decision-making around these issues is stymied by denial of the existence of social problems created or exacerbated by more than a decade of austerity, which has seen the removal of funding from many preventive services and the paring back of many other social care services.

In the absence of the political will to tackle these new social evils, it is important to ensure that social workers and other public and third sector workers are aware of the true nature and extent of social problems people face in the UK today. This is where this book comes in. It provides a critical overview of some key 'wicked' problems, with up-to-date data and insights, and suggestions for action. Chapters are written by experts in the field and Dr Selwyn Stanley has curated an accessible and vital guide to contemporary social problems in the UK. It deserves to be read by every practitioner to help equip them for the task ahead.

Martin Webber
Professor of Social Work
University of York
February 2022

Acknowledgements

Pulling this book together has been a mammoth task that would not have been possible but for the unstinted commitment of the authors and their arduous effort to develop the content for the various chapters contained within. I thank every single person for adhering to deadlines, chapter expectations, and publisher requirements. Thanks for putting up with the numerous emails and the constant back and forth of communication necessitated by our mutual desire to do the best for this venture. It's been a pleasure to collaborate with you all and a joy to see the finished product.

I acknowledge with gratitude the endorsements and feedback received from senior colleagues Tony Gilbert, Steve Hothersall, Karen Roscoe, and Martin Partridge. A very special thanks to Prof. Martin Webber in particular, for the foreword penned by him.

I thank Rebecca Brennan, Senior Publisher at Routledge for the initial feedback on several chapters and her helpful comments for improvement. To Chris Parry Editorial Assistant and the publishing team at Routledge, I owe a mountain of gratitude for their guidance in refining this publication.

Finally a word of thanks to the wife for keeping the coffee flowing and the daughter for staying out of my hair!

Thank you all.

Selwyn Stanley

1 Social Problems

Exploring the Landscape

Selwyn Stanley

Introduction

What do we call something that is experienced by large sections of society is aversive in nature and generates distress? Well, a social problem of course! Should we refer to them as social problems or social issues or social issues that are problematic? The matter is straightforward; while all social problems are social issues that need amelioration, the reverse is not always true. For instance, while crime as a social issue is certainly a problem to be addressed, the increase in cohabiting couples is a social issue that is not essentially considered to be a social problem in contemporary society. We have in this book preferred to use the term social problems more because of its predominant use in the sociology literature rather than for any other reason. The term *social problem* emerged in the 19th century; the social problem being the relationship between labour and capital (Schwartz, 1997). The term was later broadened to encompass a wide range of issues that were attributed to social 'pathology' and 'deviance.' Defining social problems is problematic and it has been observed that "there is no adequate definition of social problems within sociology, and there is not and never has been a sociology of social problems" (Spector and Kitsuse, 1977: 1).

Social Problems – the Nature of the Beast

Several authors have attempted to define social problems, and each has provided a different lens through which to view them. What then are the key features associated with our understanding of social problems?

1 They are experienced by large sections of society
   This has been a central theme for considering a social issue to be 'problematic' and has been considered by several authors in early conceptualisations of social problems (e.g., Fuller and Myers, 1941; Horton and Leslie, 1970). We will see through statistical evidence provided in this text how several issues be it poverty, substance misuse or domestic violence for instance are widely prevalent and have repercussions for masses of people.
2 They are viewed as deviation from acceptable social norms
   This criterion is a common element that features in the definition of a social problem offered by several sociologists (Merton and Nisbet, 1961; Eitzen and Zinn, 2000; Mahoney, 2003). This is often the case when certain ideals cherished by a society are violated. Crime for example while widely prevalent in all societies is undesirable and penalised through social institutions developed to combat its

DOI: 10.4324/9781003166887-1

various manifestations. While alcohol use is acceptable in many societies, crossing the threshold into the realm of misuse is frowned upon and brings immense hardships to people involved.

3 They generate distress

The experience of being affected by a particular social problem is unpleasant (Eitzen and Zinn, 2000) and viewed as adverse and undesirable by the individual or group within its radius of influence. It is accompanied by harmful consequences and has a debilitating influence on people. Family breakdown for instance is accompanied by traumatic experiences for people involved, particularly children.

4 Social problems limit human potential

The experience of poverty may limit the availability of opportunities and access to much needed resources and have wide-ranging consequences in terms of maximising one's potential. Child abuse has traumatic effects with lifelong consequences for those who have experienced it ranging from academic under-achievement and impact on employment later on.

5 The universality of social problems

All societies experience social problems; they however tend to vary by nature and extent. Some of them are common such as poverty or substance misuse but may differ in their extent and manifestation across societies. Many of them are unique to certain societies such as child labour or female infanticide which are not prevalent in western societies.

6 Social problems change and emerge over time

The advent of HIV/AIDS in the mid-1980s and the recent COVID-19 pandemic are examples of how health-related social problems affect societies the world over and are of fairly recent origin. The advancement of technology has given birth to cybercrime, a term unknown a few years ago.

7 They tend to be long-standing and persistent

Poverty and prostitution are examples of long-standing social problems that have become deeply entrenched in several societies in spite of concerted efforts for control and eradication. Parrillo (2002) suggests that this could be because of the interconnectivity between social problems or that someone benefits from their perpetuation.

8 The interdependence of social problems

Social problems tend to be multi-determined or multi-factorial in nature. There is a relationship between many social problems that often makes it difficult to unravel cause and effect. Substance misuse for instance may lead to ill health which, in turn, could limit employment, thereby perpetuating the poverty cycle. This interconnectivity is frequently the reason why it is difficult to eliminate them altogether.

9 Social problems have solutions.

Mahoney (2003) considers this to be a key characteristic of a social problem. This may appear to be a rather 'idealistic' contention as in the case of several issues that have been long-standing and pervasive such as poverty or prostitution. It is however possible to deal with or manage such issues if not eliminate them altogether.

10 They incur huge costs to society

Every society incurs huge costs, both direct and indirect, in taking efforts to eliminate or manage social problems that are experienced by large sections of its population. Enormous amounts of resources are pumped in to deal with housing issues, combat drug trafficking and misuse or alleviate poverty.

Contemporary societies are characterised by heterogeneity and diversity in terms of the sub-cultures, social hierarchies, and socio-economic classes that coexist within. This makes it almost impossible to arrive at an objective consensus regarding what constitutes a social problem, its causal factors, and approaches to remediation, as each group has its own subjective understanding, interpretation, and experience of it. Often there is a positioning of each social group as 'us' (ingroup) and 'them' (outgroup) vis-à-vis a particular social problem. For example, migrants may perceive their mobility to another country as legitimate in order to flee from political oppression or in search of a better quality of life, whereas they may be perceived by native habitants as people who take away welfare benefits and jobs that rightly belong to the locals. This then could put social groups in conflict and result in discriminatory attitudes and harassment of the perceived outgroup immigrants in this case.

The Development of Social Problems

Social constructionism is an approach that believes that people develop knowledge of the world in a social context, and that what we perceive as reality depends on shared assumptions of a particular event. Spector and Kitsuse (1977) use a social constructionist approach to discuss the development of social problems in relation to claims-making activities used by influential social groups. They suggest stages in the development of social problems and a natural history through which they evolve. It would be useful to briefly explore this now.

Stage 1: Emergence and Claims Making

A social problem emerges when an influential social entity such as policy makers, politicians, activists, or the media acknowledge the existence of an issue that merits concern owing to perceived public distress and seek remedial action. These influential groups indulge in campaigns and take other measures to influence public perceptions relating to the issue that causes concern. These influential groups engage in making claims relating to the 'adverse' or undesirable attributes of the phenomenon and heighten public concern through raising awareness about the ramifications of the issue. As various claims are made, this stage is referred to as the claims-making process. Not all efforts to turn a particular social issue into a social problem succeed and is determined to a large extent by the influential nature of the claim makers, the resources used to address the issue, and the emerging public perception relating to the social problem.

Stage 2: Legitimacy

In this stage, the social entity seeks to legitimise their claim with policy makers and the Government through advocacy, lobbying, and campaigns. Empirical evidence is offered in support of their claims and to legitimise them in the eyes of the government.

Stage 3: Renewed Claims Making

Two things can occur at this stage. First, there could be a positive response from the government and other social agencies accepting claims about this stage. However, this is likely to be rejected on the grounds that enough is not being done or strategies to deal with the problem are inadequate. Second, there could be an outright rejection of the claims, heightening tensions and resulting in disenchantment. Claims are then revised and re-asserted by the claim makers and fresh demands made for mitigation.

Stage 4: Development of Alternative Strategies

Despite renewed claims making, social change groups often conclude that the government and established interests are not responding adequately to their claims. Stage four is marked by claimants' "contention that it is no longer possible to 'work within the system' …" and then attempt to develop alternative institutions and strategies (Spector and Kitsuse, 1973: 156).

Social Problems, Social Policy, and the Welfare State

The emergence of the Welfare State dates back to 1601, when Poor Laws were put in force in the UK. However, it was the post-world war era in the 1940s and the publication of the Beveridge report in 1942 that the concept transformed into its current avatar. The report identified five major problems which prevented people from bettering themselves. They were want (caused by poverty), ignorance (caused by a lack of education), squalor (caused by poor housing), idleness (caused by a lack of jobs, or the ability to gain employment), and disease (caused by inadequate health care provision).

The recommendations were for a system that would be:

- comprehensive – cover all problems relating to poverty, from birth to death
- universal – available to all
- contributory – paid into from wages
- non-means tested – available to all, even if unable to pay
- compulsory – all workers were to contribute

BOX 1.1 ELIZABETHAN POOR LAW (1601)

It envisaged a compulsory poor rate to be levied on every parish and from property owners and the creation of 'overseers' of relief. Two types of relief were provided: **Outdoor relief:** the poor would be left in their own homes and would be given either a 'dole' of money on which to live or be given relief in kind such as clothes and food.

Indoor relief: the poor would be taken into the local alms house; the ill would be admitted to hospital; orphans were taken into orphanages; and the idle poor would be taken into the poorhouse or workhouse where they would be sent to work

Source: Victorianweb.org

The challenge of addressing the 'Five Giants' led to the establishment of the Welfare State under the then Labour Government. A key function of the Welfare State is to frame social policy and provide health and other services to cater to the needs of its citizens. The Welfare State upholds humanitarian principles based on Equality, Equal opportunity, Need, Freedom, and rights (Aravacik, 2018). Provision of a minimum income guarantee to individuals and families to facilitate the prevention of certain social risks, and to offer good living conditions to individuals in society through enunciation of measures of social welfare is also within the purview of the state (Briggs, 1961).

BOX 1.2

Social policy is concerned with the ways societies across the world meet human needs for security, education, work, health, and well-being. Social policy addresses how states and societies respond to global challenges of social, demographic, and economic change, and of poverty, migration, and globalisation.

Source: London School of Economics

Social policies are formulated by the state to deal with social problems and are strategies of macro intervention that seek to mitigate social problems experienced by a sizable section of the population. Social policy refers to programmes and efforts taken to address the needs of individuals through the provision of welfare measures (Yerkes et al., 2019). Hagenbuch (1958) holds that social policy is an effort to make sure that individuals have minimum standards and opportunities. The aim of social policies is to find solutions for problems associated with urbanisation, environment, health, and education for all segments of society such as people with disabilities, older people, women, children, and immigrants. Social policy hence envisages the provision of health-related services, social security and family welfare measures, and provisions to deal with problems related to the environment, unemployment, and poverty that affect the lives of people. These services and support include child and family support, schooling and education, housing and neighbourhood renewal, income maintenance and poverty reduction, unemployment support and training, pensions, health, and social care. Social policy aims to identify and find ways of reducing inequalities in access to services and support between social groups defined by socio-economic status, race, ethnicity, migration status, gender, sexual orientation, disability, and age, and between countries (Platt, 2021). It aims to promote the welfare of individuals through legislative provisions to ensure peace, social justice, and equality between different groups (Kennett, 2004). The basic principles that underpin social policies are social needs and social problems, equal rights and social justice, efficiency, equity and choice, altruism, reciprocity and obligation, and division, difference, and exclusion (Deacon, 2007).

It must however be noted that policies and legislations by themselves cannot effectively eliminate social problems and multi-pronged efforts need to come into play to deal with them. These would involve a combination of micro and macro strategies of intervention. For instance, drug misuse needs to be tackled through a combination of appropriate policies, education of at-risk groups, and measures to rehabilitate and mainstream people already in the throes of addiction.

Social Problems and Globalisation

According to the International Labour Organisation, globalisation refers to the progressive integration of societies and economies and is driven by new technologies, new economic relationships, and the national and international policies of a wide range of actors, including governments, international organisations, business, labour, and civil society. Globalisation has been accompanied by the internationalisation of social problems, as issues that arise in one part of the world creates problems in others. Increased internet connectivity facilitates the swift communication of ideas and the ease of travel and transportation has resulted in increased mobility of people and cultural exchange. Critics of cross-border migration allege that it causes social tensions and ideological conflict and threatens cultural diversity, local traditions, and customs. The free movement of labour has helped the UK to fill job vacancies in industries such as fruit picking and the NHS. However, immigration has also placed greater stress on UK housing and other public services such as transportation and education. Infectious diseases such as tuberculosis, HIV, and the more recent Covid have spread globally owing to increased population mobility. People move across different parts of the world for various reasons: poverty, wars, famine, environmental degradation, and there has been a rise of newer social problems, including human trafficking, the organised drug trade, and arms smuggling (Dominelli, 2010).

BOX 1.3

Human trafficking is currently a billion-dollar industry and is the third-highest income earner after arms and drug smuggling.

Source: Lyons et al., (2006)

We now have data that indicates that globalisation has strongly contributed to the improvement of the economic and living situation in some countries while adversely impacting others. For instance, a decline of people living in absolute poverty fell from 31% of the world's population to 20% (Held and McGrew, 2016). It has also been reported that between 1981 and 2001, the percentage of rural people living on less than one dollar a day decreased from 79% to 27% in China, 63% to 42% in India, and 55% to 11% in Indonesia (Bardhan, 2006). On the other hand, the indication is that poverty in Sub-Saharan Africa has risen from 290 million to 415 million, and at the end of the 19th century, the ratio of average income in the richest countries to middle income in the poorest was nine to one (Martell, 2017).

Social Movements, Social Problems, and Social Change

A social movement is a purposeful and organised effort by a significant number of people to change (or resist change in) some major aspect or aspects of society. Examples of social movements include those supporting civil rights, gay rights, trade unionism, environmentalism, and feminism. They involve collective action and focus on social change and seek to make a difference to some aspect of society that is perceived to be afflicted by a social problem. While social movements address a particular social problem and champion a cause, they do not necessarily bring solutions to it.

An important social reform movement in the 19th century was the British anti-slavery movement. It has been estimated that between 1700 and 1810 British merchants transported almost three million Africans across the Atlantic. The Society for the Abolition of the Slave Trade propagated the British anti-slavery movement through the distribution of abolitionist books, pamphlets, prints, and artefacts. It had its own network of local contacts ('agents' and 'country committees') scattered across the length and breadth of the country. Thomas Clarkson, a sort of 'travelling agent,' provided a vital link between London and the provinces, organising committees, distributing tracts, and offering advice and encouragement to hundreds of grass-roots activists. Anti-slavery resistance during the last decades of the 18th century resulted in the abolition of the slave trade in the British Atlantic world in 1807. The reasons for the end of the slave trade were many, but one recognisable feature of the movement was an increasingly vocal public rejection of the institution. The public critique of slavery was inspired by ideas about religious and natural equality. It found its voice in the burgeoning literacy and print culture of the Anglo-American world. The 1832 Reform Act, coupled with popular abolitionist momentum, proved the decisive factor in legally ending the institution of slavery in Britain and its American colonies.

Another important movement in the early 20th century was the extension of voting rights to women which was granted following a protracted struggle by several social organisations. The most militant advocates for women's suffrage became known as Suffragettes. In 1903, the Women's Social and Political Union (WSPU) was founded by Emmeline Pankhurst and her two daughters to demand the vote for women. Until 1914, when the First World War broke out, they campaigned energetically, and sometimes violently, to achieve this aim. Suffragettes were responsible for breaking the windows of 10 Downing Street, burning buildings, and damaging paintings in public galleries. They were often prepared to go to prison for their cause or even put their own lives in danger. When the First World War broke out, many women took jobs normally undertaken by men. The huge numbers of men needed to fight the war resulted in women being employed as gas workers, coal heavers, transport workers, and ambulance drivers. When the war ended, the tremendous war effort of these female workers was rewarded by the introduction of a bill that allowed women over 30 years to vote in parliamentary elections. The National Union of Women's Suffrage Societies (NUWSS) led by Millicent Fawcett, an organisation that did not support the radical activities of the WSPU was also instrumental in building up legal and constitutional support for the enfranchisement of women.

Political Forces and Social Problems

A recent example of how political decisions can disproportionately affect particular groups and generate problems for them is Brexit, which decided the exit of the UK from the European Union (EU). Let me illustrate this further.

BOX 1.4

Brexit is an abbreviation formed from two English words: 'Britain' and 'exit' and refers to the withdrawal process of the UK from the EU based on a referendum dated June 23, 2016, to leave the EU. Brexit took place at 11 p.m., January 31, 2020, when the UK formally was no longer a constituent of the EU.

Brexit and Impact on Women

A report published by the Scottish Government (2020) titled 'Brexit: social and equality impacts' has argued that the UK's decision to leave the EU will disproportionately affect women and exacerbate gender inequality. The Women's Budget Group (WBG) has conducted extensive research into the economic impacts of Brexit on gender equality and observes that Brexit "will hit women hard, leading to lost jobs, cuts to services and a squeeze on family budgets." For many women, particularly the poorest, black and minority ethnic (BAME) women and disabled women, the UK Government's EU (Withdrawal Agreement) Bill of October 2019 could mean job losses, cuts to services, squeezed family budgets, and reduced legal protections (Table 1.1).

Brexit and Impact on People with Disabilities

The potential adverse impacts of Brexit on disabled people in the UK have been highlighted by disabled peers in the House of Lords. On a debate on 'Brexit: Disabled People,' Baroness Scott of Needham Market underlined the negative effects of the loss of EU structural funds, the potential weakening of anti-discrimination laws, the potential loss of the Blue Badge scheme, and the impact on the care sector, for disabled people. Other disabled peers also campaigned vigorously against a 'no-deal Brexit,' which was considered 'disastrous' for disabled people, in particular due to impacts on social care recruitment (Table 1.2).

Minority Ethnic People:

Brexit is likely to have a negative impact on minority ethnic communities—in particular, their household incomes, spending power, career prospects, and legal rights. Furthermore, since the EU referendum in June 2016, there has been evidence of rising

Table 1.1 Potential social impacts of Brexit on women

Cuts to Women's Health Services
Cuts in benefits and public services
Need to take up more unpaid caring
Loss of women's funding (ESIF)
Loss of affordable housing
Reduced spending power
Increased vulnerability to job losses

Table 1.2 Potential social impacts of Brexit on people with disabilities

Reduced health services
Reduced social care services
Loss of disability funding (ESIF)
Loss of health care (EHIC card) and social security coordination
Loss of accessible housing
Reduced transport services
Impact on food, fuel, and medicines

Table 1.3 Potential social impacts of Brexit on black and minority ethnic people

---
Cuts in benefits and public services
Increased racism and hate crimes
Reduced spending power
Discrimination against EU nationals of colour
Vulnerability to job losses
Loss of affordable housing
Lack of BAME funding (ESIF)

---

levels of racism, xenophobia, and intolerance. The marked rise in recorded hate crime since the 2016 EU referendum in England and Wales has not been reported in Scotland or Northern Ireland. However, the UN Special Rapporteur on Racism has identified a Brexit-related growth in "explicit racial, ethnic and religious intolerance" and a stark increase in hate crimes across the UK since the referendum. A nationwide survey by Opinium in May 2019 reveals that 71% of people from ethnic minorities have experienced racial discrimination (an increase from 58% in January 2016) and that online racism has doubled since 2016 (Table 1.3).

Having laid out some of the basic features of how social problems emerge in a socio-cultural-political context, I hope has introduced the reader to some of the rudiments in understanding the nature of social problems. It is now appropriate to give you a glimpse of what lies further ahead, within these pages.

What Is This Book All About?

Well, it is about social problems, several of them; 11 to be precise. These are social problems that are prevalent not only in the UK but manifested in contemporary societies elsewhere as well. They are in fact not the only social problems that societies experience and there are several others such as terrorism and climate change that have not been discussed here, not because they are less important but as they may not find significant readership among the student population of the social sciences. The problems that have been included in this text are common everyday issues such as poverty, substance misuse, family dissolution, and youth offending. While the focus of these issues is the UK and its four constituent nations, the book would be of interest to those elsewhere as well. The issues that have been included typically find a place in most sociology courses, and the topics can be accessed individually as standalone or read in conjunction with others. Each social problem is seated within a separate chapter that follows a common basic structure that includes:

- setting the context and providing a background.
- providing statistics to establish prevalence and magnitude.
- exploring terminology, myths, and misconceptions unique to the problem being discussed.
- implications for people: individual, family, society (psychosocial issues).
- linkages with other social issues/problems (causes-consequences).
- theoretical explanations/frameworks.
- policies and legislation have then been detailed.

A comprehensive and multi-dimensional perspective of each social problem has hence been provided. It is hoped that the reader will find this chapter layout to provide an easy-to-access reading experience.

Special mention needs to be made of the next chapter in this textbook as it stands out from the others and does not deal with a 'particular' social problem. It however is a good starting point that would enable the reader to begin to make sense of social problems and deals comprehensively with issues relating to causation. These for instance include the role of social forces including economics, geopolitics, and culture. It also looks at internal factors such as the role of the self and agency besides biological and psychological factors and thus provides a multi-factorial understanding of how the dynamic interplay of several factors manifest in the complexity associated with social problems.

Chapter 3 explores *poverty* as an enduring social problem, offering some critical understanding of what it means in the UK as both a concept and a lived experience. The author presents a range of definitions, measures, and theories that have been put forward to elucidate what poverty is and what causes it, which, in turn, have influenced what has been put in place to address it. The chapter argues that the way poverty is understood alters according to the prevailing social and cultural context and that in recent years there has been a propensity in the UK to present its causes and consequences as due to the individual flaws and imprudent choices of 'the poor.' The chapter considers the implications of this to the way people who live with poverty are perceived in society and how they perceive themselves, offering some thoughts on Universal Basic Income as a possible solution and some concluding comments intended to challenge the personal deficit discourse of poverty that dominates in society today.

The chapter on 'Fractured families' discusses the causes and consequences of family breakdown and its impacts on individuals and society. It begins by exploring the importance of families, the various emerging family structures within the UK, and the triggers of family breakdown—particularly in the wake of the COVID-19 pandemic. The authors draw on statistical information, theoretical frameworks, and current evidence to analyse factors that contribute to family breakdown. They also highlight the causal associations between family breakdown and negative outcomes for affected individuals and societies. An overview of various strategies and interventions which are being used to manage and mitigate the negative impacts of family breakdown are also discussed.

Intimate Partner Violence or Domestic Violence is an issue of deep concern and an emotive issue that has serious implications for all involved. The chapter addresses issues such as the battered women syndrome besides exploring the oft asked question: 'why doesn't she just not leave?' It locates the issue within the sociocultural context of patriarchy and looks at historical aspects in relation to the problem. The chapter comprehensively deals with policies and legislations and the Domestic Abuse bill in particular. Different theoretical perspectives on domestic violence are offered and the issue is viewed through a structural lens, a feminist perspective, and an ecosystems framework.

Teenage pregnancy as a public health and a social problem is the focus of Chapter 6. Drawing from their own research of working with different groups of teenagers in the UK, the authors present a convincing picture that teenage pregnancy is not concentrated in one section of a society rather combination of multiple deprivations, social exclusion, poverty, and lack of political will to address social situations holistically have negative effects on teenagers' sexual health outcomes. They discuss the broader social, cultural, environmental, and health challenges faced by teenagers. The chapter argues that not confronting multiple socially disadvantaged positions of young women and men can lead to intergenerational cycle of poverty that needs to be addressed at micro and macro levels.

The chapter on 'Child abuse, child neglect and safeguarding children' addresses the issue of child protection. Having defined a 'child' and how child abuse is defined in law and policy, the chapter considers challenges to gathering knowledge about the extent of child abuse and briefly sets out the historical context. It then explores different aspects of child abuse and considers some of the overlap between different 'categories' of abuse. The theoretical basis for understanding child abuse is considered, and the 'wicked' and complex nature of the problem. Theoretical approaches are discussed, leading to a consideration of risk and protective factors, addressing the wide range of social and economic circumstances under which children grow up and parents rear their children. The Scottish system of Children's Hearings is compared with the approach in England and Wales, which follows a different approach in which children and their welfare are the focus of concern, but children are much less present in person.

The chapter on 'Youth Offending' turns the spotlight on an issue of increasing concern within the UK. The context is set by looking at definitions in defining the concept, and the prevalence and magnitude of the problem are presented by some stark official statistics. The chapter deals at length with several risk and protective factors that may prevent or increase the vulnerability of young people in terms of being drawn into offending behaviours. The gang culture and its charm for young people have been considered at length by the authors. The highlights of the chapter are the links made to other issues such as racial identity, social deprivation, mental health issues, and substance misuse. Current UK policies in dealing with this problem have been explored and strategies for prevention and reduction of offending behaviour by young people have also been elaborately considered.

Alcohol misuse is an issue that societies the world over grapple with. The author in this chapter begins with an overview of related concepts such as dependence, misuse, and addiction. The addiction cycle has been drawn into the discussion and is then followed by some alcohol-related statistics drawn from the four constituent nations of the UK. Some interesting facts are presented pertaining to alcohol consumption during the Covid lockdown period before moving on to sociocultural and religious influences on consumption behaviours. An elaborate section on theoretical perspectives seeks to offer causal explanations from a biological, psychological, and sociological standpoint. Alcohol-related harm, social costs of misuse and implications for mental health, and parental alcohol misuse for children have been dwelt upon. Consumption patterns relating to gender, young persons, and older people are other issues dealt with. The final section deals with recent policies and legislations in the four UK nations that seek to address the issue of alcohol misuse.

The next chapter on 'Drug Misuse' highlights a complex and emotive issue within the UK. Within the chapter, the reader will be introduced to topics that will explore the social, political, and economic cost of drug misuse in the UK. The chapter also presents the key theoretical and operational models that surround drug misuse, exploring interventions such as harm reduction and behaviour modification approaches as concepts for treatment. Finally, the authors take a nuanced and critical position in relation to legislation, policy, and practice relating to drug misuse in the UK.

The chapter on 'suicide and self-harm' deals with these issues in relation to social theory, epidemiology, societal attitudes, law and ethics, and management strategies. Suicide and self-harm rates are explored from a national and international perspective. The authors examine self-harm and suicide grounded in theory and practice, taking account of both societal and individual domains. The aim is to explore the conceptualisation of suicide and self-harm and relate it to the evidence base. The chapter commences with suicide models and aims to equip the reader with a framework to explore this sensitive topic; Durkheim is used to allow readers to challenge their knowledge and attitudes. The authors have attempted to address the consequences of self-harm and suicide for the individual and their family unit. Media portrayal, assessment, prevention strategies, legislation, and knowledge and attitudes to suicide are explored.

Homelessness is a complex social problem of considerable moral, cultural, political, and socio-economic importance and has been explored elaborately in Chapter 12. The authors present statistical information to establish the magnitude of the problem in the UK. They convincingly make the point that homelessness is not merely 'an absence of housing issue' but is a more complex problem with links to others such as substance misuse, mental health, poverty, unemployment, and crime. Besides exploring causative factors, the consequences, and adverse outcomes associated with homelessness, the authors present an analysis of the structural conditions, doctrines, regulations, and laws that govern and give shape to legislation and housing policy. Case studies have been presented to outline micro and macro strategies of intervention that could help tackle the problem.

The final chapter on multicultural societies puts a lens on how different aspects of diversity and discrimination impact individuals and communities. Using case studies to illustrate the various community tensions which manifest in different forms of discrimination including hate crimes and hate incidents, the chapter explores theoretical models to contextualise the impact of these. The chapter takes an intersectional approach, considering a wide range of inequalities, including the impact of domestic violence and abuse, HIV, mental health, and substance misuse. Including a focus on public policy across the four nations of the UK to illustrate the differences in legislation, the chapter reflects on the work still to be done in each country and concludes with practical examples on how to build inclusive communities and workplaces.

Working on this book has been an enriching experience and the contributors hope that the book now in your hands will provide you with useful nuggets of information relating to a range of commonly encountered social problems in the UK. We wish that this book will add an impetus to your thirst to probe deeper into social problems that are of specific interest to you. As you turn these pages, we hope that the content within will help develop a better understanding of social processes and factors that go into the manifestation of social problems.

Points to Ponder

1 If social problems affect individuals, how do individuals in turn influence them?
2 Consider how newer social problems have emerged with the passage of time and the reasons thereof.
3 Imagine a society where there are no social problems. What would it look like? Is this possible?

Individual Tasks

1 Take a look at the table of contents of this book. Now, make a list of social problems that have not been dealt with in this book.
2 What are the social problems that are widely prevalent in the city that you live in?

Small Group Activity

In small groups, make a list of various social problems. Now, reorder the list in terms of which ones you would want to eliminate in order of priority? Now share with other groups the reasons for your priority. Have all groups identified the same problems?

References

Aravacik. E.D. (2018). Social policy and the Welfare State. In Açıkgöz, B. (Ed.), *Public Economics and Finance*. IntechOpen, DOI: 10.5772/intechopen.82372. Available from https://www.intechopen.com/chapters/64579

Bardhan, P. (2006). Does Globalization Help or Hurt the World's Poor? *Scientific American, 294*, 84–91.

Briggs, A. (1961). The Welfare State in Historical Perspective. *European Journal of Sociology/Archives Européennes de Sociologie/Europäisches Archiv Für Soziologie, 2*(2), 221–258.

Deacon, B. (2007). *Global Social Policy & Governance*. London: Sage.

Dominelli, L. (2010). Globalization, Contemporary Challenges and Social Work Practice. *International Social Work, 53*(5), 599–612.

Eitzen, D.S., and Zinn, M.B. (2000). The Missing Safety Net and Families: A Progressive Critique of the New Welfare Legislation. *The Journal of Sociology & Social Welfare, 27*(1), Article 4. Available from https://scholarworks.wmich.edu/jssw/vol27/iss1/4

Fuller, R.C., and Myers, R.R. (1941). The Natural History of a Social Problem. *American Sociological Review, 6*(3), 320–329.

Hagenbuch, W. (1958). *Social Economics*. Welwyn: Nisbet, p. 205.

Held, D., and McGrew, A. (2016). *The Global Transformations Reader*. Cambridge: Polity Press, pp. 440–480.

Horton, P.B., and Leslie, G.R. (1970). *The Sociology of Social Problems*. New York: Appleton Century Crofts.

Kennett, P. (Ed.). (2004). *A Handbook of Comparative Social Policy*. Northampton, VT: Edward Elgar Publishing.

Lyons, K., Manion, K., and Carlsen, M. (2006). *International Perspectives on Social Work: Global Conditions and Local Practice*. Basingstoke: Palgrave.

Mahoney, J. (2003). Knowledge accumulation in comparative historical research. In Mahoney, J., & Rueschemeyer, D. (Eds.), *Comparative Historical Analysis in the Social Sciences*, Cambridge: Cambridge University Press. pp. 131–174.

Martell, L. (2017). *The Sociology of Globalization* (2nd Ed.). Cambridge: Polity Press.

Merton, R.K., and Nisbet, R.A. (1961). *Contemporary Social Problems: An Introduction to the Sociology of Deviant Behavior and Social Disorganization*. New York: Harcourt, Brace & World.

Parrillo, V.N. (2002). *Contemporary Social Problems* (5th Ed.). London: Allyn and Bacon.

Platt, L. (2021). What Is Social Policy? Available from https://www.lse.ac.uk/social-policy/about-us/What-is-social-policy

Schwartz, H. (1997). On the Origin of the Phrase 'Social Problems'. *Social Problems, 44*, 276–296.

Scottish Government. (2020). *Brexit: Social and Equality Impacts*. Available from https://www.gov.scot/publications/social-equality-impacts-brexit/pages/17/

Spector, M., and Kitsuse, J.I. (1973). Social problems: A re-formulation, *Social Problems*, *21*(2), 145–159.

Spector, M., and Kitsuse, J.I. (1977). *Constructing Social Problems*. Menlo Park, CA: Cummings Pub. Co.

Spector, Ms., and Kitsuse, J.I. (2001). *Constructing Social Problems*. New Brunswick, NJ: Transaction.

Yerkes, M.A., Javornik, J., and Kurowska, A. (2019). *Social Policy and the Capability Approach*. Bristol: Policy Press.

2 Understanding and Making Sense of Social Problems

Will Hay

Introduction

Social problems constitute a form of behaviour, condition, or state of affairs of special concern, which affect whole communities rather than a few isolated individuals. A social problem thus corresponds to what Mills (1959) called a 'public issue', rather than a 'personal trouble'. In this regard the terms 'public' and 'social' are interchangeable. In human terms, the social problems discussed in this book are undoubtedly detrimental to our sense of well-being, those of the people directly concerned and arguably of society as a whole. They do not occur accidentally and we frequently find them puzzling, depressing or grim; sometimes all three at once. Their unnerving natures often bring us up short. The dismaying aspect of social problems for social life has meant that they have long been of concern. Indeed, it is possible that they are intractable and will thus be with us for all time.

Though, in many ways, social problems are lofty subjects, taught, studied, and debated in classrooms, universities, and colleges, they are also the stuff of everyday life. Often interrelated, they raise their heads in a variety of contexts and we encounter them in numerous ways. They are part of what it means to be human. They are in this very real, lived-in sense, simultaneously of private and public concern. The array of social problems contained in this volume figure regularly and prominently in social media of all description, though the ways in which they are presented and discussed inevitably differ markedly from each other. Unsurprisingly, they are the subject of much contentious debate in the cut and thrust of Parliament. They are also the topic of many radio and television documentaries, and they form the backbone of many a stage play, film, or television drama. Their political, social, and cultural significance cannot therefore be underestimated.

The Study of Social Problems

The social scientific study of social problems, both in terms of subject matter and method of enquiry, took off in earnest with several empirical studies of crime, drug taking, homelessness, and what was then termed 'deviance' in Chicago in the 1920s. If we take this body of work as our starting point, social scientists from various disciplines have been seeking to understand and make sense of social problems in all their varying forms for a century. If there is a single message that can be taken from the received ideas handed down to us over these years, it is that the study of social problems is a rich and varied field, spanning several disciplines, with no commonly agreed set of principles

> **THE CHICAGO SCHOOL IN THE 1920S**
>
> The School put the sociological exploration of social problems on the social scientific map by introducing:
>
> - new sociological concepts;
> - new social theory; and
> - new methods of investigation.

or procedures to reconcile diverse points of view within academic disputes. Seeking to account for these differences has entailed drawing upon several precepts, ideas, and a range of competing theoretical perspectives. Originating in the groundbreaking work of Blumer (1971), there is, for example, much contention as to whether social problems consist of 'objective' situations and conditions with identifiable causes or whether they are 'social constructions'; the products of processes by which certain acts get defined as problematic and troublesome. Whether we think social problems are objective or social constructions changes how we interpret the evidence available. If we hold the view that social problems are 'factual', 'observable', and 'measurable', we are more likely to approach data as adequate portrayals of what is going on in the real world. We might call this a 'realist' stance. In this way concrete questions can be asked of data: how prevalent is the problem? who is most affected? when and where? What is likely to be of importance to social constructivists, however, is not whether data is 'reliable' or 'valid', but how the discussion is shaped, what has been included and omitted within the discourse, what is being claimed and how so-called 'social problems' come to be addressed in political and policy circles.

Though driven by different socially scientific interests and modes of analysis, both positions in their different ways nourish our knowledge of social problems. Though they articulate the issues associated with social problems differently, both in terms their orienting ideas and assumptions, they are a shared feature of the social problems discourse. Each claim is worthy of attention not just for the reasoned arguments presented, but for the socially scientific authority that each is able to wield. To study social problems—to understand and make sense of them in all their complexity—is therefore to embark upon a particular kind of exploratory and analytic enterprise. It involves making sense of different narratives and the way these are laid out. It also involves looking beyond the headlines that feature in the media on a daily basis. To understand social problems requires us to ask a range of intricate questions, three of which are of special importance.

1 Why and under what conditions do we behave in certain ways that would seem detrimental not only to ourselves, but also to our families, circle of friends, and to society in general?
2 What does the very presence of social problems and the havoc that they produce tell us about the norms and values of society?
3 Given their seemingly intractability, what should be done to ameliorate their worst effects?

There are multiple takes on each of these questions. In terms of the first, what is a convincing explanation as to the causes and necessary social conditions to foster a particular social problem for one commentator may not hold so much credence for another. With regard to the second, not all observers of social problems see the moral issues that they raise in the same way. This is especially true within debates conducted between realists and those of a social constructivist persuasion. Similarly, huge disagreements exist concerning the policies, procedures, and legislation that need to be fostered and pursued to prevent, treat, and control social problems. It follows that any attempt to understand the issues that lie at the heart of social problems necessitates constantly weighing competing explanatory claims, moral positions, and political and practical related concerns in the balance.

At this point, it should be noted that there is no general or distinctive theory of social problems. Rather what we have is a piecemeal range of explanatory and interpretive frameworks upon which the study of social problems is founded. This is not surprising. Social problems are too varied, too multifaceted, too complex, and too wide-ranging for a grand theory to emerge that would neatly and satisfactorily explain all their different aspects. Making sense of social problems can thus never be one-dimensional, nor can our knowledge and understanding of the problems contained in this book be reduced to a particular disciplinary, stand alone, framework. To understand social problems requires an analysis of how different frameworks of understanding within disciplines relate to and interact with one another. It also requires us to establish how, when appropriate, they might be brought together to show their mutual dependence rather than simply dealing with each of them in isolation or in competition with each other.

Causation

Of the many themes that weave in and out of the social problems discourse, there is perhaps none more important than that of causation. To speak of causation is to refer to the relationship that exists between particular events, actions, or processes and their results. In going about our everyday lives, we work primarily on the assumption that when such and such happens this will be the result. That is to say, one situation, event or action leads to another. We call this cause and effect.

The attempt to establish what constitutes a cause and what causes particular effects (poverty, ill health, homelessness), or forms of harmful or troublesome behaviour (misusing drugs, being violent), has long been a key feature within the social problems literature. Causes are primarily of two kinds: direct and indirect. Direct causes are those situational factors that motivate people to take specific forms of action in the here and now to achieve a set of ends using particular forms of means. A fairly straightforward example is an offender who breaks into premises for financial gain. Indirect or 'background' causes refer to situations or conditions such as bad parenting, poverty, or abuse that together form a psychosocial causal chain, which in turn predispose people such as our offender towards motivating actions. They are, in effect, what criminologist Wikstrom (2017) has called 'causes of the causes'. What may be perceived as the cause may only be connected in some way rather than being causally explanative in nature. For example, alcohol misuse does not, per se, cause crime or homelessness in any direct sense, but they often occur together.

NECESSARY AND SUFFICIENT CAUSES

Necessary and sufficient causes are frequently referred to when addressing questions of causation. The key point is that factors such as poverty which has clear links to various social problems increasing the likelihood of their manifestation is neither a **necessary** causal factor, nor is it a **sufficient** explanation to account for the social problem in question in and of itself.

Establishing the causes of social problems is therefore hardly simple. When we are addressing questions of causation we are perhaps, at best, talking of identifying particular associations and conditions, with which to form judgements about causality. Approaching the issue in this way nonetheless provides us with a useful schematic frame of reference with which to ask a range of analytic questions:

i   do the various associations and conditions precede the social problem?
ii how robust is the association?
iii do the associations and conditions become more influential in forging attitudes and behaviour with increased exposure to them?
iv are the associations and conditions coherent and consistent with attempts to identify the source of other social problems?

The Framing of Social Problems

Though the quest to establish the causes of social problems constitutes a very rich field encompassing a number of disciplines, it is, nonetheless, possible to discern two socially scientific frameworks that have been particularly influential. The first considers social problems in light of the bio-psychological make-up of individuals with which to make sense of people's everyday experiences. The second draws primarily upon sociological insights and focuses upon wider socio-political and socio-economic conditions, situations, and the societal relationships within which people and social problems are situated. Each mode of enquiry assumes a wide range of reference and is ambitious in terms of reach and scope. Each of them differs in their basic assumptions and perceptions as well as methods and general theoretical and conceptual orientation.

The ways in which each of these frameworks differ cannot, however, be pushed too far. There are, for example, several important overlaps. It is a truism that humans are by nature social beings. Though its focus is upon the individual and the scientific study of people's thoughts, feelings and behaviours, social psychology seeks to place the self within a societal context with a particular focus on social influence and culture. By the same token, sociologists interested in 'structural' forces frequently acknowledge the importance of agency. We are not, after all, programmed automatons, but creatures of flesh and blood. We frequently make decisions on the spur of the moment, impulsively and perhaps without too much thought, if any, of the consequences, as is the case, for example, in a great deal of crime and other high-risk situations. At the same time, we are also capable of making reasoned decisions which weigh up the costs, benefits, and outcomes, which require, as Kahneman (2011) has pointed out, cognitive effort and attention. We have, then, as individuals, free will to act on the world, but only within certain structural constraints and restrictions.

Internal Factors, the Self, and Agency

Though, as the metaphysical poet John Donne put it, no one person is an island, each of us are individuals with our set of differences, personalities, characteristics, and above all our own unique sense of self. As established, we are all, for the most part and to a greater or lesser extent, conscious, rational, and autonomous beings able to reflect and act upon the social world in meaningful ways. Far from being passive recipients, we are able to understand and appreciate not only what we do, but also how we might do things better, differently, more thoughtfully, or more virtuously. We are sometimes at a loss to understand some forms of behaviour, especially acts which seem to be hell-bent on self-destruction or momentous acts of violence and abuse which cause severe, prolonged, or lasting harm to others. Given our general sense of bemusement or contempt for such actions, as a starting point, it seems reasonable to ask whether behaviour of this kind is a result of abnormal brain structures that have gone awry in some way or another due to neurological, chemical, hormonal, or genetic imbalances.

Biology and Behaviour

Mental health is of increasing public and political interest, especially with regard to reducing the mental health inequalities that exist in mental illness (see Public Health England (2021a)). There are several studies within the field that have also sought to establish the role that neurochemistry plays in the mental health of the populace, particularly with regard to anxiety and depression. Some individuals are more susceptible to depression than others. Those with reduced thyroxine levels and raised cortisol levels, for example, are more likely to be show signs of stress and depression. As we know, depression, in turn, is associated with persistent insomnia, feelings of helplessness and worthlessness and social isolation, all factors that figure highly in accounts of why people contemplate suicide.

SOCIAL PROBLEMS AND THE BODY

Some people are, more prone to medical conditions such as obesity, diabetes, and cardiovascular disease. But what biological factors determine what **kind** of person we become? Are certain people more vulnerable or predisposed to particular cognitive processes or forms of action? In short, is it possible to explain human nature and human behaviour in terms of physiological laws?

Special attention in the neurological field has been devoted to the role that dopamine and serotonin play in the way that people feel, think, and act in the social world. Associated with reward and pleasure, both chemicals transmit electrical impulses between nerve cells and thus carry messages to different parts of the brain, which affect various physiological systems, cognitive processes, mood, and behaviour. These 'feel-good' chemicals are similar to opiates and generate similar effects such as numbness, relaxation, and a feeling of well-being, all factors that may well trigger and help maintain behaviour seen to be addictive. It is worth noting, for example, that the taking of alcohol and drugs both increase dopamine levels. Increasing both substances over a substantial amount of time results in less pleasurable feelings, which, Durrant et al. (2009) intimate, may lead to an increase in craving and even a loss of control over the substance. In a study of 120 people, half of whom had a dependence on cocaine, Ersche et al. (2011) found that the part of the brain most associated with rewarding behaviour—was markedly enlarged in cocaine users. The conclusion drawn from this was twofold. First, that alterations in the brain predate cocaine abuse. Second, that enlarged brain reward system renders individuals more vulnerable or prone to taking the drug and thus much more likely to become addicted even in the face of the harmful consequences of doing so.

Central to the study of the relationship between biology and human society has been the role played by biological metabolic structures and hormonal factors. There are two hormones in particular that have been regularly commented upon to explain social problems: oestrogen and testosterone, which are the prime determinants of biological sex characteristics. The part they play in psychological functioning has been of particular interest in a variety of fields; hormones being one vehicle by which some have sought to explain similarities and differences between the sexes in the rates that they create or experience particular social problems. Testosterone levels have, for example, been considered to be of prime importance in terms of determining sexual motivation and behaviour as well as aggressive and antisocial tendencies.

The third area of interest concerns the role that genes may play in troublesome behaviour. Human beings, as we know, are made up countless sets of genes inherited from our parents. They account anatomically for the colour of our eyes and our hair, our body shape, our propensity to contract certain illnesses and a good deal else besides. There is little of controversy here. Whether genetic predispositions can account for social problems other than those associated directly to anatomy and health is, however, quite another matter. According to Agrawal et al. (2012), there seems to be some evidence that genetics can indeed play at least a part in substance misuse. Whilst, they concluded, there is no single gene that causes addiction in any straightforward deterministic sense, they have argued that alcohol, nicotine, cannabis, and other illicit drug dependence are influenced by multiple genes of modest, cumulative, and interactive effect that shape the liability to addictive behaviour.

Reservations have, however, been expressed concerning the dangers of overplaying the part that biology determines behaviour. As Pilnick (2002) has noted, with new genetic knowledge comes an increasing risk that we begin to see ourselves and others not only as the sum of our genes, but also simply as an expression of our genetic make-up. As she points out, this is problematic for social scientists, since it minimises the role of social factors in explaining the characteristics of individual members of society. Further still, genetic determinism casts several question marks over whether social problems can ever be prevented or ameliorated, making any attempt to intervene a futile exercise. Moreover, whilst it is reasonable to assume that genes play an important role in any analytic framework to explain social problems, it is also the case that other aspects of the self are perhaps more significant or relevant in explaining why some people have more propensity to engage in troublesome forms behaviour than others. To establish what these might be involves delving into the insights offered by psychology, that branch of the social and medical sciences whose prime aim is to shed light on the inner, subjective experience of individuals and the meaning that individuals attach to their acts.

Psychological Factors

To speak of internal factors as somehow causing or being connected to a social problem leads to questions concerning the mental states, thought processes, feelings, emotions, values, behaviours of those who are suicidal, commit crime, drink to excess, become homeless, or experience the breakup of one's family. In examining why people do what they do, we often make use of concepts associated with the mind, seeking to explain conduct by way of various intentions, desires, motives, and reasons. To speak about internal factors is also to raise questions revolving around individual autonomy, culpability, and responsibility. The attempt to understand the internal factors associated with social problems and the attempt to apply psychological insights into people's perceptions of social problems has led to a wide range of theories and a number of divergent approaches and methods. It is possible to point to at least four modes of enquiry, each of which brings different aspects of social problems sharply into view.

The first of these is concerned with the conditions under which healthy growth development of individuals takes place and the implications for individuals if such conditions have been absent or lacking in some way. We have long thought of life as consisting of certain stages, with infancy and childhood being, arguably, the most important stage of all for human growth and development. We can go as far as to say that childhood is a central component of an internalised, moral process, the impairment or absence of which may have profound adverse consequences both psychologically and socially. Cer-

> **PSYCHOLOGY**
>
> Psychology's contribution to our knowledge and understanding of social problems is essentially threefold:
>
> 1 It is capable of conveying a great deal about the foundations of human behaviour in terms of social conditioning, the forging of identities and personalities, how one regards oneself, motivation, and a good deal else in terms of individual psyches.
> 2 It can tell us much about the psychological effects on the individuals who create or experience the social problem in question.
> 3 As an applied as well as a theoretical discipline, psychology also has much to say concerning the amelioration of social problems, especially with regard to face-to-face methods of intervention.

tainly, several leading lights in psychology including Freud, Bowlby, Erikson, and Piaget have thought so. Between them they have produced several 'classic' texts, the ideas contained in which are cited time and time again within the social problems discourse. As a collective they have had much to say of interest and importance about the role that childhood plays in the development of moral reasoning, the awareness of others' needs, the development of trust, the formation of a conscience, the importance of developing secure attachments, and the self-imposed constraints that all of us from time to time place upon ourselves and much else besides.

Taken together, what these studies suggest is that social problems encountered in adolescence and adulthood may well be the bitter fruits of seeds sown in infancy and childhood. There is some indication that this might well be the case, with numerous studies reporting that disturbed attachment in childhood does indeed carry over into adult life. Securely attached children, it has been shown, are much more likely to be classed as having better mental health, to divorce less and to experience physical and sexual abuse, financial adversity, suffer from depression, phobias, alcohol or drug abuse, and other traumas and hardships.

It is a truism that whilst we share much in common, each of us perceives and acts upon this social world of ours in very different ways. There are, of course, incalculable reasons for this being so. In part, it is because each of us has our own personality and temperament, which brings us to the second strand in what psychology has to offer in why some people engage in 'risky' behaviour and others do not. Theoretical frameworks based upon temperament and personality types have figured prominently in the study of social problems. Interest has been generated, for example, in the links between temperament, adjustment, and adaptation in the context of marital relationships, separation and divorce, as well as crime. It is, however, in the field of addiction that theories of personality and temperament are at their most pronounced, with so-called 'addictive personality theory' figuring particularly prominently. Those with addictive personalities have, at various times, been described as being rebellious, egocentric, pleasure seeking, unable to deal with frustrations, having a sense of faulty logic and being markedly irresponsible, and immature. Along similar lines, Leeds and Morgenstern (1996) have spoken of those with 'addictive personalities' as being escapist, impulsive, dependent, devious, manipulative, emotionally immature and self-centred. In line with the psychoanalytic tradition, this way of thinking about addiction views the underlying personality pathology to be due to developmental problems and views addiction as a symptom of underlying personality weaknesses, inadequacies, and deficits.

The third aspect of long-standing interest to psychologists concerns the forming of attitudes; that is to say, the range of positive or negative feelings that we hold about people, events, objects, or issues. The cognitive dimension of attitude formation in particular has been widely studied. For Maio et al. (2018), attitudes, not only influence how we process information and interpret situations, but also predispose us towards particular forms of behaviour. Take the issue of domestic violence and abuse. Violent behaviour against women is much more likely if the male perpetrator holds certain ideas based upon, inter alia, notions of distinct gender roles, and a sense of a hierarchy. These include thinking and feeling himself superior to his partner; according her a low status; and feeling sexually and physically entitled to use violence as a method of control. Central to cognition and the formation of attitudes and beliefs is the process of moral reasoning. As Kohlberg (1976) has observed, moral reasoning is guided and forged in large measure by notions of justice and rights, and it is precisely these aspects that would seem to be lacking for the most part in the perpetrators of domestic violence.

The socialisation process is amongst the most important psychodynamic mechanisms for passing on attitudes and beliefs from one generation to the other, and it is this process that constitutes the fourth contribution from psychology. It is within the socialisation process that we learn from birth through to adolescence the normative values, duties, and obligations that are placed on us and the rules that need to be complied with both as an individual and as a member of society. The general aim is, of course, within this process of enculturation, to develop a willingness within us to abide by the rules set of our own disposition. In this regard, the norms that we generally like to pass on are built upon a set of ethical and moral codes that stress particular values, affirmations, and ways of behaviour. The law, culture, politics, age, social background, peer group, and social networks are all important mechanisms in this transmission. So, too, is family life. As a general rule, familial codes place an emphasis upon specific virtues including the need to treat people with dignity and respect, and to care for one another. The reality in some families could not be starker. Some domestic violence, for example, is a norm within certain households. As Jewkes (2002) has argued, experiences of violence in the home as a child reinforces for both men and women the normative nature of violence, thereby increasing the likelihood of male perpetration and women's acceptance of abuse. In short, domestic abuse may well be a direct consequence of the failure of socialisation and emotional development within the family. The influence of 'atypical' development within the socialisation process also finds expression with regard to problem behaviour associated with substance misuse. Children and young people are much more at risk of experiencing problems with alcohol and drugs if there is a history within the family of parental substance misuse, parental failure to provide cognitive stimulation in the home, parental abuse, excessive parental criticism, inconsistent discipline, parental disengagement with their children's schooling and parental psychiatric problems.

External Factors, Cultural, Socio-economic, and Environmental Conditions

Whereas the bio-psychological interest in the genesis of social problems centres on the internal life of individuals, 'structural' interest focuses upon the external factors and social forces that are at work in society as a whole. There are three dimensions that can be extracted from within structural accounts of social problems that are of particular importance to our understanding of them.

> **SOCIOLOGY**
>
> Sociology's contribution to our knowledge and understanding of social problems is also essentially threefold:
>
> 1 It provides the 'big picture' needed to identify the **structural causal mechanisms** of social problems;
> 2 It can tell us much about the sociological **effects** on whole groups of people and communities who create or experience the social problem in question.
> 3 It has much to say concerning the ways in which social problems **ought** to be tackled in legislative and social policy terms.

Culture

Though highly abstract and as such subject to elusiveness, references to culture figure prominently within our everyday social world. Reference to consumer culture or drug culture is commonplace and easily grasped what we mean by them. Culture in its widest sense, constitutes an ensemble of rules, meanings, belief systems, ideals, values, norms, and a body of ethics that 'structure' a society. For Seidman and Alexander (2001), culture constitutes an ideological force, which provides both meaning and substance to individuals and communities as a whole. It is culture that helps shape our sensibilities, mentalities, and attitudes towards social problems. In these terms, culture is an all-enveloping element in the infrastructure and institutional framework in which we absorb, assimilate, and affirm particular ideas about problematic behaviour, especially with regard to what is morally acceptable and what is not. Culture is also instrumental in how the social problem should be tackled. The oft repeated refrain to be 'tough on crime', for example, owes as much to cultural attitudes to crime as it is a political one. At a more grounded level, culture not only affects the ways in which individuals view the nature and form of social problems, but also what help they may seek as well as the type of help sought.

Of course, culture is neither a monolithic entity, nor is it timeless and unchangeable. On the contrary, culture is multifaceted and subject to change over time. In terms of the former, attitudes, values, and beliefs towards particular social problems all play out differently in different cultural contexts. As regards the latter, we hardly need reminding those numerous cultural changes to our social and economic fabric have occurred in the last few decades, much of it politically and ideologically driven. These changes have complex, multiple, and interacting sources. The changes in our sensibilities along the way make it impossible not to weigh these changes in the balance when seeking to account for the patterns and trends of the social problems we are currently experiencing. Tracking and tracing them over time can show the influence and impact that they have had on the type of social problems that we have experienced and understood them in the past as well as present society.

Cultural forms exist, therefore, not as a discrete background phenomenon against which to foreground social problems, but are firmly embedded within all strands of society, allowing for certain social problems not only exist, but in some instances, flourish.

Socio-economics

Economics, it is conventionally said, is all about maximising utility and enhancing human capital. This covers a wide terrain. Welfare economics, for example, is concerned with the ways in which resources, goods, and services are distributed to benefit society as a whole. As with culture, economics is not only of relevance to the creation of social problems and, therefore, to their analysis, but also to their solution. All of the social problems discussed in subsequent chapters have an economic dimension, though of course some more pronounced than others. In terms of living standards, life chances are distributed, created, and determined to a great extent by the political economy and one's socio-economic position. Although complex and inter-related, robust empirical evidence abounds as to the links between, for example, crime, drug misuse, homelessness, domestic violence, ill physical and mental health, and a host of other underlying problems variously conceived as poverty, economic insecurity, and exclusion. As Public Health England (2021b) has noted, starting in many cases even before the child is born and accumulating over time, disadvantages and social inequalities and inequities surrounding social determinants such as housing, education, and employment accrue over a life course, resulting in a reduced quality of life, poorer health outcomes and early death for many people.

Panning out still further as Wilkinson and Pickett (2009) have demonstrated, the prevalence and intensity of social problems vary both within and between countries. The more unequal the society, the more social problems it is likely to experience. More equal societies have higher average life expectancy, lower levels of infant mortality, lower rates of obesity, and higher rates of literacy obesity than highly unequal developed countries. In addition, they found that trust and social mobility were also higher the more egalitarian the society. Meanwhile, many social problems are shown to be higher amongst less equal societies, including higher rates of crime, imprisonment, teenage births, drug and alcohol addiction, and mental illness.

Time, Place, and the Geopolitical Environment

It is within the communities, neighbourhoods, and environment within which people live and spend their time that gives culture and economics particular meaning and substance. As subsequent chapters will show regional differences exist across all of the social problems discussed along the urban rural divide as well as on other geopolitical differences associated with class, gender, and race. Various data have shown that the geographical distribution of social problems is far from randomly distributed, but heavily clustered in particular areas. People, for example, in the most deprived areas are five times more likely to contract tuberculosis than in the least deprived areas, four times more likely to die prematurely from cardiovascular diseases, and over twice as likely to die of cancer than people living in the least deprived areas. Suicide rates between the most and least deprived areas of England are almost twice as high in the most deprived areas compared with the least (ONS 2021). The rates of drug misuse in Scotland are much higher than in the other countries that make up the UK. When it comes to England, in 2019–2020, the north-west has the highest number of admissions to hospital due to poisoning by drug misuse, followed by the south-east, with London perhaps surprisingly having the lowest number of admissions.

How might these figures be best explained? In terms of crime, Bottoms and Wiles (2002) have provided two types of explanation. First, that patterns of association may lead to one being influenced by others to commit offences. Second, that the social area itself might influence a person's daily routine, social activities, thought processes, even personality, to the extent that someone's propensity to commit crime is intrinsically affected and in certain situations is greatly increased. What is of central importance to Bottoms and Wiles is thus the question of the relationship of the place of the offence to the offender's habitual use of time and space and, by extension, how an offender's life patterns might influence the location of offending behaviour and vice versa. It would be surprising if this analysis did not apply to other social problems, even those without a direct connection to crime.

Censoriousness, Values, and Morality

In living out our lives we assume, unless there is good reason to believe otherwise, that those with whom we come into contact are rational and reasoned people who are morally responsible for the actions that they have freely chosen to carry out. There are a plethora of acts, freely chosen or not, that are thought wrong and thus frowned upon by society. These break, consciously or unconsciously, rationally, or irrationally, the moral and social codes that most of us seek to live by. Acts which we find particularly distasteful—the abuse of children, for example, fall most easily into this category. The sense of disconsolation that all too often come in their wake are illustrative that something is not quite right. They are representative sociologically of what Durkheim called the 'conscience collective'; that amalgam of collective sentiments, values, and social mores contained in society's laws and moral codes that bind civil society together and into which citizens of society are socialised. Specific anti-social acts in the sense outlined by Durkheim could be said to be symptomatic of a much broader social malaise, their very presence and expression suggesting that there is a breakdown in the customary social conventions and social order of society. As Durkheim might well have put it, they have a function insofar as they alert society to the threats that they pose to the cultural and moral fabric of society.

> **MORAL PHILOSOPHY**
>
> Questions regarding causation, whether these be couched in a biological, psychological, or sociological framework, also raise several questions that look to moral philosophy for practical answers. Among the many moral questions that can be asked, one stands out perhaps more than any other: what **ought** to be done, both morally as well as politically, about the social problems that society has to face?

There are various ways in which such acts are censured, renounced, or prohibited. More often than not acts that are anti-social receive a sanction in some way or other. Some acts—those thought to be anti-social and seen in a negative light as being boorish or out of control in some way—may simply be viewed with moral disapproval. When thought serious or severe enough, certain acts become criminalised and as such subject to penal sanctions. Informed by ideas of rehabilitation, deterrence, or retribution, these range from fines, through to community sentences such as probation orders, through to periods of imprisonment. To break social codes in this way is not simply to fall short of the social standards to which we are all encouraged to adhere, but to challenge the very values and norms that prevail in society. In short anti-social and troublesome behaviour, especially when it involves particularly harmful criminal behaviour—domestic violence, breaking into people's homes, the trafficking of people, to take but three examples—naturally produces hostile reactions and feelings of anger and resentment.

The question thereby arises as the degree to which social problems pose a serious threat to the social solidarity and cohesiveness of society, which cohere around a sharing of common values, beliefs, and norms about what is thought good, desirable, useful, worth striving for and maintaining. Solidarity hints at people sharing the same kind of belief systems and engaging in similar kinds of activity. Certainly, we share certain rules of conduct that, in the main at least, we all follow. But only up to a point. Far from sharing the same sets of beliefs and values, the opposite often seems to be true. Similarly, the degree to which systems are integrated and the extent to which systems are dependent upon each other are both open to question. Social relations rarely run as smoothly as that to which we might aspire. We live in a society permeated and divided from top to bottom by conflict. Some examples upon which we can draw relate to the unequal relations that exist between men and women or between different ethnic groups. Yet others relate to inter-generational conflict. Still others to class conflict, brought about by differential distribution in the resources that are available to us. This represents a specific conception of society. According to this view society is not unitary, bound together by a common cause, but a plurality of competing groups and / or individuals all vying for power from within and between different social groupings and vantage points.

So viewed, social problems are not caused by bio-psychological defects but by conflictual relations that permeate society as a whole. The claim is that such conflicts are all too frequently an expression of social inequality, arising inevitably out of a sense of alienation and disaffection. The limitations of arguing that we live in a consensual and socially cohesive society are very much in evidence. To put this simply, there exists a distinct lack of social cohesion in broad swathes of social life. In a certain sense, social problems represent a breakdown in social order. Indeed, any exploration of social problems is incomplete without reference to the view that an established order based upon common and cohesive morals, values, and beliefs exists within society. In terms of moral sensibilities, we all readily accept that all kinds of abuse are simply wrong; racism, too. It is scarcely questionable that crime is an unwelcome feature of society, that children should be brought up in loving and caring environments, that people should not exploit others and a good deal else besides. There is thus at the very least an argument to be made that certain social problems threaten, in one way or another, this consensus. This, in turn, perhaps naturally leads to a sense of public concern and for remedial action to be taken in order to establish the most orderly set of social relations possible within what is self-evidently a complex and deeply divisive social world.

> **INTERVENTION**
>
> Intervention to reduce the risks and threats posed by social problems is essentially of three kinds:
>
> **Primary intervention** refers to legislation and large scale policy-making including providing funding streams and conduction campaigns to alter mind-sets, with the overall aim of stopping the social problem occurring in the first place;
>
> **Secondary intervention** concerns reducing the impact of the problem in question that has already occurred by detecting, implementing, and treating the problem;
>
> **Tertiary intervention** aims to reduce or soften the full effects of social problems by helping people manage and improve the quality of their lives in order for them to function better. All three are governed by legislation and government policy documents and practice guidelines.

Amelioration The persistent nature of social problems has meant that the need to do something about them has a prolonged and continuous one. Culturally, no society can tolerate the harms that social problems bring with them. The same is true when it comes to tackling the various inequalities and inequities that exist in fields such as health, the criminal justice system, housing, and social services based on race and ethnicity, gender, class, or some other socio-economic factor, which breach fundamental and deep-seated notions of justice and fairness. It is for these two reasons alone that various policy initiatives with various degrees of vitality have over the years been launched to prevent and lessen their worst effects.

In short, we can understand social problems not just as a set of ethical or moral issues, but also in terms of policy-making and their political nature. Though aligned to particular ideological and party-political positions, politicians from all sides recognise that something must be done to protect the public from the harms caused by social problems, to improve the lives of all its citizens and to protect the most vulnerable amongst us, to bring down crime, reduce the amount of harm caused by drug misuse, alleviate the problems associated with the fragmentation of families, bring down homelessness figures or reduce rising numbers of mental health related problems. The key question that differentiates political parties is not whether such and such a social problem should be tackled, but how this should be done, what priority should be given to the problem, and how much should be invested in their resolution. Are some groups more deserving or need our more immediate attention than others? Should health inequalities take precedence over reducing crime, substance misuse, or homelessness? Choices and tough decisions are therefore to be made, often without any clear guidance concerning the basis for making such decisions.

Taking Stock

The main aim of this chapter has been to provide multifactorial material from within the social problems discourse with which to increase our knowledge and understanding of social problems. In drawing together the threads, there are eight points in particular that have emerged from the account offered, which we might usefully note.

1 Social problems from a number of disciplinary angles and from a range of competing methodological, theoretical, and philosophical perspectives, which vary in range, detail, scope, and ambition. This requires the need to ground the ways in which we think about social problems not just in the empirical world of facts and figures using robust measuring tools, but also the processes by which social problems get defined, analysed, and acted upon.
2 Their causes are multiple, the result of an amalgam of variables some bio-psychological other sociological in nature, which may or may not coincide with one another, but certainly interact in a variety of complex ways. What is more, the boundaries between the different spheres, like lines in the sand, are not easily drawn.
3 Social problems are intrinsically circumstantial with the severity and effects of social problems being more acutely felt by different people at particular times and in particular socio-political and socio-economic eras.
4 Understanding and making sense of social problems cannot rest on standards of judgement, or a particular theoretical account which is set in stone, fixed, and immovable. There is no specific thesis to be devised, nor a single line of argument to be pursued.
5 Compositional differences occur not only between people but also between environments and situations. The bio-psycho-social circumstances of humans also

vary considerably with regard to their age, needs, and wants, to their personalities, moral, and ethical frameworks, to their gender, class, and racial background as well as their socio-cultural, socio-political circumstances.
6   The passage of time and the lifespan of individuals is of central importance to our understanding of social problems. The experience of some social problems may be relatively short-lived, whereas others may last for years. This makes questions such as how agents perceive the situation within which they find themselves, the decisions that they make at particular points in their lives and why some people persist with troublesome behaviour whilst others desist from such courses of action of crucial importance.
7   The full picture is therefore only made visible by examining the ever-changing interaction that exists between individual agents from different backgrounds, genders, 'races', socio-economic status and the wider cultural, and geo-socio-political environment within which individuals find themselves.
8   Ideological, economic, moral, practical arguments can all be made in support of putting resources into one particular social problem rather than another, with no one line of argument trumping the others. What is more, there will always be fiscal constraints, just as there will always be competition between various spheres of policy including education, employment, health, work and pension and the department of work and pensions for resources.

In sum, social problems as a field of study is alive and well. It clearly has much to offer in terms of its social scientific role and the insights it brings to our knowledge and understanding of troublesome and difficult behaviour. That social problems are laden with moral, political, socio-economic, and cultural significance is scarcely in doubt. By its nature, the social problems discourse and the knowledge it generates goes to the very heart of debates on what is acceptable in normative terms to society and what is not. Perhaps above all else, what has also been shown is that making sense of social problems and dealing with them satisfactorily is far from being a simple or straightforward matter. Social problems are intricate and complex phenomena. There remains, then, an appreciable amount of work still to do. One of the main objectives in the chapters that follow is to enhance our knowledge and understanding of social problems still further, in such a way as to be meaningful and relevant to the world within which we all live.

Analytic Questions for Consideration

1   What is the purpose of studying social problems?
2   Why and under what circumstances do social problems occur?
3   Is it possible to identify the causes of social problems with any degree of precision?
4   In what ways, if any, do social problems threaten the values and norms of society?
5   Given their intractability, how might social problems best be alleviated?

Social Problems in Numbers (A Quiz)

1   In the year ending March 2020, what percentage of people aged 16 and over said they had been a victim of a crime at least once in the last year?
2   Which area of England had the highest suicide rate in 2021?

a   North East
b   North West
c   West Midlands
d   London
e   South West

3   There were 234,795 marriages in England and Wales in 2018, which is a decrease of 3.3% compared with 2017, and the lowest number since 2009 (232,443).

    a   how many years on average are people likely to stay married?
    b   what percentage of marriages are likely to end in divorce?

4   For the 12-month period to year ending March 2020, the police recorded 758,941 domestic abuse-related crimes (1 in 3 women and 1 in 4 men), an increase of 9% from 2019. Which of the following groups of women has the highest percentage of recorded crimes?

    a   Single
    b   Separated
    c   Cohabiting
    d   Divorced

5   Over recent years, the rate of conception for women under 18 years of age has been falling steadily. What percentage has it fallen between 1993 and 2018?
6   In the year ending 2019, what percentage of people aged 18 to 74 years said that they have experienced at least one form of child abuse, whether emotional abuse, physical abuse, sexual abuse, or witnessing domestic violence or abuse, before the age of 16 years?
7   Has the number of children (aged 10–17) who received a caution or sentence for criminal offences committed risen or fallen between 2010 and 2020?
8   In England and Wales data shows that in 2020 there were 7,423 alcohol-specific deaths. Is this an increase or a decrease in numbers from 2019?
9   What percentage of adults aged 16–59 said that they have taken illegal drugs at some point in their lifetime?
10 How many million people were living in poverty (living in households with income below 60% of inflation-adjusted median income) in 2019/2020 after housing costs were deducted?

Answers to the Statistical Questions and Sources

1   13%, falling steadily over the last few years and down from 17% in the year ending March 2014.
    Source: Office for National Statistics
    https://www.ons.gov.uk/peoplepopulationandcommunity/crimeandjustice/bulletins/crimeinenglandandwales/yearendingseptember2021
2   (a) The North East with 13.3%, followed by the South West with 11.2%, the lowest being London with 7.0%
    Source: Office for National Statistics, Suicides in England and Wales: 2020 Registrations
    https://www.ons.gov.uk/peoplepopulationandcommunity/birthsdeathsandmarriages/deaths/bulletins/suicidesintheunitedkingdom/2020registrations

3. (a) 12 years

   (b) 33%

   Source: Office for National Statistics, Marriages in England and Wales: 2018
   https://www.ons.gov.uk/peoplepopulationandcommunity/birthsdeathsandmarriages/marriagecohabitationandcivilpartnerships/bulletins/marriagesinenglandandwalesprovisional/2018

4. (b) Separated with 18%, followed by divorced with 13%, single 12%, and the lowest cohabiting with 7%.

   Source: Office for National Statistics Domestic Abuse in England and Wales Overview: November 2020.
   https://www.ons.gov.uk/peoplepopulationandcommunity/crimeandjustice/bulletins/domesticabuseinenglandandwalesoverview/november2020

5. 60%

   Source Nuffield Trust, Teenage Pregnancy
   https://www.nuffieldtrust.org.uk/resource/teenage-pregnancy

6. 20%—8.5 million people.

   Source: Office for National Statistics, Child Abuse Extent and Nature, England, and Wales: year ending March 2019.
   https://www.ons.gov.uk/peoplepopulationandcommunity/crimeandjustice/articles/childabuseextentandnatureenglandandwales/yearendingmarch2019

7. 19,000 children were cautioned or sentenced during this period, a fall of 82%, with a 12% fall in the year ending December 2018. First time entrants to the criminal justice system has fallen by 84%, though the average custodial sentence has increased by seven months over this period from 11.3 months to 18.6 months.

   Source: Youth Justice Board, Ministry of Justice
   https://assets.publishing.service.gov.uk/government/uploads/system/uploads/attachment_data/file/956621/youth-justice-statistics-2019-2020.pdf

8. An increase of 19.6%.

   Source: Alcohol for Change UK, Alcohol Statistics
   https://alcoholchange.org.uk/alcohol-facts/fact-sheets/alcohol-statistics

9. 34.2%.

   Source: Home Office, Drug Misuse: Findings from the 2018/19 Crime Survey for England and Wales
   https://assets.publishing.service.gov.uk/government/uploads/system/uploads/attachment_data/file/832533/drug-misuse-2019-hosb2119.pdf

10. 14.5m, 4.3m of whom were children.

    Source: UK Parliament, House of Commons Library
    https://commonslibrary.parliament.uk/research-briefings/sn07096/

Selected Further Reading

Competing Perspectives

Crone, J.A. (2015) *How Can We Solve Our Social Problems?* (Third edition), London: Sage.
Etzioni, A. (1976) *Social Problems*, London: Prentice-Hall.
Kendal, D. (2013) *Social Problems in a Diverse Society*, New York: Pearson.
Rubington, E., and Weinberg, M. (2011) *The Study of Social Problems: Seven Perspectives* (Seventh edition), OUP USA.

Policy and Practice

May, M., Page, R., and Brunsdon, E. (2001) *Understanding Social Problems: Issues in Social Policy*, Oxford: Blackwell.

Sullivan, T.J. (2014) *Introduction to Social Problems* (Tenth edition), Needham Heights: Allyn and Bacon.

Social Constructionism

Berger, P.L., and Luckman, T. (1966) *The Social Construction of Reality: A Treatise in the Sociology of Knowledge*, London: Penguin.

Best, J. (2020) *Social Problems* (Fourth edition), New York: Norton.

Holstein, J.A., and Miller, G. (2011) *Reconsidering Social Constructionism: Debates in Social Problems Theory*: Rutgers, NJ: Transaction Publishers.

Spector, M., and Kituse, J.I. (2009) *Constructing Social Problems*, New Brunswick, NJ: Transaction Publications.

The Human Life Course

Cohen, S. (2002) *Folk Devils and Moral Panics: The Creation of Mods and Rockers* (Third edition), London: Routledge.

Lopata, H.Z., and Levy, J.A. (2003) *Social Problems across the Life Course*, Oxford: Rowman and Littlefield.

Structure and Agency

Archer, M.S. (1995) *Realist Social Theory: The Morphogenetic Approach*, Cambridge: Cambridge University Press.

Bronfenbrenner, U. (1979) *The Ecology of Human Development: Experiments by Nature and Design*, London: Harvard University Press.

Giddens, A. (1984) *The Constitution of Society: Outline of the Theory of Structuration*, Cambridge: Polity.

References

Agrawal, A., Verwies, K. Gillespie, N., Heath, A., Lessove-Schlaggar, C., Martin, N., Nelson, E., Slutske, W., Whitfield, J. and Lynsky, M. (2012) 'The genetics of addiction – a translational perspective' in *Translational Psychiatry* 2: e140.

Archer, M. (1995) *Realist Social Theory: The Morphogenetic Approach*, Cambridge: Cambridge University Press.

Berger, P. and Luckman, T. (1966) *The Social Construction of Reality: A Treatise in the Sociology of Knowledge*, London: Penguin.

Best, J. (2020) *Social Problems* (Fourth edition), New York: Norton.

Blumer, H. (1971) 'Social Problems as Collective Behaviour' in *Social Problems* 18(3): 298–306.

Bottoms, A. and Wiles, P. (2002) 'Environmental Criminology' in M. Maguire, R. Morgan, R. Rainer (Eds.), *The Oxford Handbook of Criminology*, Oxford: Clarendon Press.

Cohen, S. (2002) *Folk Devils and Moral Panics: The Creation of Mods and Rockers* (Third edition), London: Routledge.

Crone, J. (2015) *How Can We Solve Our Social Problems?* (Third edition), London: Sage.

Durrant, R., Adamson, S. and Todd, F. (2009) 'Drug use and addiction: evolutionary perspective', in *Australian and New Zealand Journal of Psychiatry* 43(11): 1049–1056.

Ersche, K., Barnes, A., Jones, P., Morein-Zamir, S., Robbins, T. and Bullmore, E. (2011) 'Abnormal structure of frontostriatal brain systems is associated with aspects of impulsivity and compulsivity in cocaine dependence', *Brain: A Journal of Neurology*, 134(Pt 7): 2013–2024. https://doi.org/10.1093/brain/awr138

Etzioni, A. (1976) *Social Problems*, London: Prentice-Hall.

Giddens, A. (1984) *The Constitution of Society: Outline of the Theory of Structuration*, Cambridge: Polity.

Jewkes, R. (2002) 'Intimate partner violence: causes and prevention', in *The Lancet* 359: 1423–1329.

Kahneman, D. (2011) *Thinking, Fast and Slow*, London: Penguin.

Kendal, D. (2013) *Social Problems in a Diverse Society*, New York: Pearson.

Kohlberg, L. (1976) 'Moral stages and moralisation' in T. Lickona (ed.) *Moral Development and Behaviour*, New York: Holt, Rinehart, and Winston.

Leeds, J. and Morgenstern, J. (1996) 'Psychoanalytic theories of substance abuse' in F. Rogers, J. Morgenstern, and S.T. Walters (eds.), *Treating Substance Abuse: Theory and Technique*, pp. 68–83. NY: Guilford.

Lopata and Levy (2003) *Social Problems across the Life Course*, Oxford: Rowman and Littlefield.

Maio, G., Haddock, G. and Verplanken, B. (2018) *The Psychology of Attitudes and Attitude Change* (Third edition), London: Sage.

May, M., Page, R. and Brunsdon, E. (eds.) (2001) *Understanding Social Problems: Issues in Social Policy*, Oxford: Blackwell.

Miller, G. and Holstein, J. (eds.) (1993) *Constructionist Controversies: Issues in Social Problems Theory*, New York: Aldine de Gruyter.

Mills, C. (1959) *The Sociological Imagination*, Oxford: Oxford University Press.

Office of National Statistics (2021) https://www.ons.gov.uk/peoplepopulationandcommunity/birthsdeathsandmarriages/deaths/bulletins/suicidesintheunitedkingdom/latest

Pilnick, A. (2002) *Genetics and Society: An Introduction*, Buckingham: Open University Press.

Public Health England (2021a) https://www.gov.uk/government/publications/health-matters-reducing-health-inequalities-in-mental-illness/health-matters-reducing-health-inequalities-in-mental-illness

Public Health England (2021b) https://www.gov.uk/government/statistics/health-inequalities-dashboard-march-2021-data-update/health-inequalities-dashboard-statistical-commentary-march-2021

Rubington, E. and Weinberg, M. (2011) *The Study of Social Problems: Seven Perspectives* (Seventh edition), NY: Oxford University Press.

Seidman, S. and Alexander, J. (2001) *The New Social Theory Reader: Contemporary Debates*, London: Routledge.

Sullivan, T. (2014) *Introduction to Social Problems* (Tenth edition), Needham Heights: Allyn and Bacon.

Wikstrom, P.-O. (2017) 'Character, Circumstances, and the Causes of Crime: Towards an Analytic Criminology' in A. Liebling, S. Maruna and L. McAra (Eds.), *The Oxford Book of Criminology* (Sixth edition), Oxford: Oxford University Press.

Wilkinson, R. and Pickett, K. (2009) *The Spirit Level: Why Greater Equality Makes Societies Stronger*, London: Allen Lane.

3 Poverty

The social problem of all time?

Elizabeth Richards

Introduction

Making sense of contemporary society and the everyday world in which we live is rooted in making connections between personal experiences of social phenomena and wider social contexts. Poverty has been and remains a contested social issue and the intention of this chapter is to put forward some critical understanding of poverty in the UK as both a concept and a lived experience. As a concept it features in a raft of academic research since the late 19th century and in recent years it has come to dominate public discussion on policy, provision, and practice with children, families, and the wider population. As a lived experience, it can be seen as one of the most enduring social issues, with recent estimates indicating that at some stage in their lives one in three people in the UK has experienced poverty and, despite claims made to the contrary by some in power, this figure has been rising in recent years (Joseph Rowntree Foundation, 2021). Initially, this chapter puts poverty in the UK in Global context, going on to outline something of its impact in the UK, historically. It goes on to explore a range of definitions, measures and theories that have been put forward to help explain what the causes and consequences of poverty are, examining some of the solutions and responses that have been put in place by various political administrations and non-governmental organisations since World War 2. Without doubt, it can be argued that poverty is a multi-faceted issue with which many, if not all the social problems presented in this edited collection are or have been connected; consequently, it might be considered *the* social problem of all time.

Poverty: a global concern

Poverty is an issue with which many international and supra national non-governmental organisations are constantly grappling. Globally, latest statistics show that almost 690 million people live with extreme poverty, on less than $1.90 a day; in 2017, 24.1% of the world lived on less than $3.20 a day and 43.6% on less than $5.50 a day. Two thirds of the world's poor people are children and young people under the age of 18, and women represent the majority of poor people in most regions. Approximately seven in ten people older than 15 who live with extreme poverty have no – or only basic – education, and approximately 22% of the world's population live with multidimensional poverty. In 2020, for the first time in 20 years, global extreme poverty was expected to rise due to the impact of the COVID-19 pandemic, adding to the forces of conflict and climate change which were, even before this, slowing the progress of poverty reduction across the world (World Vision, 2020).

DOI: 10.4324/9781003166887-3

The impact of poverty in the UK

Whilst it clearly impacts life chances in developing countries, poverty is also an issue that produces a whole range of undesirable outcomes for people in the UK. It is implicated in the development of chronic diseases and diet-related problems connected with poorer physical health and well-being across the lifespan, as well as reduced life expectancy (Marmot Report, 2010). Those living with poverty are over three times more likely to suffer from mental health problems, indeed poverty can be both a cause and a consequence of poor mental health (Elliott, 2016). Suicide is also more prevalent in those who live with poverty and deteriorating mental health may partly be explained by the stresses of living with poverty and the stigma and shame that can accompany this. Evidence suggests that poverty can also be a consequence of family breakdown, worklessness, and drug and alcohol misuse, however it is far too simplistic to state categorically that these issues are the primary cause of poverty, indeed no empirical evidence has been produced by successive governments in the UK to suggest that they are, although they are consistently represented as such in some media and by some politicians (Shildrick, 2018; Gordon, 2016). Matters such as *food poverty and insecurity*, not considered significant at the end of the 20th century have also come to the fore in the UK in recent years, identified as having a plethora of adverse effects on health and well-being, as does *fuel poverty* and living in the insecure housing and the overcrowded conditions often caused by poverty (Daly and Kelly, 2015). All these issues are connected to mental and physical health problems in the adult population, but also in children and young people.

Poverty in childhood

It is estimated that one in five children lives with persistent poverty in the UK. Children and young people can be particularly susceptible to the effects of poverty as they rarely have access to income themselves. Children who live with poverty are less likely to do well at school or go on to further or higher education and more likely to end up in unskilled and unsecure employment. They can find themselves excluded from social and cultural activities, which can impact self-esteem, mental health, and result in bullying (Daly and Kelly, 2015).

Other social issues relating to poverty are also specifically associated with childhood – child abuse, youth offending and teen parenthood – and there is evidence to suggest that child abuse, in terms of absence of care and supervision, is more prevalent amongst families who live with poverty, although by no means is the abuse of children confined to such families (Parton, 2014: 184). Youth offending too, is very much associated with poverty, and young people who live with poverty are more likely to be arrested, charged, convicted, and handed a custodial sentence. They are also more likely to be the victims of crime and many young people caught up in offending – who are often damaged by childhood trauma or mental health problems linked to poverty – find little account is taken of this, their age or socio-economic status in the criminal justice system (Muncie, 2015). Links between poverty and early parenthood are also well established, indeed, the UK has some of the highest teen pregnancy rates in the global north, with young women in the lowest socio-economic quintile almost ten times more likely to become pregnant than their more affluent counterparts (Stapleton, 2010). Low birthweight babies, prematurity, and higher infant mortality are also associated with teen motherhood (Stapleton, 2010), although it must be noted that for all families who experience it, poverty can result in lower birthweight in babies and higher infant mortality, as well as impaired cognitive and physical development in children (Spencer, 2018).

Poverty in the UK: historical context

It is over 600 years since concern about pauperism and poverty prompted legislative intervention in the form of various poor laws to alleviate it.

BOX 3.1 POOR RELIEF

In the late 18th and early 19th century two forms of poor relief were prevalent across the UK; outdoor relief (which came in the form of parish assistance to paupers who continued to live in their own homes) and indoor relief – poorhouses that offered shelter to paupers and other distressed persons (Englander, 1998).

In the 19th century, early poor laws came under scrutiny and powerful criticisms were levelled at poor relief in the UK – outdoor relief in particular – for causing more problems than it solved in undermining incentives to work and in demoralising citizens. In the 1834 Poor Law Amendment Act – considered at the time to be the 'single most important piece of social legislation ever enacted' (Englander, 1998: 1) – the administration of poverty alleviation became centralised, and provision to address it was underscored by *the principle of 'less eligibility'*; meaning that those who needed to claim poor relief *must* enter the workhouse and *must never* be better off than those who were working, even in the most menial forms of labour (Novak, 1988). At this point, poverty was understood essentially as a private matter and only to be addressed by some form of state intervention when people found themselves in the most acute circumstances and even then, support was expected to be minimal to disincentivise dependency and indolence.

The establishment of poverty as a social problem

Comprehensive surveys undertaken by two pioneers of poverty research in the UK, Charles Booth (1840–1916) and Seebohm Rowntree (1871–1954) in late 19th-century London and York were instrumental in establishing the idea that poverty was a social problem that required a more considered response.

BOX 3.2 SEEBOHM ROWNTREE

Seebohm Rowntree's work in particular established that a 'poverty line' or 'minimum income' existed below which it was judged that families and individuals would not be able to survive. Rowntree established the concept of 'primary' poverty, indicative of this destitute state; and 'secondary' poverty, a state said to be experienced by '*families whose total earnings would be sufficient for the maintenance of merely physical efficiency were it not that some portion of it is absorbed by other expenditure, either useful or wasteful*' (Rowntree, 1901: x original emphasis).

The work of these pioneers formed the beginning of the idea that "matters [such as poverty] previously deemed to be private were now viewed as a legitimate part of the 'public sphere'" (Fraser, 2009: 162). Thus, they required more supportive state intervention and that definition, measurement, and statistical evaluation was pivotal to that.

Defining poverty

Fundamentally, poverty might be defined as lacking in resources to sustain life and so termed 'absolute'. This was a definition utilised by Booth and Rowntree and that largely prevailed in the UK for most of the 20th century, however, the work of Peter Townsend was instrumental in altering this, identifying poverty as relative to the existing social conditions. For Townsend:

> Poverty can be defined objectively and applied consistently only in terms of the concept of relative deprivation… Individuals and families can be said to be in poverty when they lack the resources to obtain the types of diet, participate in the activities and have the living conditions and amenities which are customary, or at least widely encouraged or approved, in the societies to which they belong.
> (1979: 31)

In essence, relative poverty relates to the social norms prevalent in a particular society at a particular time; so for example, if it is understood to be the norm to live in a home with an internet connection, anybody who cannot afford one might be deemed to be living in relative poverty.

BOX 3.3 POVERTY: ABSOLUTE OR RELATIVE?

Most commonly, poverty has been considered in dichotomous terms as either absolute or relative. Whether it should be understood as a state of destitution where the most basic necessities, such as food, shelter, warmth, clothing, and sanitation are lacking, or whether it should be viewed as contextual and contingent on the society in which people live is a matter for debate (Platt, 2020).

With this in mind, the dichotomy between absolute and relative poverty can be somewhat misleading as it belies the complexity of poverty and 'both judgement (about what actually constitutes…a poverty line) and context (…what…is acceptable in the surrounding society) necessarily have a bearing' on how poverty is perceived and experienced over time (Platt, 2020: 159).

In 2014, The Joseph Rowntree Foundation (JRF) put forward the following definition of poverty:

> Poverty is 'When a person's resources (mainly their material resources) are not sufficient to meet their minimum needs (including social participation'.
> (cited in Goulden and D'Arcy, 2014: 3)

JRF argue that whether people have enough resources to meet their needs is impacted by several issues including their income; the kind of services they have access to; their health and education; the cost of childcare or social care, leisure; the cost of living (especially of essentials such as food, heating, housing, and transport); what kind of credit they can access, and what debt they end up with.

Poverty measurement

Measuring poverty is essential if action is going to be taken to improve the lives of those currently living with – or at risk of falling into – poverty. It is also essential to ensuring that those individuals, families, communities, and areas of the UK that have historically been left behind are supported to improve their situation. Income measurement is regarded as one of the clearest indicators of socio-economic status and poverty, enabling direct comparison with other countries, but also allowing domestic comparisons over time (Hansen and Kneale, 2013). The Households Below Average Income (HBAI) survey, produced annually by the Office of National Statistics is the primary source of data about household income and inequality in the UK (Department for Work and Pensions (DWP), 2021). Currently, the two income measures used by UK governments are:

1. Relative low income: the number of people living in households with income below 60% of the median in *that year*.
2. Absolute low income: the number of people living in households with income below 60% of (inflation-adjusted) median income as compared with a base year (in the UK, usually 2010/2011).

The first measure compares the households with the lowest incomes against the rest of the population in a particular year; the second looks at whether living standards at the bottom of the income distribution are improving over time. Income can also be measured either before or after housing costs are deducted (BHC or AHC). It is notable that poverty levels are generally higher in measures of income *after* housing costs as people who live with poverty are disposed to spend a higher proportion of their income on housing.

BOX 3.4 MEDIAN INCOME

Median income is defined as the midpoint between the highest and lowest incomes. There is a considerable difference between weekly median incomes across the UK. In 2019 the median income of the devolved nations are as follows: England £574.00; Scotland £563.20; NI £521.30; Wales £509.00 (Francis-Devine, 2020).

Recent poverty statistics

All four UK devolved nations produce poverty statistics, however, they do not all follow the same criteria or timeframes, so comparisons between them are not straightforward. Using the 60% measure most commonly used:

- England: In 2018, 18% of the population lived in relative income poverty (RIP) before housing costs (BHC), rising to 22% once housing costs are accounted for (AHC). This equates to approximately 11.7 million people BHC and 14.5 million AHC (Francis-Devine, 2020).
- Scotland: Between 2016 and 2019 17% of the population (900,000 people) were living in RIPBHC, whilst 19% of people (1.02 million people) were living in RIPAHC (Scottish Government, 2020).
- Wales: Between 2017–2018 and 2019–2020, 23% of all people in Wales were living in relative income poverty AHC – the figures are presented as percentages only and the data is divided by social group (Welsh Government, 2020).
- Northern Ireland: Measurements compare relative poverty and absolute poverty BHC. Latest statistics show that between 2018 and 2019 19% of people were living in relative income poverty BHC, equating to 350,000 individuals; 16% of people in NI (approximately 303,000) were considered to be in absolute poverty BHC (Department for Communities, 2020).

Statistics are an important factor in understanding the extent of poverty at a given time and place; they are part of a mechanism to hold governments to account and there is a simplistic appeal in adhering to 'poverty line' measurements, but they can be confusing. One of the greatest criticisms levelled at them is that they do not measure standard of living and so understanding of poverty as a social problem necessarily must entail something more than measuring 60% of median income.

BOX 3.5 POVERTY: A NEW MEASUREMENT?

In 2016 the Social Metrics Commission (SMC), an independent group of experts established a new poverty measure, to help produce a clearer understanding of the nature and experiences of poverty for differing family forms. The new measure takes account of both income and material resources, including the available liquid assets that families have; this measure also includes the inescapable costs that some families face which make them more likely than others to experience poverty, such as the extra cost of disability; childcare; rental, and mortgage costs. The SMC have also broadened their poverty measure to include an assessment of overcrowding in housing and rough sleeping, as well as presenting a more detailed analysis of the depth and persistence of poverty for those experiencing it, with the intention of highlighting the differences in experiences of those living with poverty and those living above the poverty line. The SMC argues that its approach constitutes the most accurate way to measure poverty which can provide a basis of consensus building and for taking action (SMC, 2021). Nevertheless, it is still the more standardised measure of 60% that current UK governments choose to employ.

Who are 'poor people' and why are they likely to be living with poverty?

Across all the countries of the UK evidence suggests that working age adults who live in social rented accommodation are more likely to be in relative income poverty when compared to those who are owner occupiers or renting privately (Ministry of Housing,

Communities, and Local Government, 2018). Living in a workless household also increases the chances of relative income poverty for working-age adults, as does living in a family with more than three children (CPAG, 2021). Women are at higher risk of poverty than men in the UK, but this is by no means universal. Evidence from the Poverty and Social Exclusion (PSE) Survey in 1999 suggested single women pensioners were at substantially more risk of experiencing poverty than their male counterparts, however, recent evidence suggests that this has reduced somewhat and it is lone mothers who experience the highest levels of poverty. Subsequently, the 2012 PSE Survey identified that two thirds of lone mothers were income poor (cited in Dermott and Pantazis, 2018).

People from Black, Asian, and Minority Ethinic (BAME) groups are also more likely to live in relative income poverty. Recent figures suggest that whilst income has fallen across all households from non-white ethnic groups since 2008, persistent poverty is particularly prevalent amongst the Pakistani. Bangladeshi and Black African and Black Caribbean communities (Karlsen and Pantazis, 2018). Coming from a household where there is someone with a disability also increases the likelihood of living in relative income poverty for both working-age adults and children (Shahtahmasebi et al., 2011).

Theories and concepts

One of the central debates in poverty as a social problem focuses on what actually makes people poor and there are a range of theories that claim to explain that.

Traditional sociological theories of poverty

Poverty as a social problem *per se* has not always been at the forefront of sociological thought, rather foundational theorists of sociology tended to be preoccupied by various forms of inequality. Karl Marx (1818–1883), writing in the mid-19th century for example, focused on the volatile capitalist mode of production as pivotal in fuelling and sustaining economic inequality. For Marx, two classes had evolved in modernity: the capitalist class, comprising industrialists, bankers, and merchants, supported by salaried managerial, technical, and supervisory staff and some elements of the established landed aristocracy. They sat in opposition to the working classes, who were largely dependent on the wages paid by the capitalist class. From this perspective poverty is caused by both the instability of capitalism and the exploitation of the working classes by their employers. A key feature of Marx's analysis is his argument that 'inequality is neither fixed nor necessary' and poverty might be addressed by fundamental changes to the capitalist mode of production (Townsend, 1979: 80).

Writing at the turn of the 20th century, a second foundational theorist of sociology, Max Weber (1864–1920), highlighted the impact of power, prestige, and status on generating and maintaining inequality. From Weber's perspective, considerations such as profession, ethnicity, education, income, and religion are all material to the unequal distribution of resources, causing inequality which, in turn, impacts an individual's power to control the further allocation of resources and so generates poverty. From both Marx' and Weber's perspectives, inequality and thus poverty might be addressed by the emergence of a more progressive, egalitarian society, and improved social relations at both its structural and personal levels (ibid).

Emile Durkheim (1858–1917), a third foundational sociological theorist, subscribed to a somewhat different view. Durkheim emphasised the necessity of inequality to encourage individuals to conform to the social roles and moral obligations that make up all societies. Writing in the late 19th and early 20th centuries, Durkheim argued that in order to fill all the positions that are of functional importance to society, the financial reward for undertaking them needs to be inequitable because inequality is what makes individuals endeavour to improve their occupational status. This in turn improves their social and economic condition and so allows them the opportunity to rise out of poverty. Clark and Cochrane (1998) argue this explanation situates poverty as a feature of society that is not only socially necessary but desirable because it acts as an incentive for people to try harder to succeed. Any attempt to intercede to ameliorate poverty as a social problem will prevent such efforts and result in people living with poverty losing the moral urge to fend for themselves.

Marx, Weber, and Durkheim are foundational sociological theorists; however, they still have resonance in the analysis of poverty as the antecedents of more recent thinking, which has concentrated more explicitly on the differential influence of psychology, social structure, and agency in explaining the pervasiveness of poverty over time.

Psychological explanations for poverty

Understood in terms of the 'naturalising perspective' or the 'nativist' perspective, this theoretical approach posits the idea that biological factors lead directly to poverty (Turner and Lehning, 2007). Evidence for this was gleaned originally from IQ testing, although the value of such tests and their connection with poverty is now largely refuted in academic circles, yet there are some that still advocate that poverty is 'natural and inevitable' and the result of the unequal, distribution of levels of intelligence, attributing the success of the middle classes to their superior intellect. Related psychological theories focus on the differential language development and acquisition of children who live with poverty – as compared with their better off counterparts – and its impact on employability when children reach adulthood. There also the theory that people who live with poverty have failed to develop specific traits, for example the need for achievement, affiliation and power, which presents a barrier to success in the workplace, in turn impacting financial success (McClelland cited in Steinmann, Ötting, and Maier, 2016). Concentration on personal traits and personality characteristics position the problem of poverty with 'poor' people themselves and tend to towards individualistic explanations for poverty, even when environmental factors are mooted, meaning that poverty is understood as ultimately attributable to individual characteristics.

Social structural explanations for poverty

Social structural theories of poverty put forward the idea that rather than natural and inevitable, or indeed the result of individual characteristics, poverty exists largely due to the way in which social relations are organised. From this perspective, poverty is best explained as being caused by social, economic, and political factors which put people at more risk of poverty and are largely outside the control of the individuals and families. Variations in incidences of poverty are accounted for by spatial and temporal differences in these factors. Social structural explanations for poverty, particularly rooted in class relations, largely dominated poverty analysis and responses to poverty in the post-World War 2 (WW2) era in the UK, when the welfare state was introduced, however other social divisions such as gender, race, disability, age, and sexuality have also entered the frame, since it is argued they engender discrimination and oppression manifest in sexism, racism, disablism, ageism, and heterosexism at various levels of society. Such discrimination and oppression can be a barrier to engaging in the labour market equitably, to equal participation in society and to individuals, families, and social groups accessing the resources that will lift them out of poverty (Thompson, 2018).

Agentic explanations for poverty

Agentic explanations for poverty contrast with social structural explanations because they consider poverty to be caused by factors within the control of individuals. From this perspective culture and personal behaviour are viewed as the primary determinants of poverty. Having been prominent during the 19th century, agentic/individual explanations for the existence and persistence of poverty began to re-emerge in 1950s USA to describe the dispositions and habits of some social groups. In the 1970s this began to inform understandings of poverty the UK and since then individualistic explanations of poverty have come increasingly to the fore, focussing variously on the character of 'poor' people, their inabilities and incapacities, or their lack of appropriate socialisation. This locates the cause of poverty in the attitudes, behaviour, morals of 'poor' people and focuses on the decisions and actions of individuals and what they do – or do not do – to influence their personal situation, however it takes little account of structural inequalities and their impact on perpetuating poverty (Clarke and Cochrane, 1998).

The welfare state

Since 1945, the welfare state has often been constructed as fundamental to the amelioration of poverty. The welfare state, however, is not a monolithic institution, it is shaped by political ideology and this in turn impacts what the state does to and for people who live with poverty (George and Wilding, 1994). There have been a number of political administrations in power since 1945 and each has put forward differing views of the causes of poverty and these in turn have resulted in differing welfare solutions to address it.

BOX 3.6

Social democratic ideology sees the state as central to the evolution of a more equitable society and advocates state intervention and socially responsible policies to support those in need and 'the pursuit of social justice through the gradual reform of the – predominantly capitalist – market economy' (Alcock and May, 2014:232)

BOX 3.7

Neo-liberal ideology sees individual responsibility, self-sufficiency and engagement with market principles as the most appropriate and efficient way for individuals and families to generate income and sustain themselves. The state's role should be limited to providing institutional frameworks for the private market sector and the private domestic sphere to operate (Alcock and May, 2014).

Social democracy and poverty

Prior to World War 2 (WW2) mass poverty and unemployment were recurring features of UK society and the reduction of poverty as a policy objective was a factor in the creation of the post WW2 welfare state. The welfare state has been closely associated with Social Democracy; a political ideology influenced by the *Fabian* tradition of the early 20th century.

Introduced between 1945 and 1951 during a Labour administration, at its inception the British welfare state was rooted in an economic model of full employment and state regulated nationalised industry developed by John Maynard Keynes, and the recommendations of a 1942 report entitled 'Social Insurance and Allied Services' produced by social economist William Beveridge. Poverty at this time was defined by Beveridge as 'want' and a prime concern of the newly formed welfare state was the establishment of a National Insurance scheme to abolish want and maintain people's income throughout various stages in their lives. Supported by a system of taxation and redistribution of wealth, this offered a safety net to which all who worked would contribute and could benefit. National Assistance: non-contributory provision to support disabled, sick, aged, and other persons, was also established, replacing previous poor laws and rather than 'welfare benefits' – a term utilised nowadays that perhaps gives the impression the recipient is being paid something advantageous that others are not – the focus was on 'social security'. Poverty relief in this form was framed as a universal human *right* to which any civilised society should aspire (Taylor, 2007).

Social security

A stated intention of the 'social security' provided by the welfare state was to ameliorate poverty and the worst effects of capitalism and for the following 30 years welfare policies were underpinned by a *Social Democratic Consensus* which promoted an orientation to welfare provision rooted in egalitarian principles, supplemented by a citizenship rights discourse. Poverty was understood to be caused by structural inequality, largely rooted in class relations, however, despite the introduction of family allowances and maternity benefits said to support women, the original social security system was predicated on systematic discrimination *against* women, being underpinned by two primary assumptions: 'that the proper role of women was as wives and mothers, and that the economic status of women should be that of dependence on men' (Novak, 1988: 153). As such, the experience of women at the hands of the welfare state was one of continuing poverty. A similar situation existed for other social groups and resulted in the marginalisation of BAME communities, disabled and elderly people, along with unskilled workers, who constituted the majority of people who lived with poverty in the post WW2 era.

Neo-liberalism and poverty

From the 1970s there was a marked shift away from social democratic towards neo-liberal political ideology in welfare policy and agentic/individualistic explanations for poverty began to dominate policy decisions.

BOX 3.8

It should be noted at this point that between 1979 and 1997 attempts to promote social justice and to address poverty as a social problem were not in evidence in policy debates and it is notable that only one of the numerous reports produced about welfare actually featured the word 'poverty' (Gordon, 2016).

Note: Between 1979 and 1997 attempts to promote social justice and to address poverty as a social problem were not in evidence in policy debates and it is notable that only one of the numerous reports produced about welfare actually featured the word 'poverty' (Gordon, 2016).

Successive Conservative administrations from 1979 to 1997 adopted a neo-liberal approach, situating the causes of poverty emphatically as rooted in the individual deficit of 'poor' people. For Conservatives, who embraced neo-liberal ideas, the post WW2 social democratic consensus was positively harmful to individual and social well-being. Provision of universal (and sometimes unconditional) welfare benefits was criticised as a barrier to both individual and national economic prosperity and accused of stifling the competition and freedom necessary for individuals and families to thrive (Beresford, 2016). State benefits were framed as 'hand outs' that featherbedded the idle, encouraged a dependancy culture and immoral behaviour, which in turn was argued to perpetuate poverty. The promotion of individual *responsibility*, rather than *rights,* particularly for those of lower socio-economic status, began to inform policy decisions. Thus the welfare state, hitherto seen as something of a champion of those living with was reformulated as the 'enemy of the poor'.

Neo-liberal ideology has continued to dominate policy debates on poverty: in the New Labour administration 1997–2010, it took on a mantle of *Third Way* ideology and in successive Conservative administrations since 2010, it has become associated with some of the most minimal and, indeed, punitive responses to poverty (Beresford, 2016).

The social construction of poverty

Both social democracy and neo-liberalism are examples political ideologies that understand the causes of poverty from very different perspectives; social democracy favours structural explanations; neo-liberalism favours individual/agentic. Whilst theories of both structure and agency can help to explain the causes of poverty, it is the theoretical perspective of 'social constructionism' that has helped more recently to illuminate what poverty means. From a social constructionist perspective, there is no one way to understand poverty, rather it is constituted by the ideas and beliefs about what it is and what causes it that are dominant in society *at that time* and *in that place*. Social constructionists point to the influence of language – spoken or written – and other symbolic systems of representation, such as are articulated through various forms of imagery, to describe, define, classify, characterise, and otherwise distinguish what causes poverty and who 'poor' people are (Phillips and Hardy, 2002: 3).

From a social constructionist perspective language and images relating to poverty are not merely communicative, they are conduits for the exercise of power and create 'discourses' to which social meanings, values, and norms are attached. Social constructionists argue that the process(es) by which understandings of poverty are produced, disseminated, and received lead to the dominance of particular ideas and beliefs about its causes, reflecting prevailing social fears, doubts, and concerns. None of this accidental, objective, or neutral and new discourses of poverty do not just replace the old, they reconstitute and reshape them, sometimes subtly, others less so. New understandings of poverty are then constructed, influencing how people make sense of it, which can have a profound effect on how those who live with poverty are understood by wider society and how they see themselves. Just as importantly this can alter what those in power believe is best done to address their situation and increasingly it is not poverty that is constructed as the social problem, but 'poor' people themselves.

BOX 3.9 LABELLING 'POOR' PEOPLE

Since the 19th century, there have been a series of labels that have been utilised to describe 'poor' people as a section of UK society who are understood to exist within or below the working classes. This group has been referred to variously as the 'submerged social stratum' the 'social residuum'; the 'unemployables' the 'dangerous classes'; the 'hard to reach'. Latterly the terms 'chav' and 'welfare scrounger' have entered common parlance. Such labels have constructed and reconstructed the idea that there is a class of people who are different from and subordinate to the rest of us. In recent years these people have been referred to in derogatory terms as 'the underclass' (Welshman, 2014).

Poverty and the 'underclass'

Welshman (2014) charts the development of the concept 'underclass', from 1880 to the present. In the 1950s and 60s a 'culture of poverty' thesis developed in the USA that began to individualise poverty, attributing it to the behavioural characteristics of families emanating from certain marginalised sections of society, fuelling the idea that poverty was handed down from generation to generation. This in turn influenced British perceptions, dominant in Conservative/neoliberal discourse in 1970s UK that 'problem families' existed who had "a number of inter-related difficulties – of temperament, intelligence, money, and health" (Joseph cited in Welshman, 2014: 124). This it was argued caused a 'cycle of deprivation'. Whilst there is little empirical evidence such a culture or cycle did – or does – exist, the idea persisted, conflating poverty (as lack of money) with poverty (as lifestyle choice). Having several iterations between 1979 and 1997 when the Conservative party were in power, terms such as 'transmitted deprivation' leading to a 'dependency culture' emerged in political, social, and cultural discourse. More recently, the work of American sociologist Charles Murray is implicated in the further development and maintenance of the idea that an 'underclass' exists in UK society. Again, with little evidence, this began to inform policy decisions during the New Labour administration between 1997 and 2008 in their conceptualisation of 'problem families' and became further consolidated in the public psyche when the Coalition and more recent Conservative administrations came to power from 2010, where the term 'troubled family' emerged as a dominant discourse of the causes of poverty (Welshman, 2014).

New labour, poverty, and third way ideology

Between 1997 and 2010 New Labour's approach to poverty attempted to fuse social democratic and neo-liberal ideology into a 'Third Way,'

> **BOX 3.10**
>
> The Third Way is a pragmatic political ideology claiming to combine the pursuit of economic growth with concern for the less fortunate. From this perspective the most effective way to meet the needs of citizens is to reconceptualise the welfare state as the *social investment state*, advancing "*human capital*" wherever possible' rather than providing direct income maintenance (Giddens, 1998: 117).

On the one hand, addressing poverty as a social problem and promoting social justice is seen as a legitimate policy objective and this was manifest in the introduction of a range of welfare services directed primarily at families, as well as a commitment to the eradication of child poverty, which became a central policy objective. On the other, an individualistic conditionality – that financial support from the state must be predicated on engaging in paid work – emerged. For New Labour it became not a matter of providing cash 'hand outs' to the poor (the way in which welfare benefits had come to be seen in the previous 20 years), but a more limited 'hand up'. The welfare state was reconstructed as 'enabler', rather than 'provider' to facilitate 'work for those who can work, security for those who can't' (Blair, 1999: 13). Instead of the *rights* discourse prevalent post-WW2, more emphasis was placed on individual *responsibility* to encourage 'independence, initiative, and enterprise for all' (Blair, 1999: 13). During New Labour's tenure the 'poor' and the 'not poor' were reconstructed as the socially 'excluded' and 'included' (Levitas, 2005).

Poverty and 'social exclusion'

The origin of the concept 'social exclusion' first arose in 1970s France but since the 1990s it has been closely associated with poverty in the UK. However, whilst more traditional conceptions of poverty tend to focus on wealth and the lack of financial resources that individuals or households have at their disposal, social exclusion has been conceptualised in terms of lack of social participation and social integration by some individuals and social groups.

> **BOX 3.11 SOCIAL EXCLUSION**
>
> Three discourses of social exclusion came to dominate public consciousness from 1997, becoming the driver for New Labour strategies to address poverty in its reconstituted form. A moral underclass discourse (MUD) related to moral deficit; a social integrationist discourse' (SID) related to lack of paid work; a redistributionist discourse (RED), related to structural inequality (Levitas, 2005). All three

> provide differing explanation for who might be considered 'poor' and 'excluded' and why and were operationalised to justify policy responses to those who live with poverty, but both the MUD and SID discourses began to dominate from the early 2000s. From then, any financial welfare benefits provided by the state became evermore conditional on searching for and engaging in paid work.

Levitas (2005) argues that a key problem with conceptualising poverty as 'social exclusion' is that it divides society into a socially included *majority*, and a socially excluded *minority*, disguising structural determinants of poverty by constructing it as essentially a peripheral, individual problem, easily addressed. All the excluded minority need to do to shift from excluded to included is alter their behaviour and 'play by the rules', either by acting in a more morally acceptable way or by engaging in paid work. In recent years, these two issues have become conflated, so not engaging in paid work has increasingly been understood as a moral failing and people who do not work are pathologised, regardless of the reason.

The 'othering' of the poor

The idea that there is a socially included majority and a social excluded majority is reflected in the way in which people who live with poverty are constructed as 'other' to the norm.

> **BOX 3.12**
>
> 'Othering' is a process by which dominant groups situate themselves in opposition to those less powerful by ascribing to them pathological qualities whilst characterising their own identities, attitudes, and behaviours as 'normal' and 'right'. Lister (2020) argues that the 'Othering' of the poor has been propagated by the powerful 'non-poor' – politicians, media executives, professionals, and other officials – who have maintained their own powerful status by continually collectivising and condemning people who live with poverty, constructing them as deficient in multifarious ways.

For Lister 'the poor' are a section of society who do not seem to count for anything, despite being persistently measured, categorised, and classified. This allows them to be treated without dignity or respect; more importantly it denies them a voice to participate in socio-political decision making, arguably a fundamental social need and, indeed, a right for anyone living in a democratic society.

Cultural representations of poverty

Cultural representations of poverty presented via the media fuel 'common-sense' beliefs about 'poor people' that demonise them and both language and imagery are operationalised to polarise people into strivers and skivers, deserving and undeserving. Rather than documenting living with poverty, such representations paint only a partial picture, placing the *behaviour* of poor people rather than the injustice of poverty centre stage. It is not so much that people who live with poverty are not heard, but they are heard selectively, and their voices and opinions lack influence to impact their material circumstances which 'reflects and reinforces the powerlessness of 'the poor' (Lister, 2020: 190–191).

BOX 3.13 POVERTY PORN

Evidence of selectivity in hearing the voices of people who live with poverty has been marked in recent years by the emergence of a new television genre dubbed 'poverty porn' that purports to illuminate the public about issues related to poverty and its causes. In news, reality TV and in documentaries poverty has increasingly been represented as a moral failing, evoking reactions from the public and other commentators ranging from pity to disgust. In programmes such as *Benefits Street* (2013) and *On Benefits and Proud* (2013), the voices of people who live with poverty are heard but are amplified when they are seen to make impudent demands for state financial support, with a lack of indebtedness toward those who pay the taxes that fund their lifestyles. In other programmes, the public have been invited to make moral judgements on what people living with poverty and people claiming welfare benefits need and deserve and their possessions have been scrutinised (Jensen, 2014).

'Poor' has come to mean 'flawed' and people who live with poverty are understood to be distinguishable from 'normal people' in society by behaviour and characteristics that infer they are inferior to the wider population. This behavioural understanding of poverty feeds the 'underclass' discourse that has been deployed to justify both the distribution and restriction of financial support and services, and the rhetorical use of the 'respectable' poor and the 'just about managing' has been mobilised to construct a perceived disreputable poor as the 'enemy within'.

Poverty in recent policy

Since 2010 welfare policy has been underpinned by three distinct but interrelated discourses: 'Austerity' 'Broken Britain,' and 'The Big Society.'
Austerity and Poverty
'Austerity' was an economic course set in place by the new Conservative/Coalition administration in 2010 in the wake of the 2008 worldwide financial crash.

BOX 3.14

Austerity: "a form of voluntary deflation in which the economy adjusts through the reduction of wages, prices, and public spending to restore competitiveness, which is (supposedly) best achieved by cutting the state's budget, deficits" (Blyth, 2015: 2). This is intended to augment business confidence and encourage the reinvestment that stimulates job growth, bringing the UK back to economic success.

A discourse of 'Austerity' puts forward the idea that the UK cannot afford to support people who live with poverty, they must help themselves by engaging in paid work. Mirroring the neo-liberal ideology prevalent between 1979 and 1997, the economic conditions from 2008 provided the ideal justification to validate cuts in all forms of welfare funding underpinned by the argument that spending was unaffordable, unsustainable, and indeed created a 'dependency culture,' preventing individuals from seeking paid work. Although there was a claim that the 'most vulnerable' would be supported, from 2010 it was 'fairness' in so far as *everyone* must play their part in returning the UK to economic prosperity, including those who could least afford it, that dominated policy decisions.

Poverty and 'Broken Britain'

A dominant discourse that has emerged since 2010 is that Britain is somehow 'Broken,' fragmented and undermined by:

> Irresponsibility. Selfishness. Behaving as if your choices have no consequences. Children without fathers. Schools without discipline. Reward without effort. Crime without punishment. Rights without responsibilities. Communities without control. Some of the worst aspects of human nature tolerated, indulged—sometimes even incentivised—by a state and its agencies that in parts have become literally de-moralised.
>
> (Cameron, 2011 – Prime Minister David Cameron's 'Fight Back' speech after the 2011 Tottenham Riots)

Poverty myths

On the basis of such powerful, deliberate, and calculated rhetoric, poverty myths have taken hold in public and political discourse that have gained the status of truth and have become more and more central to policy debates, which Shildrick (2018) argues masks the complex social, psychological, economic, political, and cultural causes of poverty. One report: *Breakthrough Britain*, published by the Centre for Social Justice, – set up in 2007 by former Conservative Party leader (and subsequent Secretary of State for Work and Pensions) Iain Duncan Smith – claimed to identify the five primary causes of poverty:

Family breakdown
Economic dependency and worklessness
Educational failure
Drug and alcohol abuse
Serious personal debt

Reiterated in countless political speeches by Conservative politicians and commentators in the popular press, these particular social problems have continually been represented as the determinants of poverty, although Gordon (2016) observes that they have not actually been identified as its main causes in any other research and no scientific evidence was offered by the Centre for Social Justice to support their claims. Nevertheless, such reports form the basis of poverty myths that make it seem as though these issues have an irrefutable causal relationship to poverty.

Poverty, work, and worklessness

It can often be difficult to disentangle poverty from related issues, such as worklessness, but whilst there are connections, the fact that they are conflated can obscure the complexity of both. Whilst poverty is very much connected with unemployment (and the consequent receipt of welfare benefits), not all people who are out of work are poor, neither are all those experiencing poverty unemployed.

BOX 3.15 THE PRECARIAT: THE NEW DANGEROUS CLASS

An argument has emerged recently that it is not worklessness, but employment precarity that occupies a central position in explaining the persistence of poverty and a new class of poverty subjects has emerged whose defining characteristic is a distinctive relationship with the world of work which reduces them to constant precarity in the labour market (Standing, 2016). Standing identifies "flexible" labour contracts; temporary jobs; labouring in casual or part/time work and/or working for employment agencies as furthering the work precarity that reduces people to poverty. He also observes that 'the precariat' are often exploited in the workplace, being required to undertake large amounts of residual work and preparation that largely goes unpaid. When this is taken into account, the 'precariat' are often working for far less than the minimum wage and, due to the types of work contract they are obliged to take, are not entitled to those benefits usually associated with secure paid work, such as pensions and paid holidays. They are also exploited outside the workplace, being required to retrain on a regular basis and have an education level greater than is usually expected for the labour they perform, also having to network, apply for, and take jobs that may be unsuitable to avoid being sanctioned by an overly punitive welfare benefits system.

Nevertheless, since 2010 poverty solutions have been underpinned by the Coalition and Conservative administrations' argument that paid work is the best route out of poverty. This has been incentivised, however, not by improving pay and conditions nor expanding training opportunities, but by framing welfare benefits as 'morally corrosive' and people that claim them as morally defective (Wiggan, 2012). A return to the *principle of less eligibility* – dominant in the mid-19th century – has ensued, whereby it is argued that anybody who is not in paid work must never be better off than someone who works (Pantazis, 2016). Entitlement to benefits has been constrained by the Welfare Reform Act (2012) which introduced Universal Credit, replacing Child Tax Credit, Housing Benefit, Income Support, income-based Jobseeker's Allowance (JSA), income-related Employment and Support Allowance (ESA), and Working Tax Credit. Universal Credit also established a benefits cap (currently 20,000 in Scotland, Wales, Northern Ireland and England outside of the Greater London area (where the cap is £24,000). Personalisation of disability benefits has also been extended, which has often meant disabled people must meet a much higher qualification threshold. Similarly, there has been a reduction in the disability element of Children's Tax Credits and a cut in Child Tax Credits for children born after April 2017. All these changes have disproportionately impacted the poorest sections of UK society.

The Big Society and charitable responses to poverty

The Big Society, it is claimed:

> represents 'a huge culture change—where people … don't always turn to officials, local authorities or central government for answers to the problems they face but instead feel both free and powerful enough to help themselves and their own communities'.
>
> (Cameron, 2010)

Reflecting the anti-welfare ideology prevalent since 2010, the concept of a 'Big Society' and a 'small state' places much more emphasis on voluntary and community approaches to poverty alleviation. Neo-liberal policy decisions of successive Conservative administrations have included swinging cuts to local authority budgets, which has meant that many public services have been closed or drastically reduced. Since then, charitable provision has come much more to the fore, reflective this 'Big Society' ideology. One area where this is particularly evident is food (Caplan, 2016). Since the inception of the welfare state in the UK hunger has not been considered a pressing social problem, however recent research suggests that families are increasingly unable or barely able to feed themselves and parents often go without enough to eat at times in order to make sure their children are fed, skip meals, and in some cases have to resort to food banks (Daly and Kelly, 2015).

Food banks

Foodbanks are charitable (non-governmental) organisations, staffed by volunteers, providing food parcels – generally containing non-perishable packet and tinned food – that are intended to meet the immediate needs of people with insufficient food to eat themselves, or to feed their children. The food is often donated by the public or large food providers, such as supermarkets and wholesalers, who offer foodstuffs that are still fit for consumption but legally can no longer be sold (Surmen et al., 2021). In 2021, there are more than 1,052 independent food banks across the UK, in addition to 1393 administered by the Trussell Trust. Foodbanks were very much on the periphery prior to 2008, indeed in 2008 the Trussell Trust distributed less than 42,000 emergency food packets but this increased to over 1.5 million in 2018–2019 (Figure 3.1).

In 2014, a report by an All-Party Parliamentary inquiry into hunger and food poverty in the UK was published *Feeding Britain: A strategy for zero hunger in England, Wales, Scotland and Northern Ireland*. It was deeply critical the contemporary welfare benefits system, which, although claiming to provide a safety net for the poorest in society, has failed to do so, stating that is a considerable matter for concern when an increasing number of citizens who live with poverty have no alternative but to rely on charity to gain access to even the most basic of necessities like food (Caplan, 2016); of equal concern is the shame and stigma attached to visiting food banks and to poverty more widely (Garthwaite, 2016).

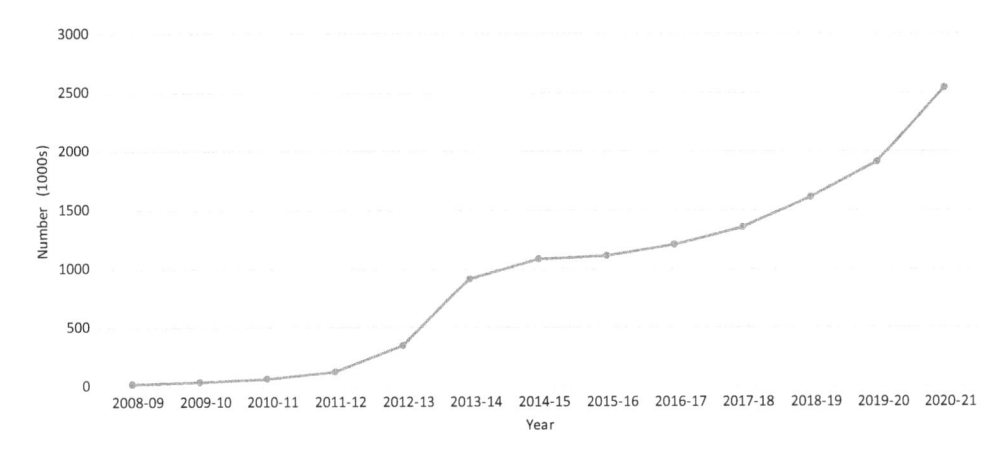

Figure 3.1 Trussell Trust emergency three-day food parcels 2008–2021.

The stigma and shame of poverty

> 'because poverty is often taken to be the result of individual failure … it is replete with possibilities for shaming'.
>
> (Walker, 2014: 49)

A universal and longstanding norm is that properly functioning individuals and families *ought* to be able to make their way in the world and provide for and look after their children. When this does not happen, this puts in place conditions for judgements to be passed by others – and indeed one's self – on shortcomings that people living with poverty are often powerless to influence; this in turn can create stigma. Walker (2014) conceptualises shame as 'stigma bureaucratised'. Exploring the psycho-social effects of poverty, he suggests that not only are people ashamed of their poverty, they also feel they are 'explicitly shamed by other people and in public discourse' (121). Walker argues further that shame is intensified for those claiming financial support when others show disapproval of them. This encourages some people to deny their own poverty and so ask for little or nothing for fear of the stigma and shame associated with doing so. What is significant is that people are often prevented from fulfilling potential as an individual, parent, family, or community member because of their feelings of shame and they become personally discouraged and dissatisfied with their failure to fulfil their own goals. This can negatively impact self-confidence, affecting and often inhibiting decisions and behaviour, making it seem as though they are not interested in trying, providing further barriers to individuals being able to lift themselves out of poverty.

Possible solutions to tackling poverty in the UK

In recent years proposed solutions to tackle poverty have been varied, but most have focussed on paid work. In her ethnographic research, Toynbee (2003) suggested that the introduction of a minimum wage had the potential to ameliorate poverty and close the gap between the poorest and the wealthiest in UK society. The minimum wage (introduced in 1998) has been increased regularly since. The introduction of stronger legislation to reduce employment precarity, improve job security, and guarantee the entitlement to in-work remuneration, holiday pay, and pensions might also provide something of a solution to poverty. Wilson (2021) points to campaigns for a living wage as being central to the reduction of poverty and commitments by businesses to paying the living wage have become more widespread. Despite all of this, poverty and income inequality has increased.

Reducing poverty might also be achievable by reform of tax laws and closing loopholes to eliminate tax avoidance by the most affluent sections of society, however one suggestion has been for a Universal Basic Income (UBI) to be introduced.

BOX 3.16 UNIVERSAL BASIC INCOME

This is the idea that every adult, regardless of employment or other status receives stipend to cover basic living costs. It is argued that such a scheme has potential to reduce poverty, improve living conditions, and play a part in achieving a more socially just society in the UK. In May 2021, the Welsh government announced its intention to run a pilot UBI scheme, so that all adults regardless of their means would be entitled to a regular sum of money to cover the basic cost of living (Hayward, 2021). There are, however, concerns that UBI would prove a disincentive for people to work, be too expensive and politically unpopular, and it may be perceived as providing handouts to those who may seem to give nothing in return. A trial of Basic Income conducted by the Finnish government produced no evidence to suggest that BI does disincentivise work, primarily because 'it is unlikely that people will cease to desire material possessions beyond that which they will be able to afford with a BI'. Evidence also suggested very little variation between the number of days employment undertaken by those who received BI and those who received regular unemployment benefits; indeed, it was found that there were health and well-being benefits that accompanied the receipt of BI resulting in 'significantly less stress and better health' in participants (Morley et al., 2019: 15).

Clearly there is a significant cost element to the provision of BI, however the UK is one of the richest nations on earth by GDP (Gross Domestic Product), indeed latest figures indicate that between 2017 and 2018, GDP in England increased by 1.4%, the highest increase of the four countries in the UK. Northern Ireland had the lowest growth between at negative 0.5%, while Wales grew by 1.3%, and Scotland increased by 0.9% (ONS, 2020).

Conclusions

Poverty has been and remains a contested concept and the way in which it is defined, measured, theorised, and given meaning is integral to understanding how it is addressed in law, policy, provision, and practice. This in turn will impact the lived experiences to those people who live with poverty. Evidence suggests that economic inequality is detrimental to both those who live with poverty and society as a whole and rather than a social problem, poverty should be viewed as a social harm and a preventable social harm at that. The total number of people in the UK living with poverty is now more than 15 million, approximately 23% of the population (SMC, 2021). In 2020, 700,000 more people in the UK, including 120,000 children, have been forced into poverty as a result of the COVID-19 crisis. 700,000 people have also been prevented from falling below the poverty line by a temporary rise of £20-a-week to boost to universal credit, introduced in April 2020 to help claimants cope with the extra costs of the pandemic. This indicates that the existence of poverty in the developed nations of the UK *is a choice made by those in power*. £20 per week is not a lot of money for one of the richest nations in the world, but this will cease as soon as the Pandemic is declared over. In the prevailing social context, if responses to COVID-19 can teach us anything, governments can find the resources to address the most pressing of social threats. The key is for poverty itself - rather than the people who live with it – to be conceptualised or indeed reconceptualised as such a threat.

Quiz

1 What fraction of the world's poor people are children and young people under the age of 18?
2 The work of which two pioneers of the 19th century first established poverty as a social problem?
3 True or false: the term relative poverty refers to lacking in resources to sustain life?
4 In 2020, Median Income in England was:

   a   £509.00
   b   £574.00
   c   £521.30
   d   £563. 20

5 Both social democracy and neo-liberalism are examples political ideologies that understand the causes of poverty from very different perspectives; social democracy favours ....; neo-liberalism favours ....
6 True or false. There is overwhelming evidence that the primary causes of poverty are: Family breakdown; Economic dependency and worklessness; Educational failure; Drug and alcohol abuse; Serious personal debt.
7 Who are 'the precariat?'

   a   people who don't want to work
   b   disabled people who cannot work
   c   people who are exploited both inside and outside the workplace
   d   people who rely on welfare benefits as their sole income

8 In recent years proposed solutions to tackle poverty have been varied, but most have focussed on ....
9 True or false: Stigma and shame can mean those who live with poverty feel they are explicitly shamed by other people and in public discourse.
10 Evidence suggests that economic inequality is detrimental to both those who live with poverty and society as a whole and rather than a social problem, poverty should be viewed as a .... and a .... at that.

Answers

1. Two thirds
2. Charles Booth and Seebohm Rowntree
3. False: The term relative poverty relates to the social norms prevalent in a particular society at a particular time. Anybody who cannot afford one or more of them might be deemed to be living in relative poverty.
4. (b) £574.00
5. (i) structural explanations; (ii) individual/agentic.
6. False: There is NO overwhelming evidence that the primary causes of poverty are: Family breakdown; Economic dependency and worklessness; Educational failure; Drug and alcohol abuse; Serious personal debt.
7. (c) people who are exploited both inside and outside the workplace.
8. paid work
9. True: Stigma and shame can mean those who live with poverty feel they are explicitly shamed by other people and in public discourse.
10. (i) social harm; (ii) preventable social harm.

Group/individual exercises

1. Poverty: An individual or social problem?
   For more than 40 years individualist accounts have dominated perceptions of what causes poverty. Consider how much power you think people who live with poverty have to alter their own financial situation.
2. Food Poverty
   Food poverty is a relatively new phenomenon. Consider whether charitable responses, such as foodbanks, are an effective way to tackle poverty.
3. Universal Basic Income (UBI)
   Consider the arguments for and against the introduction of Universal Basic Income as a response to poverty.

Supplementary reading

Lansley, S. & Mack, J. (2015). *Breadline Britain: The Rise of Mass Poverty.* Oneworld Publications.
Lister, R. (2020). *Poverty* (2nd ed). Polity.
O'Connell, R., Knight, A. & Brannen, J. (2019). *Living Hand to Mouth: Children and Food in Low-income Families.* CPAG.
Shildrick, T. (2018). *Poverty Propaganda: Exploring the Myths.* Policy Press.

Helpful websites for information on issues related to poverty:

Citizens Advice: https://www.citizensadvice.org.uk
Full Fact: https://fullfact.org
Equality Trust: https://equalitytrust.org.uk/
Health Foundation: https://www.health.org.uk/
Living Wage Foundation: https://www.livingwage.org.uk/
Social Metrics Commission: https://socialmetricscommission.org.uk/

Organisations that work with people who live with poverty:

Child Poverty Action Group (Child Poverty): https://cpag.org.uk/
Crisis (Homelessness): https://www.crisis.org.uk/
Fareshare (Food poverty): https://fareshare.org.uk/
Joseph Rowntree Foundation (Poverty and Social Change): https://www.jrf.org.uk/
National Energy Action (Fuel Poverty): https://www.nea.org.uk/

References

Alcock, P. & May, M. (2014). *Social Policy in Britain* (4th ed). Palgrave Macmillan.
Beresford, P. (2016). *All Our Welfare: Towards Participatory Social Policy*. Policy Press.
Blair, T. (1999). Beveridge revisited. A Welfare State for the 21st Century. In: R. Walker (Ed.), *Ending Child Poverty: Popular Welfare for the 21st Century* (pp. 7–20). Policy Press.
Blyth, M. (2015). *Austerity: The History of a Dangerous Idea*. Oxford University Press.
Cameron, D. (2010, July 19). *The Big Society Speech*. Retrieved June 6, 2022, from https://www.gov.uk/government/speeches/big-society-speech
Cameron, D. (2011, August 15). *PM's Speech on the Fightback after the Riots*. Retrieved June 6, 2022, from https://www.gov.uk/government/speeches/pms-speech-on-the-fightback-after-the-riots
Caplan, P. (2016). Big society or broken society? Food banks in the UK. *Anthropology Today*, *32*(1), 5–9.
Clarke, J. & Cochrane, A. (1998). The social construction of social problems. In: E. Saraga (Ed.), *Embodying the Social: Constructions of Difference* (pp. 3–42). Routledge.
CPAG. (2021). *Child Poverty Facts and Figures*. Retrieved July 19, 2021 from https://cpag.org.uk/child-poverty/child-poverty-facts-and-figures
Daly, M. & Kelly, G. (2015). *Families and Poverty: Everyday Life on a Low Income*. Policy Press.
Department for Communities (2020, September 3). *Households below Average Income: Northern Ireland 2018/19*. Retrieved June 10, 2021, from https://www.communities-ni.gov.uk/system/files/publications/communities/hbai-2018-19.pdf
Department for Work and Pensions. (2021, March 25). *Households below Average Income: For Financial Years Ending 1995 to 2020*. Retrieved May 15, 2021 from https://www.gov.uk/government/statistics/households-below-average-income-for-financial-years-ending-1995-to-2020
Dermott, E. & Pantazis, C. (2018). Which men and women are poor? In: E. Dermott and G. Main (Eds.), *Poverty and Social Exclusion in the UK: The Nature and Extent of the Problems* (pp. 17–40). Policy Press.
Elliott, I. (2016). *Poverty and Mental Health: A Review to Inform the Joseph Rowntree Foundation Anti-poverty Strategy*. Mental Health Foundation.
Englander, D. (1998). *Poverty and Poor Law Reform in Nineteenth-Century Britain, 1834–1914: From Chadwick to Booth*. Routledge.
Francis-Devine, B. (2020, March 31). *Poverty in the UK: Statistics*. Retrieved from https://commonslibrary.parliament.uk/research-briefings/sn07096/
Fraser, D. (2009). *The Evolution of the British Welfare State* (4th ed). Palgrave Macmillan.
Garthwaite, K. (2016). Stigma, shame and "people like us": an ethnographic study of Foodbank use in the UK. *Journal of Poverty and Social Justice*, *24*(3), 277–289. https://doi.org/10.1332/175982716X14721954314922
George, V. & Wilding, P. (1994). *Ideology and Social Welfare*. Harvester Wheatsheaf.
Giddens, A. (1998). *The Third Way*. Polity Press.
Gordon, D. (2016). Measuring poverty. In: E. Dermott and G. Main (Eds.), *Poverty and Social Exclusion in the UK: The Nature and Extent of the Problems* (pp. 17–40). Policy Press.
Goulden, C. & D'Arcy, C. (2014, September 14). *A Definition of Poverty*. Retrieved from https://www.jrf.org.uk/report/definition-poverty

Hansen, K. & Kneale, D. (2013). Does how you measure income make a difference to measuring poverty? Evidence from the UK. *Social Indicators Research, 110*(3), 1119–1140. Retrieved June 6, 2022 from https://link.springer.com/article/10.1007%2Fs11205-011-9976-5

Hayward, W. (2021, June 9). *Plan Set Out for 5,000 People to Take Part in Universal Basic Income Trial in Wales*. Retrieved August 28, 2021 from https://www.walesonline.co.uk/news/wales-news/universal-basic-income-wales-ubi-20769221

Jensen, T. (2014). Welfare common-sense, poverty porn and doxophy. *Sociological Research Online, 19*(3), 3. Retrieved June 6, 2022 from https://doi.org/10.5153/sro.3441

Joseph Rowntree Foundation. (2021). *UK Poverty 2020/21: The Leading Independent Report*. Retrieved November 20, 2021 from https://www.jrf.org.uk/report/uk-poverty-2020-21

Karlsen, S. & Pantazis, C. (2018). Better understandings of ethnic variations. Ethnicity, poverty and social exclusion. In: E. Dermott and G. Main (Eds.), *Poverty and Social Exclusion in the UK: The Nature and Extent of the Problems* (pp. 115–134). Policy Press.

Levitas, R. (2005). *The Inclusive Society: Social Exclusion and New Labour*. Palgrave Macmillan.

Lister, R. (2020). *Poverty* (2nd ed). Polity.

Marmot, M. (2010, February 11). *Fair Society Healthy Lives: The Marmot Review*. Retrieved June 6, 2022 from https://www.instituteofhealthequity.org/resources-reports/fair-society-healthy-lives-the-marmot-review/fair-society-healthy-lives-full-report-pdf.pdf

Ministry of Housing, Communities and Local Government. (2018). *English Housing Survey 2017–2018*. Retrieved July 18, 2021 from https://assets.publishing.service.gov.uk/government/uploads/system/uploads/attachment_data/file/856046/EHS_2017-18_SRS_report_revised.pdf

Morley, C., Ablett, P. & Mays, J. (2019). A universal basic income: What difference might it make? *Social Alternatives, 38*(2), 12–18.

Muncie, J. (2015). *Youth and Crime* (4th ed). SAGE.

Novak, T. (1988). *Poverty and the State*. Open University Press.

ONS. (2020). *Regional Economic Activity by Gross Domestic Product, UK: 1998 to 2018*. Retrieved August 28, 2021 from https://www.ons.gov.uk/releases/regionaleconomicactivitybygrossdomesticproductuk1998to2018

Pantazis, C. (2016). Policies and discourses of poverty during a time of recession and austerity. *Critical Social Policy, 36*(1), 3–20. Retrieved from https://doi.org/10.1177/0261018315620377

Parton, N. (2014). *The Politics of Child Protection: Contemporary Developments and Future Directions*. Palgrave Macmillan.

Phillips, N. & Hardy, C. (2002). *Discourse Analysis: Investigating Processes of Social Construction*. SAGE.

Platt, L. (2020). Poverty. In: G. Payne and E. Harrison (Eds.), *Social Divisions: Inequality and Social Diversity in Britain* (pp. 149–174). Policy Press.

Rowntree, B.S. (1901). *Poverty: A Study in Town Life*. MacMillan and Co. Retrieved June 6, 2022 from https://archive.org/details/povertyastudyto00rowngoog/page/n7/mode/2up

Scottish Government. (2020). *Poverty and Income Inequality in Scotland 2016–19*. Retrieved April 18, 2021 from https://www.gov.scot/publications/poverty-income-inequality-scotland-2016-19/

Shahtahmasebi, S., Emerson, E., Berridge, D. and Lancaster, G. (2011). Child disability and the dynamics of family poverty, hardship and financial strain: Evidence from the UK. *Journal of Social Policy, 40*(4), 653–673. Retrieved June 6, 2022 from https://doi.org/10.1017/S0047279410000905

Shildrick, T. (2018) *Poverty Propaganda: Exploring the Myths*. Policy Press.

Social Metrics Commission. (2021). *Responses to the 2020 Report – Poverty and Covid 19*. Retrieved August 27, 2021 from https://socialmetricscommission.org.uk/

Spencer, N. (2018). Social determinants of child health. *Symposium: Social Paediatrics, 28*(3), 138–143. Retrieved June 6, 2022 from https://doi.org/10.1016/j.paed.2018.01.001

Standing, G. (2016). *The Precariat: The New Dangerous Class*. Bloomsbury Academic.

Stapleton, H. (2010). *Surviving Teenage Motherhood*. Palgrave Macmillan.

Steinmann, B., Ötting, S. K. & Maier, G.W. (2016). Need for affiliation as a motivational add-on for leadership behaviors and managerial success. *Frontiers in Psychology, 7*, 1–18. Retrieved June 6, 2022 from https://doi.org/10.3389/fpsyg.2016.01972

Surmen, E., Keleman, M. and Rumens, N. (March 5, 2021). Ways to care: Forms and possibilities of compassion within UK food banks. *The Sociological Review.* 1–17. Retrieved June 6, 2022 from https://doi.org/10.1177/0038026121991330

Taylor, G. (2007). *Ideology and Welfare.* Palgrave Macmillan.

Thompson, N. (2018). *Promoting Equality: Working with Diversity and Difference* (4th ed). Palgrave.

Townsend, P. (1979). *Poverty in the United Kingdom: A Survey of Household Resources and Standards of Living.* Penguin.

Toynbee, P. (2003). *Hard Work.* Bloomsbury.

Trussell Trust. (2016) *End of Year Stats.* Retrieved November 28, 2021 from https://www.trus-selltrust.org/2016/04/15/foodbank-use-remains-record-high/

Trussell Trust. (2021). *End of Year Stats.* Retrieved November 28, 2021 from https://www.trus-selltrust.org/news-and-blog/latest-stats/end-year-stats/

Turner, K. & Lehning, A.J. (2007). Psychological theories of poverty. *Journal of Human Behavior in the Social Environment, 16*(1–2), 57–72. Retrieved June 6, 2022 from https://doi.org/10.1300/J137v16n01_05

Welsh Government. (2020, March 25). *Relative Income Poverty: April 2019 to March 2020.* Retrieved April 18, 2021 from https://gov.wales/relative-income-poverty-april-2019-march-2020-html

Welshman, J. (2014). *Underclass: History of the Excluded since 1880.* Bloomsbury Academic.

Wiggan, J. (2012). Telling stories of 21st century welfare: The UK Coalition government and the neo-liberal discourse of worklessness and dependency. *Critical Social Policy, 32*(3), 383–405. Retrieved June 6, 2022 from https://doi.org/10.1177/0261018312444413

Wilson, S. (2021). *Living Wages and the Welfare State: The Anglo-American Social Model in Transition.* Policy Press.

World Vision. (2021). *Global Poverty: Facts, FAQs, and How to Help.* Retrieved September 2, 2021 from https://www.worldvision.org/sponsorship-news-stories/global-poverty-facts#facts

4 Fractured families

Causes and consequences of family breakdown

Ayomide Oluseye and Aaron F. Mvula

What is a family and why is it important?

Families come in all types and are constantly evolving. These constant changes in family types and structures can put a strain on family cohesion, leading to family breakdown. Although family breakdown can have significant implications for individuals experiencing it, it is rarely seen as a social problem. This is because the associations between family breakdown and negative outcomes are complex and not always linear. For example, many non-traditional family units function well and are sometimes more protective for individuals than traditional family units (such as in the cases of domestic violence, sexual abuse, and intimate partner violence). Additionally, not all negative outcomes associated with family breakdown are inevitable or widespread. As such, the associations between family breakdown and social problems are relatively understudied and under-discussed in the literature.

There are many definitions of the term 'family,' and these definitions tend to be interpreted based on biological, cultural, or statistical perspectives. Nevertheless, it is important to first identify what a family is. Buchanan and McConnell (2017) define a family as a unit consisting of a couple (same-sex or heterosexual) with their blood-related or adopted children. This definition identifies the members constituting a family and allows us to observe the social relationship and dynamics that occur within the family unit. Families have been in existence since the beginning of time. The reason why humans form families is due to their need for social belonging and identity. The family also serves as a foundation for educating, socialising, and guiding its members to adhere to societal laws and norms (Buchanan & McConnell, 2017). While it is not all families that provide a safe and supportive environment, many agree that the family plays a key role in an individual's social, psychological, and behavioural development (Allan et al., 2001). The family is therefore believed to be crucial in contributing to order, stability, and social development.

BOX 4.1 THE MODERN FAMILY

The family structure is constantly evolving such that there are now different types of families being depicted in mainstream shows. Some of the different family types in popular TV shows are:

Sex Education: In this popular Netflix show, the relationship between Otis and his mother depicts a single-parent family.

DOI: 10.4324/9781003166887-4

> **YOU:** In season three, Dante, the blind librarian, and his partner Lansing, depict a cohabiting same-sex couple relationship.
> **Meet the Adebanjos:** The funny British sitcom revolves around the lives of an immigrant family and it depicts the traditional nuclear family.
> **Doctor Foster:** In this British drama series, Simon, his wife (Kate) and their daughter; Gemma (his ex-wife) and son, Tom depict a blended family.
> **Kermit the Frog and Miss Piggy:** Kermit and Miss Piggy from the British Muppet show were never married but were in a long-term relationship and we can depict them as a cohabiting couple.
> What other family types or structures can you identify from your favourite TV shows?

In the UK, there has been an 8% increase in the number of families in the last decade such that there are now about 19.4 million family units (Office for National Statistics (ONS), 2020). Also, due to recent demographic shifts and economic trends in society, there has been a decline in the traditional concept of family, such that diverse family structures are now emerging (e.g., single-parent families, same-sex families, and stepfamilies).

Emerging family structures in the UK

Over the last few decades, the UK has witnessed major shifts in family structures, particularly in its formation and dissolution (Allan et al., 2001; Benson & McKay 2017). Although married couple families remain the dominant family type in the UK, in a report published by the ONS (2020; see Figure 4.1), the authors note a decline in the percentage of married-couple families and state that lone parenthood families now make up 14.7% of families. There has also been a rise in cohabiting family units such that they are now the second-largest family type in the UK (see Figure 4.1).

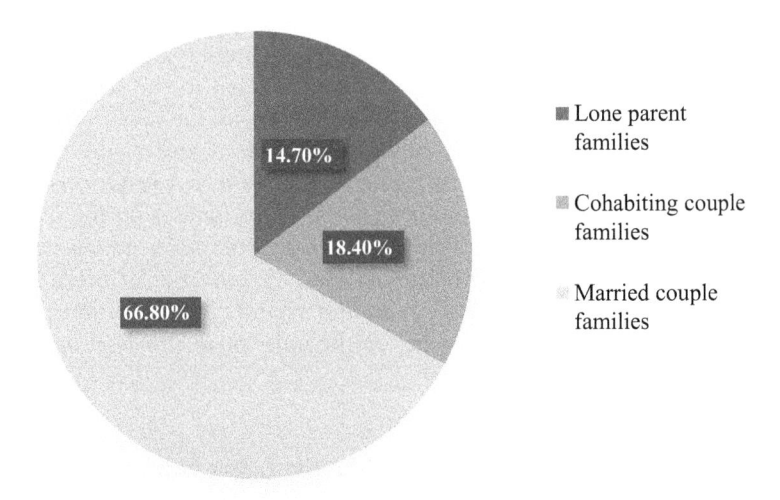

Figure 4.1 Percentage distribution of family structures in the UK.

COVID-19 pandemic and its impact on families in the UK

Although the narrative of 'we are in this together' has featured in the UK and many other countries (Cantillon et al., 2021), the impact of COVID-19 can be more subjectively explained. Lebow (2020c, 2020b) narrates that the impact of the COVID-19 pandemic on individual and family life has been pervasive. It has created rigid boundaries between the nuclear family and members of the outside family thereby reducing the social interactions and social support that might be important to married couples in conflict (Lebow, 2020a).

Also, studies that have examined the impact of the pandemic on family and marriage have produced mixed results (Besschetnova et al., 2021; Seifman, 2021). To some extent, these studies suggest that staying and working from home, as a result of the COVID-19 restrictions has strengthened family commitment. Seifman (2021) states that the pandemic has compelled families and couples to live in much closer and continual contact than they would normally do, thereby bringing them together. To substantiate this, Rivett (2020) reports that in one of the surveys focusing on UK family therapist reflections on relational lockdown and relational trauma in the time of coronavirus, four out of five parents thought that their family had gotten closer as a result of lockdown.

On the other hand, however, the pandemic has also skyrocketed divorce (Besschetnova et al., 2021; Seifman, 2021). Savage (2020) and Seifman (2021) report that divorce applications and break-ups were found to be skyrocketing across the UK during the lockdown with some law firms reporting a 122% increase in divorce inquiries between July and October 2020. Other than spikes in divorce, the pandemic has also created tense environments within households due to the introduction of work into family homes. As Lebow (2020a) opines, frequently blurred boundary between work and home life provides new opportunities for conflict. From these discussions, it can be deduced that the pandemic has had a two-fold effect on the family, strengthening it on one end, and predisposing families to increased conflicts and breakdown on the other.

Family breakdown

No matter how ideal a family is, there will be periods of conflicts and hardships. Thus, the survival of a family depends on how the parties involved in the family decide to resolve the matters at hand. Family breakdown remains one of the major problems that the UK faces, which profoundly affects individuals who have experienced it (Amato & Patterson, 2017). This chapter defines family breakdown as the process whereby relationships within a family fail and come to an end. This focuses on the intentional ending of relationships rather than bereavements. Before looking at the several reasons why families break down, it is important to understand the processes involved in family formations and dissolutions. This will provide an understanding of the different types of family breakdowns and their potential impact on the individuals involved.

Theories explaining family breakdown

Early theorists of dissolution have often focused on the causes of breakdown by looking at the characteristics of partners within the relationship. More recently, there has also been a focus on how families might experience a dissolution. In this section, four theories will be explored namely, Duck's dissolution model, Scharp's theory of family distancing, Social learning theory, and Attachment theory. Duck's dissolution model and Scharp's theory of family distancing focuses on the dynamics involved in a family breakdown between partners, and parent-child relationships. Additionally, the Social Learning theory and Attachment theory explains how family breakdown can affect the third party's (i.e., children) socio-behavioural outcomes.

Duck's dissolution model

This model was initially developed by Steve Duck in 1988 and remodified in 2006 (Rollie & Duck, 2006). This model is based on individualistic cultures where separation and divorce are not stigmatised and easily obtainable. According to Duck's dissolution model, there are five main stages leading up to a relationship (in this case, family) breakdown (Rollie & Duck, 2006) and these are namely; The intrapsychic phase, the dyadic stage, the grave-dressing stage, the social stage, and the resurrection stage.

1   **The Intrapsychic Stage**
    This is the first phase of breakdown where individuals brood over the unsatisfactory nature of their relationships, find possible solutions to it and confide in other individuals (through venting) (Duck & Wood, 2006). Here, a person's sense of dissatisfaction may not move to the next stage if the problem is resolved during the process of reflection and venting (Rollie & Duck, 2006). This is very common in relationships. However, if an individual is still dissatisfied with their partner's shortcomings and is unable to resolve this through reflection and venting, they move to the next stage.
2   **The Dyadic Stage**
    At this stage, individuals discuss their dissatisfaction with their partner with hopes for a resolution (Duck & Wood, 2006). Several confrontations may occur during this period and two possible outcomes can occur. The first possible outcome might involve a constructive approach wherein both parties resolve the problem, while the second outcome may involve both parties proceeding to being unable to resolve their differences (Rollie & Duck, 2006). This lack of resolution may begin the spiral into a breakdown.
3   **The Social Stage**
    This is the third phase where both partners begin to involve their social networks (such as friends, extended family, counsellors/therapists) in the possible process of mending the relationship or finding support. During this period, these social networks may cast blame and unveil other problems which can either resolve the problems or further hasten the dissolution process (Fine & Harvey, 2006). However, it is widely believed that once a relationship reaches this phase, a breakdown is inevitable (Fine & Harvey, 2006).
4   **The Grave-dressing Stage**
    This phase involves the process of reflexivity as to why the relationship broke down (Duck & Wood, 2006). This often involves minimising one's fault and over-emphasising the fault of the other partner. In many family breakdowns, this stage involves a period of grief over the loss of the family, anger and resentment towards the other partner, and limited attention for the children involved.

5 **The resurrection Stage**

This stage often involves a process whereby individuals move on from the relationship and forge a new path for themselves (Rollie & Duck, 2006). This can be by finding a new hobby or entering another relationship or marriage.

Scharp's theory of family distancing

In Duck's model, the discussion focused mainly on relationship breakdown between partners (in this case, parents). However, Scharp's theory looks at how family breakdown occurs between parents and their children. Although parent-child relationship breakdowns are under-researched, there is evidence to show that a family can further breakdown when children begin to distance themselves from their parents, due to the negative experiences encountered within the family relationship (Scharp & Dorrance Hall, 2017). There are many reasons why children may become estranged from their parents. This can be due to parental divorce, substance misuse, neglect, and violent parent relationships.

Unlike parents or partners who can dissolve their families in a one-time event through a divorce, there are no final processes for parent-child dissolutions (Scharp, 2019). It has been suggested that the process of family breakdown between parents and their children, often occur over an extended period and involve an act of distancing, comprised of reduced social interactions, and interdependence (Scharp et al., 2015). According to Scharp (2019), the process of parent-child breakdown can involve;

- Reduced communication quality, where the depth of information discussed is minimalised.
- Reduced communication quantity, where there is limited or no social interaction between parents and children for extended periods.
- Reduced physical contact where children keep their physical distance from their parents.
- Reduced emotion where familial feelings towards parents become greatly diminished.

However, rarely do breakdowns occur without having consequences for the individuals involved in the process. Using Social learning theory and Attachment theory, this chapter will show the impacts of family breakdown on the parent–child relationship and child development.

Social learning theory

The social learning theory was developed by American-Canadian psychologist, Albert Bandura in 1977 and this theory is based on the premise that learning occurs through our interaction with others and the social world within which we live (Grusec, 1994). According to Bandura and McClelland (1977), people learn new behaviours through observational learning, imitation, and modelling. These authors posit that when people are in an environment, they pay attention (observational learning) to how people behave (modelling) and retain these behaviours in their memories. At a later time, individuals enact the behaviour (imitation) that they have observed and if this imitated behaviour is met with a negative consequence, the individual is less likely to continue to behave in that way (Akers & Jennings, 2016). However, if the behaviour has rewarding attributes, it becomes reinforced as part of an individual's social attribute (Akers & Jennings, 2016).

As the family is the primary social institution where children learn how to interact, parents are believed to have a major influence on the behaviour of children (Abbassi & Aslinia, 2010). In a family setting, children are surrounded by caregivers (in this case parents) who provide examples of behaviours (through their social interactions) for children to observe and imitate (Abbassi & Aslinia, 2010). By observing parental behaviour, children can acquire new patterns of behaviour even in situations that do not directly involve them (Grusec, 1994); and model the behaviour they have learnt. This implies that parental modelling of both negative and positive behaviours can be learnt by children and thus provides an explanation of how family breakdown can shape a child's behavioural outcome through direct and indirect forms of socialisation. For instance, in the events leading to a family breakdown, children may observe hostility between parents and inter-parental conflicts and begin to model these behaviours in their social interactions (Abbassi & Aslinia, 2010). Additionally, after a family breakdown, children transition from a two-parent household to a single-parent household. In many single-parent households, the father is largely absent to work alongside the mother to encourage the reinforcement of positive behaviours and discourage negative modelling of behaviours (Mooney et al., 2009). As a result, children may lack the structure, guidance, and discipline, needed for their social development and adjustment. This can make them prone to problem behaviours in later life (Akers & Jennings, 2016).

Attachment theory

The attachment theory was developed by British psychologist and psychiatrist, John Bowlby in 1969 and it emphasises the impacts of parent-child attachment on socio-behavioural competence in children and adolescents (Rholes & Simpson, 2004). According to Bowlby, children are born with attachment behaviours that help to ensure close contact with their main attachment figure (in this case parents) (*ibid*). Howe (2012) explains that to stimulate caregiving responses from their attachment figures, children engage in certain behaviours such as crying, eye contact, and smiling. When parents respond, an interaction engagement occurs, resulting in the child forming an "attachment bond." This attachment bond enables children to develop an "internal working model" which informs their understanding of the world and how they interact with others (Howe, 2012). When conditions such as separation and family breakdown occur, the closeness between children and their parents are threatened and this can result in emotional distress and negative behaviours (such as delinquency, conduct disorder, and depression) (O'Gorman, 2012). This shows how attachment bonds are integral to the emotional and behavioural development of children and adolescents.

Examining the concept of parent-child attachment further, Mary Ainsworth, a psychologist, proposed that an individual's relationship with their attachment figure influences other social relationships and shape how individuals interact with their social world (Howe, 2012). She developed a classification system to label attachment experience among children and identified four patterns namely; secure, insecure/disorganised, insecure/ambivalent, and insecure/avoidant (Howe, 2012). Based on her classifications, when children have a positive attachment with their attachment figures (i.e., parents), they perceive the parent as a source of security and have confidence in their parent's support and responsiveness. This helps to promote resilience and healthy well-being among children. Individuals with positive attachments to their parents are thus less likely to engage in risky behaviours (Bretherton & Munholland, 2008). In contrast, when there is poor attachment quality between parents and their children, this can lead to insecure, anxious, ambivalent, and avoidant attachments where children are unable to sustain relationships and view themselves as unlovable (*ibid*). This can contribute to increased deviant behaviours and poor psycho-social adaptations in children and adolescents.

The above theories explain how relationships break down and the impacts that it can have on the individuals involved; however, it does not provide in-depth explanations as to why relationships break down. This will be discussed in the following section of this chapter.

Why do families break down?

According to Benson (2010), the factors which cause and contribute to family breakdown are varied and complex, existing at both family and personal levels and influenced by a wide variety of social factors (see Figure 4.2 for illustration). This chapter attempts to analyse and improve understandings of how these factors affect family breakdown:

The influence of individualism

Daly and Scheiwe (2010) assert that contemporary discourses about family life focus on the societal impacts on personal relationships such as how post-industrialisation has given rise to the detraditionalisation and individualisation of social life. Evidence from the literature suggests that over the past ten decades, there has been a move towards greater individualism in values and practices in Western societies (Heu et al., 2019). The

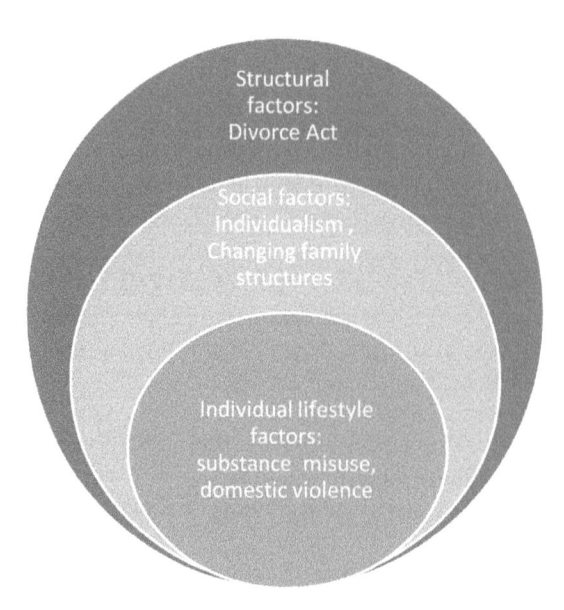

Figure 4.2 Key factors causing family breakdown.

individualism-collectivism construct plays a significant role in understanding ways in which cultures differ and how culture influences what people think and how they think (Daly & Scheiwe, 2010). According to Hoftede et al. (2010);

> *Individualism pertains to societies in which the ties between individuals are loose: everyone is expected to look after him- or herself and his or her immediate family [while] Collectivism as its opposite pertains to societies in which people from birth onward are integrated into strong, cohesive in-groups, which throughout people's lifetime continue to protect them in exchange for unquestioning loyalty'.*

(italics as original, p. 92)

This is not to suggest that the collectivist culture and its practices are extinct, as different ethnic groups have migrated into individualistic societies but still hold values and practices that are common in collectivistic societies (Daly & Scheiwe, 2010). However, this shift in values and practice to individualism has had impacts on social institutions like families. Central to individualism is the emphasis placed on self-fulfilment and personal autonomy (Lawrence, 2019). As a result, individuals living in individualist societies are less likely to sacrifice their self-interests for group gain. It is therefore not unsurprising that highly individualist societies tend to have higher divorce rates (see for example: Heu et al., 2019; Lu et al., 2006).

Comparatively, research evidence suggests that in collectivist societies, divorce or family breakdown is rare as the values and practices embedded in these societies act as protective factors to family breakdown (LeFebvre & Franke, 2013). In collectivist societies, there is a greater emphasis on group loyalty, interdependence, and concern about the needs and interests of others (Hoftede et al., 2010; Lu et al., 2006). These collectivist perspectives influence family relationships and divorce decisions, suggesting that people from these cultures are more likely to stay and resolve their problems or remain in a family even if it no longer serves their interests (LeFebvre & Franke, 2013). The individualistic and collectivist approaches may therefore explain how different cultural perspectives and values affect family breakdown.

The influence of the Divorce Act

BOX 4.2 THE CHANGING FACES OF DIVORCE LAWS

Did you know that the very first mention of divorce in England can be traced back to Henry VII of England and his separation from his wife Catherine of Aragon?

Over the years, divorce has taken on many faces.

18th and 19th century: The Act of Parliament granted divorces; however, in the events of a divorce, the woman's properties were given to the man.

1857: The Matrimonial Causes Act granted divorces via the High Court in London. To obtain a divorce, men and women had to prove their partner's adultery, however, women had to prove additional faults such as rape or incest before obtaining a divorce. The divorce petitions were also held in public court which meant everyone could attend and hear the '*dirty little secrets.*'

> **1923–1937:** In 1923, Women no longer needed to prove additional faults to obtain a divorce. In 1937, The Act was also improved upon such that people could get divorced within the first three years of marriage.
>
> **1969:** The Divorce Reform Act was introduced. People could now obtain a divorce if they had been separated for two to five years (two years if both partners want a divorce and five years if only one partner wants a divorce). This law also introduced the idea of "no-fault" in divorce.
>
> **1989:** Individuals were allowed to obtain a divorce within the first year of marriage as opposed to waiting for three years.
>
> **1996:** The Family Law Act modernised divorce by introducing mediation and restraining orders. This law has been heavily criticised.
>
> **2004:** The Civil Partnership Act allowed same-sex couples to be able to obtain a divorce. This Act is almost similar to other types of divorce laws in England and Wales.
>
> **2020:** The Divorce, Dissolution and Separation Act will remove the need to provide evidence of marriage breakdown and only require a statement from either party, stating that the marriage has broken down.

Divorce is one of the main pathways to family breakdown. Across the UK, a major factor that has been noted to facilitate increments in lone parenthood is the Divorce Reform Act of 1969 and 1996 which introduced the idea of *"no-fault"* in marriage (Benson, 2013). Although not all single parenthood is as a result of family breakdown, parental separation remains one of the main routes to lone parenthood. Before the Divorce Reform Act, divorce laws were often fault-based and individuals could only get a divorce if their partner was found guilty of committing a marital offence such as adultery (Benson, 2010). However, the introduction of *"no-faults"* which has removed the need to establish fault has made divorce easier to obtain (Fahey, 2012) (see Box 1.2 for how the divorce laws have evolved over the years). This is evidenced by increases in divorce rates in Wales and England from 24,000 in the 1960s to 111,000 in 2014 (ONS, 2016), and from 1,830 to 9,030 in Scotland (Mikolai & Kulu, 2019).

As these current divorce laws also allow individuals to divorce based on marriage breakdown, reasons such as increased disharmony, incompatibility, and growing apart have been cited for grounds of divorce, making it much easier to leave unhappy marriages (Centre for Social Justice, 2019). According to the Centre for Social Justice (2019), 45% of British adults cite growing apart as a contributing factor to their experience of family breakdown. Similarly, in a study by Lampard (2014) that focused on stated reasons for relationship dissolution in Britain, it was revealed that two-fifths of the participants reported partners having 'grown apart' and a fifth having 'nothing in common' as the reasons for the breaking up. This ease in obtaining a divorce, albeit good, also mean that the family unit is becoming increasingly fragile.

The influence of changing family structures

Historical evidence suggests that the UK has witnessed some structural modifications and changes in perspectives towards marriage and family life. According to the ONS

(2020), there has been a 3.1% increase in the number of cohabiting families and a 66.8% decrease in married-couple families since 2009 (*ibid*). This shows a declining trend in the number of married-couple families and an increasing trend in the number of cohabiting family units. Berrington et al. (2015) assert that cohabitation first began as a prelude to marriage, however, over the years, it has evolved as an alternative to marriage. They further argue that as individuals are more likely to cohabit given its growing popularity, many people are now having their first child while cohabiting as opposed to within a marriage union. This has led to a 4.8% increase in the percentage of dependent children living within cohabitation unions since 2009 (ONS, 2020). While cohabiting is becoming widely accepted as a family unit, these unions are often unstable as children born within this family unit are more likely to experience parental separation before the age of five when compared with their counterparts in a married couple family (Kiernan & Mensah, 2010). This suggests that cohabiting relationships are more likely to be susceptible to dissolution and result in lone parenthood. As projections suggest that cohabiting families will become the dominant family type in the UK by 2031, drawing from current demographic trends, it can be implied that more children will likely experience transitions in their families from formations to dissolutions (ONS, 2020).

Those who strongly argue that the rise of cohabiting has contributed to the increase in family breakdown base their arguments on the strength of the relationship commitments in the different family formations (Berrington et al., 2015; Kiernan et al., 2011). Studies have shown that couples within a marriage union tend to be more resilient in facing crisis and stressful situations, as such, they are less likely to be susceptible to dissolution and result in lone parenthood (Kiernan et al., 2011; Lampard, 2014).

The use of relationship commitment in comparing cohabiting and marital relationships have however been contested. Berrington et al. (2015) argue that the relationship dynamics in cohabitation and marriage has changed over time such that cohabitation relationships now reflect a much higher level of commitment than previously known. Notwithstanding, as more children are now living in families other than married couple units, the potential threat of family breakdown and its potential consequent impact on the children involved are of imminent concern.

Domestic violence and family breakdown

Intimate partner violence is a widespread violence affecting many families. The World Health Organisation (2021) states that globally, 27% of women aged 15–49 years have experienced either physical or sexual violence by their partners. In Britain, domestic violence remains a significant problem and is one of the main reported causes resulting in family breakdown (Chandan et al., 2020). A quantitative study by Gravningen et al. (2017), using data from Britain's third National Survey of Sexual Attitudes and Lifestyles (Natsal-3) reports that among the 706 men and 1,254 women who experienced family breakdown, 16% of women and 4% of men cited domestic violence as the reason for their family dissolutions. Similarly, a comprehensive analysis of the consequences of family Breakdown in Britain by the Centre for Social Justice (2019) revealed domestic abuse/violence to be among the main causes of family breakdown. These incidences of domestic violence significantly increased during the COVID-19 pandemic, leading to more breakdown in many families and contributing to the spike in divorce applications in the UK (Chandan et al., 2020).

Substance misuse and family breakdown

Evidence from research indicates that there is a strong connection between disrupted family relationships and substance misuse (Holland et al., 2014; Skinner et al., 2021). However, substance misuse affects each family and family member uniquely (Holland et al., 2014). While substance misuse may not be the direct cause of family breakdown, it indirectly contributes to it. There is evidence to suggest that the impact of substance misuse on family dynamics can be extensive, ranging from minor inconvenience to interpersonal violence and increased social problems (Skinner et al., 2021; Whittaker et al., 2020). Not only does substance misuse contributes to domestic violence, but it also affects the parenting capacity of individuals which may result in neglect or abuse of children (Skinner et al., 2021; Whittaker et al., 2020). This has the potential to disrupt family structures and relationship dynamics.

Consequences of family breakdown

The main concern with family breakdown is the impact that it can have on the well-being of the individuals experiencing it, particularly the children involved (Brewer & Nandi, 2014; see Figure 4.3). There is evidence to show that a range of negative consequences can occur in children's lives due to family breakdown (Panico et al., 2019; Wadman et al., 2020). These consequences range from behavioural problems, poor academic performance and self-esteem, poorer social adjustment, to risky sexual behaviours, and crime (Benson & McKay, 2017; Wadman et al., 2020).

While many studies have been carried out showing the negative associations between family breakdown and negative child outcomes (Amato, 2005; Amato & Anthony, 2014; Panico et al., 2019), it has been argued that these relationships are not directly causal. Some studies have argued that not all children experience negative outcomes as a result of family breakdown as some children tend to benefit more from parental separation due to reduced parental conflicts and amicable co-parenting (Amato, 2005; Booth & Amato, 2001). From these studies, it appears that it is not family breakdown in itself that leads to negative outcomes among children, but the interplay of risk factors

Childhood	Adolescence	Young Adulthood
•Conduct Disorder	•Poor sibling and social relationships	•Homelessness
•Resentment towards parents	•Risky sexual behaviours	•Unemployment
•Poor social adjustments	•Poor mental health •Educational disruptions	•Substance Misuse •Union Dissolutions

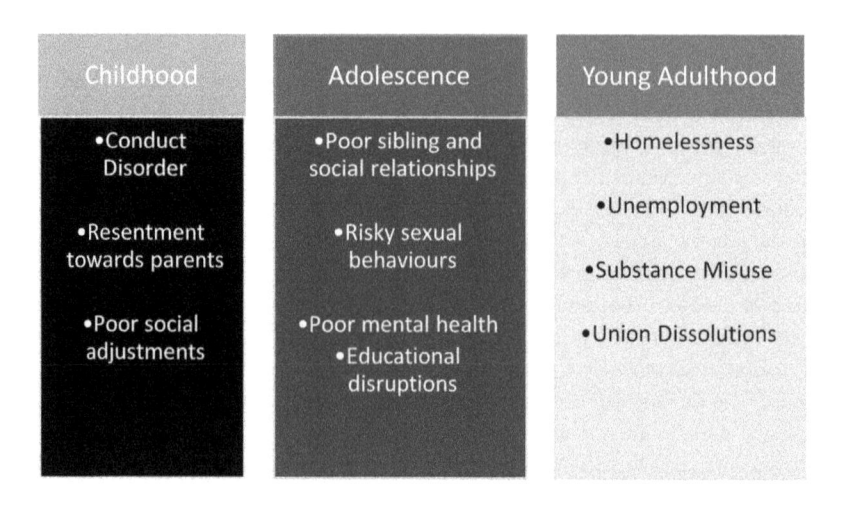

Figure 4.3 Family breakdown and lifecycle.

involved in family transitions (from formation to dissolution). It is therefore important to understand how these family transitions predispose children to negative social and psychological outcomes in the short and long term.

As family breakdown occurs in a series of process which begins before the breakdown and last beyond the breakdown, understanding it as a process rather than an event is fundamental to providing insights into how it can affect the well-being of children. In the following paragraphs, we provide an overview of how the processes involved in family transitions can affect child(ren) outcomes.

Reduced quality in parent–child relationships

Family breakdown is an important family stressor for both the parents and the child. When families break down, parents may experience psychological distress and begin to focus on their recovery, which can extend for a long period (Tosi & van den Broek, 2020). In the process, the resident parent can become emotionally unavailable, inconsistent in their parenting and rely on the child for support, reducing the time and parental attention that is given to them (Mooney et al., 2009; Tosi & van den Broek, 2020). This can affect the child's relationship with the resident parent, resulting in lower levels of affectionate behaviour, poorer communication, and more erratic discipline (Amato, 2005; Amato & Anthony, 2014).

Also, due to changes in the family structure, there is a tendency for contact with the non-resident parent to decline over time (Goisis et al., 2019). Though figures vary, there is evidence to suggest that despite increases in shared custody, about 17–30% of adolescents lose touch with their non-resident parents after a family breakdown (ONS, 2018). Thus, children are less likely to receive adequate parenting and form a stable relationship with the non-resident parent (Goisis et al., 2019). This can have implications for their self-esteem, psychological adjustment, and academic performance (Wadman et al., 2020); leading to the development of behaviour problems.

Links have also been established between parental involvement and academic performance (Fomby, 2011; Goisis et al., 2019). In a literature review by Desforges and Abouchaar (2003), it was noted that parental involvement has positive effects on the educational achievement of children, irrespective of the quality of school attended. Cohort studies in the UK also indicate that children who experience family breakdown are at a greater risk of educational underachievement and leaving school early (Amato, 2005; Brewer & Nandi, 2014). Another study by Bernardi and Boertien (2016), also noted that even though their grades were not affected, children who experienced a family breakdown were less likely to complete their secondary education. These studies thus imply that family breakdown can affect the educational achievement of children experiencing it.

Limited economic resources

The economic circumstances of families can decline after a family breakdown, and this can have an impact on child well-being and outcomes. According to Fisher and Low (2009), when a couple separates, their income can drop by more than a tenth, leading to financial difficulties. In a study by Brewer and Nandi (2014) exploring partnership dissolution, using data from the British Household Panel Study (BHPS), both authors noted that one in five resident parents fall into poverty due to a reduction in family income. Even with the introduction of welfare benefits (such as spousal support and child maintenance), this may not always resolve the loss of one parents' income from the household, further highlighting the financial impacts of family dissolutions (Brewer & Nandi, 2014). As a result, single parents are more likely to alternate between employment and end up in welfare benefits (Spencer, 2005). It is estimated that about 22% of children are living in single-parent households (ONS, 2020). Data gathered from the ONS 2018 note that children in single-parent families are more likely to live in poverty (44%) than in couple parent families (24%). Statistics suggest that in most cases following a family breakdown, the mother becomes the primary resident parent as only 10% of lone parents are fathers (ONS, 2015). Due to a relative lack of economic independence among women as they are more likely to be in lower-paid jobs and work part-time (Mariani et al., 2017); increased caring responsibilities, living costs, and unemployment consequences are likely to be more severe for women than for men (Spencer, 2005). As a result, they tend to be more disadvantaged in terms of poverty.

When there is a family breakdown, one parent has to move out of the joint home and are more likely to move into poorer environments or experience homelessness due to poor finances (Brewer & Nandi, 2014). This may explain why lone parents account for a significant proportion of individuals applying for help with homelessness and welfare benefits (ONS, 2020). When parents experience homelessness and financial difficulties due to family breakdown, it can significantly impact the health, education, and life chances of their children (Brewer & Nandi, 2014). Children who experience homelessness are more likely to experience absenteeism in education, have reduced access to healthcare (such as immunisation and vaccinations), and be more predisposed to stress, anxiety, and behavioural problems (Spencer, 2005). Thus, family breakdown can expose children to poorer socioeconomic conditions, higher levels of deprivation (Goisis et al., 2019), and contribute to child poverty levels in the UK.

The downward move in socio-economic status and housing situations can have a significant impact on child outcomes. A recent study exploring lone parenthood and childhood development proposed that lower income and resources have a greater impact on negative child outcomes than poor parenting (Harkness et al., 2020). Similarly, studies have shown that children who live in poorer households and environments are more likely to exhibit antisocial behaviour and have psychological and academic problems (Benson & McKay, 2017; Wadman et al., 2020); externalise, engage in delinquent behaviours (such as stealing, drug use, and crime) and be more likely to struggle with homelessness and unemployment in adulthood (Spencer, 2005). Considering that lone parenthood reduces the financial resources available to children, it is therefore not unlikely for it to have negative consequences on their well-being.

Increased parental conflict

The pre-separation process preceding family breakdown often involves a heightened level of inter-parental conflict and hostility due to disagreements regarding child custody, residency, and contact (Amato & Anthony, 2014). This can put children at risk of maladjustment and impact the parent-child relationship. Studies that have examined parental conflict preceding family breakdown and its impacts note that children may struggle with feelings of distress and resentment towards their parents, leading to high levels of discord in parent-child relationships (Benson & McKay, 2017; Mooney et al., 2009). These disruptions in parent-child relationships can have long-term emotional and behavioural consequences for children.

Inter-parental conflicts can also impact a child's psychological well-being. Children may feel a sense of responsibility for being the source of conflict and feel helpless in resolving conflict, consequently leading to a higher predisposition to anxiety in adulthood (Goisis et al., 2019). There is also evidence to show that adolescents are more actively affected by parental conflict preceding family breakdown as they often tend to exhibit behavioural problems and suffer from adjustment problems in school and in establishing social relationships (Amato, 2005; Amato & Anthony, 2014).

As highlighted in the Social Learning theory, inter-parental relationships can influence the nature of other social relationships, particularly within the family. In terms of family relationships, inter-parental conflicts can lead to negative sibling relationships as children tend to model the maladaptive behaviour witnessed at home to their siblings (O'Gorman, 2012). Additionally, due to increased conflict and a breakdown in parent–child relationships, adolescents are more likely to move out of their family home (Benson, 2010; Smith, 2007). As young people are often ill-equipped to secure their accommodation, they are more likely to become homeless, end up sleeping rough and survive through stealing, drug dealing, and prostitution (Bramley & Fitzpatrick, 2018; Smith, 2007) This shows how the home environment preceding family breakdown can play an important role in the child(ren)'s development and adjustment.

Relocation

Increased mobility due to family breakdown can also affect children's well-being and development. Studies have suggested that a change in physical circumstances such as home and school can have academic and social implications for children (Desforges & Abouchaar, 2003). Students who experience school mobility are at an increased risk of school suspension and lower achievement due to difficulties in adjustments (Desforges & Abouchaar, 2003). Family breakdown can increase the likelihood of physical relocation which can lead to change in homes, schools, and loss of social support such as friends. When there is a family breakdown, individuals (particularly children) may have to move several times before they find suitable accommodation (Goisis et al., 2019). This may further estrange the child from the non-resident parent. Some studies have shown that children may long for a reconciliation with estranged parents and carry this desire for an extended period, often going to extreme lengths to establish a relationship with an estranged parent (see Box 4.3).

BOX 4.3 HOW FAR WILL YOU GO TO RECONCILE WITH AN ESTRANGED PARENT?

When British rapper, Maya (popularly known as M.I.A) was young, her parents separated. In 2005, she titled her first album 'Arular' after a political code name that her estranged father used during his time as a politician in Sri Lanka.

She did this because she hoped that one day, he would google his name, see an album using his name, be curious to search about it and reach out to the owner of the album. Her dreams came true! Before the release of her album, her father emailed her saying: "This is Dad. Change the title of your album. I'm really proud."

Source: https://en.wikipedia.org/wiki/Arular

Additionally, while parents who have custody of the child are more likely to retain the joint home, they may eventually have to move out due to the sale of the house or the inability of the resident parent to maintain the house mortgage (Feijten & Mulder, 2010). This can increase residential mobility for children involved in family breakdowns. As negative financial impacts are more likely to occur due to family breakdown, children are also more likely to move to poorer neighbourhoods, predisposing them to poor health conditions and behavioural problems (Spencer, 2005).

In many instances, a change in residence or school may occur at the same time, causing a child to face multiple stressors. While many studies have not analysed the links between mobility and its negative effects on children, Haynie and South (2005) in their examination of the effects of school and residential mobility found that school changes were more likely to have smaller networks and experience stress in building new relationships.

Societal-related harm

Can family breakdowns harm society? Several scholars have argued that the social and economic burden of family breakdown for society may occur directly or indirectly due to associations with other social problems. Some of these associations to other social problems are discussed below:

Increased juvenile behaviour

Family breakdown has been identified as a pathway to poverty, crime, social welfare burden, and homelessness. In a comprehensive review of research evidence by (Amato, 2005), they noted that children who experienced family breakdown were at increased risk of behavioural problems, and, drug and alcohol abuse in adolescence and adulthood. Similarly, a 2018 study by Pasqualini et al. (2018) on family transitions, noted that family breakdown increased alcohol consumption in boys and emotional difficulties in girls. These poor psychological adjustments can contribute to heightened crime rates among young people experiencing a family breakdown. A study conducted by Smith (2007) noted that children who experience family breakdown are nine times more likely to become young offenders, accounting for 70% of all young offenders. Similarly, a more recent study among 60 young offenders and at-risk individuals in Croydon also noted that 72% of its participants had experienced family breakdown.

Increased incidences of homelessness

> **BOX 4.4 HOMELESSNESS AMONG YOUNG PEOPLE**
>
> Across the UK, young people below the age of 25 years accounted for around a quarter of households applying for help with homelessness.
>
> **England:** Between April 2017 and March 2018, 21% of young people seeking help for homelessness were aged 16 to 24 years.
>
> **Scotland:** Between April 2017 and March 2018, 25% of young people seeking help for homelessness were aged 16 to 24 years.

> **Wales:** For households under homelessness relief duties, 28% of applicants were below the age of 24 years between April 2017 and March 2018.
> **Northern Ireland:** Between April 2018 to September 2018, 32% of individuals applying for homelessness were between the ages of 16 to 25 years.
> Source: UK Homelessness; 2005–2018, ONS (2018).

Young people are also likely to experience homelessness due to family breakdown (ONS, 2020) (see Box 4.4). This is often because they may consider their new home environment unwelcoming and decide to search for a safer and more welcoming environment by leaving home. Homelessness among young people (due to departure from the family home) can have a detrimental impact on them with long term implications for their education, employment prospects, and drug use (Bramley & Fitzpatrick, 2018). It can also predispose individuals to use illegal and psychoactive substances to cope with daily stress (Smith, 2007). This can contribute to poorer socio-behavioural health outcomes among them and consequently increase the healthcare cost associated with homelessness (Bramley & Fitzpatrick, 2018).

Increased dysfunction

Family breakdown can lead to a vicious cycle of dysfunction. In a longitudinal study by Amato and Patterson (2017), children who experienced family breakdown were 16% more likely to have a union dissolution in adulthood. The study also noted that *'young people from unstable families tend to form unstable unions, whereas young people from stable families tend to form stable [relationships]'* (p. 730). This shows how family breakdown can impact the stability of the next generation.

Increased taxpayer costs

While family breakdown can negatively impact the individuals involved, it also brings financial costs to the taxpayer. It is estimated that the government spends approximately 46 billion pounds in managing family breakdown and there has been a 24% increase in these figures since 2009 (Centre for Social Justice, 2015). The effect of separation on family incomes and living standards has wide-reaching implications for the economy, as a majority of lone parents rely on state welfare, housing benefits, and struggle with unemployment (Mariani et al., 2017). This can contribute to a higher impact on levels of child poverty in the UK.

> **BOX 4.5 THE CHICKEN AND THE EGG QUESTION**
>
> Are families breaking down due to social problems or are social problems leading to family breakdown?
> Some scholars (**Team A**) argue that family breakdown leads to social problems like crime, homelessness, and behavioural problems

> Some scholars (**Team B**) argue that the reverse is the case as they believe that social problems like alcohol misuse, poor relationships, and poor economic conditions, leads to family breakdown
>
> Others (**Team C**) argue that these two issues (family breakdown and social problems) are two sides of a coin.
>
> [Diagram: Family Breakdown ⇄ Social Problems]
>
> What **Team** are you on?

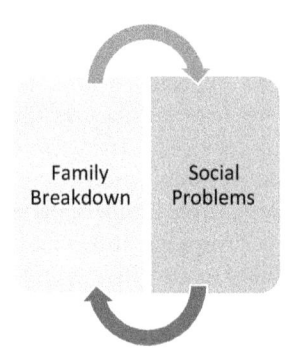

Interventions for family breakdown; policies, services, and support

The experience of family breakdown can be traumatic. It is, therefore, important that interventions and access to services are made available to help families overcome the negative effects of family breakdown (Parkinson & Robinson, 2011). There is no simple strategy or approach to solve the issue of family breakdown and this is mostly because there appears to be a lack of consensus as to the root of family breakdowns and how it should be tackled (see Box 4.5). Nevertheless, the UK Government has introduced a series of policies and legal reforms to manage the impact of family breakdown. Some of these include:

Legal reforms

The UK government helps families going through a breakdown to manage conflicts and achieve a workable parental arrangement that emphasises the rights of children to parental care and support. The most recent legislation in the UK, and the most relevant to mitigating the negative impacts of family breakdown, is the Family Law Act 1996 which governs divorce and marriage. It is expected that the mediations required and made available by the law, will help to ensure that the child remains in contact with the non-resident parent and ease conflict within families headed for divorce (Parkinson & Robinson, 2011). However, research evidence suggests that not all children may benefit from contact with both parents following divorce or parental separation, particularly if they had a poor relationship with the parent or if the parent was abusive (Mooney et al., 2009). These differences in family dynamics are thus taken into consideration when deciding the best measures for families undergoing a breakdown.

Social reforms

To improve the livelihoods of individuals and provide them with the adequate tools to function as effective members of society, it is important to prevent family breakdown and the negative impacts that it has on individuals. Benson and McKay (2017) suggest that measures targeted at helping to prevent family breakdown should include conflict resolution strategies and relationship support, as this can go a long way in influencing people's behaviour towards adopting a supportive view of commitment and family. There are a number of social assistance programs that intervene in family life to prevent family breakdown or help families going through a breakdown. Some examples are:

- Family mediation council aimed at helping families going through a breakdown to reach mediation (Parkinson & Robinson, 2011).
- Family advice and information service which aims to facilitate support networks, manage family distress (between parents and children); encourage cooperative parenting between families and avoid divorce-related conflicts. These also involve school-based support programs which help to support students going through family transitions (Centre for Social Justice, 2011).
- Troubled families programme (TFP), established in 2012 which is a targeted intervention for families at risk of breakdown. It is a family intervention approach where a nominated key worker is assigned to each family to gain an understanding of a family's interconnected issues and design a plan of action (Lambert & Crossley, 2017). Evidence suggests that the TFP administered by the Ministry of Housing, Communities and Local Government (MHCLG) has improved familial dynamics and relationships (Lambert & Crossley, 2017).
- Supporting families programme, an intervention proposed in March 2021, is the second phase of the Troubled families programme. This programme will focus on building the resilience of families vulnerable to breakdown by empowering families to find their solutions to family problems (GOV.UK, 2021).

Conclusion

This chapter has explored the evidence-base on family, family breakdown, its impacts, and proposed mitigations. It concludes by proposing a critical reflection on the future sustainability of the family. Current statistics show that that there has been a 4.2% reduction in family breakdowns in the last decade (ONS, 2021). While this shows promise, as discussed in this chapter, the evidence suggests that family breakdown has significant implications for individuals, families, and society. It is, therefore, necessary to put structures in place that ensure the proper functioning and sustainability of the family.

First, there is a need to conduct more qualitative and longitudinal research on the impact of family breakdown across individuals' lifespans. This will help to better articulate the needs of individuals going through a breakdown and contribute to effective intervention design. Second, there is also a need for policymakers and professionals to begin to consolidate and synthesise evidence on the effectiveness of interventions in managing and preventing family breakdown. This will go a long way in providing insights on how strategies and programmes can be better implemented for maximum impact.

Finally, as the family serves is a foundation for an individuals' social, behavioural, and emotional development, it is important that national, local, and professional authorities' partner with individuals to help navigate family issues and mitigate family breakdown. In this way, more person-centred approaches to family breakdown interventions can be designed and implemented. It is hoped that this chapter will further discourse on family breakdown, and ignite a more critical analysis on the subject matter.

Quiz: fractured families: causes and consequences of family breakdown

A True or false

1. Family breakdown has never been a problem in the UK
2. No matter how ideal a family is, there will be periods of conflicts and hardships.
3. Cause and contribute to family breakdown are diverse and complex
4. Substance misuse affects each family and family member the same
5. Family breakdown only affect parents involved
6. The Divorce Reform Act of 1969 and 1996 has strengthened families and made them more stable in UK
7. All children who experience family breakdown have bad outcomes

B Pick appropriate response

8. Which of the following defines a Family?

   a   Biological factors
   b   Cultural factors
   c   All of the above
   d   None of the above

9. Which of the following is both the cause and a consequence of family breakdown?

   a   Growing apart
   b   Domestic violence
   c   Substance misuse
   d   All of the above
   e   None of the above

10. What is the fastest emerging type of family unit in the UK?

    a   Lone parent families
    b   Married couple families
    c   Cohabiting families

11. What theory discusses how poor parent child relationships can lead to family breakdown?

    a   Social learning theory
    b   Scharp's theory of family distancing
    c   Attachment theory
    d   Duck's Dissolution Model

12   What divorce Act introduced the idea of *'no-faults?'*
   a   The Matrimonial Causes Act
   b   The Family Law Act
   c   The Divorce Reform Act
   d   The Civil Partnership Act
   e   The Divorce, Dissolution, and Separation Act

C **Fill in the Gap with any of the following: individualistic, increase, collectivist, or decrease.**

13   The number of married couple families are on the .... while those in cohabiting family units are on the .... in UK.
14   Family breakdown are more common in .... societies compared to .... societies.

Answers

1. False; 2. True; 3. True; 4. False; 5. False; 6. False; 7. False; 8. c – All of the above; 9. b – Domestic violence; 10. c – Cohabiting families; 11. b – Scharp's theory of family distancing; 12. c – The Divorce Reform Act; 13. Decrease, Increase; 14. Individualistic, Collectivist

Group activities

- Develop an intervention idea (service, policy, or law) that can help to tackle the issue of family breakdown.
- Pick one of the theories discussed in the chapter and critique its propositions for family breakdown.
- Do you think that there is any benefit that can be derived from a family breakdown?
- Apart from the factors discussed in this chapter, what other factors contribute to family breakdown?
- Are social problems (such as domestic violence, alcohol misuse, behavioural problems) a cause of family breakdown or an effect of family breakdown?

Points for reflection

- What does family mean to you? Who constitutes a family and who does not constitute a family? Discuss.
- Do you think that the predominant definitions of the term family is too narrow? If so, how would you define the term family?
- What do you think are the advantages of the different family structures mentioned in the chapter?

Organisations working in the topic area

Centre for Social Justice (CSJ)
https://www.centreforsocialjustice.org.uk
Office for National Statistics (ONS)

https://www.ons.gov.uk/
Department for communities and local government
https://www.gov.uk/government/organisations/ministry-of-housing-communities-and-local-government

Helpful topic-related websites (links to policies, theoretical content, etc.)

Britain's future plans to support families: https://www.gov.uk/government/publications/supporting-families-2021-to-2022-and-beyond/supporting-families-2021-22-and-beyond

Family and Household statistics: https://www.ons.gov.uk/peoplepopulationandcommunity/birthsdeathsandmarriages/families/bulletins/familiesandhouseholds/2020

Young people and homelessness: https://centrepoint.org.uk/youth-homelessness/

Supplementary reading

Centre for Social Justice (2019). *Why Family Matters: A Comprehensive Analysis of the Consequences of Family Breakdown*. United Kingdom: The Centre for Social Justice.

Centre for Social Justice (2020). *Family Structure Matters*. United Kingdom: The Centre for Social Justice.

Scharp, K. M. (2019). "You're not welcome here": A grounded theory of family distancing. *Communication Research*, 46(4), 427–455.

References

Abbassi, A., & Aslinia, S. D. (2010). Family violence, trauma and social learning theory. *Journal of Professional Counseling: Practice, Theory & Research*, 38(1), 16–27.

Akers, R. L., & Jennings, W. G. (2016). Social learning theory. In A. R. Piquero (Ed.), *The handbook of criminological theory*, 230–240. Oxford: John Wiley & Sons.

Allan, G., Hawker, S., & Crow, G. (2001). Family diversity and change in Britain and Western Europe. *Journal of Family Issues*, 22(7), 819–837.

Amato, P. R. (2005). The impact of family formation change on the cognitive, social, and emotional well-being of the next generation. *The Future of Children*, 75–96.

Amato, P. R., & Anthony, C. J. (2014). Estimating the effects of parental divorce and death with fixed effects models. *Journal of Marriage and Family*, 76(2), 370–386.

Amato, P. R., & Patterson, S. E. (2017). The intergenerational transmission of union instability in early adulthood. *Journal of Marriage and Family*, 79(3), 723–738.

Bandura, A., & McClelland, D. C. (1977). *Social learning theory* (Vol. 1). Englewood Cliffs, NJ: Prentice Hall.

Benson, H. (2010). *Family breakdown in the UK: It's not about divorce*. Bristol: Community Family Trust and the Centre for Social Justice.

Benson, H. (2013). *Unmarried parents account for one-fifth of couples but half of all family breakdown*. Cambridge: Marriage Foundation.

Benson, H., & McKay, S. (2017). *Family breakdown and teenage mental health*. Cambridge: Marriage Foundation.

Berrington, A., Perelli-Harris, B., & Trevena, P. (2015). Commitment and the changing sequence of cohabitation, childbearing, and marriage: Insights from qualitative research in the UK. *Demographic Research*, 33, 327–362.

Bernardi, F., & Boertien, D. (2016). Understanding heterogeneity in the effects of parental separation on educational attainment in Britain: Do children from lower educational backgrounds have less to lose? *European Sociological Review*, 32(6), 807–819. https://doi.org/10.1093/esr/jcw036.

Besschetnova, O. V., Fomina, S. N., Shimanovskaya, Y. V., Sizikova, V. V., Karpunina, A. V., & Konstantinova, N. P. (2021). Divorce in post-epidemic society: reasons and consequences. *Laplage em Revista*, 7(3D), 65–72.

Booth, A., & Amato, P. R. (2001). Parental predivorce relations and offspring postdivorce well-being. *Journal of Marriage and Family*, 63(1), 197–212.

Bramley, G., & Fitzpatrick, S. (2018). Homelessness in the UK: Who is most at risk? *Housing Studies*, 33(1), 96–116.

Bretherton, I., & Munholland, K. A. (2008). Internal working models in attachment relationships: Elaborating a central construct in attachment theory. In J. Cassidy & P. R. Shaver (Eds.), *Handbook of attachment: Theory, research, and clinical applications* (pp. 102–127). New York: The Guilford Press.

Brewer, M., & Nandi, A. (2014). *Partnership dissolution: how does it affect income, employment and well-being?*

Buchanan, T. M., & McConnell, A. R. (2017). Family as a source of support under stress: Benefits of greater breadth of family inclusion. *Self and Identity*, 16(1), 97–122.

Cantillon, S., Moore, E., & Teasdale, N. (2021). COVID-19 and the pivotal role of grandparents: Childcare and income support in the UK and South Africa. *Feminist Economics*, 27(1–2), 188–202.

Centre for Social Justice (2011). *Strengthening the family and tackling family breakdown: Fatherlessness, dysfunction and parental separation/divorce.* A policy paper by the Centre for Social Justice. Retrieved from: https://www.centreforsocialjustice.org.uk/wp-content/uploads/2011/10/StrengtheningtheFamily.pdf.

Centre for Social Justice (2015). *Fully committed? How Government could reverse family breakdown.* Retrrieved from: https://www.centreforsocialjustice.org.uk/library/fully-committed-how-government-could-reverse-family-breakdown.

Chandan, J. S., Taylor, J., Bradbury-Jones, C., Nirantharakumar, K., Kane, E., & Bandyopadhyay, S. (2020). COVID-19: A public health approach to manage domestic violence is needed. *The Lancet Public Health*, 5(6), e309.

Daly, M., & Scheiwe, K. (2010). Individualisation and personal obligations–social policy, family policy, and law reform in Germany and the UK. *International Journal of Law, Policy and the Family*, 24(2), 177–197.

Desforges, C., & Abouchaar, A. (2003). *The impact of parental involvement, parental support and family education on pupil achievement and adjustment: A literature review* (Vol. 433). DfES London.

Duck, S., & Wood, J. T. (2006). What goes up may come down: Sex and gendered patterns in relational dissolution. *Handbook of divorce and relationship dissolution*, 169–187.

Fahey, T. (2012). Small bang? The impact of divorce legislation on marital breakdown in Ireland. *International Journal of Law, Policy and the Family*, 26(2), 242–258.

Feijten, P., & Mulder, C, H. (2010). Gender, divorce and housing—a life course perspective, In D. Reuschke (Ed.), *Wohnen und Gender. Theoretische, politische, soziale und räumliche Aspekte* (pp. 175–193). Wiesbaden: VS Verlag für Sozialwissenschaften.

Fine, M. A., & Harvey, J. H. (2006). Divorce and relationship dissolution in the 21st century. *Handbook of divorce and relationship dissolution*, 3–11.

Fisher, H., & Low, H. (2009). Who wins, who loses and who recovers from divorce. *Sharing Lives, Dividing Assets.*

Fomby, P. (2011). Family instability and school readiness in the United Kingdom. *Family Science*, 2(3), 171–185.

Goisis, A., Özcan, B., & Van Kerm, P. (2019). Do children carry the weight of divorce? *Demography*, 56(3), 785–811.GOV.UK (2021). Supporting families. Retrieved from: https://www.gov.uk/government/collections/supporting-families.

Gravningen, K., Mitchell, K. R., Wellings, K., Johnson, A. M., Geary, R., Jones, K. G., Clifton, S., Erens, B., Lu, M., & Chayachinda, C. (2017). Reported reasons for breakdown of marriage and cohabitation in Britain: Findings from the third National Survey of Sexual Attitudes and Lifestyles (Natsal-3). *PLoS One*, 12(3), e0174129.

Grusec, J. E. (1994). Social learning theory and developmental psychology: The legacies of Robert R. Sears and Albert Bandura. In R. D. Parke, P. A. Ornstein, J. J. Rieser, and C. Zahn-Waxler (Eds.), *A century of developmental psychology* (pp. 473–497). Washington: American Psychological Association. https://doi.org/10.1037/10155-016.

Harkness, S., Gregg, P., & Fernández-Salgado, M. (2020). The rise in single-mother families and children's cognitive development: Evidence from three British birth cohorts. *Child Development*, 91(5), 1762–1785.

Haynie, D. L., & South, S. J. (2005). Residential mobility and adolescent violence. *Social Forces*. 84(1), 361–74.

Heu, L. C., van Zomeren, M., & Hansen, N. (2019). Lonely alone or lonely together? A cultural-psychological examination of individualism–collectivism and loneliness in five European countries. *Personality and Social Psychology Bulletin*, 45(5), 780–793.

Hoftede, G., Hofstede, G. J., & Minkov, M. (2010). *Cultures and organizations: software of the mind: intercultural cooperation and its importance for survival.* McGraw-Hill.

Holland, S., Forrester, D., Williams, A., & Copello, A. (2014). Parenting and substance misuse: Understanding accounts and realities in child protection contexts. *British Journal of Social Work*, 44(6), 1491–1507.

Howe, D. (2012). Attachment theory. *Social work theories and methods*, 75.

Kiernan, K., McLanahan, S., Holmes, J., & Wright, M. (2011). Fragile families in the US and UK. *Universidad de Navarra: Center for Research on Child Wellbeing, Woodrow Wilson School of Public and International Affairs.(WP11–04FF)*.

Kiernan, K., & Mensah, F. (2010). Partnership trajectories, parent and child well-being. *Children of the 21st century: The first five years*, 77–94.

Lambert, M., & Crossley, S. (2017). 'Getting with the (troubled families) programme': A review. *Social Policy and Society*, 16(1), 87–97.

Lampard, R. (2014). Stated reasons for relationship dissolution in Britain: Marriage and cohabitation compared. *European Sociological Review*, 30(3), 315–328.

Lawrence, J. (2019). *Me, me, me?: Individualism and the search for community in post-war England.* Oxford University Press, USA.

Lebow, J. L. (2020a). The challenges of COVID-19 for divorcing and post-divorce families. *Family Process*, 59(3), 967–973.

Lebow, J. L. (2020b). Family in the age of COVID-19. *Family Process*, 59(2), 309–312. https://doi.org/10.1111/famp.12543.

Lebow, J. L. (2020c). COVID-19, families, and family therapy: Shining light into the darkness. *Family Process*, 59(3), 825–831. https://doi.org/10.1111/famp.12590.

LeFebvre, R., & Franke, V. (2013). Culture matters: Individualism vs. collectivism in conflict decision-making. *Societies*, 3(1), 128–146.

Lu, L., Gilmour, R., Kao, S. F., & Huang, M. T. (2006). A cross-cultural study of work/family demands, work/family conflict and wellbeing: The Taiwanese vs British. *Career Development International*.

Mariani, E., Özcan, B., & Goisis, A. (2017). Family trajectories and well-being of children born to lone mothers in the UK. *European Journal of Population*, 33(2), 185–215.

Mooney, A., Oliver, C., & Smith, M. (2009). Impact of family breakdown on children's wellbeing: Evidence review.

Mikolai, J., & Kulu, H. (2019). Union dissolution and housing trajectories in Britain. *Demographic Research*, 41, 161–196. https://www.jstor.org/stable/26850647

Office for National Statistics (ONS) (2020). Families and households in the UK: 2020. Retrieved from: https://www.ons.gov.uk/peoplepopulationandcommunity/birthsdeathsandmarriages/families/bulletins/familiesandhouseholds/2020#:~:text=There%20were%202.9%20million%20lone,over%20the%20last%2010%20years.

Office for National Statistics (ONS) (2016). Divorces in England and Wales: 2016. Retrieved from: https://www.ons.gov.uk/peoplepopulationandcommunity/birthsdeathsandmarriages/

divorce/bulletins/divorcesinenglandandwales/2016#:~:text=In%202016%2C%20the%20 number%20of%20divorces%20of%20opposite%2Dsex%20couples,in%202015%20 (Figure%202).

O'Gorman, S. (2012). Attachment theory, family system theory, and the child presenting with significant behavioral concerns. *Journal of Systemic Therapies, 31*(3), 1–16.

Panico, L., Bartley, M., Kelly, Y. J., McMunn, A., & Sacker, A. (2019). Family structure trajectories and early child health in the UK: Pathways to health. *Social Science & Medicine, 232,* 220–229.

Parkinson, L., & Robinson, N. (2011). *Family mediation: Appropriate dispute resolution in a new family justice system.* Bristol: Family Law.

Pasqualini, M., Lanari, D., & Pieroni, L. (2018). Parents who exit and parents who enter. Family structure transitions, child psychological health, and early drinking. *Social Science & Medicine, 214,* 187–196.

Rholes, W. S., & Simpson, J. A. (2004). Attachment theory: Basic concepts and contemporary questions. In W. S. Rholes & J. A. Simpson (Eds.), *Adult attachment: Theory, research, and clinical implications* (pp. 3–14). New York, NY: Guilford Publications.

Rivett, M. (2020). Relational lockdown and relational trauma† in the time of coronavirus: A reflection from a UK family therapist. *Family Process, 59*(3), 1024–1033.

Rollie, S. S., & Duck, S. (2006). Divorce and dissolution of romantic relationships: Stage models and their limitations. *Handbook of divorce and relationship dissolution,* 223–240.

Savage, M. (2020). Why the pandemic is causing spikes in break-ups and divorces. Retrieved from: https://www.bbc.com/worklife/article/20201203-why-the-pandemic-is-causing-spikes-in-break-ups-and-divorces (29th October 2021).

Scharp, K. M. (2019). "You're not welcome here": A grounded theory of family distancing. *Communication Research, 46*(4), 427–455.

Scharp, K. M., & Dorrance Hall, E. (2017). Family marginalization, alienation, and estrangement: Questioning the nonvoluntary status of family relationships. *Annals of the International Communication Association, 41*(1), 28–45.

Scharp, K. M., Thomas, L. J., & Paxman, C. G. (2015). "It was the straw that broke the camel's back": Exploring the distancing processes communicatively constructed in parent-child estrangement backstories. *Journal of Family Communication, 15*(4), 330–348.

Seifman R. (2021). COVID-19 impacts on marriage and divorce. impakter. https://impakter.com/covid-19-impacts-on-marriage-and-divorce/

Skinner, G. C., Bywaters, P. W., Bilson, A., Duschinsky, R., Clements, K., & Hutchinson, D. (2021). The 'toxic trio'(domestic violence, substance misuse and mental ill-health): How good is the evidence base? *Children and Youth Services Review, 120,* 105678.

Smith, I. (2007). Being tough on the causes of crime: Tackling family breakdown to prevent youth crime. United Kingdom: Centre for Social Justice. Retrieved from: https://www.centreforsocialjustice.org.uk/wp-content/uploads/2018/03/causes_of_crime.pdf.

Spencer, N. (2005). Does material disadvantage explain the increased risk of adverse health, educational, and behavioural outcomes among children in lone parent households in Britain? A cross-sectional study. *Journal of Epidemiology & Community Health, 59*(2), 152–157.

Tosi, M., & van den Broek, T. (2020). Gray divorce and mental health in the United Kingdom. *Social Science & Medicine, 256,* 113030.

Wadman, R., Hiller, R. M., & St Clair, M. C. (2020). The influence of early familial adversity on adolescent risk behaviors and mental health: Stability and transition in family adversity profiles in a cohort sample. *Development and Psychopathology, 32*(2), 437–454.

Whittaker, A., Martin, F., Olsen, A., & Wincup, E. (2020). Governing parental drug use in the UK: What's hidden in "hidden harm?". *Contemporary Drug Problems, 47*(3), 170–187.

World Health Organisation (2021). Violence against women: key facts. Retrieved from: https://www.who.int/news-room/fact-sheets/detail/violence-against-women.

5 A domestic violence pandemic

Outlining victim and perpetrator perspectives

Helen Holmes

Introduction

In December 2019, the Government was elected with a manifesto commitment to "support all victims of domestic abuse and pass the Domestic Abuse Bill," initially introduced in the last Parliament. The Bill aims to ensure that victims have the confidence to come forward and report their experiences freely, safe in the knowledge that the state will do everything it can, both to support them and their children and pursue and prosecute the abuser.

In this chapter, domestic abuse is used interchangeably with intimate partner violence (IPV). A definition of domestic violence will be offered, alongside a brief history of domestic violence in the UK, to help contextualise the problem. Statistical data, according to the World Health Organization and others (WHO, NHS, social services), will provide some clarity in relation to the growing magnitude of the current domestic violence pandemic, including mortality data, hospitalisation, gender, age, etc. Theories are important not only because they offer different explanations for the phenomenon of domestic abuse but because each approach has clear implications for responses and interventions by practitioners and policymakers. This can undermine the quality of service provision, safety and initiatives for social change. Six different theoretical models will be outlined in terms of domestic violence, namely: the individualist model, structural, feminist, post-structuralist, family systems and social ecological. Firstly, let's turn to look at the Domestic Abuse Bill (2020).

There are an estimated 2.4 million victims of domestic abuse each year, aged between 16 and 74 years old, two-thirds of whom are women, whilst over one in ten of all offences documented by the police are domestic abuse related, as reported by the Home office (Domestic Abuse Bill, 2020). There is a genuinely urgent, current and ongoing need for growing awareness, training and appropriately safe and effective interventions to properly help us all to keep women safe who are in relationships involving the power dynamic recognised as IPV. This desperate need is brought into sharp relief especially due to the COVID-19 pandemic, with more time spent in the family home with far fewer outlets for family members of differing ages to socialise and be involved with a variety of activities. The lack of psychological space present during non-COVID-19 life becomes corroded and feelings usually invested in other activities and relationships escalate into abusive and dangerous situations. Women may not have any control over access to money or other freedoms, finding themselves exposed more acutely to damaging influences from their partners. Mothers who find the courage to leave their abusive partners, have nowhere left to go, with governmental decisions to close refuges, possibly leading to nothing but dangerous and fatal entrapment. Public displays

DOI: 10.4324/9781003166887-5

of violence against women are sadly too regular occurrences, as tragically witnessed in the disappearance and murder of Sarah Everard in South London, in March 2021. The Police crime, sentencing and courts Bill (March 2021) and Social care reform Bill (March 2021) are of interest.

Defining domestic violence/intimate partner violence in the UK?

A statutory definition of domestic abuse has been created through the Domestic Abuse Bill (2020), which is based on the existing cross-government definition. The definition of domestic abuse is presented in two parts. The first part deals with the relationship between the abuser and the abused. The second part defines what constitutes abusive behaviour.

The Domestic Abuse Bill (2020) sets out two criteria governing the relationship between the abuser and the abused. The first criteria states that both the person who is carrying out the behaviour and the person to whom the behaviour is directed towards must be aged 16 or over. Abusive behaviour directed at a person under 16 would be dealt with as child abuse rather than domestic abuse. The second criteria state that both persons must be "personally connected." The definition ensures that different types of relationships are captured, including ex-partners and family members. In 2012, following a public consultation, the age limit in the cross-government definition of domestic abuse was lowered from 18 to 16, to recognise that young people can experience abuse in their relationships. The lines between domestic abuse and child abuse need not be blurred. A personal relationship between the victim and perpetrator is key to the definition of domestic abuse. This is how domestic abuse is generally understood amongst the public and agencies. People who are "personally connected" are defined as: intimate partners, ex-partners, family members or individuals who share parental responsibility for a child. There is no requirement for the victim and perpetrator to live in the same household.

Broad categories are listed, which capture a range of different abusive behaviours, including physical, emotional and economic abuse. The Domestic Abuse Bill (2020) specifically includes economic abuse to demonstrate that it is a distinct type of abuse. Statutory guidance provides further details on the different types of abuse and abusive behaviours, included within those categories. The guidance will also recognise that the majority of victims of abuse are female.

Economic abuse involves behaviours that interfere with an individual's ability to acquire, use and maintain economic resources such as money, transportation and utilities. It can be controlling or coercive. It can make the individual economically dependent on the abuser, thereby limiting their ability to escape and access safety.

> **BOX 5.1 ECONOMIC ABUSE REFERS TO**
>
> - having sole control of the family income.
> - preventing a victim from claiming welfare benefits.
> - interfering with a victim's education, training, or employment.
> - not allowing or controlling a victim's access to mobile phone/transport/utilities/food.
> - damage to a victim's property

Domestic Abuse Bill and children

The Bill also recognises that domestic abuse can impact on a child who sees or hears or experiences the effects of the abuse and it treats such children as victims of domestic abuse in their own right where they are related to either the abuser or the abused. Further questions relevant to the above definition are examined in what follows. There was recognition of the devastating impact that domestic abuse can have on children exposed to it in their own home. Part 1 of the Bill provides that a child who sees or hears, or experiences the effects of, domestic abuse and is related to the person being abused or the perpetrator is also to be regarded as a victim of domestic abuse. This will help to ensure that locally commissioned services consider and address the needs of children affected by domestic abuse.

One of the key functions of the Domestic Abuse Commissioner is to encourage good practice in the identification of children affected by domestic abuse and the provision of protection and support for these children. Other measures in the Bill help better protect both the victims of domestic abuse and their families, including the provisions in respect of Domestic Abuse Protection Orders and the Domestic Violence Disclose Scheme.

A gender-neutral definition of domestic abuse is used, to ensure that all victims and all types of domestic abuse are sufficiently captured, and no victim is excluded from protection or access to services. The supporting statutory guidance will provide more detail on the features of domestic abuse, including recognising that the majority of victims are women. This is also emphasised in the Violence Against Women and Girls Strategy and the National Statement of Expectations, which sets out how local areas should ensure victims of violence and abuse against women and girls get the help they need.

The guidance is aimed at statutory and non-statutory bodies working with victims and perpetrators and commissioning services, including the police, local authorities and the NHS to increase awareness and inform their response to domestic abuse. It will also be aimed at support organisations working with victims.

History of domestic violence in the UK

Historically, abuse to women has been viewed as an acceptable aspect of marriage (Erez, 2002). During the mid-1800s, most legal systems accepted wife beating as a valid expression of a husband's authority over his wife, using the "rule of thumb," established by Sir Francis Buller, known as "Judge Thumb." This meant that a husband could beat his wife with a stick not thicker than his thumb (Women's Aid, 2008) allowed by old British Common Law (Dipty, 2009). It was only in the 1970s that domestic violence was defined as a crime, justifying intervention by the criminal justice system (Erez, 2002).

Facts and statistics in relation to domestic violence

Official statistics show the number of incidents of domestic abuse recorded by the authorities every year. However, the problem appears much bigger than shown in official statistics, as many involved including children don't tell anyone about the abuse, and they are not recorded as crimes.

BOX 5.2 KEY STATISTICS ABOUT DOMESTIC VIOLENCE IN THE UK (WHO, 2021)

Each year nearly 2 million people in the UK suffer some form of domestic abuse – 1.3 million female victims (8.2% of the population) and 600,000 male victims (4%).

Each year more than 100,000 people in the UK are at high and imminent risk of being murdered or seriously injured as a result of domestic abuse.

Women are much more likely than men to be the victims of high risk or severe domestic abuse: 95% of those going to Marac or accessing an Idva service are women.

In 2013–2014, the police recorded 887,000 domestic abuse incidents in England and Wales.

Seven women a month are killed by a current or former partner in England and Wales.

130,000 children live in homes where there is high-risk domestic abuse.

62% of children living with domestic abuse are directly harmed by the perpetrator of the abuse, in addition to the harm caused by witnessing the abuse of others.

On average victims at high risk of serious harm or murder live with domestic abuse for two to three years before getting help.

85% of victims sought help five times on average from professionals in the year before they got effective help to stop the abuse.

Myths and misconceptions relating to domestic violence

There are many myths and deep-rooted misconceptions relating to domestic violence. Box 5.3 presents some of these as listed by Women's Aid.

BOX 5.3 MYTHS ABOUT INTIMATE PARTNER VIOLENCE

MYTH: Alcohol and drugs make men more violent.
FACT: Alcohol and drugs can make existing abuse worse, or be a catalyst for an attack, but they do not cause domestic abuse.

MYTH: If it was that bad, she would leave.
FACT: Women stay in abusive relationships for many different reasons, and it can be very difficult for a woman to leave an abusive partner – even if she wants to.

MYTH: Domestic abuse always involves physical violence.
FACT: Domestic abuse as an incident or pattern of incidents of controlling, coercive, threatening, degrading and violent behaviour, including sexual violence, coercive control; psychological and/or emotional, physical, sexual and financial abuse; harassment; stalking; and/or online or digital abuse.

> **MYTH:** He can be a good father even if he abuses his partner – the parents' relationship doesn't have to affect the children.
> **FACT:** An estimated 90% of children whose mothers are abused witness the abuse.
>
> **MYTH:** Abuse or violence of any kind is never the victim's fault.
> **FACT:** Abuse or violence of any kind is never the victim's fault. Responsibility always lies with the perpetrator alone.
>
> **MYTH:** Domestic abuse is a private family matter, and not a social issue.
> **FACT:** Violence and abuse against women and children incur high costs for society.
>
> **MYTH:** Women are just as abusive as men.
> **FACT:** Women are more likely than men to experience multiple incidents of abuse, different types of domestic abuse, sexual violence and family violence such as forced marriage, female genital mutilation and so-called "honour crimes."

In order to understand this phenomenon, it would be helpful to look at relevant theories about domestic violence, namely the individualist approach, structural, feminist, family systems and social-ecological perspectives.

DV and minority ethnic groups

Domestic violence has received increasing government and public attention especially through the Covid pandemic, giving a raised voice to Women's Aid and other women's organisations committed to campaigning around violence against women and children for the past three decades. Equally, attention has again focused on issues of racism and race equality in a European context where racialised discourse around refugees and asylum seekers has become common place. Both of these separate debates converge and have pertinence for any discussion on domestic violence and the experiences of women from black and minority ethnic (BME) communities. Male violence against women from ethnic minorities is the focus of this section.

The problem of domestic violence is a taboo at the best of times, and within social groups suffering from constant discrimination, discussion of the subject tends to be avoided as far as possible. In England, 40 of the approximately 240 refuge support services are specialist refuges striving to meet the needs of differing groups of BME women and children. Despite increasing numbers of BME women accessing DV services, research shows that the success of such services in ensuring a woman-centred environment has not been mirrored in the area of race equality. Given that many groups of BME women are still under-using DV services and experiencing racism in mainstream services, which are not sensitive to their cultural, religious and other needs, the challenge of ensuring equality for all service users remains unmet and something that needs to be considered by all working in the DV sector.

Research shows that despite having equal opportunities policies in place, implementation is often weak and few services in the study were able to provide details of how they created a safe environment for BME women and children. Of concern also was the "colour-blind" approach adopted by many workers who stated that "we treat all women alike regardless of culture" – reducing racism to culture was something that was commonly done by many services. Some services also considered anti-racism as being of little concern to them because BME women did not use their services. These issues clearly have implications for the development of good practice within DV services. It is important to highlight that an emphasis on diversity alone (though an important step) does not ensure equality for women and children from BME groups. Ensuring equality requires a more proactive look at every aspect of the service, from employment practices right through to service delivery.

Similarly, when working to ensure diversity, it is important not to make assumptions about homogenised groups but recognise the complex and multiple needs of a changing population – for instance, the needs of a South Asian woman born in the UK are likely to be somewhat different from those of a woman born and raised in the sub-continent. Equally, the needs of different groups are likely to shift and change and it is important to reflect this fluidity in service responses, which can build sensitivity by consulting and involving BME women and children rather than making assumptions about them to acknowledge the specific needs of BME women.

While recognising that the BME groups encountered by DV services will vary depending on country and locality, the research highlighted a number of issues about the needs of BME women that are important to consider in service responses. For a range of reasons, BME women require a high level of support over a longer period of time. This can include mediation with statutory agencies, interpreting and specialist counselling. Immigration law and absence of settled immigration status continue to impact particularly viciously on the lives and choices of BME women. It can often determine whether a woman actually seeks help as well as shape the service response that she receives – many refuge services in England have to discriminate against some women due to their immigration status. This issue is of increasing relevance in most European countries with refugee and asylum seeker populations – however, it was found in England that many DV workers are uninformed about the issues faced by refugee women.

BOX 5.4 INTIMATE PARTNER VIOLENCE BY ETHNICITY

5.7% of 16–74-year-olds in England and Wales reported having been a victim of domestic abuse in the previous 12 months.

People of mixed ethnicity (12.9%) were more likely to experience domestic abuse than White (5.7%) or Asian people (3.8%).

People in White other ethnic groups were two times less likely to experience domestic abuse than White British people (2.9% compared with 5.9%).

Source: Actionaid (2020)

Theoretical understandings of domestic violence

Although the idea of empowerment lies at the heart of the anti-domestic violence movement, consensus on the defining characteristics of this construct has remained elusive. A clear and consistent definition of empowerment would promote the development of common metrics for research and evaluation and guide the development of best practices. Specific challenges have made the conceptualisation of empowerment difficult. The Empowerment Process Model addresses those challenges. This model articulates empowerment as a meaningful shift in the experience of power attained through interaction in the social world and describes the process of building empowerment as an iterative one, in which a person takes action towards personally meaningful goals; drawing on community supports, skill, knowledge and self-efficacy to move towards those goals; and observing the extent to which those actions result in progress. By incorporating both process and outcome dimensions, bridging the psychological and contextual realms and allowing for domain specificity, the model addresses challenges to a clear conceptualisation, providing a common framework that may be used as a reference point for social workers and researchers wishing to apply the construct. Let us now turn to the structural model, in what follows.

Structural model

The UN Declaration was the first international statement that defined violence against women within a broader gender-based framework and identified the family, the community and the state as major sites of gender-based violence (GBV). The statement was rooted in feminist analysis of social inequality. According to the UN Declaration, violence against women involves: any act of GBV that results in, or is likely to result in physical, sexual or psychological harm or suffering to women, including threats of such acts, coercion or arbitrary deprivation of liberty, whether occurring in public or in private life (p. 1).

GBV can include domestic violence, sexual harassment, sexual violence and rape. GBV is a deliberately broad term in order to recognise the gendered elements in nearly all forms of violence against women and girls, whether it is perpetrated through sexual violence or through other means. The use of the term "gender-based violence" provided a new context in which to examine and understand the phenomenon of violence against women. It shifted the focus from women as victims of violence to gender and the unequal power relationships between women and men that are created and maintained through gender stereotypes. A gender perspective on violence against women addresses the similarities and differences in the violence experienced by women and men in relation to vulnerabilities, violations and consequences.

In response to this declaration, various efforts have been made to respond to reduce and eliminate this violence experienced by women. Significant attention has been paid in the Northern hemisphere and high-income countries such as Canada and the US to the provision of social services to victims of GBV, such as strengthening and maintaining women's safety and their involvement in social, political and economic activities. Changes have also been made to justice sector responses and to treatment for perpetrators of GBV.

Interventions in low-and-middle-income countries have focused on primary prevention strategies to reduce the prevalence and incidence of violence against women and girls. These prevention programs use a wide range of approaches, including group training, social communication, community mobilisation and livelihood strategies. Microfinance and cash transfer programs in countries such as South Africa, Kenya and Ecuador have reported reductions in the rates of IPV. Community mobilisation programs in Uganda and Sub-Saharan Africa that aim to reduce violence at the population level through changes in public discourse, practices and norms for gender and violence, demonstrated not only reductions in physical and sexual partner abuse but also reduced incidence of HIV/AIDS.

These responses, however, have largely turned to understandings of GBV that place the causes, consequences and costs at an individual level. With the launch of the World

Health Organization (WHO) Multi-Country Study on Women's Health and Domestic Violence in 2005, the number of IPV prevalence studies increased. This research primarily from the health and medical fields has largely focused on individual-or-relationship-level factors to the exclusion of factors operating at a broader societal level. Prevalence studies from around the world have shown that IPV has a number of health consequences including injury, chronic pain, sexually transmitted diseases, depression and post-traumatic stress disorder (PTSD) to name a few. Though this research has contributed to an understanding of the prevalence, consequences and costs associated with IPV against women, its focus has been on individual behaviours and health outcomes, ignoring how patterns of violence are connected to social systems and social institutions.

Structural violence can be defined as the social arrangements that put individuals and populations in harm's way, the arrangements are structural because they are embedded in the social, political and economic organisation of our social world; they are violent because they cause injury to people (typically, not those responsible for perpetuating such inequalities). Structural violence includes a host of offensives against human dignity: extreme and relative poverty, social inequalities ranging from racism to gender inequality and the more perverse forms of violence that are uncontestably human rights abuses. In adopting a structural violence approach to understand GBV in a variety of contexts and events, our analysis underscores the importance of historical and social contexts that influence IPV towards women.

Structural violence is marked by unequal access to the determinants of health (e.g., housing, good quality health care, unemployment, education), which then creates conditions where interpersonal violence can occur and shape *gendered forms of violence* that place women in vulnerable positions. Gender is inescapably embedded in social systems and institutions. For instance, Parikh (2012) illustrates how a macro-level structural intervention (increase in the age of consent law at national and local levels) intended to address gendered HIV risk in Uganda has the unintended consequence of reinforcing gender-based social hierarchies. Despite the stated aim of protecting young women, the law reinstates patriarchal privilege and the regulation of adolescent female sexuality. Moreover, research pertaining to gender tends to regard the categories of "men" and "women" as distinct categories, not just in their biological make-up but also in their gender-specific role socialisation.

Feminist approach

Researchers and clinicians who advocate studying and/or treating females as primary perpetrators of IPV or who advocate studying and/or treating couples who choose to remain together after experiencing IPV have been labelled "anti-feminist." In this chapter, we review the ways feminist theory has changed over the years and how, frequently, when feminist theory is criticised or upheld as a guiding theory for understanding IPV, an outdated view of feminist theory is used. Through this review, we seek to clarify how it is possible to be a "feminist," based on a third wave intersectional position that emphasises social justice and advocates for eliminating essentialist practices, while rejecting patriarchy as the primary cause of IPV and embracing a variety of explanations and treatment options for individuals and couples in violent relationships. Our work is based on a more layered and complex model that "seeks both to hold violent partners accountable and to intervene to change couple interaction" (Stith et al., 2011, p. 10).

90 *Helen Holmes*

Patriarchy, referring to the "power of the fathers" (Kesselman et al., 2008, p. 10), is "the grand narrative that influences us all, often invisibly" (Dickerson, 2013, p. 102). It continues to have an important place in understanding some types of IPV. However, the historically persistent patriarchal social structure has been offered as the primary explanation of IPV (Stark & Flitcraft, 1996; for a discussion of this, see Winstock, 2013).

However, there is mounting evidence that both men and women use violence in relationships (Archer, 2000; Jose & O'Leary, 2009). Violence occurs in heterosexual and same-sex relationships. If patriarchy (or male privilege) is the primary explanation for IPV, how is female violence or violence in same-sex relationships understood? I found ourselves at odds with the brand of feminism that characterised, not only the social policy that required batterer groups for men and support groups for women, but also the implication that "most," if not "all men" were violent and "most," if not "all women," were victims. Further, troubling was the idea that if we believe that patriarchy also does men a disservice, we were letting men "off the hook," thereby not holding them fully accountable for the unearned privileges they receive by being men. In the same way, we had concerns with batterer intervention standards that prohibit providers from considering psychological contributions to male battering behaviour.

The idea of a single factor cause of male violence begs further exploration, in tandem with state standards that generally stem from an assumption of gendered violence. Let us now turn to look at the social-ecological perspective.

Social-ecological perspective

The effects on children of political violence are matters of international concern, with many negative effects well-documented. At the same time, relations between war, terrorism or other forms of political violence and child development do not occur in a vacuum. The impact can be understood as related to changes in the communities, families and other social contexts in which children live and in the psychological processes engaged by these social ecologies. To advance this process-oriented perspective, a social-ecological model for the effects of political violence on children is advanced. This approach is illustrated by findings and methods from an ongoing research project on political violence and children in Northern Ireland. Aims of this project include both greater insight into this particular context for political violence and the provision of a template for study of the impact of children's exposure to violence in other regions of the world. It is pertinent to now look at the current UK legislation. In relation to thinking about the perpetrator-victim stance of domestic and IPV, let us now turn to consider why women stay in such relationships, cycles of violence and battered women syndrome.

Attachment theory

Social policies and social work practices are increasingly influenced by attachment theory. Women who have been subjected to domestic violence by male partners are being assessed within this discourse, which takes little account of societal perspectives, which sustain injustices and power differentials. Domestic violence is known to be a major social problem but when attachment theory is applied to women and their babies in domestic violence it negates knowledge based in lived experiences. Rather attachment theory is informed by non-gendered family violence perspectives and research instruments, which frame domestic violence within an individualised perspective. In this way, women and their babies are observed and classified without regard for the societal factors, which affect them. In view of this, there is a need for critical social workers to question attachment theory and the positivist research instruments, which are being used to inform theory and practice. Particularly with regard to domestic violence as a gendered, societal issue, a broad perspective, which promotes a social justice view and the need for social change, is indispensable.

Intimate partner violence and substance abuse

The 2019 Domestic Abuse Bill proposed to establish a statutory definition of domestic abuse that includes "controlling, coercive, threatening behaviour, violence or abuse" encompassing "psychological, physical, sexual, economic and emotional forms of abuse" (HM Government, 2019). It also proposed to widen the scope of Domestic Abuse Protection Orders so that suspected perpetrators of domestic abuse can be compelled to attend "drug or alcohol treatment," as well as "behavioural change" programmes by the family courts (if petitioned by victims or other relevant third parties, such as non-governmental organisations) and magistrates courts (where the police would normally petition). It is proposed that compliance with such orders will be secured in part through electronic monitoring. Breaches of such orders will be a criminal offence, punishable by up to five years imprisonment, unlimited fine or both (ibid., p. 30). We can now turn to look at the relevant legislation.

Historically, policymaking with respect to drugs, alcohol and violence has focused on aggression in systems of drug distribution and supply (Goldstein, 1985) and violence arising from intoxication in the night-time economy (Wickham, 2012). There is an increasing acknowledgment internationally, however, of the link between substance use and IPV (Commonwealth of Australia, Department of Health, 2017; HM Government, 2017). The most recent UK Drug Strategy (HM Government, 2017) notes that women with experience of physical and sexual interpersonal violence are more likely to have drug or alcohol problems (Ellsberg et al., 2008) and that there is a higher prevalence of IPV perpetration amongst men in substance use treatment than in the general population (Gilchrist et al., 2017; O'Farrell et al., 2003).

Although heterosexual men and people in same-sex relationships also experience IPV (Bailey, 2018; Kubicek et al., 2016), the most common and severe forms of IPV are perpetrated against women by men (World Health Organization, 2013). Goldstein's (1985) tripartite model of the relationship between general violence and drugs proposed that drugs and violence could be related in three ways: psychopharmacologically, economic compulsively or systemically. The psychopharmacological model emphasises the direct effect of consuming or withdrawing from substances on violence perpetration; the economically compulsive model suggests that some drug users carry out violent crime to support their drug use; while the systemic model refers to "traditionally aggressive patterns of interaction within the system of drug distribution and use" (Goldstein, 1985, p. 497). Despite its failure to recognise either the interaction between social contexts and psychopharmacology (Parker & Auerhahn, 1998) or to consider the social and cultural contexts of substance-related offending more generally (Bennett & Holloway, 2009), Goldstein's model has nevertheless been influential in shaping how the drug/violence "nexus" is conceived in government policy and in inspiring research on the disinhibitory effects of intoxication in specific social settings (Parker & Rebhun, 1995), including the family (Parker & Auerhahn, 1998).

The impact on children

Children who experience domestic violence but are not battered themselves present behavioural and emotional problems similar to those experienced by bodily abused children and may also suffer from post-traumatic pressure syndrome later. One study states that witnessing violence involving parents is a predictor of future violence when compared with being a victim of child abuse.

The children see that this kind of behaviour is *acceptable* by their most important role models. Boys learn that battering is a way to influence loved ones without becoming exposed to more constructive alternatives. As they grow up boys usually identify with their fathers and lose respect for their mum or feel guilty for not being able to protect her. Home violence becomes a factor in custody cases.

Once beyond the abusive relationship, a woman can overcome the feelings involving inadequacy and helplessness that were brainwashed into her when being in an abusive relationship. Courts have granted modified associated with a consent decree to change custody from father to the mother when the mother later was able to demonstrate that the consent rule was signed under duress.

Why does she just not leave? Cycles of violence

It is challenging to us all, no doubt, to think about why wo/men remain in long-term domestic and IPV relationships, where mainly the female experiences the violence on multiple levels. There can be numerous reasons for a woman/mother not to leave, including fear of losing their life, fear of further violence as the male loses control, financial, love for their partner, security, loss of self-esteem, amongst many others.

Battered women syndrome

Serious, long-term domestic abuse can result in battered woman syndrome. This is considered to be a subcategory of PTSD. With battered woman syndrome, a woman may develop a learned helplessness that causes her to believe that she deserves the abuse and can't get away from it. In many cases, women don't report their abuse to the police or avoid telling friends and family about what's really going on in their intimate relationships.

Domestic abuse typically follows an extremely predictable cycle. The abuser will win over the new partner, often moving quickly into a relationship with tactics like "love-bombing," grand romantic gestures and pressuring for commitment early. Or the abuser will be emotionally or physically abusive. This often starts small, like a slap instead of a punch, or punching the wall next to their partner. Or, the abuser will feel guilty, swearing they'll never do it again and be overtly romantic to win their partner over. Or there will be a temporary "honeymoon" period, where the abuser is on their best behaviour, luring their partner into thinking that they're safe and things really will be different but abuse occurs, starting the cycle all over again.

Battered woman syndrome results in several distinct symptoms. A woman in an abusive relationship may think the abuse is her fault; hide the abuse from friends and family; fear for her life or the lives of her children; irrationally believe that the abuser is all-knowing and can see her every movement; be afraid and never know what side of their partner they'll see that day – a loving partner or an abuser.

> **BOX 5.5 FOUR PSYCHOLOGICAL STAGES OF BATTERED WOMAN SYNDROME**
>
> 1 **Denial.** The person is unable to accept that they're being abused, or they justify it as being "just that once."
> 2 **Guilt.** The person believes they caused the abuse.
> 3 **Enlightenment.** In this phase, the person realises that they didn't deserve the abuse and acknowledges that their partner has an abusive personality.
> 4 **Responsibility.** The person accepts that only the abuser holds responsibility for the abuse. In many cases, this is when they'll explore their options for leaving the relationship.
>
> Source: Healthline.com

Signs and indicators

There are several signs and indicators of someone being in an abusive relationship. These include withdrawing and making excuses not to see friends or family or do activities they once did (this can be something the abuser is controlling). They may appear anxious around their partner or afraid of their partner, having frequent bruises or injuries they lie about or can't explain, limited access to money, credit cards or a car, showing an extreme difference in personality. Additionally, they may be getting frequent calls from a significant other, especially calls that require them to check in or that make them seem anxious or have a partner who has a temper, is easily jealous, or very possessive. They may use clothing to hide bruises, like wearing long-sleeve shirts in the summer.

Legislation

Post-1970s

The 1970s brought three vital items of legislation, the Domestic Violence & Matrimonial Proceedings Act 1976, providing the police with powers of arrest for the breach of injunction in cases of domestic violence and allowed women to obtain the right to stay at the matrimonial home. The Domestic Proceedings & Magistrates' Courts Act 1978, amended the use of injunctions to prevent further violence in the home and the law, relating to matrimonial proceedings in magistrates' courts and the Housing (Homeless Persons) Act 1977, which refers to persons who are homeless or threatened with homelessness, which helped domestic violence victims with re-housing (UK Legislations).

Contemporary

In 1986, the Home Office published the first circular regarding domestic violence, named "Violence against women" clarifying that it was obligatory for the police to ensure the safety of women and children at domestic deputes (Applegate, 2006) but it wasn't until 1992 that both the Home Office Circular 60/1990 and the Association of Chief Probation Officers declared domestic violence to be a crime, giving law enforcement agencies the power to punish the abuser (Kury & Smartt, 2006). However, it did not make much of a change to the policy (Applegate, 2006).

It was not until 2005 when the Domestic Violence Crime and Victims Act 2004 was introduced, addressing these issues through the criminal law and bringing about change. The Act aims to increase the safety of domestic violence victims by providing the police with extra power to approach and deal with domestic violence more effectively. This established a new offence called "familial homicide," providing the power of arrest for minor offences of common assault and linking some criminal and civil remedies (Women's Aid). In criminal justice, there is a statutory code of practice to ensure support and protection is provided to victims of domestic violence (Applegate, 2006).

The Domestic Abuse Bill (2020)

Aims:

1. Create a statutory definition of domestic abuse, highlighting that domestic abuse includes physical, emotional, coercive or controlling and economic abuse.
2. Establish in law the office of Domestic Abuse Commissioner and set out the Commissioner's functions and powers.
3. Provide for a new Domestic Abuse Protection Notice and Domestic Abuse Protection Order.
4. Place a duty on local authorities in England to provide support to victims of domestic abuse and their children in refuges and other safe accommodations.
5. Prohibit perpetrators of abuse from cross-examining their victims in person in the civil and family courts in England and Wales.
6. Create a statutory presumption that victims of domestic abuse are eligible for special measures in the criminal, civil and family courts.
7. Clarify by restating in statute law the general proposition that a person may not consent to the infliction of serious harm and, by extension, is unable to consent to their own death.
8. Extend the extraterritorial jurisdiction of the criminal courts in England and Wales, Scotland and Northern Ireland to further violent and sexual offences.
9. Enable domestic abuse offenders to be subject to polygraph testing as a condition of their licence following their release from custody.
10. Place the guidance supporting the Domestic Violence Disclosure Scheme ("Clare's law") on a statutory footing.
11. Provide that all eligible homeless victims of domestic abuse automatically have "priority need" for homelessness assistance.
12. Ensure that where a local authority, for reasons connected with domestic abuse, grants a new secure tenancy.

As it stands the Bill includes a statutory duty to support victims only if they are in refuges or supported accommodation. However, the campaign for the amendment says that whilst this support is welcome, there is a risk – especially with limited funding – that this will create a two-tier system, with the majority of victims who remain in the family home not qualifying for this protection and potentially not receiving the support they desperately need as a result.

Summary

Domestic violence can be across genders but is currently most known about in relation to violence from men to women but the impact on children is long lasting and severe. This is arguably an institutionally accepted way of behaving, working on many detailed levels, through verbal and non-verbal communications, which need to be able to be challenged in social work practice with sensitivity alongside thought through planned strategies through to action.

Teenage relationship abuse urgently needs to be addressed through the education system and family interventions by social workers, to protect young people from being harmed. Domestic violence in relation to children clearly would be very upsetting for children to see one of their parents (or partners) abusing, attacking or controlling the other. Younger children may become anxious. They may complain of tummy aches or start to wet their bed. They may find it difficult to sleep, have temper tantrums and start to behave as if they are much younger than they are. They may also find it difficult to separate from their abused parent when they start nursery or school. Older children react differently.

Boys seem to express their distress much more outwardly, for example by becoming aggressive and disobedient. Sometimes, they start to use violence to try and solve problems and may copy the behaviour they see within the family. Older boys may play truant and start to use alcohol or drugs (both of which are a common way of trying to block out disturbing experiences and memories). In what follows the micro/macro interventions of DV will be elucidated, such as social worker role/skills and values/ethical issues in practice. On a micro-level, social workers may also grapple with the issue of what type of abuse (i.e., verbal insults, threats to safety and physical violence) constitutes domestic violence, when, for example, trying to determine if the domestic violence witnessed by a child is significant enough to warrant a report to child protective services.

It is important to address why partners remain in domestic violence relationships, since the victim role is powerful but can lack taking responsibility for the part played in the domestic situation, aiming for empowerment and decision-making towards a healthier lifestyle.

Points to ponder

Why do you think that women find themselves and stay in violent relationships?
Do you think that IPV is more prevalent in certain socio-economic groups, ethnicities, ages or educational background?
Do you think that there has always been IPV issues in society? If so, what is the root cause of IPV? If not, what has changed and why?

Quiz

1 Which recent circumstance has increased the incidence of DV?

   A Olympic games
   B COVID-19 pandemic
   C LGBTQI+ awareness raising
   D Sarah Everard's death

2 WHO stands for

   A World Hygiene Organisation
   B World Help Organisation
   C World Hybrid Organisation
   D World Health Organisation

3 The first aspect of the definition of domestic abuse is

   A What constitutes abusive behaviour
   B Whether DV is abusive
   C Who is involved with DV
   D The relationship between abuser and abused.

4 Does the Domestic Abuse Bill (2020) include economic abuse

   A No
   B Yes
   C Don't know

5 The Domestic Abuse Bill (2020) makes reference to children

   A Don't know
   B No
   C Yes

6 The Domestic Abuse Bill (2020) is aimed at

   A Statutory bodies
   B Non-statutory bodies
   C Police, local authorities and the NHS
   D All of the above

7 Does economic abuse include

   A Having sole control of the family income
   B Preventing a victim from claiming welfare benefit
   C Interfering with a victim's education, training or employment
   D All of the above

8 What is the age limit for inclusion in DV

   A 21
   B 18
   C 22
   D 16

9 Each year, how many people in the UK suffer with DV

   A 10 million
   B 7 million
   C 2 million
   D 0.5 million

Indicate if the following statements are true or false:

10 Seven women a month are killed by a current or former partner in England and Wales?
11 Each year more than 100,000 people in the UK are at high and imminent risk of being murdered or seriously injured as a result of domestic abuse?
12 Women were more likely to report being victims of domestic abuse in the previous 12 months than men.

Answers

1. B; 2. D; 3. A; 4. B; 5. C; 6. D; 7. D; 8. D; 9. C; 10. True; 11. True; 12. True

Activities

Individuals

Stop and think about your own definition of domestic violence and write it down.

Pairs

One person the victim, the other a friend who is approached and spend 5–10 minutes playing these parts and swap round.
Discuss the three most important needs of someone experiencing IPV.

Small groups

Discuss which myths about IPV you have held and any others that you can think of.
Which feelings do you think people in IPV relationships feel? Write these on a flip chart.
How do you think ethnicity influences beliefs about IPV? Discuss this in your small group.
Does religion in any way, influence beliefs about IPV? Discuss this in your small group.

Supplementary reading

Bacchus, L.J., Ranganathan, M., Watts, C. and Devries, K. (2018). Recent intimate partner violence against women and health: a systematic review and meta-analysis of cohort studies. *BMJ Open*, *8*, e019995.

Delara, M. (2016). Mental health consequences and risk factors of physical intimate partner violence. *Mental Health in Family Medicine*, *12*, 119–125.

Ellsberg, M., Jansen, H.A., Heise, L., Watts, C.H. and Garcia-Moreno, C. (2008). Intimate partner violence and women's physical and mental health in the WHO multi-country study on women's health and domestic violence: An observational study. *Lancet*, *371*(9619), 1165–1172.

Garcia-Moreno, C., Jansen, H.A., Ellsberg, M., Heise, L. and Watts, C.H. (2006). Prevalence of intimate partner violence: findings from the WHO multi-country study on women's health and domestic violence. *Lancet*, *368*(9543): 1260–1269.

Maman, S., Campbell, J., Sweat, M.D. and Gielen, A.C. (2000). The intersections of HIV and violence: For future research and interventions. *Social Science & Medicine*, *50*(4): 459–478.

Organisations working with IPV

Citizen Advice: https://www.citizensadvice.org.uk/family/gender-violence/domestic-violence-and-abuse-getting-help/
National Centre for Domestic violence: www.ncdv.org.uk
National Domestic Violence helpline: www.nationaldomesticviolencehelpline.org.uk
National Stalking Helpline: www.stalkinghelpline.org
Refuge: https://www.refuge.org.uk/
Victim Support: https://www.victimsupport.org.uk
Womens Aid: https://www.womensaid.org.uk/

Helpful websites on topics relating to IPV:

National Centre for Domestic Violence. The National Centre for Domestic Violence (NCDV) provides a free, fast emergency injunction service to survivors of domestic violence regardless of their financial circumstances, race, gender or sexual orientation.

National Centre for the Study and Prevention of Violence and Abuse. This is an interdisciplinary and inter-professional centre with an overall aim of providing a stimulating and inclusive environment in which to study and understand violence and abuse and its prevention – regardless of who it is perpetrated by, against or between.

National Commission on Domestic and Sexual Violence and Multiple Disadvantage. Breaking down the barriers. This report finds that survivors of abuse are being failed by the system meant to help them – with devastating consequences for them and their families.

National Commission on Domestic and Sexual Violence and Multiple Disadvantage. Hand in hand. A report on the impact of domestic and sexual abuse. It outlines key areas for change, including calling for support services to be trauma-informed and for more staff with lived experience to be on the workforce.

NHS Choices: Help for domestic violence – Live Well. Information and advice on domestic violence.

Rights of Women. Rights of Women provides legal advice and information to women affected by violence.

Safe Lives. Safe lives is a national charity dedicated to ending domestic abuse. Safe lives also offers training for professionals, free down loads of tools and advice and MARAC assessment.

References

Applegate, R. J. (2006). Changing local policy and practice towards the policing of domestic violence in England and Wales. *Policing: An International Journal of Police Strategies & Management, 29*(2), 368–383.

Archer, J. (2000). Sex differences in aggression between heterosexual partners: A meta-analytic review. *Psychological Bulletin, 126*(5), 651–680.

Bailey, B. (2018). Women's psychological aggression toward an intimate male partner: Between the impulsive and the instrumental. *Journal of Interpersonal Violence, 36*(11–12), NP6526-NP6546.

Bennett T., & Holloway K. (2009). The causal connection between drug misuse and crime. *The British Journal of Criminology, 49*, 513–531.

CAADA (Co-ordinated Action Against Domestic Abuse). *Key statistics on the prevalence of domestic abuse* [online]. Bristol: Co-ordinated Action against Domestic Abuse. Retrieved from http://www.caada.org.uk/policy/statistics.html

Commonwealth of Australia, Department of Health. (2017). Retrieved from https://www.health.gov.au/about-us/corporate-reporting/annual-reports?utm_source=health.gov.au&utm_medium=callout-auto-custom&utm_campaign=digital_transformation

Dickerson, V. (2013). Patriarchy, power, and privilege: A narrative/poststructural view of work with couples. *Family Process, 52*(1), 102–114. doi: 10.1111/famp.12018

Dipty, D. (2009). *The three dimensions of domestic violence*. Oklahoma: Tate Publishing & Enterprises.

Domestic Abuse Bill (2020) Retrieved from www.gov.uk.

Ellsberg, M., Jansen, H. A., Heise, L., Watts, C. H., & García-Moreno, C. (2008). WHO multi-country study, women's health and domestic violence against women study team. Intimate partner violence and women's physical and mental health in the WHO multi-country study on women's health and domestic violence: An observational study. *The Lancet, 371*(9619), 1165–1172.

Erez, E. (2002). Domestic violence and the criminal justice system: An overview. *Online Journal of Issues in Nursing, 7*(1) Jan (Online). Retrieved from https://ojin.nursingworld.org/MainMenuCategories/ANAMarketplace/ANAPeriodicals/OJIN/TableofContents/Volume72002/No1Jan2002/DomesticViolenceandCriminalJustice.aspx

Gilchrist, E. A., Ireland, L., Forsyth, A., Godwin, J., & Laxton, T. (2017). Alcohol use, alcohol-related aggression and intimate partner abuse: A cross-sectional survey of convicted versus general population men in Scotland: Alcohol use, aggression and IPA. *Drug and Alcohol Review, 36*(1), 20–23.

Goldner, V. (1999). Morality and multiplicity: Perspectives on the treatment of violence in intimate life. *Journal of Marital and Family Therapy, 25*(3), 325–336.

Goldstein, P. J. (1985). The drugs/violence nexus: A tripartite conceptual framework. *Journal of Drug Issues, 15*, 493–506.

HM Government (2017). 2017 Drug Strategy. Retrieved from https://assets.publishing.service.gov.uk/government/uploads/system/uploads/attachment_data/file/628148/Drug_strategy_2017.PDF

HM Government. (2019). Transforming the response to domestic abuse: Consultation and Draft Bill. Retrieved from https://assets.publishing.service.gov.uk/government/uploads/system/uploads/attachment_data/file/772202/CCS1218158068-Web_Accessible.pdf

Jose, A., & O'Leary, K. D. (2009). Prevalence of partner aggression in representative and clinic samples. In K. D. O'Leary & E. M. Woodin (Eds.), *Psychological and physical aggression in couples* (pp. 15–36). Washington, DC: American Psychological Association.

Kesselman, A., McNair, L. D., & Schniedewind, N. (2008). *Women: Images and realities. A multicultural anthology* (4th ed.). Boston, MA: McGraw-Hill.

Kubicek, K., McNeeley, M., & Collins, S. (2016). Young men who have sex with men's experiences with intimate partner violence. *Journal of Adolescent Research, 31*, 143–175.

Kury, H., & Smartt, U. (2006). Domestic violence: Recent developments in German and English legislation and law enforcement. *European Journal of Crime, Criminal Law and Criminal Justice, 14*(4): 382–407.

O'Farrell, T. J., Fals-Stewart, W., Murphy, M., & Murphy, C. M. (2003). Partner violence before and after individually based alcoholism treatment for male alcoholic patients. *Journal of Consulting and Clinical Psychology, 71*: 92–102.

Parikh, S. A. (2012). They arrested me for loving a schoolgirl: Ethnography, HIV, and a feminist assessment of the age of consent law as a gender-based structural intervention in Uganda. *Soc Sci Med., 74*(11): 1774–1782.

Parker R. N., & Auerhahn, K. (1998). Alcohol, drugs, and violence, *Annual Review of Sociology, 24*, 291–311.

Parker R. N., & Rebhun L. A. (1995). *Alcohol and homicide. A deadly combination of two American traditions*. Albany: State University of New York Press.

Stark, E., & Flitcraft, A. (1996). *Women at risk: Domestic violence and women's health*. London: Sage Publications.

Stith, S. M., McCollum, E. E., & Rosen, K. H. (2011). *Couples therapy for domestic violence: Finding safe solutions*. Washington, DC: American Psychological Association.

Wickham, M. (2012). *Alcohol consumption in the night-time economy* (Working Paper 55). London, England: Mayor of London, Greater London Authority.

Winstock, Z. (2013). What can we learn from the controversy over the role of gender in partner violence? *Partner Abuse, 4*(3), 399–412.

Women's Aid. (2008). *Domestic violence – A historical perspective*. Women's Aid.
Womens Aid. Challenging myths and misconceptions: Womens aid. Retrieved from https://www.womensaid.org.uk/information-support/what-is-domestic-abuse/myths/
World Health Organization (WHO). (2013). Global and regional estimates of violence against women: Prevalence and health effects of intimate partner violence and non-partner sexual violence. Geneva: WHO. Retrieved from http://apps.who.int/iris/bitstream/10665/85239/1/9789241564625_eng.pdf
World Health Organisation (WHO). (2021). Global, regional and national prevalence estimates for intimate partner violence against women and global and regional prevalence estimates for non-partner sexual violence against women. Geneva: WHO.

6 Teenage pregnancy – a social problem or public health issue?

Rajeeb Kumar Sah and Ritu Mahendru

Introduction

Teenage pregnancy is a global problem occurring in low-, middle- and high-income countries. Teenage pregnancy, also known as adolescent pregnancy, is defined as pregnancy in women aged 10–19 years at the time of the baby birth (WHO, 2004). Teenage pregnancy is not a new phenomenon and historically early marriage and having babies at younger age are considered as a social norm in many cultures. Despite the risks associated to women's reproductive health, such pregnancies within a marriage relationship are often considered as wanted pregnancies. In the past, even in the UK and other developed countries, the age at which women conceived was irrelevant, regardless of the harm it caused to the pregnant women, but it was important that the child was born within a 'wedlock'. Traditionally, marriage was perceived as an economic protection for both mothers and their children. If women conceived before marriage, societal pressures would force them to get married before the birth of the child, known as 'knob-stick marriage' or 'shotgun wedding', to ensure legitimacy and avoid any further problem in the society (Brown, 2016; Hadley, 2018). As sexual activity was largely confined to marriages, pregnancy outside of wedlock was often seen as shameful and disgrace for the mother, child and their family, which continues to remain a reality in many cultures. For such culture, the issue of pregnancy was a moral one and related to the marriage rather than the age of women at conception or childbirth. In recent years, the public and policy concerns in many developed economies, including the UK, have shifted away from marital status of the mother and are focused on the age at conception of women. However, the move has increasingly problematised teenage pregnancy in our society (Arai, 2009). The perception of teenage motherhood as a problematic issue in the UK society is inextricably linked to political, economic and moral factors, which often consider young mothers as deviant teenagers.

> **BOX 6.1 'KNOB-STICK MARRIAGE' OR 'SHOTGUN WEDDING'**
>
> 'knob-stick marriage' or 'shotgun wedding' was a forced union to compel fathers to take responsibility to ensure legitimacy of the born child and support for the mothers (Tarlow, 2017, p. 2).

During the 1960s and 1970s, significant social and sexual changes happened in the Great Britain, where politics, law and media shifted towards new individualism with growing appetite from people to live in a more liberal and permissive society, where marriage became less popular, and cohabitation was on rise (Brown, 2016). Moreover, structural changes in the economy and the need for an increased participation in education and employment extended the period of adolescence, which allowed women to make independent choices and experience sexual agency with freedom rather than within the constraints of a marriage relationship. Although teen pregnancy outside the marriage became more acceptable in the society and gained welfare support, it limited young mother's transition into the adulthood, in many cases affecting their participation in education and employment and hindering their ability to fully engage in the economic changes to pursue self-fulfilment and self-expression (Mills, 2016). Teenage pregnancy during this period was widely reported in media as a negative phenomenon causing ill-health and educational failure that perpetuates the cycles of poverty and intergenerational disadvantage. It became a major concern for politicians, policymakers and public health professionals and in the last decades of the 20th century, teenage pregnancy was seen as a significant public health issue and a dominant social problem in the UK.

BOX 6.2 THE WOMEN'S LIBERATION MOVEMENT (WLM)

The WLM in 1960s, particularly in the industrialised nations of the Western World, brought in the sexual revolution in the UK. Introduction of the contraceptive pill in 1961 and the revision of married women's property act in 1964 and 1967 abortion act which legalised abortions in the UK for women who were up to 24 weeks pregnant were some of the key contributors associated with the social and sexual changes (Cook, 2005; Freeman, 1973).

Teenage pregnancy in the UK

The UK teenage pregnancy rate is highest among the Western Europe and second only to the US in the developed world. In most European countries since 1970s, the number of teenage births and total fertility rates has been declining and the maternal age at first birth has been rising. Despite the decline in UK teenage pregnancy rates in recent years, it remains highest in the Western Europe. In 2018, the under-18 conception rates in England and Wales were lowest since the record began in 1969 at 16.8 conceptions per 1,000 women, a decline by 6.1% from the previous year and a 60% lower since 2007 (ONS, 2020a). This has further decreased in 2019 and stands at 15.8 conceptions per 1,000 women (ONS, 2021). The conception rate for women under 18 years has declined significantly for the 12th year in a row since 2007 (Figure 6.1).

BOX 6.3 TEENAGE PREGNANCY: GLOBAL OVERVIEW

Teenage pregnancies are a global problem occurring around the world with 15% of young women giving birth before the age of 18 years, an estimated 21 million women aged 15–19 years becoming pregnant every year in developing countries, and approximately 12 million of them giving birth (UNICEF, 2021; WHO, 2020).

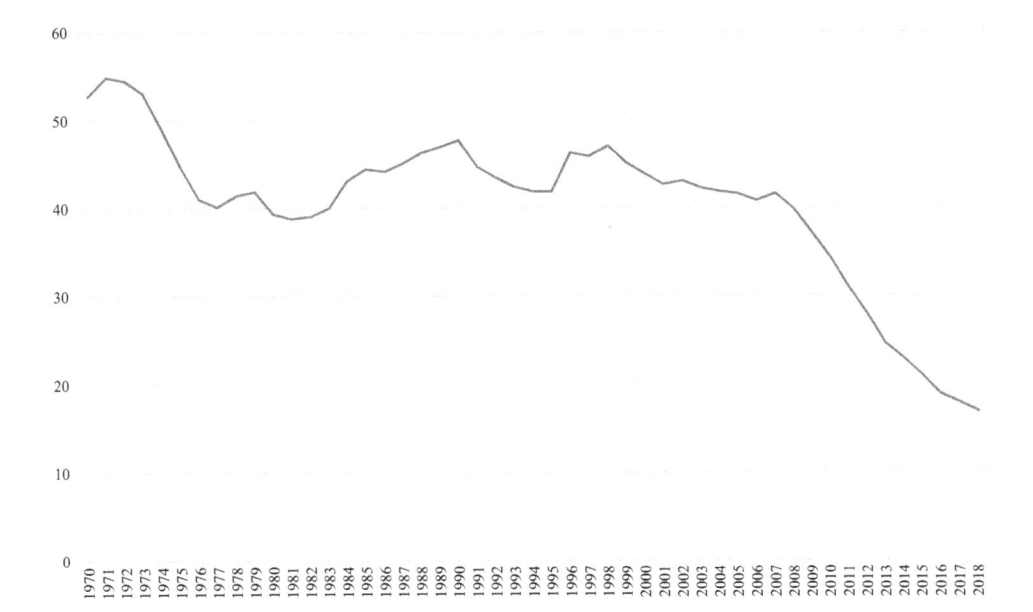

Figure 6.1 Under-18 conception rates per 1,000 women, 1969–2018, England and Wales.
Source: ONS (2020a).

The rates of teenage pregnancy across the UK vary considerably, with higher rates in the most deprived areas compared to the least deprived areas. In 2018, the under-18 conception rate for resident in the most deprived areas in England was 23.6 conceptions per 1,000 women compared to 9.5 conceptions per 1,000 women for those in the least deprived areas (ONS, 2020a). Although conception rates for women under 18 years have more than halved in the last decade, they remain more than twice as high in more deprived areas of England than less deprived areas.

Public Health Scotland (PHS, 2020) reported that the under-18 conception rates in Scotland in 2018 were 16.9 conceptions per 1,000 women, about 3.7% rise from the previous year but 60.7% decrease since 1999. In 2019, the under-18 conception rates stand at 15.6 per 1,000 women, which is 7.7% lower than in 2018 (PHS, 2021). Although teenage pregnancy rates in Scotland have reduced across all levels of deprivation, the most deprived areas in 2018 are still twice at the greater risks of teenage pregnancy.

According to the Northern Ireland Statistics and Research Agency (NISRA, 2019), the under 20 teenage birth rates in Northern Ireland have decreased from 15.52 conceptions per 1,000 females in 2008 to an all-time low at 9.03 conceptions per 1,000 females in 2016–2018. Similarly, the under 17 teenage birth rates have decreased from 2.98 conceptions per 1,000 females in 2008 to 1.39 conceptions per 1,000 females in 2016–2018. Although the teenage birth rates have been decreasing, the inequality gaps for the under 20 teenage birth rates remain very large, and the most deprived areas are six times more likely to have higher teenage birth rates compared to the least deprived areas (Carson et al., 2021). It must be noted that the statistics presented in the Northern Ireland are in the form of birth rates instead of conception rates, since the termination of pregnancy in Northern Ireland was illegal until October 2019 except where it was done to save woman's life or prevent long term or permanent physical or mental harm to the woman and then a new law came into effect on 31 March 2020 which allowed women to access abortion services without committing a criminal offence (Amnesty International UK, 2019; Sah & Robinson, 2021).

Many developing and developed countries, including the UK, are concerned about high levels of teenage pregnancy. In the UK, teenage pregnancy is regarded as one of the main contemporary social problems and it is perceived that this issue needs to be tackled to address the social and economic inequalities within different social groups of the population. While the consistent decline in teenage pregnancy is generally welcomed, it is essential to recognise that teenage mothers are not homogenous, not all teen pregnancies are unintended or unwanted, and the causes and consequences of teenage motherhood are diverse, complex and multifaceted. The causes and consequences of teenage pregnancy are neither linear nor guaranteed and the lives of young mothers are highly dependent on wider contextual factors such as personal resources, support from the families and friends, pre-pregnancy situation and post-pregnancy circumstances (Ellis-Sloan, 2019; The Scottish Government, 2016). Social exclusion, an event that severely limits young mothers' life choices and is associated with increased risk of poor socioeconomic and health outcomes of young mother and their children, is considered as one of the key causes as well as consequences of teenage pregnancy. Furthermore, teenage pregnancy is a cause and consequence of social exclusion, i.e., education and health inequality for young parents and their children (PHE, 2018b). Teenage pregnancy in contemporary society affects life chances of young people, particularly young women and their children, exposing them to vulnerabilities of intergenerational social and health inequalities and wider structural factors, such as sociocultural norms, economic policies and political system, in which they are born, grow and live.

Causes of teenage pregnancy

Teenage pregnancy is often associated with social, economic and behavioural risk factors, which also act as an independent risk factor that puts young women at the risks of teenage parenthood. It is well evidenced that social deprivation and poor educational attainment are strongly related to the higher rates of teenage pregnancy, globally. However, the causes of teenage pregnancies are complex and multidimensional and other important factors could also determine the likelihood of teenage motherhood. The report by the Social Exclusion Unit (1999) highlighted that there were three main reasons that contributed towards the high rates of teenage pregnancy in the UK: low expectations about education and job market, lack of sexual health knowledge and understanding and mixed messages about sexual activity and relationships leading to unprotected sex.

BOX 6.4 CAUSES OF TEENAGE PREGNANCY: GLOBAL OVERVIEW

Lack of information about sexual and reproductive health rights is one of the key causes of teenage pregnancy. According to UNFPA (2015), over 90% of child births to the girls aged 15–19 years in developing countries occur within early marriage where lack of or no access to contraception, family, community and social pressure to prove their fertility, lack of decision-making due to imbalance of

> power and lack of girl's education often contribute to the higher risks of teenage pregnancies. Girls receiving higher levels of education are five times less likely to become a teenage mother and have opportunities for future employment, power to negotiate their sexual and reproductive health rights and becoming financially independent to overcome the cycle of poverty.

In addition, there is strong evidence that certain groups of young people in the UK are particularly vulnerable to become teenage parents (PHE, 2019). These groups of population include, but not limited to, young people living in poverty or with single parent, those experiencing homelessness, living in care or leaving the care, who are disliked in schools or underperforming at schools, school dropouts, children of teenage mothers, teenagers involved in crime, have low expectations from the future, loss of self-esteem, have alcohol or substance misuse problems, have sex at early age, have experienced sexual abuse in childhood and young people with existing with mental health problems.

Young people today experience multiple-level risk factors that are compounded to exacerbate vulnerability and which put them at greater risk of teenage parenthood, therefore highlighting the importance of ecological approach while understanding the causes of teenage pregnancy. For example, a young woman from a poorer family with low educational attainment living in areas of greater deprivation and within a single-parent household born to a teenage mother is at much higher risk of becoming pregnant at teenage compared to other young people. In addition, young mothers with previous teenage pregnancy experiences are more likely to have repeat pregnancies in their younger age. Contraceptive use, educational attainment, history of abortion and depressive symptoms among young mothers are influential predictors for repeated teenage pregnancies (Maravilla et al., 2017). Although the available data suggest that around one-quarter of teenage pregnancies in England and Wales are subsequent pregnancies, the accurate level of repeat teenage pregnancies is not known (McDaid et al., 2017).

Social deprivation and teenage pregnancy

Social deprivation, a composite measure that includes various indicators such as poverty, young woman's education attainment, employment, health status and their parent's or household income, is considered as one of the key risk factors for the teenage pregnancy. The root cause for social exclusion among young parents is poverty and deprivation rather than early parenthood. It has been argued that young teenagers who are socially and economically disadvantaged, live in deprivation and do not see their life chances improving if they wait for a couple of years or more due to lack of educational improvements or attainment; becoming a mother can be more satisfying life events for them at that stage of their life (Cook & Cameron, 2020). In addition, if they belong to a poor neighbourhood who is deprived of opportunities and resources, aspirations of young people towards the education and employment are limited with low expectations from their life, and therefore, the risks of becoming teenage mothers are further increased to fulfil the void they experience in their life. There is clear evidence that demonstrates the linkages between social deprivation and teenage pregnancy, where teenage conceptions in socioeconomically deprived areas and areas with larger proportions of non-white populations have higher rates of teenage motherhood (Heap et al., 2020). There are many complex causes of teenage pregnancy, and it is important to understand why so many young people from socially disadvantaged and minority ethnic community do not succeed in the British community rather than simply citing it as a social or public health problem. Evidence suggests that early parenthood among socially deprived and ethnic minority communities has the potential to extend poverty and social derivation but the root cause of social exclusion among these young parents is poverty and deprivation (McDermott & Graham, 2005). There is a need to address socioeconomic and health inequalities in the community, which will eventually address the issue of teenage pregnancy and social exclusion.

Ethnicity and teenage pregnancy

Teenagers from some ethnic groups have higher rates of teenage pregnancies, especially Pakistani, Bangladeshi and Afro-Caribbean young women. ONS (2020b) reported that 73% of Pakistani, 67% of Bangladeshi and 57% of Black households' income were in the bottom two quintiles compared to the 38% of White British and 36% of White other households. Similarly, just 11% of Pakistani, 15% of Bangladeshi and 25% of Black households' income were in the top two quintiles compared to the 42% of White British and 45% of White other households. After considering for housing costs, the gaps between the minority ethnic groups and White British further widened. The link between social disadvantage and early parenthood disproportionately affects Black, Asian and Minority Ethnic (BAME) groups, which make young parents from Pakistani and Bangladeshi communities at increased risks of teenage pregnancy. The issue is further complicated as Pakistani and Bangladeshi communities' sociocultural norms and religious views do not necessarily consider teenage pregnancy as a 'problem' if the conception is within a marriage relationship (Higginbottom et al., 2006). Family relationships and religion play an important role in the sexual behaviour of young people from South Asian communities (Hennink et al., 1999). The diversity across and within minority ethnic groups indicates social, cultural and religious differences that influence sexual behaviour of the young people. Early parenthood within these communities is not necessarily seen as a barrier to educational aspirations or career opportunities but considered as a positive outcome following an early marriage, which is common, planned and culturally acceptable. Although there are significant interests in research reducing teenage pregnancy rates, little consideration is given to understand and address the issues associated with planned teenage pregnancies, which are likely to be common among these minority ethnic groups. In addition to the problematisation of teenage pregnancy, the cumulative influence of structural disadvantages, racism, poverty and risky sexual behaviour can further increase the risks of teenage pregnancy among young people from BAME groups.

Sexual abuse and teenage pregnancy

Teenagers who have been sexually abused are at an increased risk of becoming pregnant or getting someone else pregnant. Sexual abuse, alongside other forms of abuse such as physical abuse and multiple occurrences of sexual abuses in childhood and adolescence period, further exacerbates the risk of teenage pregnancy (Madigan et al.,

2014). Sexual abuse during childhood is likely to affect the developmental trajectory of the children, which may include ambiguities regarding sexual appropriateness, confused sexual boundaries, early and risky sexual behaviours and greater sexual distortions, including increased desire to become teenage mother (Noll et al., 2009). Sexual abuse has the potential to perpetuate risky sexual behaviours among teenagers by impairing their ability to negotiate safe sex or sexual relationships, and thereby leading to increase the risks of sexual violence, sex at an early age and multiple sexual partners. Abuse exposure may instigate low self-esteem and a desire to escape such environment by seeing out emotional closeness in the form of early sexual intimacy and relationships that could lead to teenage pregnancy. Sexually abused youth are also more likely to become drug dependent to cope with the traumatic experiences and engage in prostitution and survival sex to support their substance misuse (Saewyc et al., 2004). In addition, pregnancy among teenagers with a history of child sexual abuse are more likely to carry their pregnancy to term to give birth to a child and become a teenage mother compared to the teenagers from general population groups (Fortin-Langelier et al., 2019), thereby indicating the additional risks of child sexual abuse on the teenage pregnancy.

Substance misuse and teenage pregnancy

Majority of teenage pregnancies in the UK is unplanned and these unplanned pregnancies can often be associated with binge drinking of alcohol among teenagers. Research shows that there is a strong link between alcohol consumption, sex at younger age and unprotected sexual activity leading to teenage pregnancy, even after negating the effect of deprivation on the teenage pregnancy (Bellis et al., 2009). Among the young people accessing drug or alcohol services, about 1 in 12 young women under 20s is either pregnant or teenage mother and 1 in 6 young men under 25s is young father (PHE, 2019). Alcohol misuse among young people can lower personal inhibitions leading to poor judgements regarding sexual activity, vulnerability and engaging in unprotected risky sexual behaviour and later regretting the decision (Phillips-Howard et al., 2010). Maternal substance misuse at an early age is a precursor to teen pregnancy, and adolescent mothers are at heightened risk for substance abuse in the post-partum period (Chapman & Wu, 2013). Research from the US shows that adolescent pregnant women are far more likely to have experimented with alcohol, cannabis and other illicit drugs over the past 12 months before being pregnant and the substance misuse continued for many teens during the pregnancy (Salas-Wright et al., 2015). Substance misuse increases the risk for multiple sexual partners and unprotected sex and can also lead to forced sex, sexual violence, aggression and victimisation of young women putting them at higher risks of teenage pregnancy. Teenage mothers are particularly vulnerable and at increased risk for substance misuse and they are likely to have subsequent pregnancies that substance use could affect pervasively (Cornelius et al., 2004).

Consequences of teenage pregnancy

Teenage pregnancy is associated with poorer outcomes for teenage mothers and their child. Teenage pregnancy is usually a crisis for the pregnant woman and is often associated with social exclusion and poor health outcomes for the mother and the child. Social exclusion for teenage mothers often begins at an early age during childhood, with poor parenting, truancy, disrupted education and limited or lack of career prospects. Although teenage motherhood can be a positive event for some young women, the negative consequences of teenage pregnancy are widely recognised and vary from significant social issues to widespread public health problem. As teenage pregnancy prematurely halts the natural development of a young woman to adulthood, many teenage mothers complain about feeling lonely and isolated, losing independence, disconnecting with friends and experiencing challenging transition to the adulthood (Holgate et al., 2006). Young mothers are likely to bring up their children alone and in poverty and teenage pregnancy can put young parents at social and economic disadvantages and lead to physical and emotional health problems, including psychological trauma and morbidities related to abortions, exacerbating social exclusion among teenage mothers and their child.

Teenage abortions

According to the Office for National Statistics (ONS, 2020a), majority of teenage pregnancies are unplanned or unintentional and around half of them end in an abortion. Although abortions in the UK and Northern Ireland are legal, abortion rates and experiences vary depending on women's socioeconomic status and the region in which they reside. Religion, culture, familial relationships and the need of confidentiality also play an important role in decision-making towards the termination of pregnancy (Hoggart et al., 2010). Teenage women from the most deprived areas are more likely to continue with the pregnancy than undergo abortion. This may be associated with negative attitudes towards abortion and an acceptance of teenage motherhood in socially deprived areas, which are often intergenerational (Turner, 2004; Brown, 2016). Research by Lee and colleagues (2004) reported that young women's pregnancy decisions were based on the degree of social advantage or disadvantage experienced by the teenagers at the time of pregnancy. Motherhood is seen as a positive force or a way out of uncertain future for many young women who are socially disadvantaged or excluded. In contrast, young women from the least deprived or affluent areas are likely to have invested in continuing education and are more determined about their future career prospects and therefore were more likely to terminate than to deliver. The decision-making towards delivering the baby or terminating the pregnancy at teenage is not straightforward, but a complex of moral and personal reasoning (Hoggart, 2019) often shaped by the wider health inequalities and regional variations.

BOX 6.5 THE ABORTION ACT

The Abortion Act 1967 made abortions legal in Great Britain under certain specified conditions, which include the pregnancy before its 24th week, and that the continuation of the pregnancy would involve the risk greater than if the pregnancy is terminated or the termination is necessary to protect the physical and mental health of the pregnant woman (BPAS, 2013). In Northern Ireland, abortions were decriminalised in October 2019 and a new framework for lawful abortion services came into effect on 31 March 2020 (Amnesty International UK, 2019).

Adverse health outcomes associated with teenage pregnancy

Teenage pregnancy is associated with continued risky lifestyle behaviour and poor health outcomes for both teenage mother and their child. Teenage mothers are twice as likely to smoke before and during pregnancy and three times more likely to smoke throughout their pregnancy (PHE, 2019). Moreover, young pregnant females are more likely to continue with the substance misuse during and after pregnancy increasing the health risks for the child and young mothers. Teenage pregnancy may lead to poor health outcomes such as anaemia, pregnancy-induced hypertension, premature delivery, longer and difficult labour among teenage mothers (Chen et al., 2007; Jeha et al., 2015). In addition, teenage pregnancy is often cited as one of the key issues that triggers the range of mental health problems among young people. Many teenage mothers suffer from depression within a year of giving birth and experience behavioural problems such as suicidal thoughts and poor mental health problems during pregnancy and after the birth of their children (Leishman, 2007). Severe depression, attempted suicide and honour killings are some of the other risks associated with mental health problems caused by teenage pregnancy. Births and abortions associated with teenage pregnancy have the potential to impact individuals leading to wider psychological issues. Similarly, the child of the teenage mother could be born prematurely, with congenital anomalies, can have low birth weight and are at higher risks of neonatal death (Chen et al, 2007; PHE, 2019). Moreover, as a child, they have an increased risk of living in poverty and are more likely to have behavioural problems. It is argued that maternal age on itself is not a significant risk factor but many of these negative health outcomes are linked to other socioeconomic factors such as poverty, lack of education and social exclusion (Irvine et al., 1997). Besides, many of these risks could be reduced with a good quality antenatal care; however, teenage mothers are less likely to access antenatal and postnatal maternity services and are less likely to breastfeed, which may negatively impact the health outcomes of mother and child. Although reduction in teenage pregnancy rates could improve maternal and child physical and mental health and reduce health inequalities, addressing social inequalities is likely to contribute towards reduction in teenage pregnancy rates and support teenage mothers to have positive life experiences and better health and resources for future career prospects.

Education and socioeconomic impact of teenage pregnancy

Teenage pregnancy is largely believed to be a pathway for school dropouts, poverty and economic dependency and therefore is often seen as a public health concern or a social problem. Young parents are less likely to finish their education, more likely to remain unemployed, on social welfare benefit and bring up their child alone and in poverty compared to the older mothers (DH, 2013). As majority of teenage parents have an increased risk of living in poverty, they are more likely to have accidents and behavioural problems that further puts the teenage mothers and their children at the risk of social vulnerability and poor health status. The long-term prospect of teenage mothers and their children is poorer than average, and the consequences of teenage pregnancy can be felt by young mothers for rest of their life, and it has also the potential to shape the life chances of these young mothers and their children negatively (Berrington et al., 2005). There is ample evidence that young women from disadvantaged backgrounds are more likely to become teenage mothers and these mothers have higher risks of remaining disadvantaged in their adult life. Teenage mothers are less likely to be a homeowner later in life and their living standard remains comparatively poor, as they are more likely to live in a poor-quality housing. Even after adjusting for the pre-existing social disadvantage, teenage mothers are at higher risks of lower education attainment, unemployment or low incomes, difficulties with housing and familial conflicts or breakdown when compared to their peers.

Teenage pregnancy is argued to have negative impact on educational achievements of teenage mothers, but some researchers have highlighted that dropping out and educational failures predate rather than results from teenage pregnancy (Arai, 2003; Bonell, 2004). The opportunities of education and work are diminished due to the challenges with childcare responsibilities. Teenage mothers are more likely to face barriers to education, employment or training and may require positive family relationships and greater social and housing support for parent and child health. The pre-existing disadvantages of the teenage mothers are compounded by having a childbirth at the teenage, which in most cases increase the social and financial hardship, particularly in the absence of appropriate and relevant support for the teenage mothers. Therefore, the focus should be on providing support that can help teenage mothers to overcome barriers and challenges created by the pregnancy to help them succeed in education and employment, hence improving their life chances and that of their children. Moreover, the new generation of teenage parents considers pregnancy as an interruption and a pause, and they resume their education when they are ready and start working when their children become older (Brown, 2016). This shows the need to understand the consequences of teenage pregnancy using the life course approach rather than focusing on the immediate negative outcomes of teenage pregnancy.

BOX 6.6 HELPING YOUNG MOTHERS STAY IN EDUCATION

Walsall teenage pregnancy team has closely liaised with schoolteachers to support teenagers to stay in school despite facing with all sorts of barriers e.g. dropping out of school by the time teenagers get pregnant, unrealistic expectation on the girls to return to the full-time education six weeks after the birth of the child. The key is providing holistic support by understanding the needs of young pregnant women/mothers, allowing time for antenatal appointments and facilitating phased return, childcare support (LGA/PHE, 2019).

Misconceptions and stigma about teenage pregnancy

The causes and consequences of teenage pregnancy are complex and often misunderstood and distorted based on the political ideologies and preconceptions. There are various misconceptions about teenage pregnancy, such as certain groups of women are willing to become teen mothers and selected families allowing their teenage daughters to become pregnant. Other misconceptions that are widely reported in the media are the interrelationships between teenage pregnancy and welfare dependency, promiscuity and teenage mother being irresponsible (Ellis-Sloan, 2014). Moreover, there are also assumptions that teenage mothers are 'bad mothers' without skills, experience or resources that is needed to look after themselves and their child (Wilson & Huntington,

2005). Although majority of teenage mothers require social or familial support and depend on social welfare benefits following the birth of the child, there is no evidence to support the assumption that welfare provision and social housing benefits for teenage mothers are encouragement for early motherhood. Also, it is discriminatory and sexist to deliberate that teenage pregnancy is the outcome of sexual promiscuity and teen mothers are irresponsible and different compared to other mothers.

In contemporary UK society, the teenage mothers are judged by their actions, and they are frequently seen as both 'at risk' group within society as well as 'a risk' to the society (Mitchell & Green, 2002, p. 6). The problematisation of teenage motherhood by the policymakers and media increasingly portrays young mothers as a homogenous group of irresponsible, welfare-dependent single unfit parents, which has created misconceptions and stigma around teenage pregnancy within the wider society (Yardley, 2008). The stigma attached to teenage pregnancy can deter teenagers from accessing key health and social care services during and after pregnancy; as a result, they are likely to be either late or poor attendees of the antenatal and postnatal services, putting themselves and their children at the risk of negative health outcomes. The social stigma and cultural issues associated with abortion or birth can also fuel familial conflicts and wider societal problem. Evidence suggests that societal challenges are more intense for families from ethnic minority populations in the UK where teenage pregnancy outside the marriage remains unaccepted whereas the birth of a child to a teenage mother within a marriage relationship is celebrated. The problematisation of teenage pregnancy is the consequence of social structures, cultural constructions, economic projections, diverse discourses and emotive interestedness to think about our responsibility towards the young people, their children and their future rather than creating a system, which supports teenage pregnant women and mothers.

Teenage pregnancy: a social problem or public health issue

Teenage pregnancy has contributed to adverse social and public health outcomes by leaving the most vulnerable (teenage mothers and their children) behind. Scholars and activists have long argued that government's approach to tackle teenage pregnancy in the UK is often focused on the health aspects rather than wider social problem. The focus on teenage pregnancy as a major public health issue began with the commissioning of Social Exclusion Unit in 1999. Although teenage pregnancy strategy in 1999 made attempts to interrelate the relationship between social exclusion and teenage pregnancy describing social exclusion as a cause and a consequence of teenage pregnancy (SEU, 1999), researchers have argued that the government's focus remains on reducing the rates of teenage pregnancy rather than addressing the social problems that are the risk factors for teenage pregnancy. Teenage pregnancy is often associated with negative stereotypes and stigma but framing teenage pregnancy as a social problem further exacerbates stereotyping of the teenagers and ignores the complex chain of circumstances that links wider social issues with teenage parenthood. While there have been local and national initiatives to address the multifaceted nature of this issue, the government has failed to tackle the issue of teenage pregnancy using a holistic approach.

Teenage pregnancy as a social problem is seen as detrimental for teenage mothers and their offspring which has the potential to lead to social disintegration and personal failure, humiliation and hardship. The detrimental effect for young mother includes socioeconomic and educational disadvantage, negative pregnancy, poor birth outcomes and distraught parenting experiences (Macleod & Tracey, 2010). Similarly, the impact on children includes poor health and educational outcomes, intergenerational transmission of poverty and negative psychological consequences. However, many researchers argue that not all teenage mothers and their children suffer from the adverse outcomes and there is evidence that it may support teenage mother to reenergise their life chances and career opportunities (Arai, 2009). Moreover, it is argued that if teenage pregnancy leads to social disadvantage and deprivation, then government and the healthcare providers should come up with additional support to overcome those disadvantages. Macvarish (2010) concluded that the issue of teenage pregnancy has been amplified and redefined as a social problem, as it is perceived that teenage mothers fail to make a meaningful contribution to the society, in contrast to 'de-moralising' that was seen in last centuries. In addition, the public health approach has expanded the notions of teenage pregnancy associated with the harm to the teenage mother and their children and the construction of teenage mother and her child as a social threat.

Despite the recent decline in teenage pregnancy rates in the UK, it has remained highest in Europe. While considering teenage pregnancy as a public health issue, the focus remains on decreasing the teenage pregnancy rates rather than reducing the risk of social exclusion among teenage mothers (Baker et al., 2007). To achieve this, the primary focus is on the use of preventative measures that has the potential to reduce the teenage pregnancy rates. The prevention of teenage pregnancy includes delivering relationship and sex education in schools, a drive to increase the uptake of contraception use among young people and providing best antenatal and postnatal care for the teenage mothers and their children. However, the public health approach in tackling the teenage pregnancy rates is incomplete without considering the social determinants of teenage pregnancy, especially when teenage pregnancy is known to have a strong association with deprivation measures over a long period of time (McCall et al., 2014). Sexual behaviour of young people from socially deprived minority ethnic community is shaped by the structural factors around them. For example, social factors such as cultural and religious context, economic status, education and the place of residence play an important role in determining the teenage pregnancy. Therefore, it is important to understand that social problem like teenage pregnancy complements the public health issues, and therefore, these problems or issues should be tackled together taking a holistic approach.

Policies and strategies of intervention

Teenage pregnancy is an issue of intergenerational social and health inequalities affecting health and wellbeing and life chances of young women, young men and their children. The Conservative government in the 90s acknowledged the need to address the issue of teenage pregnancy in their *Health of the Nation* (HOTN) initiative, which ran from 1992 to 1997, and focussed on under-16 conception with the target to reduce the rates by at least 50% by the year 2000 (Adler, 1997). The target proved to be challenging to achieve, as the government viewed teenage pregnancy solely as a health issue with limited attention to other related issues such as socioeconomic factors, lack of effective services for contraceptives and sexual health education.

Social Exclusion Unit (1999)

The New Labour government in 1997 recognised the complexity of teenage pregnancy and took a fresh approach to address the issue by seeing teenage motherhood as a key consequence and cause of social exclusion and inequalities. The Social Exclusion

Unit (SEU, 1999) was commissioned by the New Labour government to develop a strategy to reduce the rates of teenage parenthood. Although the ten-year national target was not met, the under-18 conception rate has continued to fall since the end of this strategy. The teenage pregnancy in the UK now is at the lowest level since 1969 (ONS, 2020a). This significant decline in the teenage pregnancy has been attributed to the long-term evidence-based teenage pregnancy strategy published in 1999, which was the first comprehensive approach by the UK government to tackle the issue of teenage pregnancy. The nationally led and locally delivered strategy focussed on four key themes: (i) joined up action at national and local level; (ii) better prevention for girls and boys – improving sex and relationships education (SRE) and access to contraception; (iii) a national communications campaign to reach young people and their parents; and (iv) coordinated support for young parents (Hadley, Chandra-Mouli & Ingham, 2016). This strategy remains one of the few examples of an intervention which has successfully contributed towards reducing teenage pregnancy significantly and is considered as one of the best examples of nationally led evidence-based strategy implemented at the local level. Hadley, Ingham and Chandra-Mouli (2016) describes that the success of the strategy was associated with six key features: (i) creating an opportunity for concerted action; (ii) developing an evidence-based strategy; (iii) establishing structures and guidance for effective implementation; (iv) regularly reviewing progress; (v) embedding strategy actions in wider government programmes; and (vi) providing government leadership throughout the ten-year programme. Although the strategy ended a decade ago and more than 20 years after this strategy was introduced, policy makers have now largely acknowledged the importance of community level delivery of health, education, social care and safeguarding initiatives to addressing the issue of healthy relationships and teenage pregnancy. It is well appreciated that teenage pregnancy is a complex issue, and it needs a multi-faceted and multi-level approach to succeed in further declining of the teenage pregnancy rates in the UK. In 2010, a further guidance *Teenage Pregnancy Strategy: Beyond 2010* was published informed by updated evidence and lessons learned from the effective local practice to continue to reduce the teenage pregnancy rates (DH and DCSF, 2010). The document sets out plan to build on the existing successful strategy so that young people were able to receive information, advice and support they need to deal with sexual lifestyles and relationships and experience positive sexual health (Sah, 2017) avoiding sexually transmitted infections and unplanned teenage pregnancies.

BOX 6.7 SOCIAL EXCLUSION UNIT (1999)

The Social Exclusion Unit (SEU, 1999) was commissioned by the New Labour government to understand the reasons behind the record teenage pregnancies rate in the UK and reviewed the international evidence to develop a strategy to reduce the rates of teenage parenthood. The Strategy took a multifaceted approach to reducing rates of teenage pregnancy and addressing associated health and social problems. In 1999, a Teenage Pregnancy Unit (TPU) was established to lead the implementation of a ten-year Teenage Pregnancy Strategy (TPS), which had two specific goals:

- to reduce the under-18 conception rate by 50% from 46.6 conceptions per 1,000 in 1998 to 23.3 per 1,000 in 2010.
- to reduce the long-term risk of social inclusion of young mothers by increasing their participation in education, training or employment.

A framework for supporting teenage mothers and young fathers (2016/2019)

Public Health England (PHE) and Local Government Association (LGA) published *A framework for supporting teenage mothers and young fathers* in 2016, and updated in 2019, with an aim to help local service providers to review and provide coordinated and sustained support for young parents to build their skills, confidence and aspirations (PHE, 2019). Based on international evidence and past experiences from the local areas service providers, the framework identified ten key factors in providing strategic leadership and accountability towards addressing the issue of teenage pregnancy (Figure 6.2).

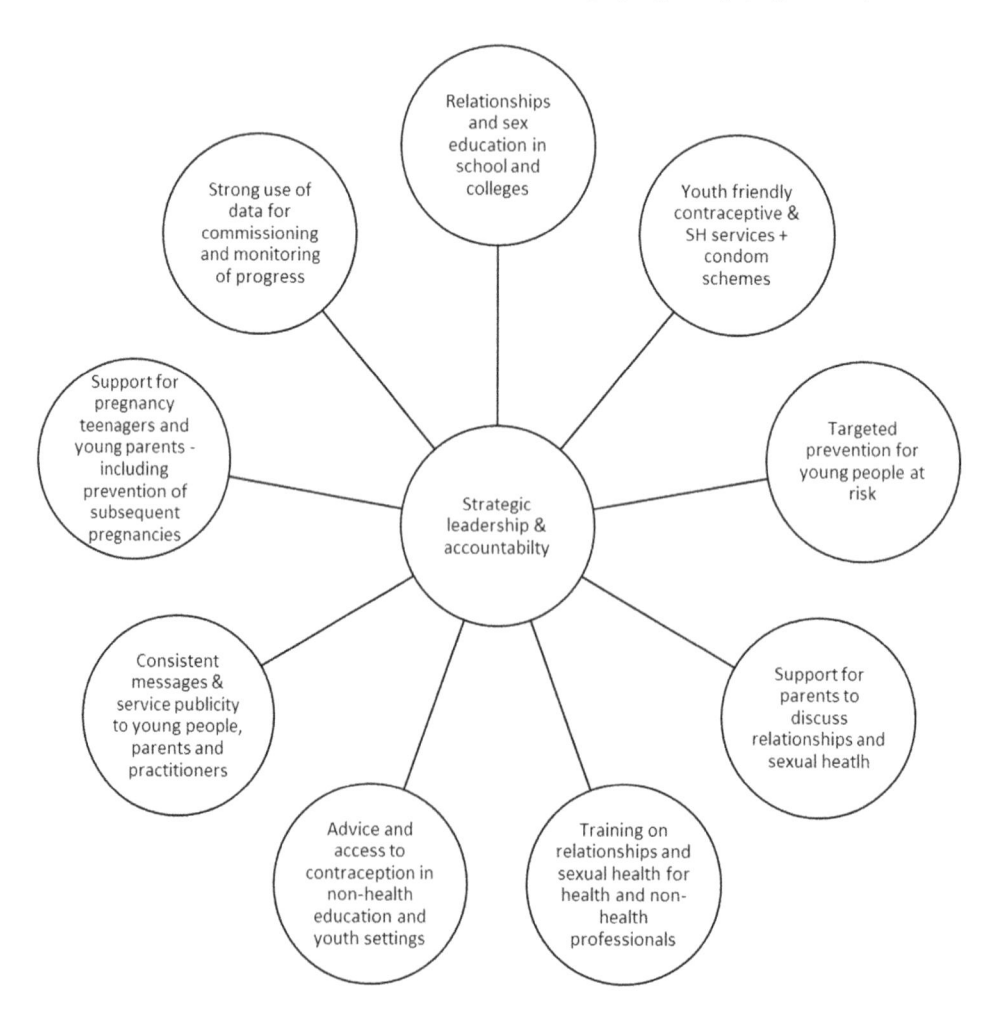

Figure 6.2 Ten key factors of effective local strategies in addressing teenage pregnancy.
Source: PHE (2019).

In 2018, *Teenage Pregnancy Prevention Framework* (PHE, 2018a) was published as a companion document to the 'Framework for supporting teenage mothers and young fathers', which was informed by the most up to date international evidence to take a multi-agency 'whole systems' approach to support local areas to assess the effectiveness of teenage pregnancy prevention programmes. The framework presented a short summary of the ten factors and reviewed them to consider key questions and identify links to relevant policies and helpful resources.

Pregnancy and parenthood in young people strategy 2016–2026 (2016)

The Scottish Government in 2016 produced their first strategy *Pregnancy and Parenthood in Young People Strategy (PPYP) 2016–2026* (The Scottish Government, 2016) with an aim to drive actions to increase opportunities available to young people to support their wellbeing and prosperity across the life course that will decrease the cycle of deprivation associated with teenage pregnancy. The strategy is based on the five guiding principles: (i) Young people at the heart of actions; (ii) Applying the social determinants of health model; (iii) Multi-agency approach and leadership; (iv) Creating positive opportunities; and (v) Evidence informed. The strategy covers many complex areas that are influenced by a large number of policies, legislation and guidance and the focus is to reflect on individual experiences, social influences and wider environmental factors to address inequalities leading to the pregnancy at young age.

Conclusion

Young people in the UK still experience higher rates of teenage pregnancy compared to their peers in high-income countries. Young people remain at the highest risk of unplanned pregnancy, there is a huge variation in teenage pregnancy rates within local authorities and at regional level, and young parents and their children are disproportionately affected by teenage pregnancy, giving rise to inter-generational inequalities (PHE, 2018a). There is compelling evidence that shows age is just one factor; however, the outcomes of a teenage pregnancy are largely influenced by the context and culture in which the pregnant women live, and the compounded effect of social and economic exclusion can pose serious health risks for the mothers and their babies. The public health policies that solely focus on the age at conception will have limited gain in reducing the cause and consequence of teenage pregnancy; however, the holistic policies aimed at reducing socioeconomic inequalities across the whole population providing adequate social and healthcare support will have a long-term sustainable and intergenerational impact on reducing teenage pregnancies as well as other public health and social issues associated with the socioeconomic inequalities.

Although these subsequent strategies have been useful in reducing the rates of unplanned teenage pregnancy and its associated poorer outcomes, there are limited discussions on addressing the social causes of the teenage pregnancy. For example, strategies support young people in social deprivation to become teenage parents; however, it does not necessarily address the issue of social deprivation directly, which is regarded as one of the key factors contributing towards unplanned teenage pregnancy. As a result, these strategies pose additional challenges, especially in the population and areas where social issues associated with the teenage pregnancy are overpowered. The initiative to reduce social exclusion to diminish the rates of teenage pregnancy is important but it is also essential that social policymakers look towards addressing the issues of social ethnic inequalities contribution towards social exclusion. The interdisciplinary nature of teenage pregnancy requires a multidisciplinary and compassionate approach to tackle the social and health issues associated with teenage pregnancy.

Points to ponder

- Teenage pregnancy rates in the UK are among the highest in the developed countries, why?
- Why teenage pregnancy is an important issue and is it a social problem or a public health issue?
- What is the impact of teenage pregnancy on young parents?
- What policies could best address the issue of teenage pregnancy?

Teenage pregnancy quiz

1. Teenage pregnancy has an impact on education of the teenage mother.

   A   True
   B   False

2. Young people below 18 years of age require parental consent to get access to contraception and pregnancy advice services.

   A   True
   B   False

3. Pregnancy and childbirth complications are the leading cause of death among girls aged 15–19 years globally.

   A   True
   B   False

4. Lack of knowledge and information about sexual and reproductive health rights is one of the key causes of teenage pregnancy.

   A   True
   B   False

5. Teenage pregnancy brings humiliation to the teenage mother and her family.

   A   True
   B   False

6. Most teenage pregnancies are .... with disproportionately ....
7. .... is considered as the key cause and consequence of teenage pregnancy.
8. In the UK, all contraceptives are provided ...... and ...., including for girls under the age of 16 in many circumstances.
9. Social Exclusion Unit highlighted that the three main reasons that contributed towards the high rates of teenage pregnancy were ...., ... and ....
10. .... weeks is the legal limit for a termination of pregnancy (abortion).
11. Becoming a teen parent increases the chances of

A   Being a single parent
B   Missing out on good times with friends
C   Less likely to finish education
D   More likely to remain unemployed
E   All of the above

12 Which of these possible factors do not contribute to teenage pregnancy are?

A   Unprotected sex
B   Peer pressure
C   Discussing about relationships and sexual health issues
D   Lack of sex education
E   Curiosity about sex

13 Which of the following groups of young people are not at the risk of teenage pregnancy?

A   living in poverty with single parent or in care or leaving the care
B   performing well at schools
C   school dropouts, low self-esteem or having low expectations from future
D   involved in crime or have alcohol/substance misuse problems
E   have experienced sexual abuse in childhood or with existing with mental health problems.

14 Which of these can help to avoid becoming a teenage parent?

A   Abstinence
B   Contraceptive use (condoms, emergency contraception or intrauterine device)
C   Talking to parents or trusted adults about making good and informed choices when it comes to sex
D   Staying in control by saying no to alcohol and drugs misuse
E   All of the above

15 Which of these following factors are not effective local strategies in addressing teenage pregnancy?

A   Relationships and sex education in schools and colleges and trainings for health and non-health professionals
B   Youth friendly contraceptive and sexual health services and condom schemes
C   Consistent messages and service publicity to young people, parents and practitioners
D   Support for young people but not for parents to discuss relationships and sexual health
E   Strong use of data for commissioning and monitoring progress of teenage pregnancy

Group activities

Case 1

Sandra is a 16-year-old girl who is currently in the care of the local authority in Liverpool and has been excluded from school. She was born when her mother was 15-year-old and her father left home when she was seven-year-old. Sandra first has sex when she was 14 years old and currently has a 19-year-old boyfriend, Jim, with whom she has been for six months. Jim is currently carrying out a community sentence for assault. Sandra has just found out that she is pregnant.

In small groups, discuss the causes and consequences of Sandra's pregnancy. What will be the challenges and support for Sandra, if she decides to give birth to the baby?

Case 2

Zainab is a 17-year-old girl from Bradford who has found herself pregnant with her first child. She had completed her GCSE with good grades, was passionate about her career and wanted to become a nurse. Coming from an extended family, she may have a lot of support around her. In fact, her older sister 19-year-old Rubina, who is married and has a one-year-old child, lives together in the extended family.

In small groups, discuss what will be the challenges and opportunities for Zainab following the news of her pregnancy.

Supplementary reading

Arai, L. (2009). *Teenage pregnancy: the making and unmaking of a problem*. Bristol: The Policy Press.
Bonell, C. (2004). Why is teenage pregnancy conceptualized as a social problem? A review of quantitative research from the USA and UK. *Culture, health & sexuality, 6*(3), 255–272.
Brown, S. (2016). *Teenage pregnancy, parenting and intergenerational relations*. London: Palgrave Macmillan.
Hadley, A. (2018). *Teenage pregnancy and young parenthood: effective policy and practice*. London: Routledge.

Useful websites

Best beginnings: for every parent, for every child. Retrieved from https://www.bestbeginnings.org.uk/
Little Lullaby: By young parents, for young parents. Retrieved from https://littlelullaby.org.uk/
NHS teenage pregnancy support: Retrieved from https://www.nhs.uk/pregnancy/support/teenage-pregnancy/
Straight Talking: Peer education. Retrieved from https://www.straighttalking.org/

References

Adler, M. W. (1997). Sexual health – a health of the nation failure. *BMJ, 314*(7096), 1743.
Arai, L. (2003). Low expectations, sexual attitudes and knowledge: explaining teenage pregnancy and fertility in English communities. Insights from qualitative research. *The Sociological Review, 51*(2), 199–217.
Arai, L. (2009). *Teenage pregnancy: the making and unmaking of a problem*. Bristol: The Policy Press.
Amnesty International UK (2019). *Abortion in Ireland and Northern Ireland*. Retrieved from https://www.amnesty.org.uk/abortion-rights-northern-ireland-timeline
Baker, P., Guthrie, K., Hutchinson, C., Kane, R., & Wellings, K. (2007). *Teenage pregnancy and reproductive health: summary review*. London: RCOG Press.
Bellis M. A., Morleo M., Tocque K., Dedman D., Phillips-Howard P. A., Perkins C., & Jones L. (2009). *Contributions of alcohol use to teenage pregnancy: an initial examination of geographical and

evidence-based associations. North West Public Health Observatory, Centre for Public Health, Liverpool John Moores University.

Berrington, A., Diamond, I., Ingham, R., Stevenson, J., Borgoni, R., Cobos Hernández, M. I., & Smith, P. W. (2005). *Consequences of teenage parenthood: pathways which minimise the long-term negative impacts of teenage childbearing*. Southampton: University of Southampton.

Bonell, C. (2004). Why is teenage pregnancy conceptualized as a social problem? A review of quantitative research from the USA and UK. *Culture, Health & Sexuality, 6*(3), 255–272.

British Pregnancy Advisory Service (BPAS). (2013). *Britain's abortion law what it says, and why*. Retrieved from http://www.reproductivereview.org/images/uploads/Britains_abortion_law.pdf

Brown, S. (2016). *Teenage pregnancy, parenting and intergenerational relations*. London: Palgrave Macmillan.

Carson, P., Blakely, H., & Laverty, C. (2021). *Health inequalities: annual report 2021*. The Northern Ireland Statistics and Research Agency (NISRA).

Chapman, S. L. C., & Wu, L. T. (2013). Substance use among adolescent mothers: a review. *Children and Youth Services Review, 35*(5), 806–815.

Chen, X. K., Wen, S. W., Fleming, N., Demissie, K., Rhoads, G. G., & Walker, M. (2007). Teenage pregnancy and adverse birth outcomes: a large population based retrospective cohort study. *International Journal of Epidemiology, 36*(2), 368–373.

Cook, H. (2005, March). The English sexual revolution: technology and social change. *History Workshop Journal, 59*(1), 109–128.

Cook, S. M., & Cameron, S. T. (2020). Social issues of teenage pregnancy. *Obstetrics, Gynaecology & Reproductive Medicine, 30*(10), 309–314.

Cornelius, M. D., Leech, S. L., & Goldschmidt, L. (2004). Characteristics of persistent smoking among pregnant teenagers followed to young adulthood. *Nicotine & Tobacco Research, 6*(1), 159–169.

Department of Health (DH). (2013). *A framework for sexual health improvement in England*. Retrieved from https://www.gov.uk/government/publications/a-framework-for-sexual-health-improvement-in-england

Department of Health and Department for Children, schools and families (DH and DCSF). (2010). *Teenage pregnancy strategy: beyond 2010*. Retrieved from https://dera.ioe.ac.uk/11277/1/4287_Teenage%20pregnancy%20strategy_aw8.pdf

Ellis-Sloan, K. (2014). Teenage mothers, stigma and their 'presentations of self'. *Sociological Research Online, 19*(1), 16–28.

Ellis-Sloan, K. (2019). Teenage mothers in later life: time for a second look. *Journal of Adolescence, 77*, 98–107.

Fortin-Langelier, E., Daigneault, I., Achim, J., Vézina-Gagnon, P., Guérin, V., & Frappier, J. Y. (2019). A matched cohort study of the association between childhood sexual abuse and teenage pregnancy. *Journal of Adolescent Health, 65*(3), 384–389.

Freeman, J. (1973). The origins of the women's liberation movement. *American Journal of Sociology, 78*(4), 792–811.

Hadley, A., Chandra-Mouli, V., & Ingham, R. (2016). Implementing the United Kingdom Government's 10-year teenage pregnancy strategy for England (1999–2010): applicable lessons for other countries. *Journal of Adolescent Health, 59*(1), 68–74.

Hadley, A., Ingham, R., & Chandra-Mouli, V. (2016). Implementing the United Kingdom's ten-year teenage pregnancy strategy for England (1999–2010): how was this done and what did it achieve? *Reproductive Health, 13*(1), 139.

Hadley, A. (2018). *Teenage pregnancy and young parenthood: effective policy and practice*. London: Routledge.

Heap, K. L., Berrington, A., & Ingham, R. (2020). Understanding the decline in under-18 conception rates throughout England's local authorities between 1998 and 2017. *Health & Place, 66*, 102467.

Hennink, M., Diamond, I., & Cooper, P. (1999). Young Asian women and relationships: traditional or transitional? *Ethnic and Racial Studies, 22*(5), 867–891.

Higginbottom, G. M. A., Mathers, N., Marsh, P., Kirkham, M., Owen, J. M., & Serrant-Green, L. (2006). Young people of minority ethnic origin in England and early parenthood: views from young parents and service providers. *Social Science & Medicine, 63*(4), 858–870.

Hoggart, L. (2019). Moral dilemmas and abortion decision-making: lessons learnt from abortion research in England and Wales. *Global Public Health, 14*(1), 1–8.

Hoggart, L., Phillips, J., Birch, A., & Koffman, O. (2010). *Young people in London: abortion and repeat abortion*. London: Department for children, schools and families.

Holgate, H., Evans, R., & Yuen, F. K. (2006). Introduction. In H. Holgate, R. Evans & F. K. Yuen (Eds.), *Teenage pregnancy and parenthood: global perspectives, issues and interventions* (pp. 1–6). London: Routledge.

Irvine, H., Bradley, T., Cupples, M., & Boohan, M. (1997). The implications of teenage pregnancy and motherhood for primary health care: unresolved issues. *British Journal of General Practice, 47*(418), 323–326.

Jeha, D., Usta, I., Ghulmiyyah, L., & Nassar, A. (2015). A review of the risks and consequences of adolescent pregnancy. *Journal of Neonatal-Perinatal Medicine, 8*(1), 1–8.

Lee, E. J., Clements, S., Ingham, R., & Stone, N. (2004). *A matter of choice?: Explaining national variations in teenage abortion and motherhood*. York: Joseph Rowntree Foundation.

Leishman, J. (2007). The range and scope of early age sexual activity and pregnancy. In J. L. Leishman & J. Moir (Eds.), *Pre-teen and teenage pregnancy: a twenty-first century reality* (pp. 7–23). Keswick: M & K Publishing.

Local Government Association (LGA)/Public Health England (PHE). (2019). *Supporting young parents to reach their full potential*. Retrieved from https://www.local.gov.uk/sites/default/files/documents/22.35%20Supporting%20young%20parents_05%20-%2027.03.pdf

Macleod, C. I., & Tracey, T. (2010). A decade later: follow-up review of South African research on the consequences of and contributory factors in teen-aged pregnancy. *South African Journal of Psychology, 40*(1), 18–31.

Macvarish, J. (2010). The effect of 'risk-thinking' on the contemporary construction of teenage motherhood. *Health, Risk & Society, 12*(4), 313–322.

Madigan, S., Wade, M., Tarabulsy, G., Jenkins, J. M., & Shouldice, M. (2014). Association between abuse history and adolescent pregnancy: a meta-analysis. *Journal of Adolescent Health, 55*(2), 151–159.

Maravilla, J. C., Betts, K. S., e Cruz, C. C., & Alati, R. (2017). Factors influencing repeated teenage pregnancy: a review and meta-analysis. *American Journal of Obstetrics and Gynecology, 217*(5), 527–545.

McCall, S. J., Bhattacharya, S., Okpo, E., & Macfarlane, G. J. (2014). Evaluating the social determinants of teenage pregnancy: a temporal analysis using a UK obstetric database from 1950 to 2010. *Journal of Epidemiology and Community Health, 69*(1), 49–54.

Mcdaid, L., Collier, J., & Platt, M. J. (2017). Unique identifiers needed to make national data sets fit for public health purposes: the example of subsequent teenage pregnancy in England and Wales. *Public Health, 153*, 58–60.

McDermott, E., & Graham, H. (2005). Resilient young mothering: social inequalities, late modernity and the 'problem' of 'teenage' motherhood. *Journal of Youth Studies, 8*(1), 59–79.

Mills, H. (2016). Using the personal to critique the popular: women's memories of 1960s youth. *Contemporary British History, 30*(4), 463–483.

Mitchell, W., & Green, E. (2002). 'I don't know what I'd do without our Mam' motherhood, identity and support networks. *The Sociological Review, 50*(1), 1–22.

Noll, J. G., Shenk, C. E., & Putnam, K. T. (2009). Childhood sexual abuse and adolescent pregnancy: a meta-analytic update. *Journal of Pediatric Psychology, 34*(4), 366–378.

Northern Ireland Statistics and Research Agency (NISRA). (2019). *Teenage birth rate for mothers under the age of 17 and 20*. Retrieved from https://www.ninis2.nisra.gov.uk/public/PivotGrid.aspx?ds=9965&lh=73&yn=2008-2018&sk=74&sn=Population&yearfilter=2100

Office for National Statistics (ONS). (2020a). *Conceptions in England and Wales: 2018*. Retrieved from https://www.ons.gov.uk/peoplepopulationandcommunity/birthsdeathsandmarriages/conceptionandfertilityrates/bulletins/conceptionstatistics/2018

Office for National Statistics (ONS). (2020b). *Income distribution*. Retrieved from https://www.ethnicity-facts-figures.service.gov.uk/work-pay-and-benefits/pay-and-income/income-distribution/latest

Office for National Statistics (ONS). (2021). *Conceptions in England and Wales: 2019*. Retrieved from https://www.ons.gov.uk/peoplepopulationandcommunity/birthsdeathsandmarriages/conceptionandfertilityrates/bulletins/conceptionstatistics/2019

Phillips-Howard, P. A., Bellis, M. A., Briant, L. B., Jones, H., Downing, J., Kelly, I. E., … Cook, P. A. (2010). Wellbeing, alcohol use and sexual activity in young teenagers: findings from a cross-sectional survey in school children in North West England. *Substance Abuse Treatment, Prevention, and Policy*, *5*(1), 27.

Public Health England (PHE). (2018a). *Teenage pregnancy prevention framework: supporting young people to prevent unplanned pregnancy and develop healthy relationships*. Retrieved from https://assets.publishing.service.gov.uk/government/uploads/system/uploads/attachment_data/file/836597/Teenage_Pregnancy_Prevention_Framework.pdf

Public Health England (PHE). (2018b). *Teenage pregnancy and young parents: report for East Sussex*. Retrieved from http://www.eastsussexjsna.org.uk/JsnaSiteAspx/media/jsna-media-documents/nationalprofiles/profileassests/Teenage%20Pregancy/Teenage-pregnancy-and-young-parents-Fingertips-Report---East-Sussex---Downloaded-Feb-2018.pdf

Public Health England (PHE). (2019). *A framework for supporting teenage mothers and young fathers*. Retrieved from https://assets.publishing.service.gov.uk/government/uploads/system/uploads/attachment_data/file/796582/PHE_Young_Parents_Support_Framework_April2019.pdf

Public Health Scotland (PHS). (2020). *Teenage pregnancy year of conception, ending 31 December 2018*. Retrieved from https://publichealthscotland.scot/media/6664/2020-08-25-teenpreg-report.pdf

Public Health Scotland (PHS). (2021). *Teenage pregnancy year of conception, ending 31 December 2019*. Retrieved from https://publichealthscotland.scot/media/8365/2021-07-06-teenpreg-report.pdf

Saewyc, E. M., Magee, L. L., & Pettingell, S. E. (2004). Teenage pregnancy and associated risk behaviors among sexually abused adolescents. *Perspectives on Sexual and Reproductive Health*, *36*(3), 98–105.

Sah, R. K. (2017). *Positive sexual health: an ethnographic exploration of social and cultural factors affecting sexual lifestyles and relationships of Nepalese young people in the UK*. Canterbury Christ Church University (United Kingdom).

Sah, R. K., & Robinson, S. (2021). Sexual health. In S. Robinson (Ed.), *Priorities for health promotion and public health* (pp. 151–174). Oxon: Routledge.

Salas-Wright, C. P., Vaughn, M. G., Ugalde, J., & Todic, J. (2015). Substance use and teen pregnancy in the United States: evidence from the NSDUH 2002–2012. *Addictive Behaviors*, *45*, 218–225.

Social Exclusion Unit. (1999). *Teenage pregnancy: report by the Social Exclusion Unit presented to Parliament by the Prime Minister by command of Her Majesty*. London: Stationery Office.

Tarlow, S. (2017). *The Golden and Ghoulish Age of the Gibbet in Britain*. London: Springer Nature.

The Scottish Government. (2016). *Pregnancy and parenthood in young people strategy 2016–2026*.

Turner, K. M. (2004). Young women's views on teenage motherhood: a possible explanation for the relationship between socio-economic background and teenage pregnancy outcome? *Journal of Youth Studies*, *7*(2), 221–238.

United Nations International Children's Emergency Fund (UNICEF). (2021). *Early childbearing*. Retrieved from https://data.unicef.org/topic/child-health/adolescent-health/#:~:text=Approximately%2015%20percent%20of%20young, age%2018%20from%202015%2D2020.&text=While%20the%20global%20adolescent%20birth, regions%20in%20sub%2DSaharan%20Africa

United Nations Population Fund (UNFPA). (2015). *Girlhood, not motherhood: preventing adolescent pregnancy*. New York: UNFPA.

Wilson, H., & Huntington, A. (2006). Deviant (m) others: the construction of teenage motherhood in contemporary discourse. *Journal of Social Policy*, *35*(1), 59–76.

World Health Organisation (WHO). (2004). *Adolescent pregnancy: issues in adolescent health and development*. Retrieved from http://apps.who.int/iris/bitstream/handle/10665/42903/9241591455_eng.pdf;jsessionid=058C35C183B1CA048602389434C45A80?sequence=1

World Health Organisation (WHO). (2020). *Adolescent pregnancy*. Retrieved from https://www.who.int/news-room/fact-sheets/detail/adolescent-pregnancy

Yardley, E. (2008). Teenage mothers' experiences of stigma. *Journal of Youth Studies*, *11*(6), 671–684.

7 Child abuse, child neglect and safeguarding children

An overview

Penelope Welbourne

Terminology and child protection: some definitions and explanations of terms used

A 'child' in the UK is defined in law as anyone under the age of 18. A child does not become a person in law, with all the rights and protections that are associated with legal personhood, until they are born (Nixon, 2010).

It is difficult to know how many children experience abuse in childhood. Children experience many kinds of negative experiences, some harmful and some not, and it is important to identify a point on the spectrum of adverse childhood experiences at which they become 'abusive'. Approaches to understanding rates of child abuse are based on different ways of asking questions about it:

- Looking at crime figures, including rates of reported crime, investigations, prosecutions and convictions for child abuse-related criminal offences,
- Asking adults in a population whether or not they experienced abuse as a child, and
- Looking at rates of referrals for assessment and intervention by child protection organisations.

These different approaches give very different estimates as to the prevalence of abuse.

In the UK, the term 'significant harm' is key to defining abuse, but this is not a precise term, and while the law attempts to capture the complex concept of harm, it does not define 'significant'. Significant harm also defines the threshold for compulsory state intervention in family life. It is defined in the Children Act 1989 as in Box 7.1.

BOX 7.1 SIGNIFICANT HARM: S31 CHILDREN ACT 1989

- 'Harm' may encompass all or any of the following: Ill treatment, which includes physical and sexual abuse, neglect, emotional abuse and psychological abuse.
- The impairment of physical or mental health.
- The impairment of physical, intellectual, emotional, social or behavioural development.
- The harm may be caused by seeing or hearing another person suffer ill treatment.

In considering whether harm is 'significant' or not, the child's health and development may be compared with that which could reasonably be expected of a similar child.

DOI: 10.4324/9781003166887-7

Children suffering or at risk of significant harm are part of the larger group of children 'in need'. This includes all children who qualify for services to promote their development and well-being under s17 of the Children Act 1989 (see Box 7.2).

> **BOX 7.2 CHILDREN IN NEED ARE**
>
> a Unlikely to achieve or maintain, or to have the opportunity of achieving or maintaining, a reasonable standard of health or development without the provision of services by a local authority; or
> b Their health or development is likely to be significantly impaired, or further impaired, without the provision of such services; or
> c They are children with a disability.

The 2018[1] Government guidance, *Working Together to Safeguard Children* (Department for Education, 2018), sets out duties and responsibilities placed on agencies and practitioners linked to their Children Act 1989 roles. It incorporates additional material addressing, for example, children's participation, reflecting developing ideas about how the rights of children should be respected. It has the force of statute: professionals involved in protecting children are expected to follow it. The wider child protection system encompasses social workers, police, education and health professionals and the courts. They may be seen as one larger system that works to investigate and assess harm, explore the best interests of the child and make provision to protect them. Court approval is required granting social workers the right to carry out a range of actions that are frequently resorted to in order to protect children in the UK, notably separating a child from its parents.

A brief overview of the historical context

Pinpointing the first recognition of child abuse as a problem in England is complex, reflecting the fluidity and complexity of child abuse as a social construct. The first legal provisions were passed that broadly required parents and carers not to abuse or ill-treat children in the late 19th and early 20th century. The Prevention of Cruelty to, and Protection of, Children Act 1889 imposed criminal penalties for cruelty to children and gave police the power to arrest anyone ill-treating a child. In 1904, the NSPCC was given the power to remove children from abusive and neglectful homes. The *Punishment of Incest Act 1908* made incest punishable in law in England and Wales, offering some protection from sexual abuse, especially to girls.

The Children Act 1908 required local authorities to appoint infant protection officers, investigating parents and carers who wilfully assaulted, ill-treated, neglected, abandoned or exposed children in a manner likely to cause unnecessary suffering or harm to their health. The foundation of the welfare state in the post-World War II era provided the organisational basis for the next steps. Improved diagnostic approaches based on medical signs of non-accidental injury (see for example Kempe et al., 1985) increased recognition of the possibility that parents could be abusive, which in turn increased recognition of the importance of understanding family functioning and the social context for abuse (see, for example, Gelles and Maynard, 1987). Forensic investigative police work and social work developed to focus on understanding the aetiology of injury and addressing child abuse developed into a medico-socio-legal problem. This model for identification and intervention remains the core of child protection work today.[2]

Categories of child abuse

In the UK, child abuse is categorised according to four types of abuse: neglect, physical abuse, emotional abuse, and sexual abuse (Department for Education, 2018). Specific more forms of abuse such as sexual exploitation, female genital mutilation (FGM), forced marriage, radicalisation, 'honour'-based harm, exploitation through 'county lines' activities involvement of children in crime, especially drug crime, and modern slavery have been added as awareness of them has evolved. What is notable about these 'newer' kinds of abuse (none of which relate to activities that are of recent origin) is that they mostly do not conform to the model of 'child cruelty' perpetrated by parents and carers that dominated the 19th and 20th century. The abusers are more likely to come from outside the family, or, in the case of FGM and forced marriage, may involve people from outside the family who share the same values.

Neglect

Child neglect is the most commonly identified form of child abuse in England and Wales. Neglect is the most common reason for making child protection plans in England (25,330 children) and the second most common reason for inclusion on the Child Protection Register in Wales (1,005 children) at 31 March 2019. The 'Working Together' guidance defines neglect as in Box 7.3.

BOX 7.3 NEGLECT

'The persistent failure to meet a child's basic physical and/or psychological needs, likely to result in the serious impairment of the child's health or development. Neglect may occur during pregnancy as a result of maternal substance abuse. Once a child is born, neglect may involve a parent or carer failing to provide adequate food, clothing and shelter (including exclusion from home or abandonment), protect a child from physical and emotional harm or danger, ensure adequate supervision (including the use of inadequate care-givers), ensure access to appropriate medical care or treatment. It may also include neglect of, or unresponsiveness to, a child's basic emotional needs'.

Some manifestations of neglect are more easily recognised because they have physical correlates, for example, failure to provide adequate food, warmth or clothing. Emotional neglect may have serious long-term consequences that do not become apparent until years later, or the effects may be misunderstood as a problem with the child, rather than a response to the care they are receiving. Children on a Child Protection Plan for neglect are more likely to be on a plan for longer: it is a less tractable problem than other categories of abuse. It also gives rise to high levels of concern: in 2019, the National

Society for the Prevention of Cruelty to Children's helpline received 12,708 calls about child neglect (NSPCC, 2021). Two-thirds were referred to another agency for intervention (Office for National Statistics, 2020).

Emotional abuse

The definition of emotional abuse from 'Working Together' is presented in Box 7.4.

BOX 7.4 EMOTIONAL ABUSE

'The persistent emotional maltreatment of a child such as to cause severe and persistent adverse effects on the child's emotional development. It may involve conveying to a child that they are worthless or unloved, inadequate, or valued only insofar as they meet the needs of another person. It may include not giving the child opportunities to express their views, deliberately silencing them or 'making fun' of what they say or how they communicate. It may feature age or developmentally inappropriate expectations being imposed on children... It may involve serious bullying (including cyber bullying), causing children frequently to feel frightened or in danger, or the exploitation or corruption of children. Some level of emotional abuse is involved in all types of maltreatment of a child, though it may occur alone'.

The definition of emotional abuse arguably makes it more difficult to identify than other forms of abuse, since it depends not only on what is done to the child but also on the (visible) impact this has on the child. 'Severe and persistent adverse effects on the child's emotional development' may not become apparent until later in life. This may be a contributory factor in making emotional abuse cases among the least likely to progress to prosecution.

Physical abuse

Physical abuse is,

> A form of abuse which may involve hitting, shaking, throwing, poisoning, burning or scalding, drowning, suffocating or otherwise causing physical harm to a child. Physical harm may also be caused when a parent or carer fabricates the symptoms of, or deliberately induces, illness in a child.

For all types of child abuse, there is an association between poverty and being on a Child Protection Plan (CPP):

"Successive studies in ... all four UK countries ... reported that children in the most deprived decile of small neighbourhoods were over ten times more likely to be on a CPP or in out of home care than a child in the least deprived decile." (Bywaters and Skinner, 2022: 67). The statistical association between a challenging socio-economic environment and child abuse has been recognised but the causal mechanism is perplexing (Bywaters et al., 2016). Possibilities include parents experiencing multiple challenges, such as chronic ill health or addiction, are more likely to live in poverty with high levels of parenting stress and families living in poverty may be subject to more surveillance.

Sexual abuse

Sexual abuse is defined not only by the type of acts that comprise sexual abuse but also by the motivation that drives it: the perpetrator pursuing their own gratification. A victim may be unaware that what is happening is abuse and may be accepting of what is being done, especially if the abuser is a trusted adult. However, children frequently experience what is done to them as distressing, embarrassing, harmful and painful, and the later impact of any sexual abuse can be severe, whether it is aversive at the time it happened or not.

The 'Working Together' definition of sexual abuse is presented in Box 7.5.

BOX 7.5 SEXUAL ABUSE

…(i)nvolves forcing or enticing a child or young person to take part in sexual activities, not necessarily involving a high level of violence, whether or not the child is aware of what is happening. The activities may involve physical contact… (and) may also include non-contact activities, such as involving children in looking at, or in the production of, sexual images, watching sexual activities, encouraging children to behave in sexually inappropriate ways or grooming a child in preparation for abuse. Sexual abuse can take place online, and technology can be used to facilitate offline abuse.

It is noteworthy that some child sexual abuse involves young people under 18. When both are children, the issue may be complicated by questions about the power relationship between abused and abuser.

An inquiry into sexual abuse by the former TV presenter J. Saville, 'Operation Yewtree', began in 2012. This revealed the extent of his abuse of children, and the extent to which he had unsupervised access to vulnerable children, including in settings such as hospital. A wide-ranging inquiry into historic child abuse was set up in 2015: the Independent Inquiry into Child Sexual Abuse (IICSA). After more than 320 days of hearing evidence, with 640 witnesses and nearly 600,000 pages of evidence, the Independent Inquiry website (which went offline during the writing of this chapter) notes, 'The information and statistics currently available do not give a full account of the scale of child abuse across England and Wales, but estimates suggest that one child in every 20 in the United Kingdom has been sexually abused'. Information is available about the IICSA but independence and reliability cannot be guaranteed (IICSA, no date). Issues with both investigation and public access to findings serve to highlight how difficult it can be to systematically explore this area of harm, which is of its nature secretive.

The low rate of conviction of sexual offenders is not encouraging:

> By its very nature, child abuse is often hidden from view and many cases don't come to the attention of the police or the courts. Of identifiable child abuse offences

recorded by the police in the year ending March 2019, around 1 in 25 resulted in a charge or summons. Of cases that did lead to a prosecution, 4 in 5 resulted in a conviction.

(Elkin, ONS, 2020: 6)

Child sexual exploitation

Child sexual exploitation (CSE) is mainly abuse by adults who are not parents or carers. While high-profile cases have often involved adult males exploiting girls, boys are also victims of CSE. The National Working Group's definition on CSE is provided in Box 7.6.

BOX 7.6

'Child Sexual Exploitation occurs when an individual or group takes advantage of an imbalance of power to coerce, manipulate or deceive a child or young person under the age of 18 into sexual activity (a) in exchange for something the victim wants or needs, and / or (b) for the financial advantage or increased status of the perpetrator or facilitator.

The victim may have been sexually exploited even if the sexual activity appears consensual. Child sexual abuse does not always involve physical contact: it can occur through the use of technology. Child sexual exploitation is a form of child sexual abuse' (NWG).

Young women who were sexually exploited and traded for sex often had little professional support and were sometimes treated as offenders rather than victims. Pressure in the 1990s and 2000s from organisations such as The Children's Society and Barnardo's eventually ended the use of 'child prostitution' in government documents, but as recently as 1997 social work services were arguing for the decriminalisation of children who engaged in sexual activity for (their own or someone else's) profit (Barrett and Pitts, 1997). In 2015, Ann Coffey (MP) was still arguing that the term should be removed from 16 pieces of legislation in which it was still being used (Topping, 2015).

Revelations about CSE in Rochdale in the early 2010s led to inquiries into the scale of the problem in the UK. Findings showed it potentially affecting children in all social groups and all areas, all ethnicities and both boys and girls. Links between CSE, online grooming and online and electronic communication, especially mobile phones, has become apparent (Home Office, 2019)

Child trafficking

BOX 7.7 CHILD TRAFFICKING

'As well as threats to the welfare of children from within their families, children may be vulnerable to abuse or exploitation from outside their families. These extra-familial threats might arise at school and other educational establishments, from within peer groups, or more widely from within the wider community and/or online. These threats can [include]: exploitation by criminal gangs and organised crime groups such as county lines; trafficking; online abuse; teenage relationship abuse; sexual exploitation and the influences of extremism leading to radicalisation' (Department for Education, 2018).

Child trafficking is defined by the NSPCC as: '…where children and young people are tricked, forced or persuaded to leave their homes and are moved or transported and then exploited, forced to work or sold' (NSPCC). An Independent Child Trafficking Guardianship scheme was introduced in England and Wales under the Modern Slavery Act 2015 but has yet to be fully rolled out (EPCAT, 2020). For young people arriving in Britain through trafficking, EPCAT has argued that services are struggling to meet demand, or even sometimes hostile to their needs as they enter a hostile immigration environment (EPCAT, 2020).

The prevalence of child abuse globally and in the UK

Understanding the prevalence of child abuse in a global context is complex because child abuse is not defined consistently by countries or cultures. Societies in which children are seen at school nearly every day, and where education, police and health professionals are trained to respond to signs of abuse, and there is an infrastructure to support children, parents and professionals through the process of investigation, may be more likely to detect and respond to abuse, and to record it. At the same time, informal support networks in communities in varied countries and cultures may also act as effective unrecorded protective systems for children.

The World Health Organization gives some bleak figures concerning abuse of children (Box 7.8).

BOX 7.8

Nearly three in four children – or 300 million children – aged two to four years regularly suffer physical punishment and/or psychological violence at the hands of parents and caregivers.

- One in 5 women and 1 in 13 men report having been sexually abused as a child aged 0–17 years.
- Precisely, 120 million girls and young women under 20 years of age have suffered some form of forced sexual contact.

World Health Organization (2020)

This is most probably an underestimate since some deaths due to child abuse will be incorrectly attributed to other causes.

There is more detailed information available about child abuse in the UK, but even here, official records probably represent a proportion of all cases of child abuse. In the year to March 2020, referrals relating to children in need rose by 4%; child protection enquiries by 125%; children requiring a child protection plan by 32%; and children in care by 24% (Foster, 2021). The reason for the increase is contested, as so much in child protection, but possible factors include rising poverty, rising need for mental health services, drug-related issues, including children being used in drug trafficking, and increased awareness of the significance of domestic violence for children. One in five adults in England and Wales are estimated to have experienced at least one form of child abuse, whether emotional abuse, physical abuse, sexual abuse or witnessing domestic violence or abuse, before the age of 16 years, and 18,706 offences of cruelty to children and young people in England and Wales were recorded by police in the year to March 2019 (Office for National Statistics, 2020).

Child abuse as an evolving social issue and a 'wicked' problem

Child abuse is a social issue for at least three reasons. Child abuse is a 'wicked' problem: one that does not dissipate as a result of interventions that are attempted to deal with it, or only partially and with difficulty. The more interventions are developed to reduce it, the more likely it is that new forms of abuse will be found or new indicators of prevalence will be uncovered. The concentration of child abuse in areas with high proportions of families living in poverty is a matter of concern, since it raises serious questions about the impact of socio-economic deprivation on children and families. Child abuse and neglect is an issue that demands concern on the part of society, not only for identified victims but for children growing up with disproportionate risk of harm (Bywaters et al., 2016; Bywaters and Skinner, 2022). A third reason child abuse is a social issue is because child abuse is also a moral issue: how far is it right to override the right to family privacy and self-determination in the interests of protecting children from parental abuse? This engages issues of individual rights and freedoms, parent and child, and cultural values.

Culture is not homogenous in any country. Children born into families that move from one culture to another need to make agile adaptation to cultural change. While becoming immersed in the new host culture, they are members of family that has brought with it the cultural values of their former home. When conflict of culture relates to the roles of parents and children, families may become subject to investigation linked to societal expectations about family life. Several such areas of cultural conflict have been identified in recent years. Examples are the right of girl children not to be subject to FGM (NHS), or parents taking them into zones of conflict: see the 2015 case of *Re X and Y*, for an example.

Some areas of conflict relate to curtailment of children's future health and cultural choices, such as FGM, others are more direct threats to life such as so-called 'honour-based' violence (Khan et al., 2017). Some practices that are now not permitted were once permitted in England, such forcing a child to accept an arranged marriage,[3] and it is noteworthy that forced marriage only became unlawful in Britain in 2014 (Gov.uk, 2014).

The intersection between adult criminal activities and child protection is another area in which our understanding of child exploitation is rapidly expanding. 'County lines' drug-dealing activities involve children being exploited by adults into carrying out criminal acts (National Crime Agency), some by children who are below the age of criminal responsibility. Child abuse is not only a 'wicked' problem in terms of solving it, it is also complex and evolving, and responding to it has to be agile and reflect the evolution of values and problems in society.

Myths and misconceptions

Child protection has been the subject of intense scrutiny for some decades. Harm to children is a highly emotive subject, which attracts both media and political interest. When a child dies after child protection services have been involved, media interest into inquiries into the death can continue for months, as in the high-profile cases of Peter Connelly and Victoria Climbie, among many others (UK Government, 2003, 2008). Some of the interest this generates can have positive effects for other children because it can stimulate a review of childcare law or the system of child protection, but it can also create and perpetuate myths about child abuse and particularly about child protection services. This is a long-standing driver of scrutiny of child protection social work (Hutchinson, 1986).

An early example of a case that had a positive effect for children in care was the distressing case of Dennis O'Neil, who died in 1945 while in the care of Newport County Borough Council, fostered at a remote farm in Wales where he was starved and beaten to death by his foster carers. The subsequent Monckton Inquiry (Monckton, 1945) led to the introduction of new regulations concerning the boarding out of children and contributed to the passing of the Children Act 1948, which in turn was largely responsible for establishing professional social work in local authority social work departments. Each local authority in England and Wales was required to have a trained Children's Officer and a Children's Committee, who were responsible for children in their care. An example of another child death that led to a substantial change in practice is that of Victoria Climbié, whose death in 2000 led to the Laming Inquiry in 2003 (UK Government, 2003), which in turn underpinned the introduction of the 'Every Child Matters' initiative (UK Government, 2003: 2) and the *Children Act 2004*. These together required agencies that work with children and young people to 'work together' more effectively to safeguard vulnerable children and young people.

These cases illustrate the potential for some degree of benefit for other children that can follow from painful child deaths. However, intense media attention on tragedies, deaths cruelty and missed opportunities to 'save' children killed by their carers can create and feed myths and misinformation about child protection social work. Complex inquiries into difficult situations do not appear to translate well into headlines and short news articles, and newspapers vary in how much emphasis is placed on accurate journalism. This makes the social work in child protection more difficult, as public misunderstanding of the role can lead to hostile attitudes and avoidance of services by parents of children who need help and support but are worried by the stigma which has been attached to it, or exaggerated stories of authoritarian intervention. The case of Sharon Shoesmith, unfairly dismissed from her post as Director of Children's Services following the death of 'Baby P' Peter Connelly (Butler, 2016), shows how disastrously individuals, as well as the whole profession, can be affected by assumptions of culpability.

Members of the public who do not come into contact with child protection services have few sources of accurate information about how they work. The duty of confidentiality prevents social workers and courts from explaining their work in detail. There is no counterbalancing sharing of positive stories about successful interventions. This unfortunately allows some myths and misconceptions about child protection social work to persist. Some examples of these are set out in Box 7.9.

> **BOX 7.9 MYTHS ABOUT CHILD ABUSE**
>
> Myth: child abuse is mainly carried out by strangers, not family members.
>
> Reality: more than 90% of physical abuse, sexual abuse, neglect and emotional abuse is carried out by people known to the child, the majority of them being parents.
>
> Myth: children who say they have been abused are quite likely to be making it up.
>
> Reality: false allegations of abuse are uncommon, and less than 10% of allegations of sexual abuse prove not to be true.
>
> Myth: children who are disabled are less likely to be abused.
>
> Reality: children with disabilities are more likely to be abused than their non-disabled peers.
>
> Myth: Sexual abuse is something that happens to girl children.
>
> Reality: both boys and girls may be sexually abused, and women as well as men can be sexual abusers.
>
> Myth: Social workers can remove children from families without any evidence of harm.
>
> Reality: Social workers sometimes remove children because they are at risk of harm, but they can only remove children with a court order when a court has carefully scrutinised evidence that shows actual or likely significant harm to the child.
>
> Myth: child abuse is about physical injury and sexual assault.
>
> Reality: not all forms of abuse involve physical contact or sexual violence. Emotional abuse and neglect are examples of abuse that may not involve abusive physical contact.
>
> Myth: parents who love their children would never harm them.
>
> Reality: sometimes even parents who love their children can fail to protect them from harm or hurt them.

Child protection: theoretical frameworks

Various theories are used in child protection work to try to understand why child abuse happens, and to identify the best way of working with an abused child and their family to identify harm, reduce the risk of re-abuse, or help a child recover from abusive experiences. Theories often suggest that certain children are at higher risk of being abused than others, although limitations on our understanding of cause and effect in child abuse means we have to be very careful about the predictions we make and how we use them. The idea that theories can be used to identify children potentially at risk of abuse or neglect has its attraction in terms of efficiency and not letting children 'slip through the net' but is not without concerns.

Munro (2019) discusses the issues associated with using predictive analytics with datasets to identify individual children at risk. There are two key aspects of any theory-based predictive model used for identifying children and families at risk. Firstly, how *sensitive* is it: does it identify many more children than are likely to be at risk, or many less? Secondly, how *specific* is it: how good is it at picking up only those children who are at risk of abuse without drawing non-abused children into the child protection 'net'. As Munro (2019) points out, both errors of over-inclusion, or false positives, and errors of under-identification, or false negatives, have serious consequences for children, families, and professionals, and indeed for the social work profession.

Gillingham (2016) argues that using large data sets to identify individual children at risk means that services can be more accurately targeted at the children most at risk. This approach is itself not without risks, since accuracy is linked to the extent to which the risk factors – and potentially protective factors – for child abuse can be identified and how effective the data sets are at capturing that data.

Theories can be used to suggest ways of reducing harm caused by abuse. Possibly one of the most widely used theories in social work is attachment theory. Attachment theory developed from the seminal work of John Bowlby (Holmes, 2014). It focuses on the relationship between carer and child, with a strong emphasis on the impact of early experience on patterning relationships between the developing child and other people and their understanding of their environment. Carers who are unable or unwilling to respond to the physical and emotional needs of the developing child contribute to the development of internalised working models of the world which may mean the child is fearful and withdrawing, or acts defensively and aggressively, or is 'clingy', or appears indifferent to others. The behaviour of the child affects the parents' behaviour too, and since the parent is already struggling to respond emotionally to the child, the possibility of neglect or abuse increases. This theory contributed a whole vocabulary for thinking about parent-child relationships and has been hugely influential in social work. A downside of the dominance of attachment theory was, arguably, social work's early focus on mothers, which may be an issue even now (Brown et al., 2009). This may have led to delay in the development of professional sensitivity to the importance of other family relationships to children and young people, such as siblings and grandparents.

Systemic theories are inherently inclusive: they address the interactions between individuals, groups, and the environment in which they live. They focus less on the fine grain of interpersonal interaction, although these are important in ecological theories too, but aim to set them in a wider context. Bronfenbrenner's ecological or bioecological theory (Bronfenbrenner, 1979) of human development incorporates consideration of the many levels of interaction between the individual and the social and wider environmental context in which they develop. Systemic approaches to children and families emphasise the constantly evolving nature of complex relationships, and the near impossibility of stasis.

Theories such as Bowlby's and Bronfenbrenners' are complex, and there is a danger that they can be applied simplistically by practitioners, and by researchers (Godwin and O'Neal, 2015). One very important thing theory such as this offer is a *language* we can use, to explore relationships and feelings and analyse how an individual's developmental trajectory is affected by influences, from the 'micro' detail of parental responding to the decisions made by politicians that affect living standards for those most dependent on state support.

Ideas about resilience are also important: the innate tendency towards recovery and nurturing what promotes recovery from adversity. Resilience offers a theory and perspective on why some children do better than others in difficult circumstances and how some parents manage to care for their children well even when experiencing stress or survive difficult childhoods themselves. Our ability to make predictions about who will thrive and who will struggle is limited, but we can try to understand which conditions or contextual factors help support safety in the present and recovery in the future (Welbourne, 2019).

These are just some examples of the many theories that one might explore. If one is interested to explore this area further, there is suggested further reading at the end of the chapter.

Risk and protective factors

Ideas about risk and protective factors come in part from observation of cases in which things went badly wrong, most significantly inquiries into child deaths, some of which have been mentioned above. Other information comes from putting together as much research knowledge as possible to look for patterns, which may be complex. The Centers for Disease Control and Prevention (CDC) in the USA have compiled a profile of risk and protective factors from research (CDC, no date). They conclude,

> Risk factors are characteristics that may increase the likelihood of experiencing or perpetrating child abuse and neglect, but they may or may not be direct causes. A combination of individual, relational, community, and societal factors contribute to the risk of child abuse and neglect.

They found that certain specific factors increase a child's risk of being abused or neglected (Boxes 7.10–7.13).

BOX 7.10 CDC RISK FACTORS FOR ABUSE

Child factors

Children younger than four years of age, children with special needs that may increase caregiver burden (e.g., disabilities, mental health issues, and chronic physical illnesses).

Parent/caregiver factors

Caregivers with drug or alcohol issues, mental health issues, including depression, young or single parents or parents with many children, with low education or income, and/or are experiencing high levels of parenting stress and economic stress.
  Caregivers living in the home who are not a biological parent.
  Caregivers who were abused or neglected as children.
  Caregivers who use spanking and other forms of corporal punishment for discipline, with attitudes accepting of or justifying violence or aggression or who do not understand children's needs or development (CDC, no date).

It is important to note that these are only *risk factors*, and some parents might fit into one or more of these categories and still be successful, loving, non-abusive parents, but it is suggested that the last point above must always constitute grounds for concern about potential child welfare issues.

BOX 7.11 FAMILY RISK FACTORS

Families that have family members in jail or prison.

Families that are isolated from and not connected to other people (extended family, friends, or neighbours).

Family violence, including relationship violence and high conflict and negative communication styles.

There are in addition environmental factors that are particularly hard for families to manage or control:

BOX 7.12 COMMUNITY/ENVIRONMENTAL FACTORS

Children living in communities with high rates of violence and crime, and easy access to drugs and alcohol.

Children living in communities with high rates of poverty, limited educational and economic opportunities and high unemployment rates, and where families frequently experience food insecurity.

Children living in communities where neighbours do not know or look out for each other and where residents move frequently.

Children living in communities with few activities for young people.

The protective factors for children are, not surprisingly, the mirror image of risk factors. To live in a family based in an area of stability and economic health, with a family that is well linked to and supported in the community and extended family, where parents value education, understand children's needs and are able to manage their own stresses without impacting on the children, and are able to get support for themselves when they need it, is to begin life with significant advantages. Present, interested caregivers who are able to set consistent boundaries, with extended family and friends who serve as positive role models are important, but so is living in a safe community with family-friendly employers and good quality education from pre-school onwards.

Some of these protective factors take years to establish, like trees, involving city planning, central government funding, public health and other health care input, policing strategies and education service improvement as well as national and local economic strategic planning. Problems that arise where support, resilience and prevention fail can be addressed at the individual level through social work input, parent counselling and education, health care to address addiction or mental health needs, targeted family support and addressing serious abusive behaviour by parents and carers through the civil and criminal justice systems as a last resort; however, there is still likely to be a negative impact on the child.

Support for parents is essential so the system for protecting children is based on enhancing child welfare through improving parenting whenever possible. The WHO advocates a multi-sectoral, multidimensional approach to child abuse, including the teaching of positive parenting skills as the best way to change parental behaviour. Legal enforcement of non-abusive parenting and 'ongoing care' for children and families are also needed but are unlikely to break intergenerational 'cycles' of abusive parenting.

> **BOX 7.13 RISK FACTORS FOR CHILD ABUSE**
>
> - gender and social inequality
> - lack of adequate housing or services to support families and institutions
> - high levels of unemployment or poverty
> - the easy availability of alcohol and drugs
> - inadequate policies and programmes to prevent child maltreatment, child pornography, child prostitution and child labour
> - social and cultural norms that promote or glorify violence towards others, support the use of corporal punishment, demand rigid gender roles or diminish the status of the child in parent–child relationships
> - social, economic, health and education policies that lead to poor living standards, or to socioeconomic inequality or instability (WHO, no date).

As well as offering support to families affected by the risk factors listed above, the WHO suggests approaches based on changing behaviour and opportunities, through education, building awareness about the harmful nature of, for example, sexual abuse, changing norms and values (including in schools, where a violence-free environment is important) and involving fathers in parenting. Prohibiting the use of violent punishment is advocated but prohibiting violence against children does not on its own protect children: there also has to be enforcement, and support.

UNICEF's Global Status Report on Preventing Violence Against Children (UNICEF, 2020), to which the WHO, UNICEF and UNESCO contributed, attempts the difficult task of formulating an overarching strategy for addressing child maltreatment. It developed the 'INSPIRE' set of evidence-based strategies for intervention (Box 7.14).

> **BOX 7.14**
>
> 'INSPIRE' is a set of seven evidence-based strategies for countries and communities working to eliminate violence against children… INSPIRE serves as a technical package and handbook for selecting, implementing, and monitoring effective policies, programmes and services to prevent and respond to violence against children.
>
> I for the implementation and enforcement of laws;
> N for norms and values;
> S for safe environments;
> P for parent and caregiver support;
> I for income and economic strengthening;
> R for response and support services; and
> E for education and life skills.
>
> Source: WHO *Global Status Report on Preventing Violence Against Children 2020*.

The legislative framework

In England and Wales, state intervention to support child safety and well-being rests on two conceptual pillars: the concept of children in need and the concept of children suffering significant harm. The first principle is that state intervention should be offered whenever possible on a consensual basis, with the consent of the parents or carers or, where the child has the capacity to consent, also the child. Secondly, the wishes and feelings of the child should be sought and taken into consideration, taking the child's level of understanding into consideration.

However, it may not be possible to work through agreement with parents, and if compulsion is needed to safeguard a child, the oversight of a court is needed to make it lawful, except in urgent cases when the police may use specific powers to keep a child safe in the short term.

The power of the police to intervene in urgent situations covers unanticipated and urgent situations in which access to a court is impossible because it would take too much time.

S46 of the Children Act 1989 applies when the police have reasonable cause to believe a child would be likely to suffer significant harm if they do not act quickly. The police have the power to place a child under police protection, but this is short-term measure only, lasting 72 hours. Without court oversight, the removal of a child from their parents has to be of short duration. The child's parents, or anyone the child has been living with, or with parental responsibility for them, and the local authority for the area the child lives in, and the one they were found in, must be informed.

The police can use this provision to remove the child from a situation where they are at risk of harm or keep them in a place where they are safe, such as a hospital, to prevent their removal to an unsafe one. The police officer must explain to the child what has been done and why, in accordance with their age and understanding, and their wishes and feelings must be ascertained. The local authority responsible for the welfare of the child must decide what further steps they wish to take to protect the child. This is the shortest of the protective measures in the Children Act 1989, lasting a maximum of 72 hours.

Social workers with concerns about the safety of a child and a need for a rapid action can apply to the courts for an Emergency Protection Order (EPO) made under s44 Children Act 1989. Courts may make additional provisions, for example, to exclude someone who presents a risk to the child from the family home so the child can stay there. An EPO lasts a maximum of eight days and can only be renewed once for a maximum of seven further days. It protects the child in the short term and gives the social worker time to gather evidence about the child's situation, health and development, any injuries they may have sustained and find out as much as possible about what has happened to them and their views.

Going to court whenever possible and giving parents time to obtain legal advice are consistent with the procedural rights of parents that are protected under Article 6;1 of the Human Rights Act 1998 (Box 7.15).

BOX 7.15 RIGHT TO A FAIR AND PUBLIC HEARING

'In the determination of his civil rights and obligations or of any criminal charge against him, everyone is entitled to a fair and public hearing within a reasonable time by an independent and impartial tribunal established by law. Judgement

> shall be pronounced publicly but the press and public may be excluded from all or part of the trial in the interest of morals, public order or national security in a democratic society, where the interests of juveniles or the protection of the private life of the parties so require, or to the extent strictly necessary in the opinion of the court in special circumstances where publicity would prejudice the interests of justice'.

When a longer period of time than that given by an EPO is required, a local authority may apply for an interim care order under s38 of the *Children Act 1989*, which permits the local authority to arrange a safe place for the child if they cannot return home. It should not last longer than 26 weeks, the statutory timeframe for reaching a final court hearing to settle the outcome of the case. Placement on an interim care order may be within the child's extended family if this can be arranged safely for the child, or in other accommodation such as with foster carers or (less commonly in the UK) in a residential care setting.

An alternative and less intrusive order is the Child Assessment Order, made under s43 of the 1989 Act, which compels parents or carers to comply with directions given by the court regarding investigation or assessment, for example, an assessment of a medical or psychiatric condition, or of physical development. Unlike the interim care order and EPO, this does not involve the removal of the child from the family home other than for the purposes of assessment and investigation.

A court may, at the end of a case typically lasting up to 30 weeks (the statutory time frame is 26 weeks, but this is not always attainable), decide to make no order at all or (among the legal options available, depending on the child's best interests) make a 'full' care order, lasting until the child is 18 if not discharged before, or if they are to remain within the child's extended family network but not with parents, a special guardianship order, both *Children Act 1989* provisions. Special guardianship is most likely when care by a relative or other carer linked to the child and/or family is a viable option. Care orders may entail the child being placed with foster carers or non-parent relatives. Finally, if an adoption order is made, under separate adoption legislation, the *Adoption and Children Act 2002*, this creates a lifelong change to the child's legal status, transferring parental responsibility in full to the adopters and ending it for anyone who held it before.

This is a brief and not exhaustive account but gives an outline of the orders most likely to be used in child protection cases.

Protecting children in Northern Ireland

The child protection system in Northern Ireland (NI) is very closely aligned with that in England and Wales, being based on the same concepts of significant harm as the threshold for compulsory intervention in family life, and a shared approach to child abuse as triggering a multidisciplinary response involving social workers, police and health as well as other services, notably education, as appropriate. It also uses the concept of safeguarding as the umbrella term to capture both child protection interventions and the provision of services to promote the well-being and development of children in need. Some of the organisations and policies underlying child protection in NI are however distinctive.

The organisation tasked with overseeing safeguarding is the Northern Ireland Safeguarding Board, set up in 2012 by the *Safeguarding Board Act 2011*. Where the *Children Act 1989* determines the scope and nature of state intervention to protect children in England and Wales, in NI, the equivalent legislation is the *Children (Northern Ireland) Order 1995*. The 'Children Order' has provided a stable legislative framework for intervention for over 20 years,

> …All the while in Northern Ireland, the Children Order has remained the compass to navigate a path for social workers in this landscape of practice which is so fraught with moral indeterminacy … and messy in its complexity…
>
> (Duffy et al., 2016: 327)

Other important documents are the strategy document 'Children and Young People's Strategy 2020–2030' (Department for Education, Northern Ireland, 2021), which sets out several outcomes sought for all children in NI: that children should have the following:

> …that we give our children and young people the best start in life, ensuring that they grow up in a society which provides the support they need to achieve their potential. This includes good health; a secure family and community environment including an adequate standard of living; education; a good physical environment; opportunities for cultural and artistic expression and to make a positive contribution to society; physical exercise; space to play; and protection from violence and harm. This Strategy aims to support the rights and improve the well-being of all our child.
>
> (*Children and Young People's Strategy* p. ii)

The Strategy uses the definition of well-being set out in the Children's Services Co-operation Act (Northern Ireland) 2015, which states this includes:

- Physical and mental health
- Enjoyment of play and leisure
- Learning and achievement
- Living in safety and with stability
- Economic and environmental well-being
- Making a positive contribution to society
- Living in a society which respects their rights
- Living in a society in which equality of opportunity and good relations are promoted.

Both England and Wales and NI have Children's Commissioners, whose roles are to safeguard and promote the rights and best interests of children and young people. In both jurisdictions, the rights and well-being of particularly vulnerable groups, such as children in care and care leavers, are subject of particular scrutiny. Children's participation and input into the functioning of services to protect them and The Northern Ireland Commissioner for Children and Young People have issued advice on how public sector bodies can best engage with children and young people. The Commissioner Office's publication 'Participation with Children and Young People: Advice to Public

Bodies' underlines the high importance placed on participation and 'voice' for children and young people in Northern Ireland.

Assessments of possible risk and harm to children are carried out by the Health and Social Care Trust (HSCT) Gateway Service. If there is reason to believe there may be a criminal aspect to the harm suffered, they may implement the Joint Protocol, which governs joint working between the police and social workers, and refer the case to the NI Police Service for joint investigation. The underpinning assessment framework for all children in NI who are or may be in need of support services is the UNOCINI framework: Understanding the Needs of Children in Northern Ireland (2011), which was under review at the time of writing. This is the equivalent framework to the England and Wales 'Framework for Assessment of Children in Need and their Families', discussed above.

Comparison with the Scottish system of children's hearings

The protection of children in Scotland is distinct in significant respects from that of England and Wales and Northern Ireland. Scotland has a legislative system for responding to child abuse based around Children's Hearings. It is built upon principles established by the Kilbrandon Report of 1964, the main one being that children and young people who offend, as well as those who require care and protection, should equally be considered 'children in need' (Scottish Government, no date).

Each Panel has three trained Panel Members who receive training and independent legal advice to assist them in making decisions about children but who have the power to make independent decisions. The Scottish Children's Reporter Administration receives referrals for children and young people who are believed to require 'compulsory measures of supervision' and decides whether the child or young person needs to be referred to a Hearing Scottish Children's Reporter Administration, no date). The grounds for referral are broadly defined and include:

- The child suffers from lack of parental care, or is falling into bad associations, or is exposed to moral danger, or is beyond the control of their parent/carer (relevant person).
- The child, or another child in the same household, has been the victim of an offence such as sexual abuse, assault or neglect.
- They are a member of the same household as a person who has offended against a child or young person.
- They have failed to attend school without reasonable excuse, or have committed an offence, or abused solvents, drugs or alcohol.

If the grounds for referral are not accepted, or the child or young person does not understand due to their age or ability, the case may be heard by the Sheriff Court. A distinctive aspect of the Scottish Children's Hearings system is the expectation the child will be present, whereas in England and Wales, children who wish to attend hearings about them have to ask for permission to attend, which may not be granted. However, in England and Wales, older children involved with the family court in care proceedings are increasingly stating they wish to be present at their court hearing and instruct their own legal representative, but they remain a small minority (Ancliffe, 2020).

In Scotland, children can have a pre-hearing visit to familiarise themselves with building in which the hearing is to be held and are given a pack of information including a form 'All about Me', which they can if they wish complete and give to the Panel to tell the Panel what they want to say about themselves. Also, present at the hearing is a reporter, who is responsible for the fair conduct of the hearing, and three lay panel members. A social worker for the child is likely to be present, and possibly one or more other professionals such as a teacher. Parents or carers may also attend. Children have the right to bring a trusted person, and a solicitor (though this is not a requirement). There may also be a safeguarder present:

> Children's hearings and sheriffs appoint Safeguarders where they think there is a requirement to safeguard the interests of the child involved. The Safeguarder does an independent assessment of what is in the child's best interests and provides it to the hearing or court.
>
> (Scottish Government, no date)

One issue with expecting children to be present at a hearing about them is that consideration needs to be given to their readiness to take part in processes in which adults with professional roles and/or training are likely to dominate. Advocacy for children has been provided for in law since the 2011 Children's Hearings (Scotland) Act was passed, but only introduced in spring 2020.

Points to ponder

- What might be the rewards of being a child protection social worker?
- What would you do or say if you were told by someone you knew well that they had experienced abuse in the past, but they had never told anyone before?
- If social workers work predominantly with low-income families, what do you think that tells us about the role of social work in society in the UK?

Quiz

1. What is the definition of neglect in England and Wales?
2. How long has there been a legal concept of child abuse in England?
3. What is meant by child sexual exploitation, and how is it distinguished from other forms of sexual abuse?
4. What is meant by the acronym 'FGM'?
5. Identify one distinctive feature of the Scottish system of child protection compared with that of England Wales and Northern Ireland.
6. What proportion of sexual offences against children that lead to a prosecution by police and the CPS go on to lead to a conviction in England and Wales? (a) a quarter, (b) half, or (c) four fifths?
7. Child sexual exploitation does not often happen to boys and young men - true or false?
8. 'One in … adults in England and Wales are estimated to have experienced at least one form of child abuse, whether emotional abuse, physical abuse, sexual abuse, or witnessing domestic violence or abuse, before the age of 16 years'. One in how many?

9   What is meant by 'County Lines'?
10 Dennis O'Neil died a tragic death while in care. What happened as a result of his death that progressed the development of child protection and professional social work?
11 What happened to the Director of Social Services after the death of 'Baby' Peter Connelly?
12 Which of these statements about child protection are true: (a) the public often hear bad things about social workers failing to protect children, so the reality must be that children are harmed frequently when this could have been prevented, (b) each time a child is killed by their parents, it means a social worker has failed the child, (c) the child protection system will never prevent harm happening to every child.

Answers

1   Neglect is persistent failure to meet a child's basic physical and/or psychological needs, likely to result in the serious impairment of the child's health or development.
2   Since the late 19th century –1889 was the date of the first statute to criminalise child abuse in England.
3   Child sexual exploitation occurs when an individual or group takes advantage of an imbalance of power to coerce, manipulate or deceive a child or young person under the age of 18 into sexual activity, for financial gain or to enhance their status, possibly and/or in exchange for something the victim wants or needs. Sexual abuse involves forcing or enticing a child to take part in sexual activities, so CSE is a form of sexual abuse, but whereas perpetrators of non-CSE sexual abuse usually conceal the abuse from all others, in CSE others are involved as co-abusers. The distinction is not always sharp, especially when technology has been used for sharing images.
4   Female genital mutilation.
5   The system of Children's Hearings, also known as Children's Panels, is distinctive to Scotland.
6   c.
7   False – although in the year to March 2019, young women are around three times as likely as men to have experienced sexual abuse before the age of 16 years (UK Office for National Statistics, 2020).
8   One in *five* adults in England and Wales is estimated to have experienced at least one form of child abuse, whether emotional abuse, physical abuse, sexual abuse or witnessing domestic violence or abuse, before the age of 16 years.
9   'County Lines' refers to drug dealing and other criminal activities carried out by gangs, which use young children, sometimes as young as under 10s who are below the age of criminal responsibility in England and Wales, to carry out criminal acts. The term typically refers to criminal activities that link established criminal activities in urban areas with smaller cities and towns, and the 'County Line' is the name of the phone line that is used to take orders of drugs.
10 After Dennis O'Neil's death, the Monckton Inquiry of 1945 led to the introduction of new regulations concerning the boarding-out of children and contributed to the passing of the Children Act 1948, which in turn was largely responsible for establishing professional social work in local authority social work departments. Each local authority in England and Wales was required to have a trained Children's Officer and a Children's Committee, who were responsible for children in their care.

11   She was dismissed, but a court subsequently held her dismissal was unfair. While senior staff in child protection organisations are responsible for the services they direct, they also have to be treated fairly, even when things go wrong.
12   (a) – this is not really a statement that is definitely 'true' or 'false'. Every child that is harmed is one too many, and it is especially troubling when there were signs that more assertive intervention was needed to safeguard the child, but it was not taken. This has to be considered in the context of decision-making based on information that may be partial and difficult to evaluate; dishonestly and deception by abusers; the unpredictability of some human behaviour; social workers' responsibility to uphold the law on family rights, and the majority of cases in which children are protected from harm. But it is also true that reading reports into child deaths makes very sad and thought-provoking reading concerning situations in which the child protection system failed. (b) Not true. While there have been cases in which social workers have had enough information to enable them to act sooner and possibly save a child's life, this is not the case in every situation in which a parent or carer harms a child through abuse or neglect. (c) True. It seems very unlikely that there could ever be a child protection system with such a breadth of surveillance of parenting and resources to prevent any child coming to harm under the definition of child abuse, and it is possible that as a society we would not want such an intrusive regime. But we can learn from our own good practice as well as errors, at both personal and institutional levels, and from other services providing services to the public, including internationally. We can use research and lobby for resources to make the services we offer as good as they can be and maximise well-being through safeguarding children as effectively as possible.

Individual or small group exercises

- Identify and read one report concerning the death of a child over the age of five. How far was the child's perspective sought and heard in the period before the child died?
- What were the barriers and potential enablers to hearing the child's voice during this period?
- What do you think might have been helpful, if anything, in hearing more directly from the child?

Organisations working in the topic area

NSPCC
National Working Group Tackling Child Sexual Exploitation
National Association for People Abused in Childhood (NAPAC)
Family Rights Group

Supplementary reading

Beckett, C. (2007) *Child protection: an introduction*, 2nd Ed., London: Sage.
Parton, N. (2015) *Contemporary developments in child protection, policy challenges and Changes*, Social Sciences (online Journal Special Edition).

Norton, G. and Davies, R. (2017) *A child's journey through contemporary issues in child protection*, London: Family Law.

Smidt, S. (2013) *The developing child in the 21st century: a global perspective on child development*, London: Routledge.

Helpful and interesting topic related websites

British and Irish Legal Information Institute – https://www.bailii.org/
National Working Group Tackling Child Sexual Exploitation – https://www.nwgnetwork.org/
NSPCC Types of Abuse – https://www.nspcc.org.uk/what-is-child-abuse/types-of-abuse/
Pink Tape – A Blog from the Family Bar – http://www.pinktape.co.uk/
Report Child Abuse – https://www.gov.uk/report-child-abuse
Working Together to Safeguard Children and Families – https://www.gov.uk/government/publications/working-together-to-safeguard-children--2

Notes

1 This was the current version at the time of writing, last updated in 2020, but it is regularly updated and readers should check for the most recent version.
2 Scotland has different legal provisions discussed later.
3 Note that arranged marriage is lawful, forced marriage is not.

References

Ancliffe, S. (2020) 'The separate representation of children', *Family Law Week archive*, available at: https://www.familylawweek.co.uk/site.aspx?i=ed208839

Barrett, D. and Pitts, J. (1997) 'Child prostitution in the UK', *Crime and Justice Magazine*, no 28, 26–27, available at: https://www.crimeandjustice.org.uk/sites/crimeandjustice.org.uk/files/09627259708553131.pdf

Bronfenbrenner, U. (1979) *The ecology of human development*. Cambridge, MA: Harvard University Press.

Brown, L., Callahan, M., Strega, S., Walmsley, C. and Dominelli, L. (2009) 'Manufacturing ghost fathers: the paradox of father presence and absence in child welfare', *Child and Family Social Work*, 14, 25–34.

Butler, P. (2016) 'Sharon Shoesmith on Baby, P, child protection and the tabloid media: 'I came very close to not standing up again', *The Guardian*, August 19, 2016, available at: https://www.theguardian.com/society/2016/aug/19/sharon-shoesmith-baby-p-haringey-social-services-interview

Bywaters, P., Bunting, L., Davidson, G., Hanratty, J., Mason, W., McCartan, C. and Steils, N. (2016) 'The relationship between poverty, child abuse and neglect: an evidence review', Joseph Rowntree Foundation.

Bywaters, P. and Skinner, G. (2020) 'The Relationship Between Poverty and Child Abuse and Neglect: New Evidence', Huddersfield University, Huddersfield, available at: https://research.hud.ac.uk/media/assets/document/hhs/RelationshipBetweenPovertyChildAbuseandNeglect_Report.pdf

Centers for Disease Control and Prevention (no date) 'Risk and protective factors', available at: https://www.cdc.gov/violenceprevention/childabuseandneglect/riskprotectivefactors.html

Department for Education (2018) 'Working together to safeguard children: statutory guidance on working to safeguard and promote the welfare of children', available at https://www.gov.uk/government/publications/working-together-to-safeguard-children--2

Department for Education (Northern Ireland) (2021) 'Children and young people's strategy 2020-2030', available at: https://www.education-ni.gov.uk/publications/children-and-young-peoples-strategy-2020-2030

Duffy, J., Caldwell, J. and Collins, M. (2016) 'Reflections on the impact of the children (NI) order 1995', *Child Care in Practice*, 22(4), 327–332.

EPCAT (2020) 'Child trafficking in the UK 2020: a snapshot', available at: https://www.ecpat.org.uk/Handlers/Download.ashx?IDMF=b92ea99a-6dd8-480c-9660-e6c0f0764acf

Foster, D. (2021) House of commons briefing paper number 8543, 12 March 2021 'Children's social care services in England', UK House of Commons Library, available at: https://commonslibrary.parliament.uk/research-briefings/cbp-8543/

Gelles, R. and Maynard, P. (1987) 'A structural family systems approach to intervention in cases of family violence', *Family Relations*, 36, 270–275.

Gillingham, P. (2016). 'Predictive risk modelling to prevent child maltreatment and other adverse outcomes for service users: inside the 'black box' of machine learning', *British Journal of Social Work*, 46(4), 1044–1058.

Godwin, S. Ashiabi and O'Neal, Keri K. (2015) 'Child social development in context child social development in context: an examination of some propositions in Bronfenbrenner's bioecological theory', *Sage Open Journal*, 5(2) available at: https://journals.sagepub.com/doi/full/10.1177/2158244015590840

Gov.uk (no date) 'Forced marriage', available at: https://www.gov.uk/stop-forced-marriage

Gov.uk (2014) 'Forced marriage now a crime', available at: https://www.gov.uk/government/news/forced-marriage-now-a-crime

Gray, D. and Watt, P. (2013) 'Giving victims a voice, NSPCC and metropolitan police', summary available at: https://en.wikipedia.org/wiki/Giving_Victims_a_Voice#:~:text=Giving%20Victims%20a%20Voice%20is,the%20Operation%20Yewtree%20criminal%20investigation.&text=Numbers%20of%20alleged%20victims%20totalled,were%20minors%20at%20the%20time

Holmes, J. (2014) *John Bowlby and attachment theory*, 2nd Ed. London: Routledge.

Home Office (2019) 'Factsheet: child sexual exploitation and abuse', available at https://homeofficemedia.blog.gov.uk/2019/11/05/factsheet-child-sexual-exploitation-and-abuse/

Hutchinson, R. (1986) 'The effect of inquiries into cases of child abuse upon the social work profession', *The British Journal of Criminology*, 26(2), 178–182.

IICSA info (no date) available at: https://en.wikipedia.org/wiki/Independent_Inquiry_into_Child_Sexual_Abuse#:~:text=The%20Independent%20Inquiry%20into%20Child%20Sexual%20Abuse%20(IICSA)%20in%20England,protect%20children%20from%20sexual%20abuse

Kempe, C., Silverman, F., Steele, W., Droegemuller, W. and Silver, H. (1962) 'The battered child syndrome', *Journal of the American Medical Association*, 181, 17–24, also available at: https://www.kempe.org/wp-content/uploads/2015/01/The_Battered_Child_Syndrome.pdf

Khan, R., Saleem, S. and Lowe, M. (2017) '"Honour"-based violence in a British South Asian community', *Safer Communities*, 17(1), 11–21.

Monckton, W. (1945) 'Report by Sir Walter Monckton on the circumstances which led to the boarding out of Dennis and Terence O'Neill at Bank Farm, Minsterley and the steps taken to supervise their welfare.' cmd. 6636. London: HMSO, 1945.

Munro, E. (2019) 'Predictive analytics in child protection', CHESS Working Paper No. 2019-03/Durham University.

National Crime Agency (no date) 'County lines', available at: https://www.nationalcrimeagency.gov.uk/what-we-do/crime-threats/drug-trafficking/county-lines

NHS (no date) 'Overview – Female Genital Mutilation (FGM)', available at: https://www.nhs.uk/conditions/female-genital-mutilation-fgm/

Nixon, D. (2010) 'Should UK law reconsider the initial threshold of legal personality? A critical analysis', *Human Reproduction & Genetic Ethics*, 16(2), 182–217.

NSPCC (2021) 'Childline annual review', available at: https://learning.nspcc.org.uk/research-resources/childline-annual-review

NSPCC (no date) 'Child trafficking', available at: https://www.nspcc.org.uk/what-is-child-abuse/types-of-abuse/child-trafficking/#

NWG (no date) 'What is CSE?', available at: https://www.nwgnetwork.org/what-is-cse/
Office for National Statistics (2020) 'Child neglect in England and Wales: year ending March 2019', available at: https://www.ons.gov.uk/peoplepopulationandcommunity/crimeandjustice/articles/childneglectinenglandandwales/yearendingmarch2019
Scottish Children's Reporter Administration (no date) 'Role of the reporter', available at: https://www.scra.gov.uk/about-scra/role-of-the-reporter/
Scottish Government (no date) 'Child protection', available at: https://www.niccy.org/media/2979/niccy-participation-advice-to-public-bodies-jan-18.pdf
Topping, A. (2015) 'End use of outdated term 'child prostitution', says MP', *The Guardian* Tue January 6th, 2015, available at: https://www.theguardian.com/society/2015/jan/06/child-prostitution-term-outdated-mp-ann-coffey
UK Government (2003) 'The Victoria Climbie inquiry', available at: https://assets.publishing.service.gov.uk/government/uploads/system/uploads/attachment_data/file/273183/5730.pdf
UK Government (2003:2) 'Every child matters', available at: https://www.gov.uk/government/publications/every-child-matters
UK Government (2008) 'Haringey serious case reviews: child A', available at: https://www.gov.uk/government/publications/haringey-local-safeguarding-children-board-first-serious-case-review-child-a
UNICEF (2020) 'Global status report on preventing violence against children 2020', available at: https://www.cdc.gov/violenceprevention/childabuseandneglect/riskprotectivefactors.html
Welbourne, P. (2019) 'Safeguarding children and the use of theory in practice' in *Routledge handbook of social work theory*, eds. Payne, M. and Reith-Hall, E. London: Routledge.
World Health Organization (2020) 'Child maltreatment', available at: https://www.who.int/news-room/fact-sheets/detail/child-maltreatment
WHO (no date) 'Child maltreatment', available at: https://www.cdc.gov/violenceprevention/childabuseandneglect/riskprotectivefactors.html

Case cited

Re X and Y [2015] EWHC 2265 (Fam), available via BAILII at https://www.bailii.org/ew/cases/EWHC/Fam/2015/2265.html

8 Youth offending

Nature, causes and implications

Sally-Ann Ashton and Anna Bussu

Youth offending context and background

Defining youth offending

The term "Juvenile delinquency" is used in the academic literature to refer to young people who have committed a criminal offence (Young et al., 2017). The legal definition of "juvenile" is not universal in the criminal justice systems across European countries and around the world, and it can determine a different age-bound status of a "juvenile" in regard to criminality. Young et al. (2017) suggest that there are no specific reasons underlying these differences, but they may arise from the lack of agreed international standards. Interpretations depend on the political, historical, ideological and economic background in each country. Most European countries set their ages of criminal responsibility between 14 and 16 years. For example, 14 in Germany and Italy, 15 in Sweden, Finland and Norway, 16 in Portugal and 18 in Luxembourg; France has one of the lowest in Europe at just under at 13 years. In the US, several states are even lower at six years of age and nor was the US a signatory of UNCRC due to 22 states permitting capital punishment of individuals who had committed crimes as juveniles (Young et al., 2017).

In the UK, the Justice System classifies "juvenile offenders" as all young people aged 10–17 and "young offenders" as all young people aged 18–21 (up to their 21st birthday). However, the term "young offenders" or "youth offending (YO)" is usually more generally adopted for the full age range. In Northern Ireland, England and Wales the minimum age of criminal responsibility (MACR) is ten years old. In May 2019, the Scottish Parliament passed a law setting the Scottish MACR from 8 years to 12. This means that children under the age of 10 in Northern Ireland, England and Wales, and under 12 in Scotland cannot be arrested or charged with a crime; however, children above these ages can be arrested and taken to court if they have committed an offence. We can consider this age to be very low as children under the age of 10 do not have the complete capacity to understand the impact of their actions on other people (UNCRC, 2007). This also means that large numbers of children are being exposed to a criminal justice system, which may have harmful effects on their wellbeing and psycho-social development.

The Equality and Human Rights Commission (EHRC) has urged reforms across the UK after the United Nations' convention on the Rights of the Child (UNCRC, 2007) required that States should establish an age below which children are presumed "not to have the capacity to infringe the penal law" and also suggested that States should increase their lower MACR to the age of 12 years as the absolute minimum acceptable age and to continue to increase it to a higher age level (see the UNICEF recommendations, Box 8.1). The MACR is a crucial aspect that needs to be reconsidered in the UK to be consistent with national policies promoted and international standards adopted so far.

BOX 8.1 AGE OF CRIMINAL RESPONSIBILITY: UNICEF RECOMMENDATIONS

- Ensure that the minimum age of criminal responsibility is over 14 and continue to be increased.
- Ensure that all children and adolescents under 18 in conflict with the law enjoy the protection of the juvenile justice system in line with international standards.
- Exclude provisions that allow for lowering protection standards for certain offences or give discretionary powers to judges in deciding whether the juvenile justice system applies.

Source: UNICEF, "Legal Minimum ages and the realization of adolescents rights" retrieved from https://www.unicef.org/lac/media/2771/file/PDF%20Minimum%20age%20for%20criminal%20responsibility.pdf

---

Young offender statistics

From April 2019 to March 2020, 19,000 children in England and Wales were cautioned or sentenced. Fortunately, the number of children who received a caution or sentence has fallen by 82% over the last ten years, with a 12% fall in the last year (YJB, 2021). However, too many young people are re-offending: 73% of young people released from custody re-offend within a year (Ministry of Justice, 2015) and 38.5% of children and young people reoffend after this point (YJB, 2021). The reoffending rate decreased by 0.2% in the last year, although it remains higher than ten years ago (when it was 37.7%; YJB, 2021). The government spends large sums of money on the secure estate, including YO institutions, secure training centres and secure children's homes (MoJ, 2015). From the Youth Justice Board (YJB)[1] report (2021) it emerged that, in 2020, there were 57,600 arrests of children (aged 10–17) by the police in England and Wales (excluding Lancashire and Greater Manchester). The statistics show that the arrest of children in the UK has decreased by 74% over the last ten years, with an increase of 1% compared with the previous year.

Furthermore, in the year ending March 2020, 7.200 youth cautions were given to children in England and Wales. This is a decrease of 90% compared with the year ending March 2010, with a decrease of 16% in the last year (YJB, 2020).

BOX 8.2 YOUTH JUSTICE STATISTICS

- **Youth Justice Statistics:** Annual bulletin published by the Youth Justice Board (YJB) and Ministry of Justice (MoJ). These statics offer detailed data on the youth justice system, including offences committed, socio-demographics data of children (10–17) in the youth justice system, outcomes they have received.

- **Reoffending Statistics:** These statistics are published quarterly by the MoJ. The report provides statistics on proven reoffending for both adult and juvenile offenders, in both yearly and quarterly cohorts. The statistics are produced from data taken from the Police National Computer (PNC).
- **Knife and Offensive Weapon Sentencing Statistics:** They describe trends in the number of offenders receiving cautions and convictions for possession of a knife or offensive weapon, including threatening offences. This report is published quarterly by the MoJ's Sentencing Statistics Team.
- **First Time Entrants Statistics:** This report is enable breakdowns by gender, age group, ethnicity, police force area, offence class, and disposal type/category. The statistics are produced from data taken from the PNC.
- **Reconviction rates in Scotland:** This publication provides analyses of trends in reconviction statistics.
- **Official Research and Statistical Bulletin** on "Youth Engagement Statistics for Northern Ireland." The statistics are published by the Ireland Department of Justice (DoJ).

Categories of crime associated with youth and offending roles

Violent crimes

Violent offending has dominated recent UK government crime strategies, because an increasing number of children and young people enter the justice system for more serious and violent offences, including possession of weapons. However, it should be noted that although knife crime remains a problem in YO, crime statistics show that the majority of perpetrators and victims are adults (YJB & MoJ, 2018). In 2018, for example, children committed 21% of all knife and weapon offences (YJB, 2018).

Although violence reduction strategies in England and Wales concentrate on the relationship between weapon carrying and gangs, academic research indicates that it is individual offenders who tend to carry weapons (Oudekerk & Morgan, 2016). This is irrespective of whether they are carried for protection or force, because individuals feel vulnerable when away from their peers or group (Ashton & Bussu, 2020). A study utilising police data from Merseyside demonstrated that young people with extended offending trajectories were typically arrested initially for antisocial behaviour,[2] expressive violent offending, or non-violent income-generating offences, such as theft. Some offenders then progress to violent income-generating crimes, often in the presence of others (Ashton et al., 2021). The economic and emotional costs of juvenile offending are considerable (Box 8.3). Early identification and support for children and young people could reduce both the harm and costs of crime.

BOX 8.3 ECONOMIC COSTS OF CRIME

The total costs of crime in England and Wales in 2015/2016 to be approximately £50bn for crimes against individuals and £9bn for crimes against businesses. Violent crimes, committed by adults and young offenders, make up the largest proportion of the total costs of individual crime – almost three-quarters – but only one-third of the number of crimes. This is mainly due to the higher physical and emotional costs to the victims of violent offences (HO, 2018). Investing in prevention, early intervention and supporting young people who offend can ultimately reduce the economic costs of crime.

Co-offending

Offending in the presence of others during adolescence is recognised as both a criminal learning process and an increased criminogenic risk (Andresen & Felson, 2010). For youth, antisocial behaviour and fighting are frequently undertaken in the presence of others, and young people cite boredom, thrill seeking, and social exchange as reasons for these activities (Ashton & Bussu, 2020). Robbery and burglary are also associated with more than one offender (Hodgson, 2007) and their appearance on an adolescent's offending timeline is significant. Robbery indicates a shift from expressive to instrumental offending, and burglary requires a level of training, thus suggesting criminal exploitation by more experienced offenders (Ashton et al., 2021).

Managing and supporting those who co-offend is not straightforward because there are two distinct roles in the form of instigators and followers (McCord & Conway, 2002). These positions can be flexible depending on membership of the group. For example, a younger offender may follow the leadership of older and more experienced group members for one criminal act but may repeat what she or he has learned with peers, fulfilling the role of instigator and leader. Similarly, an individual who is capable of offending alone, may recruit accomplices for certain categories of crime and therefore, even as juveniles, present a heightened risk to their peers (Ashton et al., 2020). Establishing whether a young person acts alone, in the company of others, or offends in both styles is important not only for managing their risk but also in determining the most effective offending behaviour programme. Followers may require support with breaking away from and resisting antisocial peers, whereas those who instigate offences present different criminogenic risks to themselves and others.

County lines and child criminal exploitation

Social and environmental risk factors can increase exposure to older criminals, who present an additional risk to young people. The UK government recognises this phenomenon. Both strategy and prevention of YO have focused on a particular category of co-offending and adult criminal exploitation: the phenomenon known as "county lines". Although the term "county lines" refers specifically to the movement of drugs from urban areas to less densely populated parts of the UK, the process involves a hierarchy of criminals and the exploitation of young people at both local and national levels by criminal gangs (HO, 2016, 2018). The National Crime Agency (2019) suggests that there are over 2,000 "deal lines" in the UK, linked to around 1,000 county lines. These lines are often branded and, along with customer bases, are sometimes sold to other gangs to avoid detection by law enforcement.

Gang membership

Gang membership is used as an indicator for increased risk by a number of criminal justice agencies. This practice has been heavily criticised because it labels young people as gang involved, which in turn can impact on how they are viewed by criminal justice professionals. There is a lack of consensus, both professionally and among young people, over what constitutes a gang (Curry, 2015). Research in both England (Ashton & Bussu, 2020) and Scotland (McLean, 2017) has demonstrated that there are both delinquent peer groups, serving a social and recreational purpose; and adolescent street gangs who are more focused on violent income-generating crimes such as robbery or drug sales. Members of both groups are at risk of involvement in adult organised crime dealing with the importation and distribution of drugs, firearms, and the exploitation and trafficking of vulnerable people (Coomber & Moyle, 2018; Densley, 2012; McLean, 2017).

Whether an individual progresses from lower-level involvement to more active gang membership can depend on several different factors. As with temporary co-offending groups, not every gang member fulfils the same role, nor are their experiences of involvement the same (Pyrooz et al., 2013). Variation in the roles that young people fulfil, their level of embeddedness, and other social and psychological risk or protective factors impact on their experiences and trajectories (Dmitrieva et al., 2014). Consequently, for some young people, leaving the gang does not necessarily eradicate their level of risk or the trauma that they have experienced (Ashton et al., 2020).

UK-based models of gang involvement suggest a hierarchy of escalating criminal involvement and offending (Densley, 2012; McLean, 2017). At the lowest level are groups of youths of a similar age who engage in expressive offending behaviours, such as criminal damage, fighting, and theft for the purposes of funding drug use (Ashton & Bussu, 2020). For some, expressive aggression develops into acquisitive violent offending in the form of robbery and drug dealing (Ashton et al., 2021). At this point, criminality becomes intrinsic to the group's identity and older criminals may feature in the social networks of adolescents (Ashton & Bussu, 2020; McLean, 2017). Both categories of deviant youth are vulnerable to adult criminal exploitation. Studies consistently show that criminals who are often referred to as "elders" or "olders" typically live in the same area as the young people but are not acquainted with them (Ashton & Bussu, 2020; Densley, 2012; McLean, 2017). Criminals befriend young people on the streets with offers of drugs, designer clothes and trainers and entice them with access to expensive cars. They also beguile their victims with stories about gang life and social status (Hesketh & Robinson, 2019), often testing potential recruits with criminal tasks such as drug selling or the handling of firearms (Ashton & Bussu, 2020). By immersing young people in an alternative criminal group, the exploiters also succeed in removing them from their families and peers. They then use violence and debt bondage to control the young person further, making them feel that it is impossible to escape.

Research has shown that people stay in a gang for two years on average (Curry et al., 2014). Those who have been affiliated are likely to have experienced heightened levels of exposure to violence and victimisation (Bennett & Holloway, 2004). There are strong associations between exposure to violence and mental disorders, which can increase an individual's risk of violent offending irrespective of group membership (Flannery et al., 2001, 2006). Although young people may find it possible to leave a delinquent peer group, leaving an organised crime gang can be daunting especially since gang members threaten the families of those who are involved. Exit strategies cited by young people who had been involved with adult gangs included being caught by the police for drug dealing and trafficking and starting a serious romantic relationship. After convincing the gang members that they would not talk to the police all of four out of five individuals in the study had successfully left the gang, but all recounted how traumatic their experiences had been (Ashton & Bussu, 2020).

Risk factors associated with juvenile deviance

Social risk factors

Delinquent peers can present a criminogenic risk irrespective of whether the group constitutes a gang (Weerman, 2003). There are two ways in which antisocial peers can impact upon the behaviour of adolescents. The first is directly, either when they act opportunistically in the company of others or when they plan an offence without the knowledge of others. The second is when deviant peers in both longstanding and temporary social groups influencing attitudes to offending and criminality (Warr, 2002). Research has indicated that antisocial peer influence affects delinquent behaviour from mid-adolescence to the early twenties, whereas peer antisocial behaviour is more limited, from the ages of 16 to 20 (Monahan et al., 2009). Increasing levels of resistance to peer influence can be an effective offending intervention during mid-adolescence.

Drug use presents an increased risk of the exploitation for children and young people in several ways. It exposes young people to peer or adult drug dealers; it can lead to the accumulation of drug debts; and indicates a vulnerability to criminal recruiters (Hesketh & Robinson, 2019). Although many young people are social drug users, some use substances to mask underlying problems, such as trauma or mental disorder (Ashton & Bussu, 2020). These risks are increased during and after gang involvement because of the activities and experiences that relate to the preparation and selling of drugs. Substance use alone is not a predictor of gang membership and there are other social and environmental factors that are known to contribute to an enhanced vulnerability. In addition to delinquent peers, these include neighbourhood, family and parenting. Some factors can act as protective elements, for example, socially deprived neighbourhoods offer increased opportunity for gang recruitment, but strong family ties and parental supervision can counteract this risk (Aldridge et al., 2012). Nevertheless, young people often cite lack of opportunities for making money legally as a reason for criminal involvement (Ashton & Bussu, 2020). In response, some young people explain their involvement in drug selling as a legitimate form of employment (Hesketh & Robinson, 2019).

Psychological risk factors

There are other developmental risk factors that are relevant and which should be taken into account when supervising and supporting young people who are involved in expressive violent offending (e.g., assault or criminal damage). Low impulse control has been associated with increased group offending (Hirshi & Gottfredson, 2000). It has been suggested that individuals with lower levels of self-control are attracted to others who share the same deficit (McGloin et al., 2009). It is worth noting that the risk is dynamic and that for some individuals impulse control continues to develop into the early adulthood (Steinberg, 2010).

A number of other psychological factors can increase the risk of deviant behaviour and may also explain the start of expressive aggression and early involvement in offences such as fighting, assault, and criminal damage are often the earliest types of deviant behaviour (Ashton et al., 2021). Some of these factors are associated with the impact of adverse childhood experiences (ACEs). ACEs are measured by a ten-item score for childhood exposure to: emotional abuse, psychical abuse, sexual abuse, emotional neglect, physical neglect, gamily violence, household substance abuse, household mental illness, parental separation or divorce, and household member incarcerated (Felitti et al., 1998; Rutter, 1983). Although originally investigated in regard to poor health outcomes, subsequent research has found that ACEs have a relationship to elevated serious offending and victimisation of human trafficking (Craig et al., 2017). A large-scale study of juvenile offenders demonstrated that family violence, parental separation and divorce and an incarcerated household member were the most prevalent ACEs for both males and females (Baglivio et al., 2014). However, adolescent females in the sample presented with a statistically significant higher occurrence of sexual abuse when compared to males.

Protective factors such as lower impulsivity and thrill-seeking behaviours have been found to mediate a high score of ACEs (Craig et al., 2017), indicating that a comprehensive approach to risk and supporting young people to develop coping strategies for developmental and behavioural risks can be an effective intervention. Those young people who have experienced ACEs and who have a history of offending may require additional support and supervision. The presence of ACEs is exponentially associated with an increased risk of reoffending (Wolff et al., 2017). This is because prolonged exposure to ACEs is associated with longer-term neurological and psychological disorders, and there is an association between a range mental disorders and repeat adolescent offending. Those diagnosed with oppositional deviant disorder, disruptive behaviour disorder, and conduct disorder can present with aggression and violence; conduct disorder additionally is associated with deception and violent income-generating offences (Wibbelink et al., 2017). Some mental disorders can increase impulsivity. High proportions of young people involved in the Criminal Justice System suffer from attention-deficit hyperactivity disorder (ADHD), which can impact not only on their behaviour but also their ability to retain attention and to engage with offending interventions (Harpin & Young, 2012). Anxiety and depression are also prevalent in samples of juvenile offenders (Grisso, 2008) often in conjunction with other mental disorders. Early diagnosis and treatment are essential, because some young people report using illegal substances as a response to a mental disorder or illness in the misguided belief that this will relieve their symptoms (Ashton & Bussu, 2020).

Theoretical explanations frameworks for desistance from deviant groups

Four models have been put forward to explain the impact of a delinquent group on an individual's involvement in offending, and although generally applied to gang membership they are also relevant to co-offending and temporary criminal groups (See Box 8.4 and Curry et al., 2014 for summary).

> **BOX 8.4 MODELS TO EXPLAIN THE RELATIONSHIP BETWEEN THE INDIVIDUAL, THE GROUP AND OFFENDING**
>
> - **Facilitation** – a gang/delinquent group offers more offending opportunities and normalises delinquent behaviour as part of the group identity.
> - **Enhancement** – youth who are already delinquent are more likely to join a gang/delinquent group and then, once a member, their involvement enhances their violent and anti-social behaviour.
> - **Selection** – already delinquent youth are attracted to gangs/groups and that membership has no causal impact on their criminal behaviour.
> - **Invariance** – although gang/delinquent group membership per se is not inherently criminal or criminalising, the onset of gang membership corresponds to an increase in delinquency.

The majority of gang and group offending interventions focus on removing the individual from the influence of others. However, this approach only works effectively under the Facilitation Model because this purports that the individual is delinquent because of the opportunities and culture of the deviant group. In fact, the Enhancement Model has the most support, suggesting that delinquent individuals are attracted to a deviant group, but are not dependent upon others to offend. This would imply that young people who have been involved in gangs or co-offending groups present a continued risk after leaving or separating themselves from their peers. It is possible that the amount of influence the group depends on the individuals. It is important to establish this relationship to support young people who belong to delinquent groups and to consider their role. In respect to gangs, there are a number of individual, social and environmental risk factors that contribute to involvement and desistance (Wood & Alleyne, 2010). Furthermore, this approach reflects current practice within the field of juvenile justice and for the prevention and management of YO. They are discussed in detail below.

Models of interventions

Several theoretical frameworks and approaches have inspired national policy, programmes and intervention approaches in the UK, especially the Risk, Need, Responsivity (RNR) model,[3] developed by Andrews and Bonta (2010). This model stresses the importance of an effective *risk* assessment and that offenders' treatment should be focused on criminogenic *needs* and *responsivity* (individual abilities and commitment to being engaged in the interventions). The RNR model is based on rigorous evidence and risks/needs assessment tools produce important data that can be adopted to make effective decisions. In contrast, the good lives model (GLM) considers it essential to focus on life dimensions other than risk; for example, family, employment, leisure, community and individual well-being (Wilson & Yates, 2009). Similarly, desistance theory (see Trotter, 2016 amongst others) has argued that a focus on risk assessment and management can reduce the opportunities to promote positive changes in the people lives. These desistance approaches are more focused on "individual lives, personal trajectories, individuals' social contexts and networks" (Maruna & Mann, 2019) and how these can impact on the "crime journey". Desistance approaches have had a growing influence on probation policy and practice for both adult offenders and younger people; however, there is limited evidence about its effective for young offenders.

In some ways, these three models have different priorities but at the same time are complementary (Wilson & Yates, 2009). In this regard, a systematic review promoted by Koehler and colleagues (2013) on evaluations of correctional interventions, conducted in Europe, where two-thirds of the studies were carried out in the UK, emphasised that programmes conducted in accordance with the RNR principles (Andrews et al., 2011) indicated a reduction of 16% in reoffending against a baseline of 50%. Studies of community treatment, with small samples and high programme fidelity had larger effect.

Association with other social issues

Youth offending and racialised identity

Some social groups in the UK are disproportionately represented in the CJS. In the year ending March 2018, Black children, for example, were over four times more likely than white children to be arrested (YJB, 2018). It is particularly concerning that these groups are also over-represented in custody. It is important to recognise that this disproportionality does not mean that Black and Asian youth are involved in more criminal behaviours than their white counterparts. Problems of systemic racism in the British CJS have been highlighted (Car, 2017; YJB, 2011) and the need to recognise how the system disadvantages certain communities with a call for comprehensive support have been recognised (Wainwright & Larkins, 2020).

British Asian youth is a neglected group in research on crime victims of ethnic and cultural stereotypes (Goodey, 2001) and as well over-represented in the criminal justice system in 2019–2020, according to MoJ data. Furthermore, the Government's annual youth justice statistics show a record-high proportion of children in youth custody are from Black, south Asian and other ethnic backgrounds (YJB, 2021).

Racial profiling and the mis-association of gang and knife crime with Black British youth remains a problem in some areas of the Youth Justice System and has attracted a considerable amount of criticism in terms of policy and practice (Williams & Clarke, 2016). Again, the statistics consistently show that most young people who are involved in either knife crime or street gangs are racialised as white. Nevertheless, the over-representation of young Black males in the figures for Stop and Search and in the secure estate indicate that this particular myth still impacts on the lives of children and adolescents from African, Black British and Caribbean ancestry and their communities. The problem that gangs present for children from all ethnicised backgrounds is real. The Children's Commissioner (2019) estimated that there are at least 46,000 children in England who are involved in gang activity, and around 4,000 teenagers in London alone are being exploited through child criminal exploitation/county lines.

YO and social deprivation

The connection between social deprivation and crime is multifaceted. In effect, the people, who live in socially deprived areas, are more likely to become victims rather than offenders. This risk factor is not only about poverty but relates to the broader social context where young people are more likely to get exploited and to experience violence and abuse (Webster & Kingston, 2014). Therefore, poverty and social exclusion should be considered when assessing a young person's offending behaviour. Like other risk factors (such as child abuse, parental and sibling drug and alcohol abuse, mental disorders, disengagement from education) poverty can increase the likelihood of involvement in crime as both perpetrator and victim (Sampson & Laub, 2003; Lewontin, 2000). A perceived lack of financial and social opportunities could lead some young people to conclude that their only way of achieving their goals is though crime (Webster & Kingston, 2014). However, in a recent study of YO in England, social deprivation rating was not itself significantly correlated to offending (Ashton et al., 2021) and it is important to remember that it is the minority of young people who live in socially deprived areas who offend.

The relationship of YO to mental disorders and substance use

Offending has often been found to be associated with certain mental disorders (Fazel et al., 2008; Souverein et al., 2019) and substance misuse (alcohol and drug). Young people within the juvenile justice system are among the most vulnerable groups in society and their mental health needs are, in proportion, very high (Fazel et al., 2008; Souverein et al., 2019). Many of these young people present with complex needs such as being in care, suffering from mental and other health problems, and special educational needs. A large proportion have previously been in custody: 38% have experienced time in Youth Offending Institutions and 52% in Secure Training Centres (Home Office, 2015); and more than a third have a diagnosed mental health disorder (Taylor, 2016).

Young adult offenders are less likely than older offenders to be problem drug users, or to use harder and more harmful drugs. Nevertheless, research (Fuller et al., 2013) has shown that drinking among adolescents under the age of 18 years is associated with criminal and disorderly behaviour. Furthermore, substance use and mental disorders are considered key risk factors for violence and re-offending (Farrington et al., 2017). Alcohol misuse also has a relationship to antisocial behaviour. A longitudinal study in the UK (Young et al., 2007) found that antisocial behaviour was a predisposing factor to alcohol misuse, which has both long- and short-term impact on young people. In other studies (see for example Hammerton et al., 2017) excessive alcohol has been found to inhibit the desistance process. We need further research to understand the cause–effect relationship between antisocial behaviour and alcohol misuse, but it is widely accepted that alcohol can reduce inhibitions, impair judgement and increase the risk of aggressive behaviour for some individuals (see Box 8.2 – Youth Justice Statistics).

Current policy and responses to young offenders

Responding to early offending behaviour between the ages of 10 and 17 years is a social priority. Young people who commit crimes from an early age are more likely to become habitual offenders with long and consolidated criminal careers. In effect, many of the most prolific adult offenders began their criminal careers when they were young (Moffitt, 1993). In the long term, preventing offending behaviour at an early age is an effective way to reduce crime and improve lives.

The myth of antisocial and violent gangs of young people who are beyond treatment and help has been debunked. Researchers have long acknowledged that most adolescents who are involved in crime commit non-violent offences and have an age-limited trajectory (Farrighton, 1996; see section "Violent crimes"). Nevertheless, associations between youth, knife crime and gangs persist in the media and remain a focus for Government policy and policing.

Recently, YJB for England and Wales (2019) published standards outlining the minimum expectations for all agencies that provide statutory services to ensure good outcomes for children in the youth justice system. The main principle is considering "child first" and offender second and that young people should be treated and supported humanly when they encounter the justice system (Case & Browning, 2021; see Box 8.5). Involvement in the justice system can constitute a risk to the evolution of the child through the interruption of educational processes and socialisation. Furthermore, Youth Offending Services need to support young people to take responsibility for their actions, even in terms of trial. It is essential for the preparation of interventions to know the personality of the children, their personal, family, social and environmental resources and to provide emotional and psychological support for young people at every stage and level of the proceedings (Bussu & Patrizi, 2013; Bussu et al., 2016).

The Government policy in England and Wales has provided four principle polices to prevent offending and support children's educational engagement (MoJ, 2015):

1. Young people need education and training to enable them to return to school or college or find employment.
2. Increasing the use of "Restorative Justice" approaches where victims are able to explain the impact an offence has caused.
3. Simplifying youth sentences and making them more effective at rehabilitating.
4. Reducing the use of remand in custody for young people, and gradually making local councils responsible for the cost of remand.

The UK government also recognises the vulnerability of young people to criminal exploitation by gangs and their involvement in the sale and trafficking of drugs (Home Office, 2016; Windle et al., 2020). In this regard, the government has disseminated polices and guidelines to help to identify and protect children who are criminally exploited (HO, 2018). However, prevention programmes for criminal exploitation should be introduced in schools before the onset of adolescence (Ashton & Bussu, 2020). According to recent studies (see Ashton & Bussu, 2020), new polices need to take into consideration the impact of new technologies and social media on youth crime involvement. We can anticipate that this risk factor has increased during the COVID-19 pandemic and the lockdowns in UK. A recent study (Bell et al., 2020, 37) has highlighted the concern for some specific groups "at risk of offending or harm to others and include being groomed into gang related activities" (i.e. County Lines and criminal exploitation). In this regard, more attention is required for multidisciplinary research on the COVID-19 pandemic, especially on how criminal groups are taking advantage of this pandemic, and how it has impacted on the crime and illegal economies. According to Bell et al. (2020) and Cowie and Myers (2021), we need to monitor the impact of pandemic on young people's mental health. This observation is especially relevant for vulnerable groups with complex and high forensic risks who often have experienced ACEs, learning difficulties, and mental illness. As researchers and professionals, we need to think of new strategies for promoting personal resilience and collective protective factors to support children and young people to face pandemic-related challenges.

> **BOX 8.5 CHILD FIRST: NATIONAL STANDARDS OF THE YOUTH JUSTICE BOARD FOR ENGLAND AND WALES**
>
> The child first principle is unpacked into four "tenets", each of which includes a range of components (see Case & Browning, 2021).
>
> 1. See children as children;
> 2. Develop pro-social identity for positive child outcomes;
> 3. Collaboration with children;
> 4. Promote diversion.
>
> (See Case & Browning (2021): Child First Justice: the research evidence-base [Full report]. Loughborough University. Report. https://hdl.handle.net/2134/14152040.v1)

Prevention and reduction: offending behaviour programmes and strategies

In order to understand policies relating to the supervision of young offenders, it is necessary to consider the Crime and Disorder Act 1998. This Act prioritises crime prevention and the promotion of community safety by requiring interinstitutional partners to work together, adopting a holistic approach to crime and disorder. More recent and relevant legislations are considered in the Act 2000 "Powers of Criminal Courts", the Act 2008 "Criminal Justice and Immigration" and the Act 2012 "Legal Aid, Sentencing and Punishment of Offenders" (see Box 8.6).

There is a variety of prevention programmes and intervention strategies focused on YO. Usually, these programmes are run within local communities and involve educative agencies most important for young people, like families, school and peers. The most recent UK government strategies (Home Office, 2016; 2018) have shifted from an earlier punitive attitudes and punitive approaches (Home Office, 2011) towards supporting young people and their families. The majority of preventive programmes are focused on young people who are considered at risk, for example, because they were previously involved in crime and anti-social behaviour and/or at risk to re-offend again. Frequently, these programmes are promoted and run by council's local Youth Offending Services/Teams and by other local organisations, such as youth charities. The Crime and Disorder Act 1998 lays out statutory requirements for youth offending teams (YOTs). YOTs have an important role also to help young people who have been arrested, supporting them and their families at court, supervising community sentences and building a collaborative and supportive relationship when they are sentenced to custody. YOTs plan local strategies and services to guarantee positive outcomes for children, including sustainable desistance from crime, and also to prevent children crime involvement and/or anti-social behaviour.

Furthermore, YOTs work by adopting a multiagency and inter-professional approach, collaborating with the police, probation officers, schools and education authorities, health, housing and children's services and charities and the local community (Gov. UK, 2019; Gray, 2016). YOTs also assess children's needs and refer them to effective evidence-based interventions. In the last 20 years, evidence-based interventions for juvenile offenders within a public health framework have grown (Young et al., 2017).

Early preventative work should include parents and care givers to educate them about the impact of negative adult experiences and behaviours on their children (Baglivio et al., 2015). For example, early support for families and children who have a police call out for domestic violence or abuse could prevent violent expressive and acquisitive offending in adolescent (Herrera & McCloskey, 2001). Early prevention focusing on family problems, social inequality, economic deprivation, and juvenile offending should be prioritised to reduce the risk of engaging in offending behaviour.

An important factor that professionals (i.e., psychologists, sociologists, social workers, YOT officers, etc.) need to consider when planning effective interventions is the prevalence rate of youth in the justice system who suffer from mental disorders. The rate of mental disorders and illnesses has been found to be consistently higher for those in the youth justice system compared to the general population of adolescents (Grisso & Barnum, 2000). UK YO behaviour programmes over the last ten years have focused on building life skills and resilience (Hodgkinson et al., 2020); supporting mental health and promoting well-being (Townsend et al., 2010); preventing social exclusion, involving actively the community; developing positive and prosocial networks (Farrington, 2015; Farrington et al., 2012); promoting educational engagement (Humayun & Scott, 2015); and family-based interventions (Farrington & Welsh, 2003; Moodie et al., 2015). Offering comprehensive interventions to support those who exhibit delinquent and criminal behaviours is important and is central to the approaches such as multisystemic therapy (O'Connor & Waddell, 2015). Finally, targeted interventions based on cognitive behavioural approaches can also successfully support children and adolescents to better control their impulsivity (Piquero et al., 2016).

> **BOX 8.6 SOCIAL POLICY AND PREVENTION**
>
> - YO national policy and preventive strategies.
> - Youth crime prevention programmes (Gov.UK, 2020) (https://www.gov.uk/youth-crime-prevention-programmes).
> - Standards for children in the youth justice system (Gov.UK, 2019) (https://www.gov.uk/government/publications/national-standards-for-youth-justice-services).
> - Criminal Exploitation of children and vulnerable adults: County Lines guidance (Home Office, 2018).
> - Collaborative approaches to preventing offending and re-offending by children (CAPRICORN) (Publics Heath England, 2019).
> - Youth justice strategy: progress report (Gov.Scot, 2017) (https://www.gov.scot/publications/youth-justice-strategy-preventing-offending-getting-right-children-young-people/).
> - Prosecution of young people (https://www.gov.scot/publications/thematic-report-prosecution-young-people/).

Summary

The number of children and young people entering the youth justice system has decreased over the last ten years, but at the same time the health and social needs of those in the youth justice system are increasingly complex to manage. In this regard, we need more research and annual statistics to collect robust representative prevalence data on the health and social care needs of children and young people in all sectors of the youth justice system (Lennox & Khan, 2012) and the programme effectiveness to support them.

Furthermore, both national and local authorities and professionals need to consider new strategies and targeted programmes to support young offenders who are victims of criminal grooming, especially in deprived areas, planning pro-social activities and employment opportunities. The role of adult offenders and organised crime groups in grooming and involving children and adolescents in drug sales and violent offending is now recognised, and there has been a call for young people to be recognised as victims rather than perpetrators of crime. This aspect needs to be taken into careful consideration for policy and interventions. To design gang interventions and individual therapeutic support and to ensure that there is support who those who leave a gang. It is also essential that youth workers and YOTs recognise that leaving a gang is, in fact, the norm and that with support the majority of young people can and will cease to be involved with deviant groups (Ashton & Bussu, 2020). Professionals, supported by national and local authorities, need to plan more effective interventions, adopting a multiagency and inter-professional approach that involving schools and education authorities, health, children's services, charities, and the local community.

Points to ponder

1 What does the term "county lines" refer to?
2 What *risks factors* are associated with drug use?
3 Which mental disorders have a relationship to offending?
4 What *protective factors* can mitigate adverse childhood experiences as a risk?
5 What key elements featured in the Youth Justice Board 2019 standards for minimum expectations for agencies working with young people who offend?

Quiz

Take the following 10-item quiz

1 In the UK, the Justice System classifies "juvenile offenders" as all young people aged ____ to _____ and "young offenders" as all young people aged _____ to _____ (fill in the blanks).
2 Gang members recruit young people (true/false).
3 We do not have evidence about adult offenders and organised crime groups in grooming and involving children and adolescents in drug sales and violent offending (true/false).
4 Young people are often wrongly associated with: a) non-violent crime b) violent crime c) violent and non-violent crime.
5 The rate of mental disorders and illnesses has been found to be consistently higher for those in the youth justice system compared to the general population of adolescents (true/false).
6 The people, who live in socially deprived areas, are more likely to become victims rather than offenders (true/false).

7 What risks are associated with drug use? (open question).
8 RNR is the acronym of: (a) Risk Need Responsivity model, (b) Risk Neighbourhood Responsivity and (c) Risk Neutral Responsivity.
9 The Desistance Theory has argued that a focus on risk assessment and management can increase the opportunities to promote positive changes in the people lives (true/false).
10 We need to support young offenders, who are victims of criminal grooming, especially in deprived areas, planning pro-social activities and employment opportunities (true/false).

Answers: 1. "juvenile offenders", 10–17 years; "young offenders" – 18–21 years; 2. True; 3. False; 4. b; 5. True; 6. True; 7 (open question); 8. a; 9. False; 10. True.

Activities

Read the real "case study" below and answer and discuss in a small group, and/or individually, the following explorative questions:
"So, one of the lads who I was - one of the lads who was up here, he lived quite near me, I was good mates with him, and he's the one who kind of taught me how to, you know, whip it and that, and his family were involved in that, and his, you know, and it kind of went like that, and he said, You know, ring him, and he said Yeah, get him to come down, and then one of his family members said, You know, while you're making it, you know, you can sell it at the same time and earn a bit more money, do you know what I mean, so, say he'll pay you five hundred quid a week just for running it, then you'll get maybe a grand a week for making it, do you know what I mean, so it works out a lot, so it's kind of like the guy I'm working for's idea, you know what I mean".
(Taken from Ashton & Bussu, 2020)

Questions:

What economic, psychological, and social risk factors are referenced in the case study?
What elements would interventions need to include to comprehensively support the young person?

Further reading

Harding, S. (2020). *County lines: exploitation and drug dealing among urban street gangs*. Bristol: Bristol University press.
Pitts, J. (1999). *Working with young offenders*. (2nd ed.). Basingstoke: Palgrave Macmillan.

Service user organisations working in the topic area

The Prisons and Young Offenders Institutions (Scotland): https://www.legislation.gov.uk/ssi/2011/331/contents/made

Youth offending teams: https://www.gov.uk/youth-offending-team
Youth Justice Agency (Northern Ireland): https://www.justice-ni.gov.uk/topics/youth-justice/youth-justice-agency
Youth Justice Board (YJB): https://www.gov.uk/government/organisations/youth-justice-board-for-england-and-wales

Supplementary reading

Ashton, S., & Bussu, A. (2020). Peer groups, street gangs and organised crime in the narratives of adolescent male offenders. *Journal of Criminal Psychology, 10*(4), 277–292.

Ashton, S., Ioannou, M., Hammond, L., & Synnott, J. (2020). The relationship of offending style to psychological and social risk factors in a sample of adolescent males. *Investigative Psychology and Offender Profiling, 17*(2), 76–92.

Farrington, D. P., Gaffney H., & Ttofi M. M. (2017). Systematic reviews of explanatory risk factors for violence, offending, and delinquency. *Aggression and Violent Behavior, 33*, 24–36.

Helpful topic related websites

Youth offenders: https://www.cps.gov.uk/legal-guidance/youth-offenders
Young offenders Institution, England and Wales: https://www.legislation.gov.uk/uksi/y?sort=year
Young offenders policy: https://www.gov.uk/government/publications/2010-to-2015-government-policy-young-offenders/2010-to-2015-government-policy-young-offenders
Young offenders, Northern Ireland: https://www.nidirect.gov.uk/articles/youth-justice
Young offenders, Scotland: https://www.gov.scot/policies/youth-justice/

Notes

1 YJB is an executive non-departmental public body, sponsored by the Ministry of Justice.
2 https://www.legislation.gov.uk/ukpga/1998/37/contents.
3 Risk – the level of assessment or intervention should match the level of risk. Need – treatment or intervention should focus on those factors which are most clearly linked to offending (criminogenic needs). Responsivity – the intervention should be tailored to the needs of the individual to enhance their ability to engage.

References

Aebi, M. F., Tiago, M. M., Berger-Kolopp L., & Burkhardt C. (2017). SPACE I—Council of Europe Annual Penal Statistics: prison populations. Survey 2016. Strasbourg: Council of Europe.

Aldridge, J., Medina-Ariz, J., & Ralphs, R. (2012). Counting gangs: Conceptual and validity problems with the Eurogang definition. In *Youth Gangs in International Perspective* (pp. 35–51). New York, NY: Springer.

Andresen, M. A., & Felson, M. (2010). The impact of co-offending. *British Journal of Criminology, 50*(1), 66–81. https://doi.org/10.1093/bjc/azp043

Andrews, D. A., & Bonta, J. (2010). *The psychology of criminal conduct*: Routledge.

Andrews, D. A., Bonta, J., & Wormith, J. S. (2011). The risk-need-responsivity (RNR) model: does adding the good lives model contribute to effective crime prevention? *Criminal Justice and Behavior, 38*(7), 735–755. https://doi.org/10.1177/0093854811406356

Ashton, S., & Bussu, A. (2020). Peer groups, street gangs and organised crime in the narratives of adolescent male offenders. *Journal of Criminal Psychology, 10*(4), 277–292. https://doi.org/10.1108/JCP-06-2020-0020

Ashton, S., Ioannou, M., Hammond, L., & Synnott, J. (2020). The relationship of offending style to psychological and social risk factors in a sample of adolescent males. *Investigative Pyschology and Offender Profiling, 17*(2), 76–92. https://doi.org/10.1002/jip.1548

Ashton, S., Valentine, M., & Chan, B. (2021). The relationship of psychological and social risk factors to violent offending in a sample of adolescent males. *International Journal of Offender Therapy and Comparative Criminology*, 1–17.

Baglivio, M. T., Epps, N., Swartz, K., Huq, M. S., Sheer, A., & Hardt, N. S. (2014). The prevalence of Adverse Childhood Experiences (ACE) in the lives of juvenile offenders. *Journal of Juvenile Justice, 3*, 12–34.

Baglivio, M. T., Wolff, K. T., Epps, N., & Nelson, R. (2015). Predicting adverse childhood experiences: the importance of neighborhood context in youth trauma among delinquent youth. *Crime & Delinquency, 63*(2), 166–188. https://doi.org/10.1177/0011128715570628

Bell, G., Deshpande, M., Hales, H., Harding, D., Pendlebury, G., & White, O. (2020). Multidisciplinary research priorities for the COVID-19 pandemic. *The Lancet Psychiatry, 7*(7), e37–e38.

Bennett, T., & Holloway, K. (2004). Gang membership, drugs and crime in the UK. *British Journal of Criminology, 44*(3), 305–323.

Bussu, A., & Patrizi, P. (2013). Best practices of a promotional and restorative community.

Bussu, A., Patrizi, P., & Lepri, G. (2016). In need of a cultural shift to promote restorative justice in Southern Europe. *Contemporary Justice Review, 19*(4), 479–503. https://doi.org/10.1080/10282580.2016.1226814.

Carr, N. (2017). The Lammy Review and race and bias in the criminal justice system. *Probation Journal, 64*(4), 333–336.

Case, S. & Browning, A. (2021). Child First Justice: the research evidence-base [Full report]. Loughborough University. Report. https://hdl.handle.net/2134/14152040.v1

Children's Commissioner (2019). Keeping Kids safe. Improving safeguarding responses to gang violence and criminal exploitation. https://www.childrenscommissioner.gov.uk/wp-content/uploads/2019/02/CCO-Gangs.pdf

Coomber, R., & Moyle, L. (2018). The changing shape of street-level heroin and crack supply in England: commuting, holidaying and cuckooing drug dealers across 'county lines'. *British Journal of Criminology, 58*(6), 1323–1342. https://doi.org/10.1093/bjc/azx068

Cowie, H., & Myers, C. A. (2021). The impact of the COVID-19 pandemic on the mental health and well-being of children and young people. *Children & Society, 35*(1), 62–74.

Craig, J. M., Piquero, A. R., Farrington, D. P., & Ttofi, M. M. (2017). A little early risk goes a long bad way: Adverse childhood experiences and life-course offending in the Cambridge study. *Journal of Criminal Justice, 53*, 34–45.

Curry, G. D., Decker, S. H., & Pyrooz, D. C. (2014). *Confronting gangs: crime and community* (Third Edition). Oxford University Press.

Curry, G. D. (2015). The logic of defining gangs revisited. In Decker, S. H. & Pyrooz, D. C. (Eds.), *The handbook of gangs* (pp. 7–27). Wiley-Blackwell.

Densley, J. (2012). The organization of London's Street Gangs, *Global Crime, 13*, 42–64. https://doi.org/10.1080/17440572.2011.632497

Dmitrieva, J., Gibson L., Steinberg L., Piquero A. & Fagan, J. (2014). Predictors and consequences of gang membership: comparing gang members, gang leaders, and non–gang-affiliated adjudicated youth. *Journal of Research on Adolescence, 24*(2), 220–234. https://doi.org/10.1111/jora.12111

Farrighton, D. P. (1996). *Understanding and preventing youth crime.* Joseph Rowntree Foundation: York Publishing Services.

Farrington, D. P. & Welsh, B. C. (2003). Family-based prevention of offending: a meta-analysis. *Australian & New Zealand Journal of Criminology, 36*(2), 127–151. https://doi.org/10.1375/acri.36.2.127

Farrington, D. P., Loeber, R., & Ttofi, M. (2012). Crime prevention and public policy. In Farrington, D. P. & Brandon, C. W. (Eds.), *The Oxford handbook of crime prevention* (pp. 1–18). Oxford.

Farrington, D. P. (2015). The developmental evidence base: psychosocial research. In Crighton, D. A. & Towl G. J. (Eds.), *Forensic psychology* (2nd Ed., pp. 161–181). Wiley.

Farrington, D. P., Gaffney, H., & Ttofi, M. M. (2017). Systematic reviews of explanatory risk factors for violence, offending, and delinquency, *Aggression and Violent Behavior, 33*, 24–36. https://doi.org/10.1016/j.avb.2016.11.004

Fazel, S., Doll, H., & Långström, N. (2008). Mental disorders among adolescents in juvenile detention and correctional facilities: a systematic review and metaregression analysis of 25 surveys. *Journal of the American Academy of Child and Adolescent Psychiatry, 47*(9), 1010–1019. https://doi.org/10.1097/CHI.Ob013e31817eecf3

Felitti, V. J., Anda, R. F., Nordenberg, D., Williamson, D. F., Spitz, A. M., Edwards, V. et al. (1998). Relationship of childhood abuse and household dysfunction to many of the leading causes of death in adults: the Adverse Childhood Experiences (ACE) study. *American Journal of Preventative Medicine, 14*, 245–258. https://doi.org/10.1016/S0749-3797(98)00017-8

Flannery, D. J., Singer, M. I., & Wester, K. (2001). Violence exposure, psychological trauma and suicide risk in a community sample of dangerously violent adolescents. *Journal of the American Academy of Child and Adolescent Psychiatry, 40*, 435–442. https://doi.org/10.1097/00004583-200104000-00012

Flannery, D. J, Singer, M. I., Van Dulmen, M., Kretschmar, J., & Belliston, L. (2006). Exposure to violence, mental health and violent behavior. In Flannery, D. J., Vazsonyi, A. T., & Waldman, I. (Eds.), *The Cambridge handbook of violent behavior*. Cambridge University Press.

Fuller, E., Henderson, H., Nass, L., Payne, C., Phelps, A., & Ryley, A. (2013). Smoking, drinking and drug use among young people in England in 2012. Health and Social Care Information Centre, L.S.

Goodey, J. (2001). The criminalization of British Asian youth: research from Bradford and Sheffield. *Journal of Youth Studies, 4*(4), 429–450. https://doi.org/10.1080/13676260120101897

Gov.Scot (2017) Youth justice strategy: progress report. https://www.gov.scot/publications/youth-justice-strategy-preventing-offending-getting-right-children-young-people/

Gov.Scot (2020). Policy youth justice. https://www.gov.scot/policies/youth-justice/raising-age-criminal-responsibility/

Gov.UK (2018). Youth justice statistics: 2018 to 2019. Youth justice annual statistics for 2018 to 2019 for England and Wales. https://www.gov.uk/government/statistics/youth-justice-statistics-2018-to-2019

Gov.Uk (2019). Standards for children in the youth justice system https://www.gov.uk/government/publications/national-standards-for-youth-justice-services

Gov.UK (2020). Youth crime prevention programmes. https://www.gov.uk/youth-crime-prevention-programmes

Gray, P. (2016). 'Child friendly' international human rights standards and youth offending team partnerships. *International Journal of Law, Crime and Justice, 45*, 59–74. http://dx.doi.org/10.1016/j.ijlcj.2015.11.001

Grisso, T., & Barnum, R. (2000). Massachusetts youth screening instrument, Second Version: User Manual and Technical Report; University of Massachusetts Medical School: Worcester.

Grisso, T. (2008). Adolescent offenders with mental disorders, *The Future of Children, 18*(2):143–164. http://dx.doi.org/10.1353/foc.0.0016

Hammerton, G., Mahedy, L., Murray, J., Maughan, B., Edwards, A. C., Kendler, K. S., Hickman, M., & Heron, J. (2017). Effects of excessive alcohol use on antisocial behavior across adolescence and early adulthood. *Journal of the American Academy of Child and Adolescent Psychiatry, 56*(10), 857–865. https://doi.org/10.1016/j.jaac.2017.07.781

Harpin, V., & Young, S. (2012). The challenge of ADHD and youth offending. *Cutting Edge Psychiatry in Practice, 1*, 138–143.

Herrera, V. M., & McCloskey, L. A. (2001). Gender differences in the risk for delinquency among youth exposed to family violence. *Child Abuse & Neglect, 25*(8), 1037–1051. https://doi.org/10.1016/S0145-2134(01)00255-1

Hesketh, R. F., & Robinson, G. (2019). Grafting: "The boyz" just doing business? Deviant entrepreneurship in street gangs. *Safer Communities, 18*(2), 54–63. https://doi.org/10.1108/SC-05-2019-0016

Hirschi, T., & Gottfredson, M. R. (2000). In defense of self-control. *Theoretical Criminology, 4*(1), 55–69. https://doi.org/10.1177/1362480600004001003

Hodgkinson, R., Beattie S., Roberts R., & Hardy, L. (2020). Psychological resilience interventions to reduce recidivism in young people: a systematic review. *Adolescent Research Review, 6*, 333–357. https://doi.org/10.1007/s40894-020-00138-x

Hodgson, B. (2007). Co-offending in UK police recorded crime data. *The Police Journal: Theory, Practice and Principles, 80*(4), 333–353. https://doi.org/10.1350/pojo.2007.80.4.333

Home Office (2011). Youth Justice Statistics 2011/12 England and Wales. Youth Justice Board / Ministry of Justice Statistics bulletin.

Home Office (2015). Collection Home Office circulars 2015. https://www.gov.uk/government/collections/home-office-circulars-2015

Home Office (2016). *Ending gang violence and exploitation*. HM Government. https://assets.publishing.service.gov.uk/government/uploads/system/uploads/attachment_data/file/491699/Ending_gang_violence_and_Exploitation_FINAL.pdf

Home Office (2018). *Criminal exploitation of children and vulnerable adults: county lines guidance*.

Humayun, S., & Scott, S. (2015). Evidence-based interventions for violent behavior in children and adolescents. *Violence and Mental Health*, 391–419. https://doi.org/10.1007%2F978-94-017-8999-8_18

Koehler, J. A., Lösel, F., Akoensi, T. D., & Humphreys, D. K. (2013). A systematic review and meta-analysis on the effects of young offender treatment programs in Europe. *Journal of Experimental Criminology, 9*(1), 19–43. https://doi.org/10.1007/s11292-012-9159-7

Lennox, C., & Khan, L. (2012). Youth justice. https://assets.publishing.service.gov.uk/government/uploads/system/uploads/attachment_data/file/252662/33571_2901304_CMO_Chapter_12.pdf

Lewontin, R. (2000). *The triple helix: Gene, organism, and environment*. Cambridge, MA: Harvard University Press.

Maruna, S., & Mann, R. (2019). Reconciling 'desistance' and 'what works'. https://www.justiceinspectorates.gov.uk/hmiprobation/wp-content/uploads/sites/5/2019/02/Academic-Insights-Maruna-and-Mann-Feb-19-final.pdf

McCord, J., & Conway, K. P. (2002). Patterns of juvenile delinquency and co-offending. In Waring, E. J. & Weisburd, D. (Eds.), *Crime and social organization. Advances in criminological theory*. Vol. 10 (pp. 15–30). Transaction Publishers.

McGloin, J. M., & O'Neill Shermer, L. (2009). Self-control and deviant peer network structure. *Journal of Research in Crime and Delinquency, 46*(1), 35–72. http://jrc.sagepub.com/cgi/content/abstract/46/1/35

McLean, R. (2017). An evolving gang model in contemporary Scotland. *Deviant Behavior, 39*, 309–321. https://doi.org/10.1080/01639625.2016.1272969

Ministry of Justice (2015). 2010 to 2015 government policy: young offenders. https://www.gov.uk/government/publications/2010-to-2015-government-policy-young-offenders/2010-to-2015-government-policy-young-offenders

Moffitt, T. E. (1993). Adolescence-limited and life-course-persistent antisocial behavior: a developmental taxonomy. *Psychological Review, 100*(4), 674–701.

Monahan, K. C., Steinberg, L., & Cauffman, E. (2009). Affiliation with antisocial peers, susceptibility to peer influence, and antisocial behavior during the transition to adulthood. *Developmental Psychology, 45*(6), 1520–1530.

Moodie, K., Vaswani, N., Shaw, J., Morton, P., Orr, D., Allardyce, S., & Connelly, G. (2015). *Working with young people who offend: An examination of the literature regarding violence, substance misuse and harmful sexual behaviour*. http://www.cycj.org.uk/wp-content/uploads/2015/07/Working-with-young-people-who-offend-website-copy.pdf

National Crime Agency (NCA) (2019). *National crime agency annual report and accounts.* https://www.nationalcrimeagency.gov.uk/who-we-are/publications/329-nca-annual-report-accounts-2018-19/file

O'Connor, R. M., & Waddell, S. (2015). What works to prevent gang involvement, youth crime and violence: a rapid review of interventions delivered in the UK and abroad. The Early Intervention Foundation.

Oudekerk, B., & Morgan, R. E. (2016). *Co-offending among adolescents in violent victimizations, 2004–13.* US Department of Justice, Office of Justice Programs, Bureau of Justice Statistics.

Piquero, A. R., Jennings, W. G., Farrington, D. P., Diamond, B., & Gonzalez, J. M. R. (2016). A meta-analysis update on the effectiveness of early self-control improvement programs to improve. *Journal of Experimental Criminology, 12,* 249–264. https://doi.org/10.1007/s11292-016-9257-z

Publics Heath England (2015). A guide to community-centred approaches for health and wellbeing. https://assets.publishing.service.gov.uk/government/uploads/system/uploads/attachment_data/file/768979/A_guide_to_community-centred_approaches_for_health_and_wellbeing__full_report_.pdf

Public Health England (2019). Young people's substance misuse treatment statistics 2018 to 2019: report. https://www.gov.uk/government/statistics/substance-misuse-treatment-for-young-people-statistics-2018-to-2019/young-peoples-substance-misuse-treatment-statistics-2018-to-2019-report

Pyrooz, D. C., Sweeten, G., & Piquero, A. R. (2013). Continuity and change in gang membership and gang embeddedness. *Journal of Research in Crime and Delinquency, 50*(2), 239–271. https://doi.org/10.1177/0022427811434830

Richardson, R., Trépel D., Perry A., Ali, S., Duffy, S., Gabe, R., Gilbody, S., Glanville, J., Hewitt, C., Manea, L., Palmer, S., Wright, B., & McMillan, D. (2015). Screening for psychological and mental health difficulties in young people who offend. *Health Technology Assessment, 19*(1). https://doi.org/10.3310/hta19010

Rutter, M. (1983). Stress, coping, and development: some issues and some questions. In Garmezy, N. & Rutter, M. (Eds.), Ctr for Advanced Study in the Behavioral Sciences, Inc, *Stress, coping, and development in children* (pp. 1–41). Johns Hopkins University Press. (A slightly modified version of this chapter appeared in the "Journal of Child Psychology and Psychiatry," 1981, Vol. 22).

Sampson, R. J., & Laub, J. H. (2003). Desistance from crime over the life course. In *Handbook of the life course* (pp. 295–309). Springer, Boston, MA.

Social Mobility Commission (2019). Monitoring social mobility. https://assets.publishing.service.gov.uk/government/uploads/system/uploads/attachment_data/file/891155/Monitoring_report_2013-2020_-Web_version.pdf#page=17

Souverein, F., Van Dorp, M., De Heide, B., De Hair, K., Van Dijk, J., Van Domburgh, L., Popma, A., & Mulder, E. (2019). *Jaarrapport 2018 monitor kleinschalige voorziening Amsterdam.* Ministerie van Justitie, Dienst Justitiële Inrichtingen.

Steinberg, L. (2010). A dual system model of adolescent risk-taking. *Development Psychobiology, 2017–2024, 52*(3), 216–224. https://doi.org/10.1002/dev.20445. PMID: 20213754.

Taylor, C. (2016). Review of the youth justice system in England and Wales. https://assets.publishing.service.gov.uk/government/uploads/system/uploads/attachment_data/file/577105/youth-justice-review-final-report-print.pdf

Townsend, E., Walker, D. M., Sargeant, S., Vostanis, P., Hawton, K., Stocker, O., & Sitholeb, J. (2010). Systematic review and meta-analysis of interventions relevant for young offenders with mood disorders, anxiety disorders, or self-harm. *Journal of Adolescence, 33*(1), 9–20. https://doi.org/10.1016/j.adolescence.2009.05.015. Epub 2009 Jun 27. PMID: 19560808.

Trotter, C. (2016). Risk assessment in practice. In Trotter, G. M. C. & McNeill, F. (Eds.), *Beyond the risk paradigm in criminal justice.* Palgrave.

UNCRC (2007). Committee on the rights of the children. Forty-fourth session Geneva, 15 January 2007. https://www2.ohchr.org/english/bodies/crc/docs/CRC.C.GC.10.pdf

Wainwright, J., & Larkins, C. (2020). Race, ethnicity, young people and offending: the elephant in the room. *Social Identities, 26*(1), 128–144. https://doi.org/10.1080/13504630.2019.1684887

Warr, M. (2002). *Companions in crime: The social aspects of criminal conduct.* Cambridge University Press.

Webster, C., & Kingston, S. (2014). Poverty and crime review. https://eprints.lancs.ac.uk/id/eprint/71188/1/JRF_Final_Poverty_and_Crime_Review_May_2014.pdf

Weerman, F. M. (2003). Co-offending as social exchange: explaining characteristics of co-offending. *The British Journal of Criminology, 43*(2), 398–416. https://www.jstor.org/stable/23638860

Wibbelink, C. J. M., Hoeve, M., Stams, G. J. J. M., & Oort, F. J. (2017). A meta-analysis of the association between mental disorders and juvenile recidivism. *Aggression and Violent Behavior, 33,* 78–90. https://doi.org/10.1016/j.avb.2017.01.005

Williams, P., & Clarke, B. (2016). Dangerous associations: joint enterprise, gangs and racism. *Centre for Crime and Justice Studies.* https://www.crimeandjustice.org.uk/sites/crimeandjustice.org.uk/files/Dangerous%20assocations%20Joint%20Enterprise%20gangs%20and%20racism.pdf

Wilson, R. J., & Yates, P. M. (2009). Effective interventions and the Good Lives Model: maximizing treatment gains for sexual offenders. *Aggression and Violent Behavior, 14*(3), 157–161. https://doi.org/10.1016/j.avb.2009.01.007

Windle, J., Moyle, L., & Coomber, R. (2020). 'Vulnerable' kids going country: children and young people's involvement in county lines drug dealing. *Youth Justice, 20*(1–2), 64–78. https://doi.org/10.1177/1473225420902840

Wood, J., & Alleyne, E. (2010). Street gang theory and research: where are we now and where do we go from here? *Aggression and Violent Behavior, 15*(2), 100–111. https://doi.org/10.1016/j.avb.2009.08.005

Wolff, K. T., Baglivio, M. T., & Piquero, A. R. (2017). The relationship between adverse childhood experiences and recidivism in a sample of juvenile offenders in community-based treatment. *International Journal of Offender Therapy and Comparative Criminology, 61*(11), 1210–1242. https://doi.org/10.1177/0306624X15613992

Young, R., Sweeting, H., & West, P. (2007) A longitudinal study of alcohol use and antisocial behaviour in young people. *Alcohol and Alcoholism, 43*(2): 204–214. https://doi.org/10.1093/alcalc/agm147

Young, S., Greer, B., & Church, R. (2017). Juvenile delinquency, welfare, justice and therapeutic interventions: a global perspective. *BJPsych Bulletin, 41*(1), 21–29. https://doi.org/10.1192/pb.bp.115.052274

Youth Justice Board (2011). Youth Justice Board for England and Wales annual report and accounts 2010 to 2011. **https://www.gov.uk/government/publications/the-youth-justice-board-for-england-and-wales-annual-report-and-accounts-2010-to-2011**Youth Justice Board and Ministry of Justice (2018). Youth Justice Statistics 2017/18. https://assets.publishing.service.gov.uk/government/uploads/system/uploads/attachment_data/file/774866/youth_justice_statistics_bulletin_2017_2018.pdf

Youth Justice Board and Ministry of Justice (2019). Standards for children in the youth justice system 2019. https://assets.publishing.service.gov.uk/government/uploads/system/uploads/attachment_data/file/957697/Standards_for_children_in_youth_justice_services_2019.doc.pdf

Youth Justice Board and Ministry of Justice (2020). Youth Justice Statistics 2018/19. England and Wales, Ministry of Justice. https://assets.publishing.service.gov.uk/government/uploads/system/uploads/attachment_data/file/956621/youth-justice-statistics-2019-2020.pdf

Youth Justice Board and Ministry of Justice (2021). Youth Justice Statistics 2019/20. England and Wales, Ministry of Justice.

9 Alcohol misuse
One too many?

Selwyn Stanley

Introduction

Lowe (1990) states that 'Alcohol is the oldest and most widely used intoxicant. There are relatively few places on the surface of this planet where the inhabitants do not imbibe with enthusiasm and enjoyment' (p. 53).

Since time immemorial, people have experimented with mood-altering substances for various reasons ranging from stress relief and recreation to seeking a psychedelic or transcendental experience. One of the earliest such substances discovered by man was alcohol (from the Arabic: *al-kuhul* or *al-khol*), cherished for its intoxicating effects and mind-altering properties. Quite early in time, in a moment of *Eureka*, the primitive man discovered that ripening and rotting fruits in a warm climate produced juices that had an exhilarating influence on the mind. The discovery of yeast and its role in speeding up the process of fermentation was not far behind, and the liquid became popular in many civilisations around the world. Alcohol is one of the most used substances the world over (along with nicotine and caffeine), and its use is socially and legally sanctioned in most societies. In times gone by, alcohol consumption has found a place of significance in the courts of many kings and emperors, has simultaneously been exalted by statesmen, philosophers, poets, and writers, on one hand, and on the other, vilified as the devil's brew for the erratic and unpredictable behaviour that it often generates. While for some people drinking alcohol is not a matter of concern, what becomes worrisome is when drinking overwhelms one's daily existence, interferes with functioning, and causes harm to oneself and to others. The individual has then crossed the line into the grey shades of misuse and into the realms of addiction or alcoholism. It is this individual who is the focal point of this chapter, whose dalliance with alcohol has generated tons of scientific and empirical literature and has captivated the attention of professionals from several disciplines such as sociology, medicine, public health, nursing, and social work.

BOX 9.1 CELEBRITY ALCOHOL-RELATED DEATHS

Mickey Mantle – Professional baseball player
Stuart Cable – Drummer of 'Stereophonics'
Keith Moon – Drummer of 'The Who'
Bon Scott – Lead singer of 'AC/DC'
Richard Burton – Actor
F. Scott Fitzgerald – Author
Amy Winehouse – Singer and songwriter

Terminology: alcoholism, alcohol misuse, or dependence?

The term alcoholism was originally coined in 1849 by Magnus Huss and was used to refer to chronic continual drinking or periodic consumption of alcohol, which is characterised by impaired control over drinking, frequent episodes of intoxication, preoccupation with alcohol and the use of alcohol despite adverse consequences. The NIAAA defines alcoholism (National Institute on Alcohol Abuse and Alcoholism, USA) as when one can no longer control the use of alcohol and compulsively abuses alcohol, despite its negative ramifications, and/or experience of emotional distress when not drinking.

BOX 9.2 MYTHS ABOUT ALCOHOL

MYTH: Every person reacts to alcohol in the same way.
FACT: Many factors affect a person's reaction to alcohol – body weight, metabolism, gender, body chemistry, and the environmental context are a few.
MYTH: Eating a big meal before dinking will keep one sober.
FACT: Drinking on a full stomach will only delay the absorption of alcohol into the bloodstream, not prevent it.
MYTH: Cold showers, fresh air, or hot coffee help sober a person.
FACT: Only time will remove alcohol from the system. It takes the body approximately one hour to eliminate the alcohol in one drink. An old saying goes, "give a drunk a cup of coffee and all you have is a wide-awake drunk".
MYTH: Alcohol is a stimulant.
FACT: Alcohol is a depressant, slows down motor skills, retards behaviour, and influences movement and reaction time. That's why large doses induce sleep.
MYTH: Alcohol improves sex.
FACT: Alcohol can make people feel less uncomfortable in a social situation. Excessive consumption can lower the sex drive in both genders and result in erectile problems in men.
MYTH: I am too old to develop a drinking problem.
FACT: Many people develop problems with drinking at a later age.
MYTH: I will not have a problem as I only drink wine or beer.
FACT: Problem drinking is not about what you drink, but how it affects your life.

Alcohol dependence is another term used to refer to 'alcoholism' and is characterised by an uncontrollable urge to drink. Dependence could be manifested in terms of physical and/or psychological dependence. The International Classification of Diseases (ICD) published by the World Health Organization (WHO) is a clinical diagnostic system used globally by several countries including the UK. The most recent revision of the ICD published in 2019, ICD-11, includes alcohol dependence as the 'master diagnosis' and distinguishes this from 'Harmful Pattern of Use of Alcohol' and 'Hazardous Alcohol Use'. While 'Harmful Use' is defined as repeated consumption of alcohol leading to physical or mental harm; 'Hazardous Use' refers to repeated use of alcohol in amounts or in patterns that potentially carry the risk of future harm. Alcohol dependence is a disorder of regulation of alcohol use arising from its repeated or continuous use, characterised by a strong internal drive to use alcohol, which is manifested by impaired ability to control its use, increasing priority given to use over other activities and persistence of use despite harm or negative consequences. These experiences are often accompanied by a subjective sensation of urge or craving to use alcohol. Physiological features of dependence may also be present, including tolerance to the effects of alcohol, withdrawal symptoms following cessation or reduction in alcohol use, or repeated use of alcohol to prevent or alleviate withdrawal symptoms (Saunders et al., 2019).

The UK prefers the use of the term 'alcohol misuse' as against the use of terms such as alcohol addiction and alcoholism mostly found in the American literature. In the UK, the NICE guidelines and the NHS use the term alcohol misuse to encompass both people with alcohol dependence and those with patterns of harmful alcohol use. Simply stated, alcohol misuse refers to drinking excessively; more than the lower-risk limits of alcohol consumption (for safe drinking guidelines see Box 9.1). It is hence the use of alcohol for a purpose not consistent with legal or medical guidelines (WHO, 2020).

The addiction cycle

The individual goes through multiple stages before reaching the phase of addiction. This can occur over a short period of time or take months or years to develop. The cycle of addiction may involve moving from initial use to abuse, the development of tolerance, addiction, and relapse (Figure 9.1).

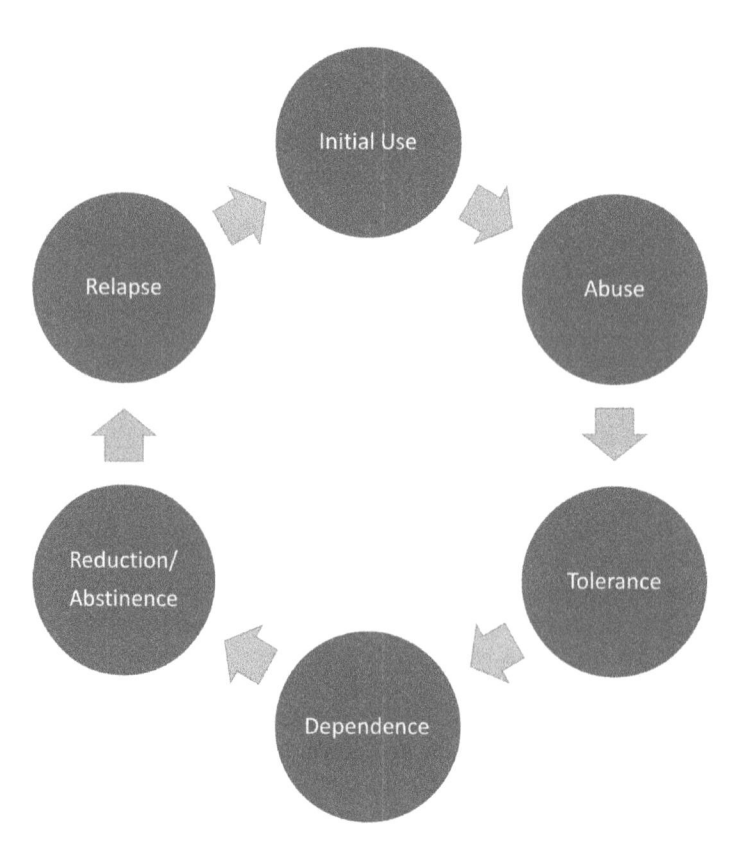

Figure 9.1 The addiction cycle.

Alcohol consumption patterns across the UK

The Global Drugs Survey (2019) included 5,400 people from the four nations of the UK and more than 120,000 from 36 countries between October and December 2018. Britons reported getting drunk an average of 51.1 times in a 12-month period – almost once a week, with the USA, Canada, and Australia closely following the UK at the top of the global rankings. Comparisons of the four UK nations indicate that around four in five adults drink and one in five are teetotallers.

In England, in 2018, 82% of adults drank alcohol in the past 12 months, with 49% of adults drinking at least once a week, with a higher proportion of men than women consumers (86% and 79%, respectively) (Health Survey for England, 2018). The proportion of men and women drinking over the low-risk drinking guidelines (Figure 9.2) of 14 units in a week varied across age groups and was most common among men and women aged 55–64 years (38% and 19%, respectively; NHS Digital, 2020).

In Scotland, in 2019, adults bought an average of 9.9 litres of alcohol, equivalent to 19 units per week for each person. One in four people (24%) drink at hazardous or harmful

Figure 9.2 Low-risk drinking guidelines.

levels (more than 14 units per week). This constitutes 32% of men and 16% of women (Scottish Health Survey, 2019).

According to the National Survey for Wales, in 2018–2019, 2% of adults were harmful drinkers and 16% of adults were hazardous drinkers; 25% of male and 12% of female drinkers consumed above the weekly guideline of 14 units per week. In relation to age, 22% of adults in the 45–64 age group consumed over the weekly guidelines when compared to 17% in the 65+ and 16% in the <44 age groups.

The Health Survey of Northern Ireland, 2018/2019, reports that over three-quarters (79%) of adults aged 18 and over drink alcohol. Over four-fifths of males (83%) were drinkers, with a tenth of males (9%) reporting that they drank heavily. Three-quarters of females (76%) were drinkers, with 2% reporting heavy drinking.

Consumption during lockdown

A survey of 2,000 people in the UK commissioned by Alcohol Change and the Alcohol Health Alliance (2020), found that 28% of people agreed to have drunk more alcohol than usual during lockdown. Younger people and those who were working were more likely to agree that they had been drinking more than those who were older or were not working. For those working from home, perhaps a drink at the end of the day is a reward for the zillions of hours spent staring at a monitor. Perhaps this also suggests that going out for work on weekdays is a good way of staying away from the bottle! 13% in this study said their typical number of units had increased, 12% said it had dropped, and 60% said it was unchanged. A considerable number of current and former drinkers (7%) stopped drinking completely during lockdown. This was more pronounced among younger people, with 11% of 18–34-year olds saying they have stopped drinking during lockdown. This is particularly encouraging and possibly reflects a growing concern over slipping into higher levels of consumption and increasing health consciousness.

The Royal College of Psychiatrists observed that nearly half (45%) of its psychiatrists had seen a rise in patients whose alcohol or drug use had contributed to a deterioration in their mental health during the pandemic (The Telegraph, 15 Nov). Data from Public Health England (PHE) show that older age groups significantly increased their alcohol intake during lockdown, with a fifth of those aged 45–74 years drinking more than 21 units a week (Institute of Alcohol Studies, 2020).

Socio-cultural influences on alcohol consumption

Socio-cultural factors largely determine how substance use and abuse are constructed, regulated, and perceived the world over. A report by the Social Issues Research Center (1998) provides good insight into socio-cultural influences on alcohol consumption. The report indicates that in all cultures, drinking is a rule-governed activity and there are certain universal norms pertaining to drinking such as proscription of solitary drinking, prescription of sociability, social control of consumption and behaviour, and restrictions on female and 'underage' drinking. It considers four main symbolic uses of alcoholic beverages: as labels defining the nature of social situations or events, as indicators of social status, as statements of affiliation, and as gender differentiators. Drinking is, in all cultures, essentially a social activity, and most societies have specific, designated environments for communal drinking. These drinking places tend to be socially integrative, egalitarian environments that facilitate social bonding and constitute a special environment, a separate social world

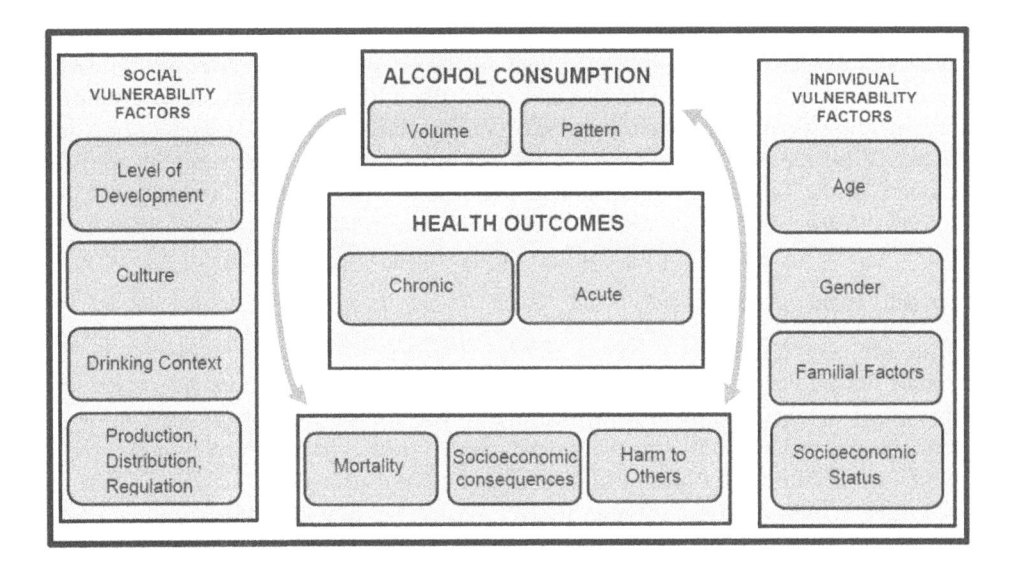

Figure 9.3 Conceptual causal model of alcohol consumption and health outcomes.

with its own customs and values. In all societies, alcohol plays a central role in transitional rituals – both major life-cycle events and minor, everyday transitions. In terms of everyday transitions, in cultures such as the UK, alcohol may be used to mark the transition from work to play, as dropping into a pub or bar at the end of a day's work. Alcohol is universally associated with celebration, and drinking is, in all cultures, an essential element of festive occasions such as weddings, birthdays, and religious festivals. Often the festivity may be used as an excuse for excessive drinking as during Christmas. In an analysis of British drinking culture, Ally et al. (2016) observe that half of British drinking occasions involve consuming only modest amounts of alcohol at domestic or family gatherings.

The environment in which one resides plays a key role in alcohol use (Figure 9.3). These relate to access and affordability factors. In some countries, it is significantly harder and more expensive to acquire alcohol. In general, the more pervasive the presence of alcohol in an environment, such as the density of pubs and alcohol selling outlets, the availability of cheap alcohol, the more likely an individual is to consume alcohol. Limiting the availability of alcohol through an increase in price leads to a reduction in consumption and, in turn, reductions in alcohol-related harm.

Religion and alcohol consumption

Religious beliefs and doctrines significantly influence social tolerance and perceptions relating to the consumption of alcohol and other substances. Islamic countries have stringent laws relating to alcohol consumption. In Western societies, on the other hand, alcohol is freely available, and wine is a socially acceptable meal accompaniment. Reference to the use of wine can be seen in Greek mythology and Hebe the adolescent daughter of the Greek god Olympus was the designated cupbearer of the gods. Ancient Syrian, Babylonian, Egyptian, and Roman civilisations have also documented the widespread use of alcohol.

Studies that have compared members of different religious affiliations (Najjar et al., 2016) indicate that non-religious individuals and Buddhists report more favourable attitudes towards alcohol use, followed by Christians and Muslims. Drinking quantity was more strongly associated with favourable attitudes to alcohol use for Buddhists and Christians than for non-religious participants. Similarly, while some authors (e.g., Charro, 2014) report that members of the Catholic faith consume more alcohol than members of the Muslim or Protestant faith, others (e.g., Desmond et al., 2013) have found that Catholicism provides a protective mechanism against alcohol consumption.

Familial influences

Family life plays a significant role in the development of attitudes and behaviours associated with alcohol consumption. Growing up in a family where heavy drinking is practiced or encouraged tends to normalise the use of alcohol, making it socially acceptable, expected, and potentially desirable. Families characterised by low levels of parental supervision or control, poor communication patterns and a lack of clearly defined rules of behaviour are some other factors associated with alcohol use in children. If children have early exposure to alcohol, they are also more likely to struggle with it later in life and the evidence indicates that those who start drinking before age 15 are five times more likely to develop alcoholism later in life than those who begin drinking at 21 (NIAAA, 2019).

Peer influences

Both primary and sub-cultures that one belongs to potentially influence alcohol consumption patterns and associated behaviours. Members of certain sub-cultures are more likely to engage in alcohol abuse, which may be actively encouraged by other members and may be a method of gaining acceptance to fit in with the rest of the crowd. The evidence suggests that there has been a decline in alcohol consumption among young people since 2005 (ONS, 2017a). Young people are however particularly vulnerable to peer influence if their immediate circle is one that encourages experimentation with alcohol and perpetuates a booze culture that is acceptable and getting 'seriously hammered' is perceived to be the 'in' thing. College undergraduates who drink heavily tend to view alcohol use as integral to the student role and feel entitled to drink irresponsibly and there is evidence that beliefs about alcohol and the college experience influence levels of alcohol consumption (Crawford & Novak, 2006).

Explanatory frameworks

One of the earliest perspectives on substance misuse, the *moral model* viewed excessive consumption to be 'wrong' and those who fall into addiction as being 'bad'. Addiction according to this notion was a result of poor choices attributed to a lack of willpower, determination or moral strength, a sign of human weakness – a defect in character. From a religious perspective, the misuser is said to indulge in 'sin' and is enslaved to a 'vice'. The Rev. J.E. Todd in 1882 published a paper titled 'Drunkenness a vice, not a disease'. Addiction was thus seen as immoral conduct where 'excessive drinking or drug use is considered freely chosen behaviour that is at best irresponsible and at worst evil' (Thombs, 1999: 4).

Biological bases

While there are complex neuro-psycho-physiological processes that have been unravelled in the context of addiction, our foray into the biology of alcohol misuse in this chapter is a rather simplistic endeavour. It is more an effort to appraise the reader of its importance and the belief that the tremendous evidence offered by neurobiology and genetics just cannot be overlooked, as these explanations occupy a position of pre-eminence in understanding the complexity of addiction.

Genetics

There is a contention within the literature of the possibility of genetic transmission in alcoholism. Goodwin's (1974) classic study compared the adopted children of alcohol-dependent parents with the adopted children of non-alcohol-dependent parents. He found that the risk of becoming alcohol dependent increased in children of alcohol-dependent biological parents. In contrast, if the adoptive parents were alcohol dependent, there was no increased risk of alcoholism in their adopted children. This work indicates that more than the family environment, genetic factors influence the risk of alcohol dependence. However, the search for a specific gene that transmits alcohol dependence across generations has been elusive and the pathways of genetic transmission have yet to be established with absolute certainty.

Neurobiology

There is ample evidence that neuro-physiological processes are involved in addictions and other compulsive behaviours (WHO, 2004). Alcohol causes changes to brain structures and their functioning, affects brain chemistry, and interferes with the brain's communication patterns. It is known that changes to the brain's cerebral cortex are associated with impaired decision-making, impulsivity, and compulsivity, which make it more likely that a person is likely to take a drink or have difficulty resisting the urge to drink. The brain's reward system is responsible for drug-seeking and cravings. People become addicted because they experience alcohol effects as pleasurable. People often drink to relieve stress, but alcohol's effect on the brain's hypothalamus creates problems with stress regulation. Since withdrawal from alcohol is itself stressful, this creates a vicious cycle. Stopping alcohol use creates stress, but the use of alcohol diminishes the brain's ability to regulate stress.

Neurotransmitters are chemicals such as serotonin and dopamine, which transmit electrical impulses between nerve cells and thus carry messages to different parts of the brain, which then affects various physiological systems, cognitive processes, mood, and behaviour. Lower dopamine levels are associated with stress and higher levels with pleasurable sensations. Alcohol ingestion seems to enhance dopamine levels, making a person feel good, who may then repeat the behaviour to experience the pleasurable sensations associated with it. It is also believed that some people have a genetic dopamine deficiency, which then motivates them to seek drugs to enhance dopamine levels and experience a state of euphoria, relaxation, and well-being (Ma & Zhu, 2014). Another neuro-biological explanation that has been empirically validated for long in the case of many types of addictions (sex, food, exercise) is that relating to the release of endorphins in the brain. These feel-good chemicals are like opiates and generate similar effects such as numbness, relaxation, and a feeling of well-being that trigger and maintain addictive behaviour. However, these neuro-biological explanations while being rooted in empirical evidence, do not consider socio-cultural and contextual factors, which are implicated in substance misuse.

Psychological perspectives

These explanations focus on psychic states, cognitive processes, and behavioural tendencies. Like the biological explanations, they attempt to answer why certain individuals are more likely than others to use substances and become addicted. The *psychoanalytic tradition*, popular in the 1900s, had several explanations to offer in relation to substance misuse, particularly cocaine and alcohol. Early Freudians such as Fenichel viewed alcohol and drug abuse in terms of instinctual gratification and pleasure-seeking behaviours owing to id impulses. Leon Wurmser attributed addictive behaviours to intrapsychic conflict, while Krystal (1988) believed that substance misusers had early experiences of psychic trauma, involving states of overwhelming affect.

The *Addictive Personality theory* has its roots in psychoanalytic explanations, which considers personality inadequacies to be the cause of addiction (Leeds & Morgenstern, 1996). Tiebout (1942) described alcoholics as being rebellious, egocentric, pleasure seeking, unable to deal with frustrations, having a sense of faulty logic, and being markedly irresponsible and immature. He saw these attributes as being adaptations to the developing disease of alcoholism rather than accounting for its causation. The theory however has not received much empirical support and years of research have failed to reveal a consistent 'alcoholic personality'.

Jellinek (1960) propounded the classic *disease model* which widely influenced the notion that 'once an alcoholic, always an alcoholic' and spawned the total abstinence approach that continues to underpin the core philosophy of groups such as AA (Alcoholics Anonymous). The notion that the 'disease' of alcoholism can be treated but not cured forms the basis of the approach that advocates total abstinence as the only option to deal with it. Jellinek distinguished heavy drinkers from 'real alcoholics' by their ability to control their drinking (i.e., stop at will or decide whether or not to drink). According to the disease model, alcoholics typically manifested tolerance (increasing intake to obtain the same high), withdrawal symptoms (adverse body symptoms during non-consumption), and either 'loss of control' or 'inability to abstain' from alcohol. These individuals cannot drink in moderation and with continued drinking, their disease is progressive and self-destructive.

Choice theory was developed by Glasser who held that people are intrinsically motivated when making choices, which forms the basis of all behaviour. This notion was then adopted by Skog (2003) and others to explain substance misuse based on choices that people make rather than any compulsion, which is one of the core tenets of the disease model. According to this theory, any behaviour directed towards future-oriented consequences necessarily involves making a choice. In the case of addiction, the user is faced with conflicting choices that change because of current preferences.

Expectancy theory holds that alcohol consumption is related to beliefs and expectations associated with drinking. Consumption is associated with positive expectancies that drinking alcohol will have positive outcomes (e.g., increase in social interaction or stress reduction) and avoidance or abstinence is associated with negative expectancies (e.g., feelings of guilt, social embarrassment, loss of job and income). Alcohol expectancies influence drinking behaviours such that positive expectancies are associated with increased drinking, while negative expectancies are associated with less drinking (Jones et al., 2001).

Social Learning Theory, developed by Albert Bandura in the mid-1970s, describes the effect of cognitive processes on goal-directed behaviour. It considers the human capacity for learning within a social environment through observation and communication. The role of reinforcement (perceived rewards), cognitive expectancies (pleasurable effects associated with drinking), modelling (observation and imitation), coping (with stress or adversity), and self-efficacy (the extent of control exercised over drinking in different situations) are key concepts in influencing substance use and misuse.

Behavioural models of alcohol misuse use the concepts of classical and operant conditioning to explain the process of addiction. Classical conditioning, also known as learning by association, is the pairing of a previously neutral stimulus with a response. These stimuli, by virtue of their pairing with the effects of alcohol consumption, become conditioned stimuli capable of eliciting conditioned responses such as consuming alcohol. Operant conditioning, or instrumental learning, on the other hand, refers to the way in which the consequences of behaviour influence the likelihood of that behaviour being repeated. Alcohol acts as a reward, or positive reinforcer, and with repetition, the association between cue (e.g., stress or a celebration), response (consumption), and reward (decrease in stress; enhanced party experience) becomes stronger. Similarly, the user may perform an operant response such as drinking to avoid impending withdrawal symptoms and the associated discomfort associated with craving (negative reinforcement).

Sociological perspectives

Sociological theories understand alcohol consumption and misuse as a societal phenomenon, having largely cultural, social, and economic origins. Such factors tend to be external to the individual, and sociological theories typically do not focus on genetic predispositions, chemical imbalances, neurological processes, or personality traits. Sociological perspectives seek explanations in social structures and processes that are environmental or 'macro' issues involving neighbourhoods, communities, and the larger society in which the individual lives. Sociological explanations emphasise the importance of certain aspects of the social environment such as the meaning, norms, perceptions, and patterns of alcohol consumption in any society and to social interaction and the influence of culture.

Social construction theory is concerned with the processes by which people describe, explain, or account for the world in which they live in (Schneider & Ingram, 1993). It believes that a great deal of human life exists as it does due to social and interpersonal influences (Gergen, 1985). A person's beliefs are created within the social context in which he or she lives and as such his or her knowledge, as a social phenomenon, develops within social interaction (Cheung, 1997). It holds that there are no absolute or universal truths and that knowledge is dependent on how society chooses to 'construct' concepts and theories and attribute meanings and explanations to various events. In the context of alcohol, constructionism influences how society perceives the use and misuse of alcohol, what norms and labels are used in this context, what behaviours are considered to reflect addiction as well as how we deal with people who engage in excessive consumption.

The *cultural identity theory* (Anderson, 1998) explains substance abuse aetiology by understanding how individual and environmental phenomena influence the construction of drug-related identities and drug abuse. The theory considers misuse as being characterised by (1) a pattern of regular and heavy use over a significant period, (2) a set of consumption-related problems (at work, or with interpersonal relationships, one's own health, and formal social control agencies), (3) previous and failed attempts to cease consumption, and (4) self-awareness as having a problem with alcohol.

The *structural-functional* paradigm (August Comte, Emile Durkheim, and Talcott-Parsons) adopts a macro view of society as a complex system comprising of various social systems and institutions that work together to promote unity, solidarity, cohesiveness, stability, and order. This is important for people to thrive and flourish and is a fundamental necessity for social existence. Chaos, instability, and alienation on the other hand disrupt society's functioning and are undesirable. Thus, from the point of harmonious social functioning, overindulgence in alcohol and drugs exerts a disruptive influence on social functioning and disturbs societal equilibrium. This potentially fosters alienation or anomie, which can in turn instigate conflict, deviance, and chaos. Social inequality has also been considered as a possible factor in influencing alcohol consumption. Pickett and Wilkinson (2009) highlight the 'pernicious effects that inequality has on societies: eroding trust, increasing anxiety and illness, (and) encouraging excessive consumption'. The authors contend that among the richest countries, it's the more unequal ones that do worse according to almost every quality-of-life indicator such as mental illness, drug, and alcohol consumption.

Social network theory focuses on the role of social networks as important channels for the development and transmission of consumption behaviours. These networks are key as alcohol consumption can both influence choice of relationships (e.g., selecting drinking buddies as friends) and be influenced by them (e.g., being pressured by peers). Members of a shared social network influence each other through persuasion, sharing information, or expressing approval. The degree of connectedness to a specific social network is positively associated with the likelihood of imbibing and reflecting the normative behaviour of that group (Alexander et al., 2001). Individuals who are linked to networks where individuals drink are at an increased risk for drinking themselves, initially and over time (Jeon & Goodson, 2016).

Family systems theory holds that all people in the family system play a part in the way family members function in relation to one other (Bowen, 1978). Alcohol misuse is viewed as a symptom of a dysfunctional family unit, not only of symptomatic dysfunction in the individual who misuses alcohol. The symptom of excessive consumption surfaces when anxiety levels are high in the family, which in turn heightens anxiety in those who are dependent on the misuser. The process of drinking to relieve anxiety, and increased family anxiety in response to drinking, can spiral into a functional collapse or become a chronic pattern. Alcohol misuse is hence viewed as the outcome of a family system having exhausted its capacity to manage anxiety and various stressors.

An *integrated perspective* that provides a rounded insight into the multi-factorial nature of substance misuse is the *bio-psychosocial* model. Influenced by the systems theory, it does not owe allegiance to any discipline or school of thought within it, nor is it identified with a single author. The model has been widely accepted across disciplinary boundaries as it offers an integrated framework to practitioners whose convictions are rooted in a multi-disciplinary approach. Being eclectic in nature, it enables them to cherry pick aspects of the model which they feel is relevant in the context of the uniqueness of the service users they encounter as well as the typicality of their life situations. It believes that the combinations, interactions, and the weightings of specific biological, psychological, and social factors are different for each individual. It thus views substance misuse behaviours and experiences as complex, variable, and multifactorial. It also takes on board the heterogeneity of service users, the unique effects of the substance on their lives, and rejects the 'one shoe fits all' approach to intervention. The objective of service delivery and intervention from this perspective is to enable service users to develop greater control over their life in general and patterns of alcohol use in particular. Abstinence therefore is seen as desirable, but not the sole objective of intervention.

Alcohol-related harm

There has been considerable debate over the years relating to the beneficial and harmful effects of alcohol consumption. In moderation (one drink a day), alcohol is associated with a lower risk of hypertension, myocardial infarction, stroke, sudden cardiac death, gallstones, and cognitive decline (Mostofsky et al., 2016). The issue of course with moderate drinking is that not many people are going to stop with just having one drink a day! Increasing alcohol intake to more than four drinks a day can increase the risk of hypertension, abnormal heart rhythms, stroke, heart attack, and death (Bell et al., 2017). Excessive alcohol consumption in fact has been associated with more than 200 types of injuries and diseases, including road traffic and domestic accidents, cancer, liver cirrhosis, stroke, alcoholic cardiomyopathy, and infectious diseases, and it has been estimated that around 6% of total deaths could be attributable to alcohol consumption worldwide (WHO, 2011). Long-term heavy drinking can cause physical changes to the brain, leading to alcohol-related brain damage and difficulties with reasoning, remembering, and understanding. Figure 9.4 depicts body organs affected by excessive alcohol consumption.

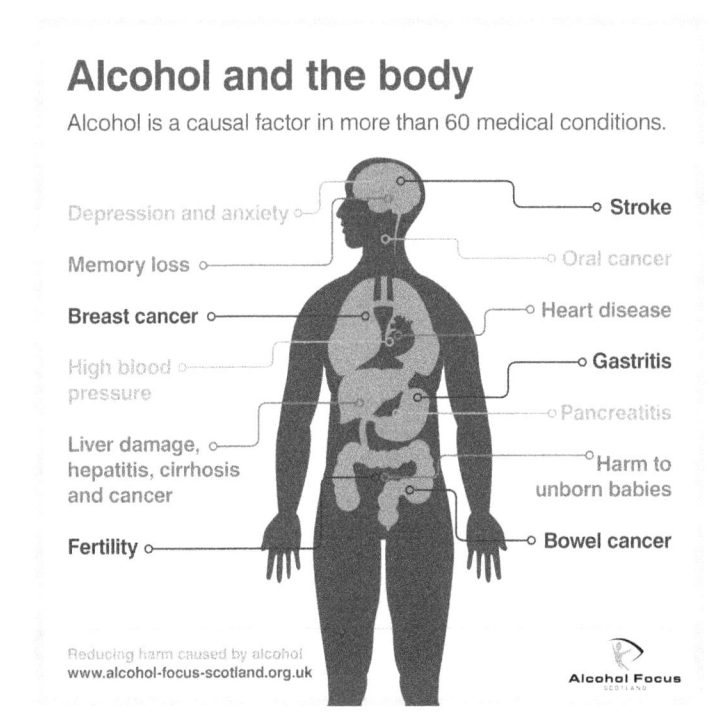

Figure 9.4 Alcohol and the body.

Besides the health consequences associated with excessive drinking, alcohol contributes to death and disability through accidents and injuries, assault, violence, homicide, and suicide (OECD, 2020). Tomlinson et al. (2016: 12) observe that 'the research supporting the relation between all forms of aggression and alcohol use is enormous [and] unequivocal', they further note that 'this relationship is likely moderated by individual difference and contextual factors [and] is most prominently demonstrated in men'. The empirical evidence also indicates the involvement of alcohol in sexual aggression perpetrated by young men (Abbey et al., 2014) and studies that have examined the role of alcohol in homicidal incidents have found that 48% of both victims as well as perpetrators had been drinking (Kuhns et al., 2014).

The overall cost of alcohol-related harm

BOX 9.3 DRINK-DRIVE LEGAL LIMITS

Failing a roadside breath test by registering over 35 micrograms of alcohol in England and Wales; over 22 micrograms in Scotland and 35 micrograms of alcohol per 100 millilitres of breath in Northern Ireland. An estimated 8,700 people were killed or injured in 2018 in Great Britain when at least one driver was over the drink-drive limit. Figures for Northern Ireland indicate that in 2018, there were 2,942 casualties attributed to drug/drink driving.

Source: Dept. of Transport (2020)

Alcohol contributes to 10% of the UK's burden of disease and death, making alcohol one of the three biggest lifestyle risk factors after smoking and obesity. Alcohol misuse is the biggest risk factor for death, ill-health, and disability among 15–49-year olds in the UK, and the fifth biggest risk factor across all ages (Burton et al., 2016). Overall, the harmful use of alcohol results in a significant health, social, and economic cost to society and ranks among the five top risk factors for disease, disability, and injury throughout the world. There are three major categories of alcohol-related health, social and economic costs (WHO, 2014b):

- the direct economic costs of alcohol consumption, such as costs to health and social care, the police and criminal justice system, and the unemployment and welfare systems.
- the indirect costs of alcohol consumption, due to lost productivity owing to absenteeism, unemployment, decreased output, reduced earnings potential, and lost working years due to premature pension or death.
- the intangible costs of alcohol consumption, for example, costs assigned to pain and suffering, poor quality of life, or costs from money spent on alcohol in families where the money should be spent on other things (Figure 9.5).

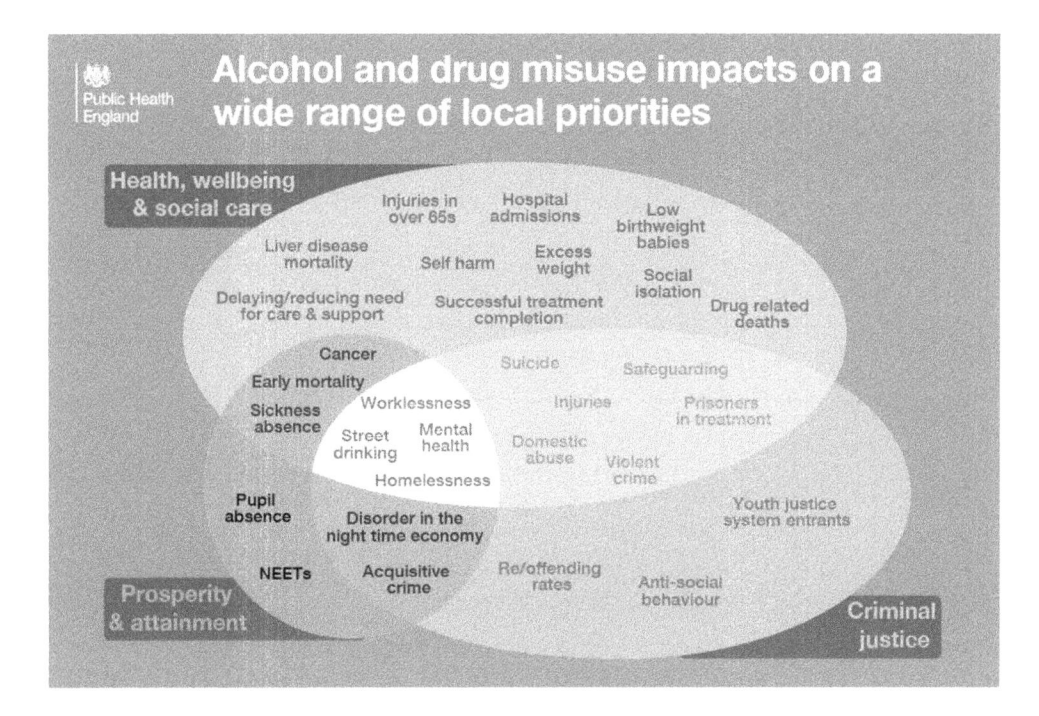

Figure 9.5 Alcohol impacts on a range of priorities.

Alcohol-related hospitalisations and deaths – UK (2018)

In 2018/2019, there were 358 thousand estimated admissions in the UK where the main reason for admission to hospital was attributable to alcohol. This was 6% higher than 2017/2018 and 19% higher than 2008/2009 (NHS Digital, 2020). Hospital admission figures are depicted in Figure 9.6 and show an increase each year.

In 2020, there were 8,974 deaths (14.0 per 100,000 people) from alcohol-specific causes registered in the UK, an 18.6% increase compared with 2019 (7,565 deaths; 11.8 per 100,000 people). More than three-quarters of alcohol-specific deaths were caused by alcoholic liver disease. Scotland had the highest rate of alcohol-specific deaths for both genders, followed by Northern Ireland, Wales, and England (ONS, 2021) (Table 9.1).

Harm to others from drinking

Harms from alcohol consumption accrue not only for the drinker but also affect others such as family, friends, and those in proximity such as in public transport. These harms may be to the health of others (e.g., injury, a family member's anxiety or depression, transmission of infection to a sexual partner), or may be social (e.g., situations resulting in assault, disorderly behaviour causing public nuisance) or economic (e.g., damage to property, money for family necessities spent on drinking; Karriker-Jaffe et al., 2018). Excessive drinking affects the family owing to financial problems, relationship issues, mental ill health, bereavement, and domestic violence. Wives of alcohol-consuming

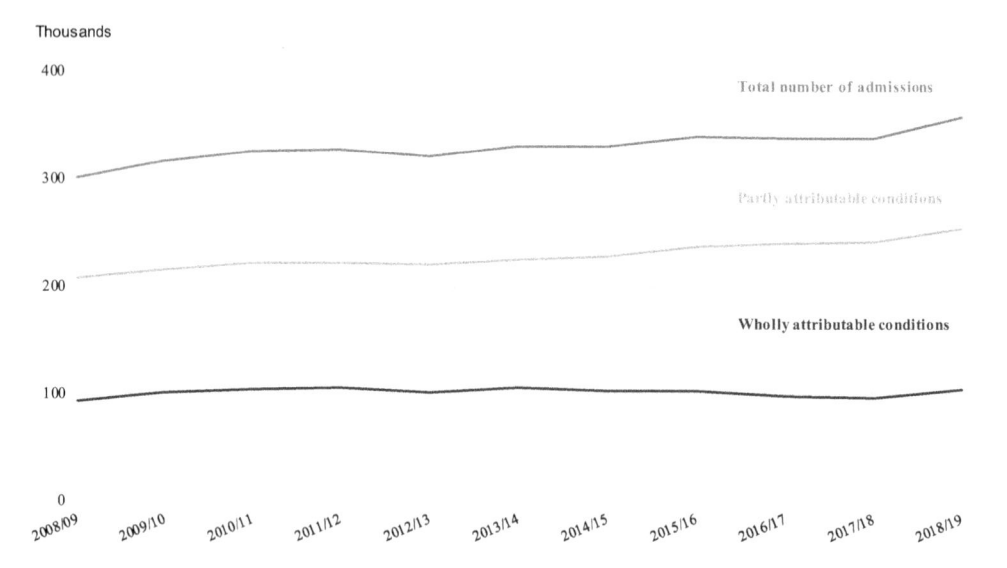

Figure 9.6 Estimated alcohol-related hospital admissions.

Table 9.1 Alcohol attributed deaths in the UK

Country	Number of deaths (2019)	Deaths per 10,000 (2019)
England	5,820	10.9
Wales	368	11.8
Scotland	1,020	16.8
Northern Ireland	336	18.8
UK	7,544	1.8

Source: ONS (2021).

spouses report lower levels of marital adjustment and poorer family interaction pattern when compared to families where alcohol is not consumed (Manning et al., 2009). It is then all these consequences taken together that makes alcohol misuse an issue of concern that affects individuals, families, and the wider society.

Alcohol and mental health

The relationship between alcohol and mental health is complex. Alcohol has been described as 'the UK's favourite coping mechanism', and many people self-medicate with alcohol to try and help manage stress, anxiety, depression, or other mental health problems (Mental Health Foundation, 2006). Depression and heavy drinking have a mutually reinforcing relationship – meaning that either condition increases a person's chances of experiencing the other (Adams, 2017). Overuse of alcohol can contribute to the worsening of symptoms of many mental health problems and, in particular, lead to low mood and anxiety. Alcohol has very close links with depression; while some use alcohol to deal with phases of depression and to self-medicate, excessive consumption by itself leads to depression (Bolton et al., 2009). There is a seven times increased risk for a suicide attempt, and this risk further increases to 37 times after heavy alcohol use (Borges et al., 2017). The risk of suicidal ideation, suicidal attempts, and completed suicide each increases two to three times among those with AUDs when compared to the general population (Darvishi et al., 2015). The prevalence of most mood, anxiety, substance, personality disorders, and thought disorders such as schizophrenia is higher in people with alcohol use disorder than in the general population (Castillo-Carniglia et al., 2019). Excessive alcohol consumption is associated with loss of motivation, reduced performance at work, school, and university and to aggravate relationship problems, all of which in turn have the potential to adversely impact the mental health status of the user.

Parental alcohol misuse (PAM): implications for children

PAM refers to a spectrum of problem drinking by those with parental responsibility for children. Figure 9.7 presents some statistics related to PAM in the UK. Most parents who consume alcohol do so in moderation and do not pose a risk of harm to children. Alcohol misuse is generally damaging to families, impacting on parents' ability to care for their children, how the family functions, and affecting children from pre-birth to adulthood. Children of parents who misuse alcohol are more likely to be living in deprivation with chaotic home environments and experience exposure to crime and toxic substances; domestic, emotional, physical, and sexual abuse; and needing to take on caring roles for younger siblings (Dube et al., 2002; McLaughlin, 2016). There is also an increased risk of a younger child being harmed because of poor hygiene, lack of safety precautions, or being left for long periods of time unsupervised, in the care of an older sibling, or with someone outside of the family who may not be appropriate (Turning Point, 2006).

PAM can lead to inconsistent and unpredictable parenting, children having to care for their parent or younger siblings, impacts on school attendance and homework, and physical and mental health impacts (Hedges & Kenny, 2018). Poor self-esteem and adjustment deficits manifest in these children (Stanley & Vanitha, 2008) and they face

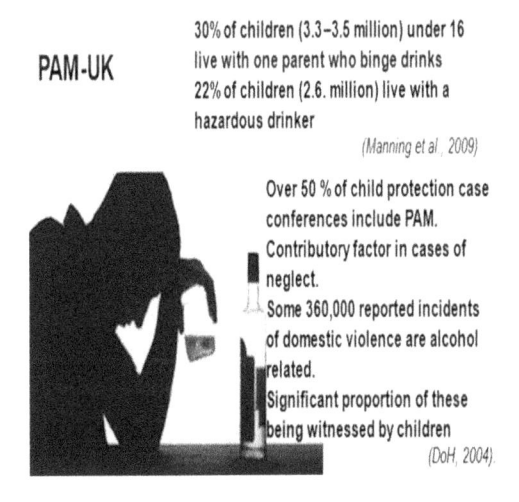

Figure 9.7 Parental alcohol misuse.

increased risks of neglect, sexual and physical abuse (Hughes et al., 2017), injury-related emergency admissions (Paranjothy et al., 2018), criminal behaviours (McKeganey et al., 2002), and suicide (Felitti et al., 1998). PAM has also been associated with problematic externalising behaviours in children such as conduct disorder, oppositional defiant disorder, attention difficulties, violent, and rebellious behaviour (McGovern et al., 2018).

There is evidence that PAM can influence drinking behaviours in young people who are more likely to develop their own problems with alcohol later in life (Burton et al., 2016). They are more likely to drink more heavily and more often and drink alone rather than with their peers (Mares et al., 2011). The *social cognitive model* (Bandura, 1986) posits that young people learn drinking behaviours from observing their parents and the resulting outcomes of consumption experienced by their parents.

Alcohol and intimate partner violence (IPV)

The involvement of alcohol has been implicated in several instances of IPV and there has been considerable debate about the precise nature of this association. A prevalent view in the IPV literature is that alcohol consumption is used as a post hoc explanation for the occurrence of IPV, to excuse aggression or provide mitigation in legal proceedings (Graham et al., 2011). Alcohol use is common among a high proportion of cases of IPV perpetration, with perpetrator substance use being found in half of the domestic homicide cases since 2011 (Gilchrist et al., 2019). While many perpetrators or victims believe that alcohol is to blame for physical and sexual abuse (Radcliffe et al., 2017), alcohol use by itself does not cause perpetrators to inflict abuse. The evidence shows that where a perpetrator is violent and abusive under the influence of alcohol, they usually show such behaviours even without alcohol or use different forms of abuse when not drinking including intimidation, coercion, control, and financial abuse (Galvani, 2004). Wives of alcoholics report higher levels of conflict, perceive more danger, and experience greater communication apprehension in their spousal relationship (Stanley, 2012).

Alcohol consumption in young people

Alcohol use and drunkenness, along with other risk-taking behaviours, tend to emerge in adolescence. Indeed, alcohol is one of the most common psychoactive substances used by adolescents and easy availability is a key factor. Decreased parental supervision, spending more time outside the home in the company of peers, and greater independence seem to lead to experimentation with alcohol for most young people between the ages of 12 and 16. Young people use alcohol to fulfil social and personal needs, enhance contact with peers, and initiate new relationships. According to the *gateway theory*, a substance user moves sequentially from alcohol and cigarettes to marijuana, which then serves as a gateway to the use of other hard drugs. There is evidence that adolescent drinking is associated with fatal and non-fatal injuries, blackouts, suicide attempts, unintended pregnancy, sexually transmitted diseases, academic failure, and violence (Perkins, 2002). Road-traffic injuries, suicide, and other forms of unintentional injury have also been linked to adolescent alcohol consumption (Maldonado-Molina et al., 2010). Alcohol consumption during adolescence could potentially result in functional and structural changes in the brain that can have lasting effects into adulthood (Sánchez-Queija et al., 2015). Early alcohol use among adolescents can also increase the risk of alcohol dependence in later life (Grant & Dawson, 1997).

Alcohol and older people

Many older people limit their alcohol use because they are unable to drink as much as they used to as the effects of alcohol were stronger. Many older adults, however, drink at levels considered hazardous or harmful where alcohol use could lead to significant physiological, psychological, or social harm. Older people in the UK experience more harm resulting from alcohol use than any other age group (ONS, 2017a). Reduction in the body water to fat ratio, a decreased hepatic blood flow, inefficiency of liver enzymes, and reduced renal clearance are some factors that accounts for lesser tolerance to alcohol in older people (NHS Health Scotland, 2006). Alcohol can worsen the symptoms of certain pre-existing health conditions, affect the progression of disease, and interact with prescribed medications besides increasing the risk of falls in older adults (Mukamal et al., 2004).

A systematic review of qualitative studies that explored older people's perceptions and experiences with alcohol (Bareham et al., 2020) states that most older adults identified themselves as 'normal' drinkers, framing their consumption as responsible. The review also found that heavier drinkers continued to drink heavily as they saw intoxication to be one of life's remaining pleasures. Further, alcohol was valued for its ability to create feelings of pleasure and relaxation, which were perceived as an important part of enjoying later life.

Alcohol Policy

The Government's Alcohol Strategy (GAS, 2012)

BOX 9.4 HOW MUCH DO HANGOVERS COST THE ECONOMY?

A nationally representative sample of 3,400 British workers about how their work had been affected both by their own drinking and the drinking of others. The study found that 42% had ever gone to work hungover or under the influence of alcohol. These workers rated their performance at work to be 39% less effective than usual. People working while hungover or under the influence of alcohol costs the UK economy between £1.2 billion and £1.4 billion a year.

Source: Institute of Alcohol Studies (2020)

The UK's alcohol policy is long overdue since its strategy the GAS was released in 2012. Some of the key features of this strategy are:

Reducing the availability of cheap alcohol: The introduction of a minimum unit price for alcohol and a ban on multi-buy promotions.

Alcohol Advertising: Curbs on irresponsible promotions in pubs and clubs were also proposed along with restrictions on media advertising.

Ensure that local areas can tackle local problems: The maximum fine for establishments persistently selling alcohol to underage drinkers was doubled to £20,000. It also suggested that making it easier to close premises found to be persistently selling alcohol to young people and to give local communities powers to introduce Early Morning Restriction Orders and to introduce a new late-night levy to ensure that businesses that sell alcohol into the late night contribute towards the cost of policing. It also mandated local powers to control the density of premises licenced to sell alcohol.

Greater industry responsibility and action in tackling alcohol misuse: It also envisaged providing support to the alcohol industry to market, advertise, and sell their products in a responsible way and deliver the core commitment to 'foster a culture of responsible drinking, which will help people to drink within guidelines'.

Challenge people to change their behaviour by giving them the information and support they need: This would involve reviewing the alcohol guidelines for adults so that people can make responsible and informed choices about their drinking and to initiate a social marketing campaign to communicate the health harms of drinking above the lower-risk guidelines.

The 'Health First' alcohol strategy (2013)

BOX 9.5

Minimum unit pricing (MUP) sets a baseline price below which no one can sell an alcoholic drink. The price is based on how much alcohol is in each drink and is seen as a step to deal with the availability of cheap and strong alcohol. The minimum price set in Wales and Scotland is 50p per unit of alcohol (10 ml); England is yet to do so. According to a report in the 'Irish Times' in July 2020, the Northern Ireland Health Minister has expressed a commitment to hold a public consultation on this issue within a year.

The WHO's review 'Alcohol: No Ordinary Commodity' is considered the definitive review of evidence on effective public policy on alcohol worldwide. However, it did not present direct or UK-specific policy recommendations. Hence, an independent group of UK experts prepared 'Health First', a UK alcohol strategy, applying the findings of the WHO document to a UK context. The goals of the policy were to (1) reduce the overall level of alcohol consumption in the population; (2) reduce the incidence of alcohol-related illness, injuries, and deaths; and (3) reduce the incidence of alcohol-related disorder, anti-social behaviour, violence, and crime. The document made 30 recommendations such as a minimum price of at least 50 p per, sale of alcohol in shops to be restricted to specific times, prohibition of all alcohol advertising and sponsorship and reducing the legal limit for blood alcohol concentration for drivers to 50 mg/100 ml.

Four nations – How evidence based are alcohol policies and programmes across the UK?

This report by the Alliance for Useful Evidence (2015) examined the evidence base that underpinned various policies across the four constituent nations of the UK. In it, the scientific evidence points clearly to action in relation to the five broad areas: pricing, availability (including licencing and sales), marketing (including promotion, product, and packaging), early intervention and treatment, and other (including drink driving, information, and education) (Figure 9.8).

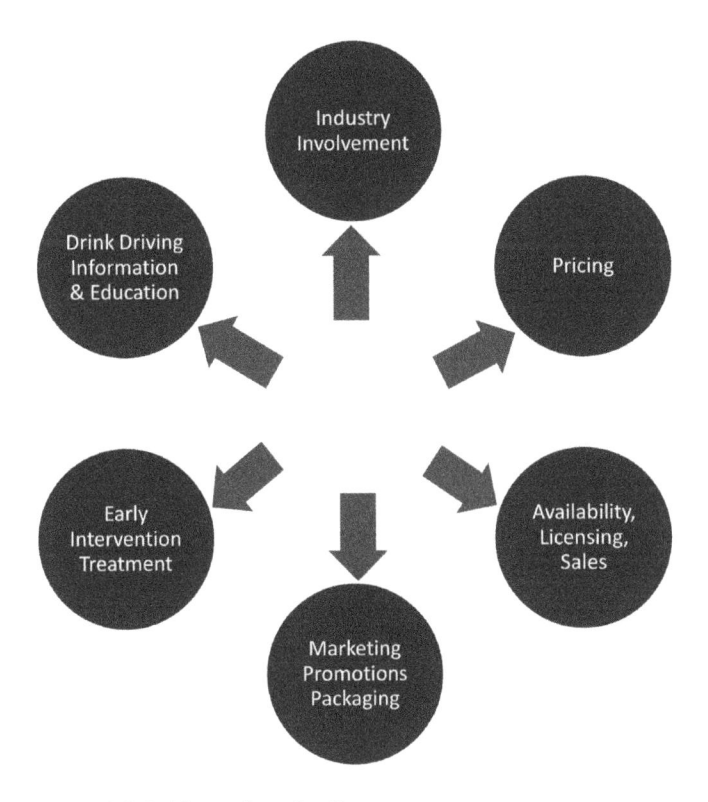

Figure 9.8 Evidence-based policy.

Recommendations of the Alcohol and Families Alliance, UK (2018)

The Alcohol and Families Alliance (AFA) in their report call for further action to address alcohol-related harms affecting children and families. It recommends the provision of evidence-based support for families affected by alcohol according to local need and inter-agency commissioning and delivery of family support services. Better training for universal service practitioners to identify parental drinking problems and signpost families to specialist support where appropriate and to develop the drug and alcohol workforce to better support families. Support for carers was recommended in terms of increase in Carer's Allowance and making carers aware of their rights and benefits. Addressing the wider role of alcohol in society, the Government should start a national conversation about our relationship with alcohol through a mass media campaign to challenge stigma and that policies should be implemented to tackle the three main drivers of alcohol harm: affordability, availability, and promotion.

Alcohol policy England

A national policy for England is long overdue and 'The alcohol harm reduction strategy for England' was enunciated in 2004. Four keyways to reduce alcohol-related harms were proposed (Foster & Thom, 2004): (1) Improved and better-targeted, education, and communication. (2) Better identification and treatment of alcohol problems. (3) Better co-ordination and enforcement of existing powers against crime and disorder. (4) Encouraging the industry to continue promoting responsible drinking and to continue to take a role in reducing alcohol-related harm.

Alcohol Framework Scotland (2018): This updated Framework has three central themes that deal with reducing consumption, enabling positive attitudes and choices relating to consumption, and supporting families and communities to deal with alcohol and associated problems. The framework endorses the SAFER package which consists of five evidence-based, high-impact strategies, which WHO recommends governments should prioritise to tackle alcohol-related harm. These seek to:

Strengthen restrictions on alcohol availability.
Advance and enforce drink driving countermeasures.
Facilitate access to screening, brief interventions, and treatment.
Enforce restrictions on alcohol advertising, sponsorship, and promotion.
Raise prices on alcohol through excise taxes and pricing policies.

BOX 9.6

The provisional 2020 to 2021 financial year total for alcohol duty receipts was £12,124 million, an increase of £286 million (2%) compared to the previous financial year.

Source: National Statistics (2020)

Wales: The ten-year (2008–2018) Substance Misuse Strategy – *Working Together to Reduce Harm* launched by the Welsh Assembly Government in 2008 sets out an agenda to reduce harm caused by alcohol, drugs, and other substances. The strategy describes four key aims:

1 Reducing the harm to individuals, their families, and wider communities from the misuse of drugs and alcohol, while not stigmatising substance misuse.
2 Improving the availability and quality of education, prevention and treatment services, and related support, with priority given to those related to alcohol.
3 Supporting evidence-based decision-making, improving treatment outcomes, developing the skills base of partners and service providers through workforce development, and joining up agencies and services more effectively.
4 Developing user-focused services and a rights basis for children and young people in both the development and delivery of the strategy.

Northern Ireland: The New Strategic Direction for Alcohol and Drugs (NSD) Phase 2 is the strategy for preventing and addressing the harm related to substance misuse in Northern Ireland. It followed on from the original New Strategic Direction for Alcohol and Drugs, which was reviewed and updated in 2011/2012. The overall aim was to: 'reduce the level of alcohol and drug-related harm'. In brief, the strategy envisages five supporting pillars that provide the conceptual and practical base for the Strategy namely, Prevention and Early Intervention; Treatment and Support; Law and Criminal Justice; Harm Reduction; and Monitoring, Evaluation and Research.

Commission on Alcohol Harm (2020) recommendations

The Alcohol Harm Commission was set up to examine the full extent of harm across the UK: the physical, mental, and social harm caused to people around the drinker, to wider society, and to the drinker themselves. The Commission mentions that the new alcohol strategy must include targeted measures to support families and protect children from harm, including alcohol-fuelled violence. It holds that the new alcohol strategy must be science-led and adopt the WHO's evidence-based recommendations for reducing the harmful use of alcohol. This includes measures on affordability – such as the introduction of MUP in England - and restrictions on alcohol advertising and marketing – such as ending sports sponsorship, better information for consumers, advice and treatment for people drinking at hazardous and harmful levels, and action to reduce drink driving. Further, it states that reducing the £3.5 bn cost of alcohol to the NHS would help to relieve pressure on the service and free up capacity to respond to the consequences of COVID-19. It also calls for addressing the stigma around alcohol use disorders, encouraging conversations about drinking to take place more easily, and creating space for people to be open about the effects of alcohol on their health and those around them.

Points to ponder

1. Consider someone known to you who has a problem with alcohol. In what ways do you think this has affected the person/his or her family?
2. Why do people who have problems with alcohol not use their 'willpower' (or human agency) to stop, regulate or refrain from problematic use?
3. Which explanatory framework (theory) in your opinion satisfactorily explain reasons for alcohol consumption? Why?
4. The government spends a huge amount of money on drug and alcohol services and at the same time allows for easy availability of alcohol. Why?
5. What effective measures can be initiated to encourage young people to engage in safe consumption practices?

Quiz

The following statements require you to fill in the blanks, state if they are true or false or to choose the options provided within brackets.

1. Physiological features of alcohol dependence include increasing _____ to the effects of alcohol, and _____ symptoms following cessation of alcohol use.
2. Growing up in a family where heavy drinking is prevalent tends to normalise the use of alcohol, making it acceptable, and potentially desirable (True/False).
3. Alcohol causes changes to brain structures and their functioning and interferes with the brain's communication patterns (True/False).
4. According to Skog's theory substance misuse has been explained based on _____ that people make rather than any compulsion.
5. The role of reinforcement, cognitive expectancies, modelling, and self-efficacy are key concepts associated with _____ theory.
6. According to _____ theory, alcohol misuse is viewed as a symptom of a dysfunctional family unit.

7 PAM can influence drinking behaviours in young people who are more likely to develop their own problems with alcohol later in life (True/False).
8 According to the _____ theory, a substance user moves sequentially from alcohol and cigarettes to marijuana and other hard drugs.
9 The ten-year Substance Misuse Strategy – *Working Together to Reduce Harm* was launched by which UK nation? (England, Wales, Scotland, Northern Ireland)
10 Safe drinking guidelines in the UK suggest that one should not consume more than ___ units of alcohol in a week (12, 14, 18, 21).

Answers:

1. Tolerance, withdrawal 2. True 3. True 4. Choices 5. Social learning 6. Family systems 7. True 8. Gateway theory 9. Wales 10. 14

Organisations related to alcohol misuse

Alcohol Change UK is a leading UK alcohol charity, formed from the merger of *Alcohol Concern* and *Alcohol Research UK*.
   https://alcoholchange.org.uk/
Beating Addictions offer a unique reference point on how to treat and overcome an addiction.
   http://www.beatingaddictions.co.uk/
Alcoholics Anonymous is concerned solely with the personal recovery and continued sobriety of individual alcoholics who turn to the Fellowship for help
   https://www.alcoholics-anonymous.org.uk/
The National Association for Children of Alcoholics (Nacoa) provides resources and support for children growing up in families where one or both parents suffer from alcoholism or a similar addictive problem.
   https://nacoa.org.uk/
The Drinkaware Trust is an independent UK-wide alcohol education charity that works to reduce alcohol-related harm by helping people make better choices about their drinking.
   https://www.drinkaware.co.uk/

Helpful websites:

Lexicon of alcohol and drug terms published by the World Health Organization:
https://www.who.int/substance_abuse/terminology/who_lexicon/en/
Nuffield Trust: Alcohol-related harm and drinking behaviour
https://www.nuffieldtrust.org.uk/resource/alcohol-related-harm-and-drinking-behaviour-1
Alcohol Change: Alcohol Policy
https://alcoholchange.org.uk/policy/policy-insights
NHS: Alcohol Misuse

https://www.nhs.uk/conditions/alcohol-misuse/
Useful websites on drugs and alcohol:
https://www.theguardian.com/society/drugsandalcohol/page/0,728603,00.html

References

Abbey, A., Wegner, R., Woerner, J., Pegram, S. E., and Pierce, J. 2014. Review of survey and experimental research that examines the relationship between alcohol consumption and men's sexual aggression perpetration. *Trauma, Violence and Abuse* 15(4): 265–282.

Adams, S. 2017. Psychopharmacology of tobacco and alcohol comorbidity: a review of current evidence. *Current Addiction Reports* 4(1): 25–34.

Alcohol and Families Alliance, UK. 2018. https://www.alcoholpolicy.net/2018/07/alcohol-and-families-alliance-calls-for-further-policy-action.html

Alcohol Framework Scotland. 2018. https://www.gov.scot/publications/alcohol-framework-2018-preventing-harm-next-steps-changing-relationship-alcohol/

Alcohol Harm. 2020. https://www.alcoholpolicy.net/2020/09/commission-on-alcohol-harm-2020-report-calls-for-science-led-alcohol-strategy.html

Alcohol Health Alliance. 2020. https://ahauk.org/news/august2020/

Alexander, C., Piazza, M., Mekos, D., and Valente, T. 2001. Peers, schools, and adolescent cigarette smoking. *Journal of Adolescent Health* 29(1): 22–30.

Alliance for Useful Evidence. 2015. http://linkis.com/org/a408x

Ally, A. K., Lovatt, M., Meier, P. S., Brennan, A., and Holmes, J. 2016. Developing a social practice-based typology of British drinking culture in 2009–2011: implications for alcohol policy analysis. *Addiction* 111(9): 1568–1579.

Anderson, T. 1998. A cultural identity theory of drug abuse. *Sociology of Crime, Law, and Deviance* 1: 233–262.

Bandura, A., & National Inst of Mental Health. 1986. *Social foundations of thought and action: a social cognitive theory*. Englewood Cliffs, NJ: Prentice-Hall, Inc.

Bareham, B. K., Kaner, E., and Barbara Hanratty, B. 2020. Managing older people's perceptions of alcohol-related risk: a qualitative exploration in Northern English primary care. *British Journal of General Practice* 70(701): e916–e926.

Bell, S., Daskalopoulou, M., Rapsomaniki, E., George, J., Britton, A., Bobak, M., Casas, J. P. et al. 2017. Association between clinically recorded alcohol consumption and initial presentation of 12 cardiovascular diseases: population based cohort study using linked health records. *BMJ* 22(356): j909.

Bolton, J. M., Robinson, J., and Sareen, J. 2009. Self-medication of mood disorders with alcohol and drugs in the National Epidemiologic Survey on Alcohol and Related Conditions. *Journal of Affective Disorders* 115(3): 367–375.

Borges, G., Bagge, C., Cherpitel, C., Conner, K., Orozco, R., and Rossow, I. 2017. A meta-analysis of acute use of alcohol and the risk of suicide attempt. *Psychological Medicine* 47(5): 949–957.

Bowen, M. 1978. *Family therapy in clinical practice*. New York: Aronson.

Burton, R. et al. 2016. The public health burden of alcohol and the effectiveness and cost-ffectiveness of alcohol control policies: an evidence review. PHE publications gateway number 2016490.

Castillo-Carniglia, A., Keyes, K. M., Hasin, D. S., and Cerdá, M. 2019. Psychiatric comorbidities in alcohol use disorder. *The Lancet. Psychiatry* 6(12): 1068–1080.

Charro, B. 2014. The role of religion and religiosity in alcohol consumption in adolescents in Spain. *Miscelá nea Comillas* 72 (140–141): 293–308.

Cheung, M. 1997. Social construction theory and the Satir model: towards a synthesis. *American Journal of Family Therapy* 25(4): 331–343.

Commission on Alcohol Harm. 2020. https://ahauk.org/commission-on-alcohol-harm-report/
Crawford, L. A., and Novak, K. B. 2006. Alcohol abuse as a rite of passage: the effect of beliefs about alcohol and the college experience on undergraduates' drinking behaviors. *Journal of Drug Education* 36(3): 193–212.
Darvishi, N., Farhadi, M., Haghtalab, T., and Poorolajal, J. 2015. Alcohol-related risk of suicidal ideation, suicide attempt, and completed suicide: a meta-analysis. *PLoS One* 10(5): e0126870.
Dept. of Transport. 2020. https://assets.publishing.service.gov.uk/government/uploads/system/uploads/attachment_data/file/864835/drink-drive-provisional-estimates-2018.pdf
Desmond, S. A., Ulmer, J. T., and Bader, C. D. 2013. Religion, self-control, and substance use. *Deviant Behavior* 34(5): 384–406.
Dube, S., Anda, R., Felitti, V., Edwards, V., and Croft, J. 2002. Adverse childhood experiences and personal alcohol abuse as an adult. *Addictive Behaviors* 27(5): 713–725.
Felitti, V. J., Anda, R. F., Nordenberg, D. et al. 1998. Relationship of childhood abuse and household dysfunction to many of the leading causes of death in adults: the Adverse Childhood Experiences (ACE) Study. *American Journal of Preventive Medicine* 14(4): 245–258.
Foster, J., and Thom, B. 2004. The alcohol harm reduction strategy for England: introduction, *Drugs: Education, Prevention and Policy* 11(5): 349–350.
Galvani, S. 2004. Responsible disinhibition: alcohol, men and violence to women. *Addiction Research and Theory* 12(4):357–371.
Gergen, K. J. 1985. Social constructionist inquiry: context and implications. In K. J. Gergen and K. E. Davis (Eds.), *The Social Construction of the Person*, 3–18. New York: Springer.
Gilchrist, G., Dennis, F., Radcliffe, P., Henderson, J., Howard, L., and Gadd, D. 2019. The interplay between substance use and intimate partner violence perpetration: a meta-ethnography. *International Journal of Drug Policy* 65: 8–23.
Global Drugs Survey 2019. https://www.globaldrugsurvey.com/gds-2019/
Goodwin, D. W., Schulsinger, F., Møller, N., Hermansen, L., Winokur, G., and Guze, S. B. 1974. Drinking problems in adopted and nonadopted sons of alcoholics. *Archives of General Psychiatry* 31(2): 164–169.
Government's Alcohol Strategy (GAS, 2012; Home Office, 2012). https://www.gov.uk/government/publications/alcohol-strategy
Graham, K., Bernards, S., Wilsnack, S. C., and Gmel, G. 2011. Alcohol may not cause partner violence but it seems to make it worse: a cross national comparison of the relationship between alcohol and severity of partner violence. *Journal of Interpersonal Violence* 26(8): 1503–1523.
Grant, B. F., and Dawson, D. A. 1997. Age at onset of alcohol use and its association with DSM-IV alcohol abuse and dependence: results from the National Longitudinal Alcohol Epidemiologic Survey. *Journal of Substance Abuse* 9: 103–110.
Health First' alcohol strategy. 2013. https://ahauk.org/resource/health-first-an-evidence-based-alcohol-strategy-for-the-uk/
Health Survey for England. 2018. https://digital.nhs.uk/data-and-information/publications/statistical/health-survey-for-england/2018
Health Survey Northern Ireland: First Results 2018/19 | *Department of Health*. [online]. https://www.health-ni.gov.uk/publications/health-survey-northern-ireland-first-results-201819 (Accessed 23 December 2021).
Hedges, S., and Kenny, C. 2018. *Parental alcohol misuse and children*. UK: Parliamentary Office of Science and Technology.
Hughes, K., Bellis, M. A., Hardcastle, K. A. et al. 2017. The effect of multiple adverse childhood experiences on health: a systematic review and meta-analysis. *The Lancet Public Health* 2(8): e356–e366.
Institute of Alcohol Studies. 2020. https://www.ias.org.uk/alcohol_alert/november-2020/
Jellinek, E. M. 1960. *The disease concept of alcoholism*. New Haven, CT: Hillhouse Press.
Jeon, K. C., and Goodson, P. 2016. Alcohol and sex: friendship networks and co-occurring risky health behaviours of US adolescents. *International Journal of Adolescence and Youth* 21(4): 499–512.

Jones, B. T., Corbin, W., and Fromme, K. 2001. A review of expectancy theory and alcohol consumption. *Addiction* 96(1): 57–72.

Karriker-Jaffe, K. J., Room, R., Giesbrecht, N., and Greenfield, T. K. 2018. Alcohol's harm to others: opportunities and challenges in a public health framework. *Journal of Studies on Alcohol and Drugs* 79(2): 239–243.

Krystal, H. 1988. *Integration and self healing: affect, trauma, alexithymia.* Hillsdale: NJ, Analytic Press

Kuhns, J., Exum, L., Clodfelter, T., and Bottia, M. 2014. The prevalence of alcohol-involved homicide offending: a meta-analytic review. *Homicide Studies* 18(3): 251–270.

Leeds, J., and Morgenstern, J. 1996. Psychoanalytic theories of substance abuse. In Rotgers, F., Keller, K. S., Morgenstern, J. (eds.), *Treating substance abuse: theory and technique,* 68–83. New York: Guilford Press

Lowe, G. 1990. Alcohol: a positive enhancer of pleasurable expectancies? In Warburton, D. M. (ed), *Addiction controversies,* 53–65. London: Harwood Academic

Ma, H., and Zhu, G. 2014. The dopamine system and alcohol dependence. *Shanghai Archives of Psychiatry* 26(2): 61–68.

Maldonado-Molina, M. M., Jennings, W. G., and Komro, K. A. 2010. Effects of alcohol on trajectories of physical aggression among urban youth: an application of latent trajectory modeling. *Journal of Youth and Adolescence* 39(9): 1012–1026.

Manning, V., Best, D. W., Faulkner, N., and Titherington, E. 2009. New estimates of the number of children living with substance misusing parents: results from UK national household surveys. *BMC Public Health* 9: 377.

Mares, S. H. W., van der Vorst, H., Engels, R. C. M. E., and Lichtwarck-Aschoff, A. 2011. Parental alcohol use, alcohol-related problems, and alcohol-specific attitudes, alcohol-specific communication, and adolescent excessive alcohol use and alcohol-related problems: an indirect path model. *Addictive Behaviors* 36(3): 209–216.

McGovern, R., Gilvarry, E., Addison, M. et al 2018. *Addressing the impact of non-dependent parental substance misuse upon children: a rapid review of the evidence of prevalence, impact and effective interventions.* UK: Public Health England.

McKeganey, N., Barnard, M., and McIntosh, J. 2002. Paying the price for their parents' addiction: meeting the needs of the children of drug-using parents. *Drugs: Education, Prevention and Policy* 9(3): 233–246.

McLaughlin, K. A. 2016. Future directions in childhood adversity and youth psychopathology. *Journal of Clinical Child and Adolescent Psychology* 45(3): 361–382.

Mental Health Foundation. 2006. Cheers? Understanding the relationship between alcohol and mental health. https://www.drugsandalcohol.ie/15771/1/cheers_report%5B1%5D.pdf

Mostofsky, E., Mukamal, K. J., Giovannucci, E. L., Stampfer, M. J., and Rimm, E. B. 2016. Key findings on alcohol consumption and a variety of health outcomes from the nurses' health study. *American Journal of Public Health* 106(9): 1586–1591.

Mukamal, K. J., Mittleman, M. A., Longstreth, W. T. Jr., Newman, A. B., Fried, L. P., and Siscovick, D. S. 2004. Self-reported alcohol consumption and falls in older adults: cross-sectional and longitudinal analyses of the cardiovascular health study. *Journal of the American Geriatrics Society* 52(7): 1174–1179.

Najjar, L., Young, C., Leasure, J. L., Henderson, C. and Neighbors, C. 2017. Religious perceptions of alcohol consumption and drinking behaviours among religious and non-religious groups. *Mental Health, Religion and Culture* 19: 1–14.

National Statistics. 2021. Alcohol Bulletin Commentary. https://www.gov.uk/government/statistics/alcohol-bulletin/alcohol-bulletin-commentary-february-2021-to-april-2021

National Survey for Wales. 2018–19. https://gov.wales/alcohol-consumption-national-survey-wales-april-2018-march-2019

New Strategic Direction for Alcohol and Drugs (NSD) Phase 2. https://www.emcdda.europa.eu/system/files/att_229803_EN_NI_New%20Strategic%20Direction%20for%20Alcohol%20and%20Drugs%20Phase%202_2011-2016.pdf

NHS Digital. 2018. https://digital.nhs.uk/news-and-events/latest-news/338000-admitted-to-hospital-as-a-result-of-alcohol-in-2017-18

NHS Digital. 2020. https://digital.nhs.uk/data-and-information/publications/statistical/statistics-on-alcohol/2020/part-4

NHS Health Scotland. 2006. http://www.healthscotland.com/documents/2134.aspx

NIAAA (National Institute on Alcohol Abuse and Alcoholism). 2019. https://www.niaaa.nih.gov/publications/brochures-and-fact-sheets/underage-drinking

OECD. 2020. Alcohol consumption (indicator). doi: 10.1787/e6895909-en (Accessed on 2020)

Office for National Statistics (ONS). 2017a. https://www.ons.gov.uk/peoplepopulationandcommunity/healthandsocialcare/drugusealcoholandsmoking/bulletins/opinionsandlifestylesurveyadultdrinkinghabitsingreatbritain/2017

Office for National Statistics (ONS). 2017b. https://www.ons.gov.uk/peoplepopulationandcommunity/healthandsocialcare/causesofdeath/bulletins/alcoholrelateddeathsintheunitedkingdom/registeredin2020

ONS (2021) Alcohol-specific deaths in the UK: registered in 2020. https://www.ons.gov.uk/peoplepopulationandcommunity/healthandsocialcare/causesofdeath/bulletins/alcoholrelateddeathsintheunitedkingdom/registeredin2020#alcohol-specific-deaths-in-the-uk

Paranjothy, S., Evans, A., Bandyopadhyay, A. et al. 2018. Risk of emergency hospital admission in children associated with mental disorders and alcohol misuse in the household: an electronic birth cohort study. *The Lancet Public Health* 3(6): e279–e288.

Perkins, H. W. 2002. Surveying the damage: A review of research on consequences of alcohol misuse in college population. *Journal of Studies on Alcohol* 14: 23–29.

Pickett, K., and Wilkinson, R. G. 2009. *The spirit level: why more equal societies almost always do better?* London: Allen Lane.

Radcliffe, P., d'Oliveira, A. F., Lea, S., Dos Santos F. W., and Gilchrist, G. 2017. Accounting for intimate partner violence perpetration. A cross-cultural comparison of English and Brazilian male substance users' explanations. *Drug and Alcohol Review* 36(1): 64–71.

Sánchez-Queija, I., Oliva, A., Jiménez, A., and Martínez-Vara de Rey, C. 2015. Longitudinal analysis of the role of family functioning in substance use. *Journal of Child and Family Studies* 25. doi: 10.1007/s10826-015-0212-9.

Saunders, J. B., Degenhardt, L., Reed, G. M. and Poznyak, V. 2019. Alcohol use disorders in ICD-11: past, present, and future. *Alcoholism Clinical & Experimental Research* 43(8): 1617–1631.

Schneider, A., and Ingram, H. 1993. Social construction of target populations: implications for politics and policy. *American Political Science Review* 87(2): 334–347.

Scottish Health Survey. 2019. https://www.gov.scot/publications/scottish-health-survey-2019-volume-1-main-report/

Skog, O. J. R. 2003. Alcohol consumption and fatal accidents in Canada, 1950–98. *Addiction* 98(7): 883–893.

Social Issues Research Center. 1998. http://www.sirc.org/publik/drinking3.html

Stanley, S. 2012. Communication apprehension and danger assessment in wives of alcoholics. *International Journal of Social Science and Humanity* 2(4): 301–304.

Stanley, S., and Vanitha, C. 2008. Psychosocial correlates in adolescent children of alcoholics—implications for intervention. *International Journal of Psychosocial Rehabilitation* 12(2): 67–80.

The alcohol harm reduction strategy for England. 2004. https://www.fai.org/sites/default/files/documents/alcoholhar_pdf.pdf

The Government's Alcohol Strategy (GAS). 2012. https://www.gov.uk/government/publications/alcohol-strategy

The Telegraph. (15 Nov.). https://www.telegraph.co.uk/politics/2020/11/15/lockdown-baby-boomers-spending-saved-money-alcohol-says-royal/

Thombs, D. L. 1999. Alcohol and motor vehicle use: profile of drivers and passengers. *American Journal of Health Behavior* 23(1): 13–24.

Tiebout, H. 1942. The private hospital and the care of alcoholic patients. *Diseases of the Nervous System*, 3: 202–205.

Tomlinson, M., Brown, M., and Hoaken, P. 2016. Recreational drug use and human aggressive behavior: a comprehensive review since 2003. *Aggression and Violent Behavior* 27: 9–27.

Turning Point. 2006. https://www.drugsandalcohol.ie/6276/1/3499-3720.pdf

Working Together to Reduce Harm. https://gov.wales/sites/default/files/publications/2019-10/substance-misuse-annual-report-and-forward-look-2019.pdf

World Health Organization. 2020. Lexicon of alcohol and drug terms. https://advocatetanmoy.com/2020/03/11/lexicon-of-alcohol-and-drug-terms-world-health-organization/

WHO. 2004. Global status report on alcohol. http://www.who.int/substance_abuse/publications/global_status_report_2004_overview.pdf

WHO. 2011. Global status report on alcohol and health. http://apps.who.int/iris/bitstream/handle/10665/44499/9789241564151_eng.pdf?sequence=1

WHO. 2014a. https://apps.who.int/iris/bitstream/handle/10665/112736/9789240692763_eng.pdf;jsessionid=0F8A61C23E9E804969F5B2E8668CA608?sequence=1

WHO. 2014b. Global status report on alcohol and health 2014. http://apps.who.int/iris/bitstream/10665/112736/1/9789240692763_eng.pdf?ua=1

10 A Bitter Pill to Swallow

Exploring and Understanding Drug Misuse in the UK

Darren Hill and Petra Salisbury

Prevalence and Magnitude

Substance use comes in all forms, and it is important we understand the amount of people using illicit drugs. The National Drug Treatment Monitoring System (NDTMS) records the numbers of people who seek treatment for their drug use in **England**. Between April 2020 and January 2021, 31,289 adults sought support for opiate-related treatment and 15,771 also approached services for other 'non-opiate'-related support – not including alcohol (NDTMS, 2021a). For young people, under the age of 18, more general figures are kept in terms of the amount of young people accessing or entering treatment; in January 2021, the total number of young people (under 18) in treatment (year to date) was 8,835 (NDTMS, 2021b).

BOX 10.1 MYTH: YOUNG PEOPLE ARE TEMPTED TO TRY DRUGS BY PUSHERS

Whilst there are many drug dealers, most young people are introduced to drugs by a friend or someone they know. Instead of pushing, most people are pulled in by curiosity, social networks, and a desire to experiment.

In **Scotland**, 10,900 adults were in drug treatment in the year 2019/2020, 36% of which was for Heroin-related issues. The statistics for young people were counted in the under 25 age group and showed 1,263 in treatment and 1,742 waiting to access services (Public Health Scotland, 2021).

NHS **Wales** collects their numbers slightly differently, having various age categories above ten years old. Recent data inform that 24,649 people were referred to treatment services, of those who attended 9,655 were for alcohol use and the remainder (6,262) were either for 'drug use' or 'not disclosed' (NHS Wales, 2021).

Northern Ireland also includes under 18s in their figures and initially breaks these down into alcohol use (1,397), drug and alcohol use (1,342), and finally drug only (1,525; DoH, 2021). Further breakdowns can be seen on the type of drugs people are using within the documents mentioned above. We must acknowledge that these figures are taken from data sets for structured treatment services and people who are seeking change; these figures do not include those who use drugs and do not seek help.

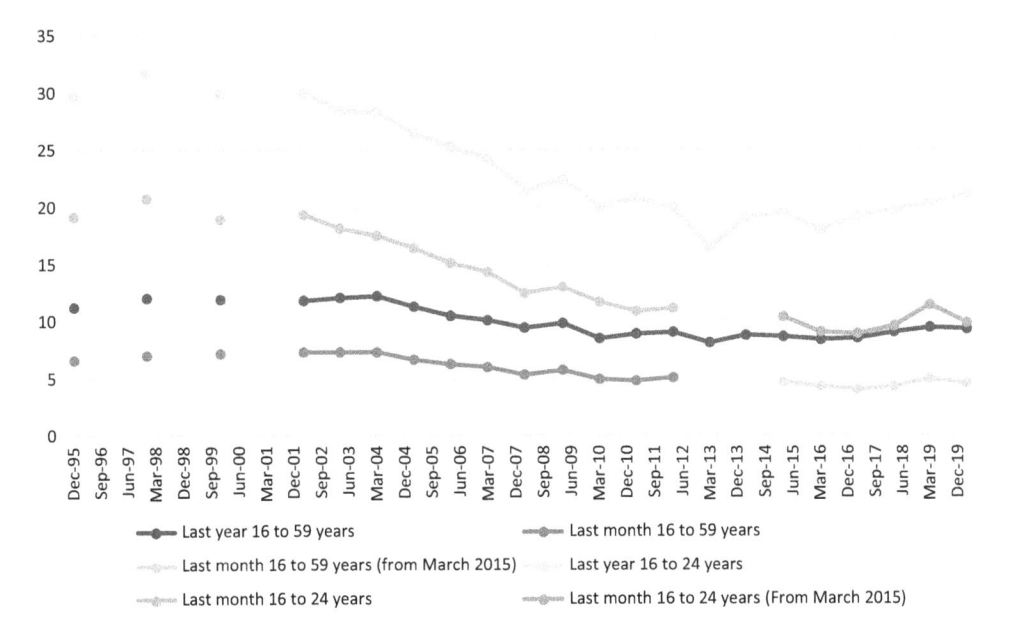

Figure 10.1 Drug misuse in England and Wales: year ending March 2020 (ONS, 2021).

Research suggests that the number of problem drug users is larger than the official treatment figures, they assert that up to 400,000 people in the UK use opiates or crack in a harmful or problematic way (Hill et al, 2016). Public Health England (2021) also estimated that in 2011 over 87,000 people were injecting drugs raising more questions as to how accurate official statistics are. The Office for National Statistics (ONS) also keeps data for England and Wales regarding the amount of people aged 16–59 who have used 'any drug' in the last year; 'any drug' refers to illegal drugs. The latest data taken from the National Crime Survey (NCS) suggests that over the last year, there has been no change from the previous year in the level of drug use amongst adults and showed that 1 in 11 adults (9.4%/3.2 million people) had used 'any drug' in the last year. In the 16–24 age group, this figure is higher at 21% or 1.3 million people in this age group. The graph below shows how the figure has changed and in most cases declined, amongst both the 16–59 group and the 16–24 group since 1996. The use in the last month's question was not asked from March 2012 but was reintroduced in March 2015 (Figure 10.1).

Terminology

When we think about the terms drug use or misuse, we must situate those terms within the broader social, medical, and criminal justice contexts within the UK. Drug use or misuse comes down to intent; a drug user is someone who takes a prescribed or appropriate drug to treat a specific ailment or medical condition. A drug misuser takes a drug to elicit an emotional or physiological effect for pleasure or recreation. There are many illicit drugs and they come in all shapes, forms, and sizes, but generally drugs fall into three overarching categories – depressants, stimulants, and hallucinogens: each having positive and negative implications. It is important to acknowledge here that drug use

Table 10.1 Positive and negative factors of stimulants, depressants, and hallucinogens

Stimulants: This group includes cocaine, crack cocaine, meth amphetamine, mephedrone, and amphetamine.
Positive Factors (Short Term): These drugs speed up the central nervous system and produce feelings of confidence and energy. People often feel the best they have ever felt (euphoria) and experience increased social functioning including talkativeness, confidence-increased humour, and empathy. They also reduce appetite and tiredness.
Negative Factors (Long Term): Stimulants can lead to cardiovascular issues and result in fatal heart problems and strokes. Hyper-active social presentation, self-reinforcing behaviour (tapping, rocking), anxiety. Withdrawal from stimulants can leave users restless, irritable, sleepless, and paranoid, anxious, and with suicidal thoughts.
Depressants: This group includes opioids, alcohol, and benzodiazepines.
Positive Factors (Short Term): These drugs can slow the central nervous system down and produce feelings of relaxation, euphoria, and general well-being. They can make the user feel warm, protected, and worry free and relieve anxiety and tension.
Negative Factors (Long Term): Social detachment, anxiety during withdrawal or detoxification. Risk issues with polysubstance misuse (alcohol–opiates–benzodiazepines) overdose and death may occur. Depressants often slow down reactions: hazards and accidents are more likely to occur in social contents. A physical dependency (recognised by medicine) that has an acute withdrawal when they are taken over extended period in large amounts, the dependency can impact on social functioning and presentation within society
Hallucinogens: This group includes LSD, magic mushrooms, and cannabis.
Positive Factors (Short Term): Hallucinogens give a heightened appreciation of the sensory experience and perceptual distortion: essentially hallucinogens are taken to induce a psychotic state.
Negative Factors (Long Term): Negative experiences can occur on hallucinogens the experience is directly related to users' mental and emotional state.

comes in different forms from recreational to problematic. Whatever the form of use; drug use or misuse ultimately aims to induce an altered state of consciousness. As we can see from the table above, a broad range of effects can be experienced from stimulants, depressants, and hallucinogens (Table 10.1).

Not all illicit drugs fit neatly into the categories above, though many of them do. Even the much-hyped emerging **New Psychoactive Substances (NPS)** tend to follow the traditional depressant, stimulant, hallucinogen model; there may be 600 of them currently available but despite the variety they tend to fall within the three major spheres of intoxicating effects explored (EMCDDA, 2020). Despite the number of NPS within the UK, there are several major key drugs that have shaped the illicit drug use landscape: spice, nitrous or nangs, and mephedrone or m-cat (Loi et al., 2015). Synthetic cannabis has become a major drug of choice for many young people and has also found a place within problematic and entrenched drug-using communities, a high proportion of dependent street-based drug users regularly using spice as an alternative to heroin and crack cocaine (EMCDDA, 2017). The use of 'nangs' or nitrous oxide is endemic in inner city areas in the UK, any walk down the road in many parts of the UK will highlight the flotsam of nitrous use, small silver canisters found in most bus shelters and scattered by many a road kerb sides. Initially, the rise of NPS was attributed to poor-quality heroin, cocaine, and ecstasy. Since the introduction of NPS, the illicit drug world like any market has responded, the quality of traditional illicit drugs such as heroin, cocaine, and ecstasy has improved, and we are at a situation where both the quantity and quality of all illicit drugs have improved.

The system of classification and scheduling for illegal drugs is a controversial one, as it is a convoluted legal process that has evolved from a moral, medical, psychological, and

Table 10.2 Legal classification of various drugs in the UK

Legal Classification	Drugs	Possession	Supply/ Production
Class A	Heroin, Cocaine, Crack Cocaine, MDMA, Ecstasy, LSD, Magic Mushrooms, Amphetamine (prepared for injection)	Up to 7 years in prison, an unlimited fine or both	Life in prison, an unlimited fine or both
Class B	Amphetamine, Cannabis, Barbiturates, Codeine, Ketamine, Synthetic Cannabinoids, Synthetic Cathinones (mephedrone)	Up to 5 years in prison, an unlimited fine or both	Up to 14 years in prison, an unlimited fine or both
Class C	Anabolic steroids, benzodiazepines (diazepam), gamma hydroxybutyrate (GHB), gamma-butyrolactone (GBL), piperazines (BZP), khat	Up to 2 years in prison, an unlimited fine or both (except anabolic steroids – it's not an offence to possess them for personal use)	Up to 14 years in prison, an unlimited fine or both
Temporary Class Drugs	Some methylphenidate substances (ethylphenidate, 3,4-dichloromethylphenidate (3,4-DCMP), methylnaphthidate (HDMP-28), isopropylphenidate (IPP or IPPD), 4-methylmethylphenidate, ethylnaphthidate, propylphenidate) and their simple derivatives	None, but police can take away a suspected temporary class drug	Up to 14 years in prison, an unlimited fine or both

social system. It follows no one logical or coherent process for assessing harm from an objective standpoint. An example of this would be the movement of Class B or C drugs to Class A via their route of administration; if you are injecting a Class B substance, it automatically becomes Class A due to the higher medical risk of the administrative method. The system of classification has also come under attack for not recognising the harm of legal drugs, such as nicotine and alcohol; Professor Peter Nutt in 2009 was forced to resign from his role as Chair of the Advisory Council on the Misuse of Drugs for suggesting that ecstasy was less harmful than alcohol. The system whilst not perfect or unitary in its methodology does provide a regulatory context and represents the evolutionary nature of prohibition and the social construction of drug misuse (Table 10.2).

The Social Context of Drug Misuse

Drug misuse is a subjective and socially constructed narrative, shaped by a complex system of morality, economics, politics, and legislation. We are not trying to be trite about such a serious issue; quite simply drugs are chemical compounds; they are neutral; they have uses that are practical, medical, and social; it is the meaning that we give to them that create a contested and socially constructed reality (Parssinen, 1983; Young, 1976). The term drug misuse is an emotive subject it conjures up evocative imagery, in both the mind of the individual and the collective imagination of society, resulting in the growth of myth and misconception. Our collective social order and reality often hinge on a narrative that sustains and promotes a battle between good and evil, right, and wrong.

The nefarious drug pusher; the degenerate and debased drug fiend; exotic powders, infernal elixirs and mind-altering potions; underpinned by the inescapable torment of the damned in their dependency and enslavement to drugs (Gossop, 2013). As a society, we have created a dualistic moral and mental framework where individuals are separated into good and bad; deserving, or undeserving, our institutions in the media, arts, and culture reinforces this narrative (Hill et al., 2018). It is a common myth and misconception that drug use, and drug misuse, centres only on poor individual decision-making; the decision to use or misuse drugs takes part in a wider social context. This individualisation of drug misuse forms part of a wider discourse within our society that seeks to isolate and compartmentalise social problems within an individual, rather than looking at wider social determinants that contribute to drug use or misuse. The need to have internal and external enemies to provide a moral framework that separates us into good and bad citizens seems to be a consistent and coherent message of modern western industrial civilisation; as society becomes more complex, so must the tools and systems that manage us and contain behaviour within acceptable parameters (Russell, 2009). Despite the move towards a judicial, moral, and political management of substances with the UK, we must recognise that since the dawn of civilisation individuals, families and communities have required the use of substances to mitigate, manage, and alleviate a range of social, psychological, and physiological needs (Escohotado, 1999). However, in forming a discussion on the social construction of drug misuse, it must be recognised that psychoactive substances form part of a larger family of chemical comforts that operate between the moral dualistic narrative of good and bad. The consumption of psychoactive substances underpins the foundations of society, they provide spiritual connection, meaning, comfort, space for breaks, and relaxation and keep us going at work. A world without psychoactive substances would be a very cold and unfriendly place to work, rest, and play.

The trade in illegal drugs is a global issue estimated to be worth between $400 and $600 billion annually; it outstrips the net worth of the global arms trade and is only beaten by the oil and gas trade in profitability (Hill et al., 2016). The world of illegal drugs follows a sound business model, it has a small number of producers, millions of dedicated and addicted consumers, and relatively small overheads (McKeganey, 2011). The illegal drug industry is flexible and adaptable and responds to the market needs of consumers rapidly. The organisations that facilitate this global trade have links to the international firearms trade, and modern slavery. Even though we have global prohibition, supported by an ongoing 'war on drugs', we remain at a stalemate, or some may view a loss and the drugs continue to flow, in increased numbers and of a higher quality.

Drug Misuse: Implications for People – a Psychosocial Perspective

The previous discussion has highlighted the social context of drug misuse; drug use or misuse in the UK sits at a moral crossroads between good and evil and right and wrong, and this moralistic social perspective forms part of our conceptualisation of substance use. Within the UK our response to drug use and misuse has taken a psychosocial turn; the complexity of the issue and the depth of the problem have led to no one response being adequate. A psychosocial perspective takes in medical, psychological, and social factors (these models will be explored later in this chapter) (Hill et al., 2016). Within the UK, the psychosocial perspective has converged on a harm reduction response to substance use as both a pragmatic and realistic response to an issue that has no one single solution (McKeganey, 2011).

> **BOX 10.2 MYTH: DRUG ADDICTION IS VOLUNTARY BEHAVIOUR**
>
> One of the popular social myths is that drug addiction is a voluntary decision. A recreational user may begin using drugs in a voluntary way, but over time things can change; recreational use may become dependent use than an addiction. Once a significant habit is formed, addiction changes the way you think and respond to events, and eventually use becomes compulsive and at times uncontrollable.

Before we explore the harm reduction philosophy, it is necessary to explore and situate drug misuse as a multi-factorial activity. Within the UK, the use of substances or illegal drugs has become a 'normal' experience, what was once a 'deviant' outsider activity can now be viewed and experienced as a 'normalised' experience and transitionary encounter for young people in the UK (Parker et al., 1998). We are not making the case that drug use is a given or that misuse and dependency are normal, just that the recreational experience of illicit drugs by young people transitioning into adult life is increasingly behaviour that is not questioned. While this is not the norm, it is perceived as being 'normal' in the lives of young people. Given such a pervasive context, not all illegal drug users engage in problematic or harmful behaviour. Problematic drug use is the use of substances that may be deemed legally or medically unacceptable, dangerous, or harmful (Ghodse, 2010). They may experience legal consequences in the form of arrest, detention, or prosecution for possession, or supply of illicit substances from criminal justice services such as the police. There are also social consequences for regular or dependent drug misuse; individuals may experience relationship problems or familial breakdown due to the prioritisation of drug misuse over social relationships. The habitual and consistent use of drugs also comes with economic consequences, illicit drugs are expensive, and habitual use can lead to debts to family, friends, financial institutions, employers, and drug dealers. Many committed drug users also experience both physical and mental health consequences as a result of drug misuse, and these issues will be explored later. To summarise, substance use becomes problematic when the consequences of use outweigh the positives, whether this be seen from a physical/mental health, legal, social, or financial perspective (Hill et al., 2016).

One of the core features of problematic substance use is the nature of addiction and dependency. Addiction and dependency are used interchangeably, but for the purpose of this chapter, let's set out some terms.

Dependency is usually attributed to a physical dependence of an illicit drug usually depressants such as opioids or benzodiazepines. Addiction refers to the complex interplay of physical dependency, psychological dependency, and the impact of social factors on long-term and continuous drug use. While it is possible to be dependent on a drug without being addicted to it, more often than not addiction follows dependency.

> **BOX 10.3**
>
> **Polysubstance Use:** Polysubstance use refers to the use of multiple substances. Polysubstance dependence or addictions are when an individual uses at least three different classes of substances and does not have a favoured substance that qualifies for dependence on its own.

Recreational drug use can be defined as the use of psychoactive substances to induce a state of relaxation, altered consciousness, heightened perception, or detachment within the mental and emotional state of the user. Recreational drug users of illicit substances tend to use these occasionally and have no regular or continuous issue with the consumption. They use illicit drug to enhance their life and find chemical comfort and relaxation in their recreational experience. As mentioned earlier this relates to an estimated 1 in 11 adults aged 16–59 (ONS, 2021). Recreational drug users advocate responsible drug use as a method for their consumption and place illegal drugs in the same context as legal drugs such as alcohol, nicotine, and caffeine. Recreational use of illegal drugs, while prohibited, is often socially tolerated and enforced by criminal justice agencies within the UK with a level of discretion.

The Costs and Consequences of Drug Misuse

The Financial Cost

Within this section, we are going to look at the costs of drug misuse moving beyond the individual, to the wider community at large. It is estimated that in the UK, illegal drugs cost society £15.4 billion in policing, health care, and crime (Home Office, 2020). Research conducted by Hay and Gannon (2006) suggests that the number of problem drug users is larger than the official treatment figures; they assert that up to 400,000 people in the UK use opiates or crack in a harmful way. McKeganey (2011) reminds us poignantly that between 60% and 70% of crime in the UK is linked to illegal drugs. The money involved in drug production and supply taints all levels of society from the street to the highest levels of the economic, social, and political world. Economic power buys access at all levels and it would be naive not recognise the influence that the world of illegal drugs has; the money from illicit drugs moves from the shadow economy to the legal economy, through a complex system of laundering and transfer that makes once unaccountable illegal money legitimate. A vast amount of police time at a regional, national, and international levels within the UK is dedicated to this pursuit. The National Crime Agency estimate that up to a £100 billion annually is laundered in the UK, with drugs playing a significant role in that figure (NCA, 2020). The National Economic Crime Centre has a system of reporting suspicious economic activity and reports over 300,000 suspicious activity reports being filed in one year (NCA, 2020a). If the outcome of prohibition and the war on drugs was to reduce the production, supply, and use of illegal drugs, it does not seem to be either effective or making major inroads to the problem. It is estimated that despite a national system of prohibition supported by policing only 5% of illegal drugs, at best, are seized by criminal justice services in the UK.

In counting the costs of drug misuse, we often forget the causation; the economic system we live within supports systemic inequality and nurtures the conditions for illicit drug use; the more unequal we have become the more unhappy, addicted, isolated, and atomised we have become as a society (Wilkinson & Pickett, 2007). It is from this perspective that we see addiction and drug misuse as both a response and a form of self-medication for economic and social inequality. The key to this context is that drug use and misuse do not impact directly on the social, political, and economic elites within the UK. Illicit drugs disproportionately affect individuals who are economically disadvantaged and drawn from working-class communities. The working-class communities that have seen their economic base for survival and existence removed through a process of deindustrialisation and marketisation; have the highest areas of drug addiction and deprivation. The greatest impact of addiction and drug misuse in the UK can be disproportionately found in the former industrial, mining, and manufacturing areas (Parker, 2005). Given this context, it is important to recognise the disproportionate impact of social class within addiction and dependency.

It is estimated that the cost of treating drug addiction and the associated physical health issues cost the NHS up to £500 million a year. Drug misuse and in particular addiction have a systemic impact on the health and wellbeing of the body, and mind; one particular complexity is the link between mental health and addiction. Half of the individuals who are using illicit drugs dependently reported a coexisting mental health problem or 'dual diagnosis' alongside their addiction issues (Hill et al., 2016). Mental health and addiction can be located as 'issues' that are intertwined within wider social and economic factors. However, we must recognise despite social causation the medical model is the dominant model for understanding mental health. The medical-psychiatric-based approach to the identification of substance misuse and mental health has seen the development of two systems that support classification and diagnosis: these systems are the World Health Organization's – *International Classification of Diseases* (ICD 10) and the American Psychiatric Association's – *Diagnostic and Statistical Manual* (DSM-V) (APA, 2013). Within the context of dual diagnosis within this chapter, we are using the DSM-V criteria as in Box 10.4:

BOX 10.4

1 An individual who has an identified substance use disorder with a co-existing psychiatric disorder that may be a secondary substance-induced mental health disorder,
2 Or a primary mental health disorder that was present before the use of substances.

Substance Misuse and Mental Health Issues

Within mental health and addiction, the term 'dual diagnosis' is a contested one, there are often passionate organisational and professional discussions over what comes first the problems with addiction or mental health. These discussions are often based on professional and institutional priorities; services are rationalised, organised, and funded by diagnostic labels. Despite medicalisation, there is compelling evidence that mental health and addiction are social and communication issues that are interlinked; this linked complexity is further supported by The Department of Health (2002) guide which describes four possible interlinked relationships (Box 10.5):

> **BOX 10.5**
>
> 1 A primary psychiatric illness precipitating or leading to substance misuse.
> 2 Substance use worsening or altering the course of a psychiatric illness.
> 3 Intoxication and/or substance dependence leading to psychological symptoms.
> 4 Substance misuse and/or withdrawal leading to psychiatric symptoms or illness.

Despite using a codified manual and having clearly demarked guidance from the Department of Health (2002): it is important to recognise that there is no one single uniform dual diagnosis presentation; it can be argued that there are many different patterns of consumption and multiple and complex presentations of mental distress. One common theme is that mental health, illicit drugs, and addiction are often interlinked and inseparable. Dual diagnosis is both a simple and a thoroughly confusing concept; within a complex world that places extreme pressure on our lived experience, we often experience conflicting mental states of varying degrees (Hill et al., 2016). As individuals seek to alleviate their mental distress, they often seek substances that can be used to medicate psychological and social distress symptoms as a form of self-medication. Often the illicit drugs individuals consume can contribute to or cause mental distress or symptoms often as a side effect. We also live in a society that is built upon economic and social inequality, in such a social context individual are often use illicit drugs to manage complex and traumatic life events, people who have experienced trauma often seek chemical comfort from illicit substances to manage and alleviate distress. The medicalisation of mental health and addiction has supported a narrative and discourse where the fault line for a 'dual diagnosis' is located within the individual. Thus, the impact of poverty and economic inequality on mental health is disguised by a complex layer of assessment, treatment, and diagnosis by medical and allied health professionals, locating the problem as an individual responsibility. In disguising the complexity of causation, it can be argued that the individualised-medicalised system protects those aspects of society that support the economic conditions that contribute to the social reproduction of mental and physical health problems.

Criminal Justice System

The UK criminal justice system, in particular prisons, has seen an increase and acceptance of illegal substances within the prison estate; this increase and normalisation mirror the normalisation of drugs within wider UK society (McKeganey, 2011). The difference we are seeing within UK prisons in the scale and severity of the problem; a wide variety of psychoactive substances are variable, which has led to an increase in difficulty in managing prisoners, as the use of substances creates a culture that nurtures violence through a system of drug debts and retribution. The range of substances available in particular new psychoactive substances such as synthetic cannabis has had a significant impact on the management of prison populations (Duke, 2020). Research highlights that up to 80% of men entering prison between the ages of 17–24 were drug users prior to entering and around 30% continued to use drug whilst in prison (Liriano & Ramsey, 2003). We discuss this because prisons can be seen as a microcosm of external society; the use and consumption of substances are systemic and endemic and have become somewhat normalised.

Harm Reduction

The promotion of a harm reduction model is an attempt to divert drug users away from criminal activity and problematic, dangerous drug use. Harm reduction also aims to engage people in community drug treatment services either by way of prescription drugs or other harm reduction interventions such as needle exchange services. The adoption of harm reduction as an approach and philosophy is a tacit if not subtle admission that drug use is not going away anytime soon. One of the biggest criticisms of harm reduction is that it acts as a sticking plaster for social, political, and economic conditions that service to sustain addiction; however, Harm reduction interventions are successful in engaging with drug users who fundamentally do not want behaviour change.

Links with Other Social Issues

The complex interplay between poverty, inequality, mental health, and physical health places problematic drug user in a high-risk category for harm and reduced life expectancy. The discourse of drug misuse cannot be viewed as an individualised issue, as we acknowledge in the wider harm reduction movement, drug use and misuse is systemic in its impact on the individual, family, community, and society. The first 50 years of UK drug policy failed to meaningfully recognise the impact of drug misuse on children and young people. The first UK national drug strategy in 1998 "Tackling Drugs to Build a better Britain" explored treatment, prevention, offending, and availability of drugs, but only mentioned children in passing, as an afterthought.

Impact on Children

Hidden Harm (2003) estimated that there were between 250,000 and 350,000 children of problematic drug users in the UK and recommended more coherent joint working practices be put in place to help reduce the impact of parental substance use on children (ACMD, 2003). Since 2008, and with the current UK Drug Strategy, children of drug users and young people are given a central place in the strategy, with specific reignition of the detrimental impact that illicit drugs have on parenting and outcomes for children and young people. More recently, this recognition of interlinked harm has developed further, with the articulation of the 'toxic trio' of drug misuse, domestic violence, and mental health, having a disproportionate impact on the social wellbeing and development of children and young people (Hill et al., 2018). We are not making the case that all parents who use drugs are bad parents. Many drug-using parents function effectively and offer 'good enough parenting'. The concept of 'good enough parenting' combined with the discourse of 'troubled families' is a clear indication that this is an area where there are shifting views, complex ethical issues, and uncertain professional practice (Hill et al., 2018). Part of the complexity lies within establishing what 'good enough parenting' looks like within any family, let alone drug-using families. Care and love are difficult components to break down; however, good enough parenting can be recognised in the need for parents to place the child's needs before theirs (Race & O'Keefe, 2017). Parental involvement in problematic drug misuse and drug dependency impacts on their ability to meet the child's needs over their daily drug-using needs.

The commitment to safeguard and uphold the rights of children combined with the rights of individuals to privacy and a family life is one of the most difficult and complex ethical situations health and welfare professionals face when encountering parental substance misuse. Despite the complexity, a pragmatic path must be chosen for the simple reason that 20% of adults entering drug treatment lived with children and 31% of adults in drug treatment reported that they were parents but were separated from children (McKeganey, 2011). Quantitative research has highlighted that the impact of parental drug use on children has been profound. Children exposed to cocaine in utero have been found to have a higher rate of premature birth, smaller head size, and lower birth weight. The follow-up study of babies exposed to in utero cocaine use has also highlighted suspicious or abnormal neurological signs at birth and deficits in mental and motor development (Lewis et al., 2004). Research undertaken with parents maintained on methadone has highlighted issues, and the use of methadone has a serious impact on neurobehavioral functioning; the effects of methadone were profound and impacted on foetal heart rate and motor activity. Even when we reduce the harm from substance use through treatment and support, there is no such thing as safe drug use, there are only safer alternatives. The impact of drug use and misuse on children and young people is significant. Qualitative studies that have collected the voices and experience of children and young people who have grown up in drug misusing families have highlighted the complex dangers and risks that children and young people face (Barnard, 2007). Many of the children normalised the violence, poverty, and degradation; they recognised that they were loved but came second place to drugs. The stories highlight lack of food, routines, violence from drug dealers, crippling debts, and most of all the lack of money and material access to the things children needed to not only survive but thrive; this social, psychological, and material degradation was underpinned by a secrecy, as the children of parental drug users are often hidden in veils of secrecy and remain loyal to their parents for fear of removal (Bancroft, 2004). So how do we respond to these complex issues of adult dependency and child welfare? Within the UK as we have alluded to previously, we operate a harm minimisation approach to drug treatment, this harm reduction approach is underpinned by a recovery model that sees abstinence as the end goal of treatment but not a prerequisite of accessing support or drug treatment services. This harm reduction model is underpinned by an operational medical, psychological, and social model of practice and their associated theoretical frameworks; we will move on to exploring these frameworks in depth within the next section of the discussion.

Theoretical and Operational Frameworks of Drug Misuse and Addiction

To understand how the UK has responded to problematic drug misuse and recreational drug use, it is important to understand the theoretical models of addiction and dependency. Drug misuse and addiction in the UK is responded to with three overarching theoretical models that of the Medical, Psychological, and Social Model (MPSM). Whilst it is important to recognise that the nature of drug misuse and addiction is contested between these models; we must recognise that the dominant model for managing drug misuse is the medical and psychiatric or psychological model of practice. These dominant systems also shape the social model of practice as they converge on a coherent system of individual adjustment and behaviour modification. Whilst it is difficult to find one overarching theory of addiction, theories that explore addiction and drug misuse can be broadly located at the individual level and the population level. The definitions of addiction vary but analysis by the European Monitoring Centre for Drugs and Drugs

Addiction suggests that the key features of addiction involves a repeated powerful motivation to engage in an activity such as drug misuse; addiction is acquired through engaging in the activity; the activity does not involve innate programming because of its survival value; and there is significant potential for unintended harm (West, 2013).

Within the UK, the problematisation of addiction as a fault line within the individual follows a consistent discourse that has been systematic. The discourse of individual responsibility is a primary driving force behind both the medical, psychological, and social models of intervention. In modelling the individual multiple theoretical positions have emerged; within this chapter, we will situate and explore the key theoretical categories of **automatic processing theories and biological/process of change theories.**

Automatic Process Theories (APT) attempt to explain and contextualise addiction by reference to individuals and their social circumstances. Individuals are regarded as possessing particular personal characteristics or residing in social environments that nurture and sustain addictive behaviour (Hyman et al., 2006). Recovery from addiction for individuals involves behaviour modification or adjustment of individual characterises or social locations. Within APT, the individual learning theories of addiction position addiction as a series of learnt behaviours derived from learning associations between cues, responses, and powerful positive or negative reinforcers (Ahmed, 2011). A key example of APT learning theory is Operant Learning Theory (OLT); OLT is a general theory of behaviour change that is built upon the premise that the presence of cues and the experience of positive and negative reinforcement increase or decrease the likelihood of a certain behaviour (Mook, 1995). OLT is a widely studied and evidence-based learning theory and underpins most models of motivational psychology and behaviour modification. Evidence supporting OLT theories of addiction includes the observation of non-human species acquiring addictive behaviour patterns (Ahmed, 2011). OLT of addiction has limitations, and it does not account for the importance of self-conscious intentions or beliefs not acquired through experience (Hyman, 2006).

The psychological model of APT has a direct link with the biological/medical model for the theoretical position of **Drive Theory (DT)**. DT is built upon the premise that addiction involves the development of powerful drives underpinned by a homeostatic mechanism (Mook, 1995) A key example of DT is the disease model of addiction. It must be recognised that the disease model is vast and goes beyond the scope of DT and has its own unique category of **Biological Theory (BT)**; however, the foundations of the disease model or medical model of addiction rely upon the concept that addiction and drug misuse involve pathological changes in the brain that result in overpowering stimulus to engage in drug misuse and addictive behaviour (Gelkopf et al., 2020).

Underpinning the APT and BT are the **Process of Change Theories (PCT)**. PCT form a core intellectual and operational context for addiction services and are a stalwart of behaviour change and modification in addiction theory. PCT focuses on the life cycle of addiction, from initial induction to drug misuse through the development of addiction, the theory looks at and explores attempts at recovery contextualising success and failure as part of an ongoing and fluid cycle subject to change. PCT focus on not only the cycle of change but also the mechanism, motivations, and desire to change within the individual.

The **Transtheoretical Model (TTM)** is one of the most widely used theoretical models of addiction that underpins policy, practice, counselling, and psychological interventions within addiction services (Prochaska et al., 1992). The stages of change,

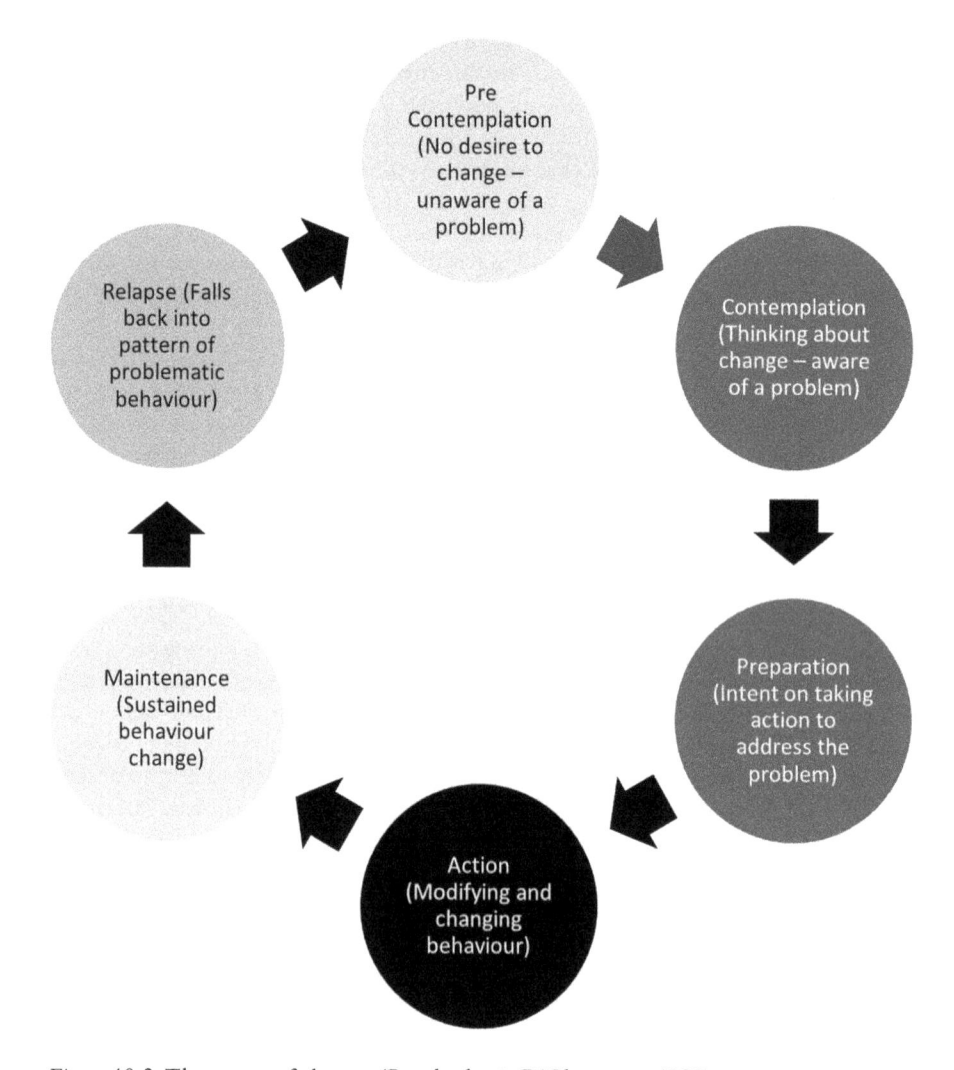

Figure 10.2 The stages of change (Prochaska & DiClemente, 1983).

processes of change, and concepts of self-efficacy and decisional balance are iconic and form part of the core logic, philosophy, and delivery of harm reduction drug addiction services in the UK (DiClemente et al., 1991). While the TTM is located at an individual level of adjustment, its theoretical operational within the processes of change recognises the importance of the social and population level of addiction. It is with this in mind that we move on to social or societal level theories of addiction (Figure 10.2).

With social theories of addiction or population modelling, there are a range of addiction theories; there are those that focus on social networks, behavioural economics, and models of communication and those that explore populations as systems. Within this discussion, we are going to focus on Social Network Theories (SNT); SNT highlight that the rates of transition into and out of addiction on the part of individuals within a group are a function and expression of the social connections between them (Valente et al., 2003). Addictive behaviours can occur in multiple levels within a social context, through families, local area groups, subcultures, and ultimately large-scale populations.

Key examples of SNT include diffusion theory which explores non-linear diffusion of innovations in illicit drugs; new psychoactive substances would be a good example of this (Ferrence, 2001). Social Contagion Theory focuses on connections between individuals and groups to chart uptake and cessation of addictive behaviours. Within the UK, the concept of individual and social models of addiction theory fit into an operational delivery context that combines both individual and social theories of addiction. Our services are contracted with medical, psychological, and social models of addiction and the interventions are undertaken at a community context. With this operational context in mind, we now move on to our next section exploring policy, practice, and the complex discourse that surrounds drug misuse in the UK.

UK Drug Policy and Legislation: From Free Trade to Prohibition

Historical Overview

The UK has had an ambivalent position with drugs and psychoactive substances; we have moved from a position of free trade to prohibition. This shift in social attitudes, policy, and legislation has been informed by three central discourses: the moral; the medical, and the criminal. Historically the UK and the Crown, through its operational arm the British East India Company (BEIC) were part of one of the first and largest international drug cartels openly and legally trading in opium and other psychoactive substances (Parssinen, 1983). British India, or to be more concise the BEIC had been the largest supplier of opium to China. It is ironic given our contemporary position of prohibition that the UK with the BEIC as a protagonist, fought several wars against China, who had tried to prohibit opium importation and smuggling. It is estimated that up to 10% of the population of China was dependent on opium during this period. We must also recognise that the process of industrialisation and urbanisation during the 18th and 19th centuries was both chaotic and unstructured; there was no national health service and narcotics provided both medical and social relief to the brutal living and working conditions of the poor and working classes. Marx remarked religion was the opium of the masses, but in truth, opium was the opium of the masses (Gossop, 2013). The sale and consumption of substances was unregulated until the mid-19th centuries when we see the rise of medicine as a professional institution. The eventual shift in attitudes towards international opium dealing came from a diminishing return on revenues and the development of a significant and vocal anti-opium lobby within the UK.

This use of moral, medical, and criminal justice narratives to shape the response to narcotics within the UK becomes part of a systemic tool for control and regulation and a consistent theme to this day. The late 19th, early 20th century sees a shift in attitudes towards the regulation and control of narcotics. The legal disciplinary capture of psychoactive substances from over-the-counter panacea for social distress and medical complaints to control by the state announces the end of an era of the comfort-given substance. The first regulation of psychoactive substances develops from a moral panic around the opium-addicted urban poor, a familiar often repeated narrative in the UK. The Public Health Act 1848 and the Pharmacy Act 1868 attempt to manage the distribution of psychoactive substances through the newly emerging medical profession. This national context was developed further by the first international drugs legislation that was enshrined in 1912 at The International Opium Convention at the Hague; the convention was signed by 12 nations including the UK. This global convention reinforced the position that the distribution of opium should be regulated by the medical profession and non-medical use was to be criminalised. The early 20th century was characterised by global conflict (World War I) and economic collapse during the great depression. Within this context of conflict and turmoil, psychoactive substances were characterised as external and foreign threats with the Regulation 40B of the Defence of the Realm Act 1914 (DORA) followed up by the Dangerous Drugs Act 1920. The legislation provided both a criminal justice context and medical role for the distribution of drugs. Throughout this period, we see the development of a deeper codification of the criminal justice and medical context of regulation and control. The Departmental Commission on Morphine and Heroin Addiction 1924–1926 or the Rolleston Report as it was headed up by Sir Humphrey Rolleston confirmed that addiction was a disease and that it should be treated by medical professionals. This report enshrined medicine as the gate keepers for addiction, its treatment, and the provision of drugs as medicines; it began a comprehensive system of treatment known as the 'British System'. The mid-20th century to the early 21st century sees another shift in the legislative and policy context; the medical discourse becomes reduced as a greater emphasis on criminal justice becomes central in the management and control of drugs and drug treatment.

Contemporary Policies

The mid to late 20th century sees a systemic shift in how health, education, justice, and broader welfare services are delivered. The creation of the NHS and the development of psychiatry as an established specialism of medicine created a radical overhaul in the provision and regulation of illicit drugs and drug dependency. Sir Russell Brain chaired the Interdepartmental Committee on Drug Addiction in 1961 and 1965, respectively, the two reports by this committee recommended the shift in treatment from general medicine; general medicine was described as facilitating addiction by creating dependency. Treatment was to be moved to the more specialised psychiatric and in patient community services; we see the beginning of addiction and mental health as a dominant discourse. During this period, drug treatment is moved in from general medical practice in the community to the special hospital and psychiatric clinic; general practitioners are placed at the centre of a moral panic where they are painted as encouraging and sustaining drug use. This policy and practice shift is also mirrored in legislation with the Dangerous Drugs Act 1967 (DDA 1967) and the Misuse of Drugs Act 1971 (MDA 1971). The MDA 1971 set clear parameters for criminal justice measures and in principle the schedules of classification and penalties reflected the potential for harm. Three classes were established (A, B, C) and drugs were allocated to them on a set criterion: whether they were being misused; whether they were likely to be misused; whether the misuse was likely in both previous cases to have or could have harmful effects sufficient to constitute a problem. The Misuse of Drugs Act 1971 has provided the foundation for all subsequent responses to illegal drugs, their prohibition, and treatment in the UK. The context for this legislation is the principle of harmfulness; however, the principle of harmfulness is not clearly established and is a hybrid of medical; social, moral, and legal models of practice. The notion of harmfulness can be considered as paternalistic and has no clear established evidence base. The MDA 1971

Table 10.3 Drug strategies in the UK

Drug Strategy Name	Year	Key Points
Tackling Drugs to Build a Better Britain	1998	• Help young people to resist use. • Protect communities from drug-related anti-social behaviour. • Treatment – enable people to seek help to live drug/crime-free lives. • Availability – stifle availability on our streets
UK Drug Strategy	2010	• Reducing demand • Restricting supply • Building recovery
UK Drug Strategy	2017	• Reducing demand • Restricting supply • Building recovery • Global Action
Strategy Harm to Hope	2021	• Break Drug Supply chains • Deliver world class treatment and recovery system • Achieve a generational shift in demand for drugs

is based more on a model of socio-moral objection rather than an empirical approach to harm or its reduction. Despite criticism, this system of classification has become entrenched as the foundation of our criminal justice response. This system remained firmly in place until the Psycho Active Substances Act 2016 which was developed in response to the mass production and development of hundreds of new psychoactive substances that the legislative framework of classification could not keep up with. The Psycho Active Substances Act 2016 still maintains the classification and schedule system for enforcement and has evolved to meet todays saturated drug market. Highlighting the agility and flexibility in the legislative response, rather than focusing on individual substances it makes all psychoactive substances subject to a criminal justice context. The late 20th and early 21st century sees not only a greater range of criminal justice response to drugs but also a shift in drug policy, and drug treatment from the specialist medical psychiatric model to a more criminal justice framework. There is a tacit acceptance that prohibition has failed in that interdiction and enforcement are tenuous. With this recognition of the failure of interdiction, the criminal justice and medical models converge upon an expanded harm reduction model of treatment; this shift is implemented through a series of UK Drug Strategies (1985, 1998, 2008, 2010, 2017; Table 10.3).

UK drug policy has flip-flopped between whether it should punish, educate, or treat its drug users and without any real success has, over time, attempted all three. Whilst the reduction of drug-related harm and good evidence-based treatment and support is welcomed and needed; harm reduction does not address the wider issues that nurture, support, and facilitate drug addiction and dependency.

Summary

The use and misuse of substances in the UK is an issue that is here to stay; drugs and illicit substances are part of our social, political, and economic fabric of our society. Given the harm caused by illicit drugs and the discussion highlighted within this chapter, the only pragmatic conclusion would be to argue for drug legalisation. We can see the compelling evidence for this, much of the harm associated with drug misuse is rooted in the policies, legislation, and criminalisation of drug use. However, tempting this proposal is we must ask ourselves this: if we legalised all drugs would addiction and dependency levels remain stable and manageable levels? It is difficult to predict the future but given the prevailing economic and social conditions of systemic inequality, we have seen drug addiction and dependency increase as society has become more fractured and individualised. The issue of drug-related harm cannot be addressed by removing barriers to access or promoting behavioural models of intervention. A more developed harm reduction model must have truly political dimension that seeks to address the social determinants of addiction at a legislative and policy level. Illicit drugs and dependency can only be minimised when people have increased access to better social and material resources, improved living conditions, and increased community cohesion. Drug dependency is underpinned by isolation, inequality, and low status in the social odder of society; to beat isolation, anxiety, and addiction, we need social solidarity and economic equity as a foundation for a good society.

Points to Ponder

Should illicit drug be legalised in the UK?
If we legalised all drugs would addiction and dependency levels remain stable and manageable levels?
What would happen to the drugs trade if drugs were to be legalised?

Reflective Points

Reflecting on the schedule of classification (A, B, C) developed in the UK to manage drug misuse.
If you had to develop a criminal justice system to manage drug misuse how would you do this?
How would you measure harm?
What system would you use, moral, medical, social, or psychological?

Quiz

State whether the following items are True or False

1 Allowing people to use drugs in your home is a crime?
2 Cannabis (weed) can only be smoked?
3 Using Cocaine can lead to weight loss?
4 Nitrous oxide is a harmless drug?

Choose the Correct Answer:

5 Amphetamines are:

a. Depressants b. Stimulants c. Hallucinogens

6 Is Heroin a

   a. Stimulant b. Depressant c. Hallucinogen

7 Magic Mushrooms are a

   a. Stimulant b. Depressant c. Hallucinogen

Fill in the Blank in the Following Items

8 _____is a highly addictive form of cocaine processed into a crystal.
9 _____is the most common mind-altering substance used during adolescence.
10 _____is a synthetic drug with stimulant and hallucinogenic effects.

Answers

1. True. 2. False. 3. True. 4. False. 5. Stimulant. 6. Depressant. 7. Hallucinogen. 8. Crack. 9. Marijuana. 10. Ecstasy.

Small Group Discussion

Activity One

Please consider the following drugs detailed below.
  What category do they belong to, are they a depressant stimulant or hallucinogen?
  Cocaine, Heroin, Magic Mushrooms, Amphetamine, Ecstasy, Spice, Ketamine.
  Do these drugs fit into one category?
  Which of the drugs would you consider a recreational drug and which drug would you view as causing dependency?

Activity Two

Each student is to take the name of a drug, and the students must decide upon themselves the order of harm for each drug. Students must make a line from least harmful to most harmful and discuss why they have done this.

  More information regarding this activity can be found by reading Chapter three Nutt, D. 2012. *Drugs Without the Hot Air.* UIT, Cambridge.

Supplementary Reading

Ghodse, H. (2009) *Drugs and Addictive Behaviour: A Guide to Treatment* (3rd Ed). Cambridge: Cambridge University Press.
Gossop, M. (2007) *Living with Drugs.* London: Ashgate Publishing.
Hill, D. Penson, W. J., and Charura, D. (2016). *Working with Dual Diagnosis: A Psychosocial Perspective.* London: Palgrave Macmillan.
McKeganey, N. (2011) *Controversies in Drugs Policy and Practice.* London: Palgrave Macmillan.
Parssinen, M. T. (1983). *Secret Passions, Secret Remedies: Narcotic Drugs in British Society 1820–1930.* Manchester: Manchester University Press.

Service user organisations working in the topic area

Adfam (Information and support for the families of drug and alcohol users): https://adfam.org.uk

Frank (General information, advice and support): https://www.talktofrank.com/

Narcotics Anonymous (12 Step Recovery Group): https://ukna.org/

References

Advisory Council on the Misuse of Drugs (ACMD). (2003) Hidden Harm. [Internet]. Available from https://assets.publishing.service.gov.uk/government/uploads/system/uploads/attachment_data/file/120620/hidden-harm-full.pdf (Accessed March 2021).

Ahmed, S. H. (2011) 'The science of making drug-addicted animals', *Neuroscience* 211, pp. 107–125.

Bancroft, H. (2004) *Parental Drug and Alcohol Misuse: Resilience and Transition among Young People*. York: JRF.

Barnard, M. (2007) *Drugs and the Family*. London: Jessica Kingsley Press.

DiClemente, C. C., Fairhurst, S. K., Velasquez, M. M., Prochaska, J. O., Velicer, W. F., and Rossi, J. S. (1991) 'The process of smoking cessation: An analysis of precontemplation, contemplation, and preparation stages of change', *Journal of Consulting and Clinical Psychology* 59, pp. 295–304.

DoH (Department of Health). (2002) *Mental Health Policy and Implementation Guide – Dual Diagnosis Good Practice Guide*. London: Department of Health.

DoH (Department Of Health). (2021) [Internet]. Statistics from the Northern Ireland Substance Misuse Database. Available from https://www.health-ni.gov.uk/publications/statistics-northern-ireland-substance-misuse-database-201920 (Last accessed March 2021).

Duke, K. (2020) 'Producing the "problem" of New Psychoactive Substances (NPS) in English prisons', *International Journal of Drug Policy*, 80. doi: 10.1016/j.drugpo.2019.05.022.

EMCDDA. (2017) *Synthetic Cannabinoids in Europe (Perspectives on Drugs)*. Lisbon: EMCDDA.

Escohotado, A. (1999) *A Brief History of Drugs: From the Stone Age to the Stoned Age*. Vermont: Inner Traditions/Bear.

Ferrence, R. (2001) 'Diffusion theory and drug use', *Addiction* 96, pp. 165–173.

Gelkopf, M., Levitt, S., and Bleich, A. (2002) 'An integration of three approaches to addiction and methadone maintenance treatment: The self-medication hypothesis, the disease model and social criticism', *Israel Journal of Psychiatry and Related Sciences* 39, pp. 140–151.

Ghodse, H. (2010) *Drugs and Addictive Behaviour: A Guide to Treatment* (3rd Ed). Cambridge: Cambridge University Press.

Gossop, M. (2013) *Living with Drugs*. 7th ed. London: Ashgate.

Hill, D., Mercer, D., and Agu, L. (2018) *Exploring and Locating Social Work: A Foundation for Practice*. Basingstoke-England: Macmillan International – Red Globe Press.

Hill, D., Penson, B., and Charura, D. (2016) *Working with Dual Diagnosis: A Psychosocial Perspective*. Basingstoke-England: Palgrave Macmillan.

Home Office. (2020) [Internet] Financial Cost of Acquisitive Crime Caused by Class a Drug Users in the UK. Available from https://www.gov.uk/government/publications/financial-cost-of-acquisitive-crime-caused-by-class-a-drug-users-in-the-uk (Last Accessed January 2021).

Hyman, S. E., Malenka, R. C., and Nestler, E. J. (2006) 'Neural mechanisms of addiction: the role of reward-related learning and memory', *Annual Review of Neuroscience* 29, pp. 565–598.

Lewis, M. W., Misra, S., Johnson, H. L., and Rosen, T. S. (2004 May) 'Neurological and developmental outcomes of prenatally cocaine-exposed offspring from 12 to 36 months', *The American Journal of Drug and Alcohol Abuse*, 30(2), pp. 299–320. doi: 10.1081/ada-120037380. PMID: 15230078.

Liriano, S. and Ramsay, M. (2003) 'Prisoners' drug use before prison and the links with crime'. In: Ramsay, M. (ed.) *Prisoners' Drug Use and Treatment: Seven Research Studies* (pg 7). Home Office Research Study 267. London: Home Office.

Loi, B., Corkery, J. M., Claridge, H., Goodair, C., Chiappini, S., Gimeno Clemente, C., and Schifano, F. (2015) 'Deaths of individuals aged 16–24 years in the UK after using mephedrone', *Human Psychopharmacology: Clinical & Experimental* 30(4), pp. 225–232.

McKeganey, N (2011) *Controversies in Drugs Policy and Practice*. London: Palgrave Macmillan.

Mook, D. (1995) *Motivation: the Organization of Action*. London: Norton.

National Crime Agency (NCA). (2020) [Internet] Money Laundering and Illicit Finance. Available from https://www.nationalcrimeagency.gov.uk/what-we-do/crime-threats/money-laundering-and-illicit-finance (Last Accessed January 2021).

National Crime Agency (NCA). (2020a) [Internet] Suspicious Activity Reports. Available from https://www.nationalcrimeagency.gov.uk/what-we-do/crime-threats/money-laundering-and-illicit-finance/suspicious-activity-reports (Last Accessed January 2021).

National Drug Treatment Monitoring system (NDTMS). (2021a) [Internet] Community Adult Treatment Performance Report. Available from https://www.ndtms.net/Monthly/Adults (Last Accessed March 2021).

National Drug Treatment Monitoring System (NDTMS). (2021b) [Internet] Community Young People (YP) Treatment Performance Report. Available from https://www.ndtms.net/Monthly/YoungPeople (Last Accessed March 2021).

NHS Wales. (2021) [Internet] Treatment Data – Substance Misuse in Wales 2018–19. Available from https://gov.wales/sites/default/files/publications/2019-10/treatment-data-substance-misuse-in-wales-2018-19.pdf (Last Accessed March 2021).

Office for National Statistics (ONS). (2021) Drug Misuse in England and Wales: Year Ending March 2020. Available from https://www.ons.gov.uk/peoplepopulationandcommunity/crimeandjustice/articles/drugmisuseinenglandandwales/yearendingmarch2020#:~:text=Any%20drug%20use%20in%20the%20last%20year&text=Findings%20from%20the%20Crime%20Survey, 9.4%25%3B%203.2%20million%20individuals (Last Accessed March 2021).

Parker, H., Aldridge, J., and Measham, F. (1998) *Illegal Leisure: The Normalization of Adolescent Recreational Drug Use*. London: Routledge.

Parker, S. (2005). *Mentor UK Coastal and Ex-mining Areas Project – A Review of the Literature*. London: Mentor.

Parssinen, M. T. (1983) *Secret Passions, Secret Remedies: Narcotic Drugs in British Society 1820–1930*. Manchester: Manchester University Press.

Prochaska, J. O., DiClemente, C. C., and Norcross, J. C. (1992) 'In search of how people change – applications to addictive behaviors', *American Psychologist* 47, pp. 1102–1114.

Public Health England (PHE). (2020) [Internet] Substance Misuse Treatment for Adults: Statistics 2018 to 2019. Available from https://www.gov.uk/government/statistics/substance-misuse-treatment-for-adults-statistics-2018-to-2019 (Last Accessed January 2021).

Public Health England (PHE). (2021) [Internet] Shooting Up: Infections among People Who Inject Drugs in the UK, 2019. Available from https://assets.publishing.service.gov.uk/government/uploads/system/uploads/attachment_data/file/953983/Shooting_Up_2020_report.pdf (Last Accessed March 2021).

Public Health Scotland (PHS). (2021) [Internet] A National Statistics Publication for Scotland. Available from https://beta.isdscotland.org/find-publications-and-data/lifestyle-and-behaviours/substance-use/scottish-drug-misuse-database/ (Last Accessed March 2021).

Race, T. and O'Keefe, R. (2017) *Child-Centred Practice: A Handbook for Social Work*. London: Palgrave Macmillan.
Russell, B. (2009) *The Prospects of Industrial Civilization*. London: Routledge.
West, R. (2013) *Models of Addiction*. Lisbon: EMCDDA.
Young, J. (1971) *The Drugtakers: The Social Meaning of Drug Use*. London: Paladin.

11 Constructing and conceptualising suicide and self-harm

Steven Jones and Rajan (Taj) Nathan

Explanatory models of suicidal behaviour

Suicide is a human tragedy and no amount of theories, statistics, or facts will change its far-reaching impact. Clinical conceptualisations of suicidal behaviour are widely prevalent. Within a medical paradigm, psychiatric diagnoses are given explanatory power. For instance, an individual's suicidal behaviour may be seen to be a consequence of a major depressive disorder or of personality disorder (Bertolote and Fleischmann, 2002). Such explanations are limited by the rigidity of the categorical approach to diagnosis. In themselves, diagnoses restrict scope for recognising an individual's unique circumstance. If the key explanatory entity for an individual's suicidal act is, for example, major depressive disorder, then there is an implicit assumption that from an explanatory perspective the individual is equivalent to all other individuals whose suicidal acts have been attributed to major depression and different to those whose acts have been deemed to be a consequence of borderline personality disorder. Empirical evidence supports an association between diagnoses such as major depressive disorder and borderline personality disorder on the one hand and suicidal behaviour on the other (Dong et al., 2019; Temes et al., 2019). However, caution should be exercised before accepting that the diagnosis is a causal entity which leads to behaviour. To the contrary, a psychiatric diagnosis is a collection of experiences and behaviours which is not necessarily underpinned by a singular causal entity that is common to all individuals to whom the diagnosis is applied. It should not come as a surprise that a collection of experiences and behaviours which includes 'recurrent thoughts of death, recurrent suicidal ideation' (as DSM-5 major depressive disorder does) or one which includes 'recurrent suicidal behaviour' (as DSM-5 borderline personality disorder does), are associated with suicidal acts (American Psychiatric Association, 2013).

Suicidal behaviour has been linked to physiological, genetic, and other biological markers (Sudol and Mann, 2017). An explanatory model based on such biological correlates may inform certain types of interventions (particularly medical ones; Hawton et al., 2015). Such a model has the potential to objectify the suicidal mind. Alternatively, explanatory models may rely on psychological processes to derive meaning. Notably, the Integrated Motivational-Volitional (IMV) model seeks to integrate the evidence base by conceptualising suicidal behaviour according to three phases (O'Connor and Kirtley, 2018). The first, or 'pre-motivational,' phase encompasses recognised vulnerabilities and environmental factors. The second, or 'motivational,' phase refers to the role of key processes such as defeat, entrapment, autobiographical memory biases, and rumination to explain the development of suicidal ideation and intent. In the final, or volitional, phase, volitional moderators such as access to means or fearlessness are seen as critical to the translation of ideation/intent into action. Such models have greater flex and therefore wider applicability. However, they still are constrained by the assumption that these processes are essential to suicidal behaviour.

All of the aforementioned models encourage a focus on the individual. In so doing, they may recognise the role of extra-individual events (e.g., in the form of a precipitating or perpetuating life events), but ultimately the explanation is brought together at the level of the individual and they do not routinely take into account latent group-level processes. Whilst explanations for suicide at the level of the individual (such as diagnostic or psychological formulations) may inform interventions for individuals, there is a risk of neglecting the wider contextual processes and thereby also failing to recognise opportunities to inform group interventions, such as policy.

BOX 11.1 EXPLANATORY PARADIGMS

Type	Context	Level	Examples
Biological	Physical matter	Individual	Genetic risk, neurochemical differences
Psychological	Mind-based processes	Individual	Integrated Motivational-Volitional model
Sociological	Societal	Groups	Durkhiemian model

Durkheim's contribution

From his empirical study of the differences in suicide rates between different societies, Emile Durkheim sought to identify collective processes that create societal conditions for these differences in rates (Durkheim et al., 2002). He used the notion of social integration to describe the degree to which the members subscribe to shared values, goals, and practices (Johnson, 1965). According to Durkheim, societies at either end of the spectrum of integration are liable to increased suicide rates (Durkheim et al., 2002). Societies characterised by low levels of solidarity can lead to a type of suicide which Durkheim called egoistic. Differences in integration may arise, for instance, due to a difference in the prevailing religion. The individualism attributed to protestant communities (as opposed to the Catholic ones which are held to involve a greater sense of community) are purported within the Durkhiemian model to create a setting for egoistic suicide (Stack, 2004). The model is not just apparent in comparisons between different communities. The same community may vary in its level of integration over time. Notably, a crisis can serve to promote integration and therefore reduce the likelihood of egoistic suicides (Bille-Brahe, 2000). At the other end of the spectrum, excessively high levels of integration are associated with suicides for the benefit of the group, so-called altruistic suicide (Stack, 2004). Examples that have been described include the act of hari-kari committed by defeated Japanese soldiers. In addition to integration, Durkheim identified the social force of regulation which may be manifest in a way that is linked to suicide. Within a fluid and unregulated community in which traditional institutions are attenuated there is a greater liability to anomic suicides. Overly regulated societies are associated, according to Durkheim, with fatalistic suicides. It stands that self-harm should be examined or explored along its sociological as well as its psychological continuums (Steggals et al., 2020). Millard (2013) suggested that self-harm is something that is psychologically self-evident and more a product of social history than it is a reflection of natural fact.

Suicide and self-harm

Exploring the works and theories of others presents an opportunity to review our individual belief systems. However, it has to be acknowledged that a full understanding of the complexities of suicide is likely to be unachievable, whether that is at an individual or a societal group level. Suicide and self-harm are multifaceted concepts that are influenced by biological, psychosocial, and socio-cultural factors (Kutcher and Chehill, 2007). A conceptual distinction between suicide and self-harm may be made, rather straightforwardly, on the basis of the outcome. But clinical experience and empirical evidence indicates that although there may be some differences, the assumption of a categorical ignores commonalities between the situations leading to different outcomes.

BOX 11.2 SUICIDE METHODS (UK, 2016)[a]

Methods	Proportion of deaths by suicide	
	Males (%)	Females (%)
Hanging, suffocation, or strangulation	58.7	42.8
Poisoning	18.3	36.2
Drowning	4.3	5.2
Falls and fractures	3.9	5.3
Other	14.8	10.5

[a]Suicides in the UK: 2016 registrations (Office for National Statistics).

BOX 11.3 SELF-HARM METHODS

Cutting	Hitting
Scratching	Swallowing
Burning	Object insertion
Scalding	Wound tampering
Poisoning	Eye enucleation
Hair-pulling	

Whilst the authors adopt a largely UK perspective, international evidence will also be presented. It is for society and interagency services to work on reducing the likelihood of completed suicides, whilst accepting that suicide will always occur and at the same time elucidating processes and system elements that contribute to causal explanations. One such potential contributory factor is knowledge and awareness gaps amongst health professionals (Jones et al., 2015; Kumar et al., 2016); furthermore, investigations have revealed that common to the circumstances contributing to an increased likelihood of a suicide outcome are deficits in clear communication.

Suicide statistics in context

Suicide is a significant public health concern with global relevance. Each year approximately three-quarters of a million people chose to end their life by suicide. There were close to 800,000 suicide deaths worldwide in 2016, equating to an age-standardized suicide rate of 10.5 per 100,000 population (WHO, 2016). Global rates differ considerably between countries from less than 5 to over 30 deaths by suicide per 100,000 (WHO, 2019). Suicide can occur throughout a person's life course. Seventy-nine percent of all suicides occurred in low- and middle-income countries (LMICs; WHO, 2016).

Major differences exist between high-income countries and LMICs. In the latter, young adults and elderly women have higher suicide rates than their counterparts in high-income countries. But middle-aged men in high-income countries have much higher suicide rates than middle-aged men in LMICs. Suicide rates are higher in males (13.7 per 100,000) than in females (7.5 per 100,000). But for females, the highest rates in some countries were above 30 per 100,000, and for males above 45 per 100,000 (WHO 2019). Whilst the male/female suicide ratio is close to 3–1 in high-income countries, the ratio is more equal in LMICs. The majority of global suicide deaths occurred in LMICs (79%), where 84% of the world's population lives. More than half (52.1%) of global suicides occurred before the age of 45. Suicide deaths among adolescents in the majority of cases (90%) were from LMICs were approaching 90% of the world's adolescents live (WHO, 2019). European age–sex-standardised rate (EASR) in 2019 was 15.5 deaths per 100,000 population, slightly higher than the 2018 figure of 14.6 per 100,000 (2017 figure = 12.8 per 100,000). This highlights an upward three-year trend in European suicide rates. For males, suicide EASR in 2019 was 23.3 per 100,000 compared to 21.9 per 100,000 in 2018. For females, the suicide EASR in 2019 was 7.6 per 100,000, higher than the rate in 2018 (7.3 per 100,000). In 2019, the suicide rate for males was over three times that for females. Europewide rates for both genders are increasing, but the gender divide remains constant (ONS, 2020).

England and Wales, Scotland, and Northern Ireland data

Care should be exercised when comparing suicide data between different jurisdictions. The definitions of suicide and burdens of proof have changed in the past decade, and it could be argued lack consistency UK wide. Suicide rates are reported by deaths per 100,000 of population. These rates however do not take account of local/regional variations that can skew the data away from suicide hot spots. Fluctuations on an annual basis must also be treated with caution; they can falsely reassure that interventions are working (or not), accepting that there are regional differences. These variations do not take into account other factors that may have a bearing on suicide raters.

In England and Wales the National Confidential Inquiry (NCI) into Suicide and Safety in Mental Health has collected in-depth information on all suicides in the UK since 1996. In Wales, changes in suicide rates over time are more volatile than those in England because of the relatively smaller number of deaths (University of Manchester, 2019). To attempt to reduce suicide rates, we first need to know how many people die each year and when and where they died. The method employed in the suicide also must be determined, with the overall aim being to reduce lethality and make interventions targeted. Protective factors for suicide must be explored at an individual level, locally and then nationally or vice versa. Local government, primary care, health and criminal justice services, third sector organizations, and all people affected by suicide have a role to play.

Deaths by suicide result in a coroner's inquest. The time taken to complete an inquest (especially during global pandemics) from the date the death occurred to the date the death will have an impact on how cotemporaneous current data sets are. Registration delays for deaths by suicide can take between six and nine months. Provisional suicide data show there were 10.7 suicide deaths per 100,000 people in Quarter 3 (July to September) 2020 in England, equivalent to 1,334 deaths registered; this rate is similar to rates seen in 2019. Wales, Northern Ireland, and Scotland report separately.

Suicide figures for Scotland show that 833 people died by suicide in 2019. When compared to 784 deaths by suicide in 2018, this suggests an upward trend (Scottish Public Health Observatory, 2020). Between 2017 and 2019 figures in Scotland for both sexes and age ranges have risen year on year. In 2009, the National Records of Scotland (NRS) that gathers information about the nature of death changed its approach, following which there was a significant increase in the percentage of poisoning deaths described as accidental, with an associated decrease in those described as being undetermined intent. This is likely to have contributed to the fall in recent years (2010–2017) in the number of officially recorded probable suicides (NRS, 2020). Approaching 32% of all probable suicides were people aged between 45 and 59 years. Over the last five years period, the proportion of probable suicides was higher in the 45–49 age groups. This change in age group shift marks another change from the late 1990s when a larger proportion was people in their late 20s to early 30s (NRS, 2020).

Northern Ireland Statistics and Research Agency (NISRA) report statistical indicators of overall mental health that monitor trends in deaths resulting from intentional (and probable) self-harm which is interest. Data are available on 'intentional self-harm and suicide.' Data from Northern Ireland in 2015 indicated 318 (245 male, 73 female) deaths that fell within the definition of suicide. This was the highest figure recorded with a small decline to 307 (228 males, 79 females) in 2018 (NISRA, 2020). But again, figures do not accurately portray the pain caused to families, even with such small downward trends.

Definitions in the Northern Ireland suicide death reports are the same as the UK definition that also includes deaths from self-inflicted injury and undetermined intent events.

Suicide rates, gender, and age

Suicide is more likely amongst men than women, in particular men in their 40s and 50s from lower UK socio-economic groups. There were 16.3 deaths per 100,000 males (992 deaths registered) equating to 5.4 suicide deaths per 100,000 females (342 deaths registered); these rates are similar to rates reported the year before. Suicide rates for men and women are statistically significantly higher in late 2020 (compared with early 2020) because of the lower number of suicides registered in April–June. The ONS suggests that this may be due to COVID-19 restrictions impacting on the coroner's service with delayed inquests. For the last 10 years, people aged 10–24 years and men aged 45–64 years have the greatest increases in suicide rates (ONS, 2020).

Implications of suicide: individual, family, community, and wider society

When an individual takes their own life it carries a significant impact for family members, the family unit, and the wider community. Those individuals who do not successfully die by suicide are liable to experience a range of feelings from feeling fortunate or regretful to have survived. They may feel that they have reached the depths of despair and feel shamed, outcast or perhaps shunned and ostracised locally. Family feelings of loss, anger, or confusion may be encountered, aligned to grief and loss. We are mindful of not using the words, successful and failed attempts that are value laden and potentially invalidating, but individuals may adopt such terms as they strive for meaning.

The journey out of despair may be long, and it requires support and no small amount of courage to overcome. Suicidal behaviour remains stigmatised at a societal level.

Ideas, thoughts, and feelings of suicide and self-harm may co-exist within the same individual, but the act can be retrospectively defined by the outcome. Self-harm rather than deliberate self-harm has become the preferred phrase. A toolkit for self-harm is available to download from the University of Manchester team based on NICE quality standards for self-harm https://sites.manchester.ac.uk/ncish/

Suicide definition – From 2018, a 'civil standard' has been applied by coroners that on the balance of probability:

- the death occurred because of a deliberate act by the deceased
- that in doing so and at all relevant times, the deceased intended the consequence would be death
    For all deaths given a conclusion of suicide, a coroner makes this decision having ruled out all other possible explanations

(ONS, 2019)

Self-harm definition – Self-harm refers to any act of self-poisoning or self-injury carried out by a person, irrespective of their motivation. This commonly involves self-poisoning with medication or self-injury by cutting. Self-harm is generally not used to refer to harm arising from overeating, body piercing, body tattooing, excessive consumption of alcohol or recreational drugs, starvation arising from anorexia nervosa, or accidental harm to oneself (NICE, 2013).

What figures do not accurately convey is individual perspectives on the many social, political, psychological, and societal impacts of suicide. They are an attempt to provide perspective, but the real value resides in initiatives that reduce suicide risk. Being mental health professionals in secondary care services, we only ever know when we got it wrong when someone attempted significant harm to themselves, or sadly ended their life. We can only guess about those whose life we intervened on and prevented an act/ attempt. It is these psychosocial avenues that interest us in our drive to become up-to-date evidence-based practitioners. This is not too dissimilar to writing an academic assignment or engaging in debate in a class or socially. We endeavour to use the best and most current evidence, to assimilate it into our thoughts, our work, and our way of being as a member of society. This is why it is important to read this chapter whilst being mindful of the many other influences that impact on self-harm and suicide such as poverty, drugs, alcohol, mental health, relationships, money, employment, and families. This is why it is so individual and unique to each personal set of circumstances, there are so many variables in operation; and each has different weightings. These weightings can vary from hour to hour and day to day.

The NCI into suicides has collected and collated suicide data (England and Wales) for over 20 years. This data has enabled a deeper understanding of the circumstances that surround death by suicide but also allowed valuable preventative or risk reduction evidence to emerge. The NCI gathers evidence from studies of mental health services, primary care, and accident and emergency departments. NCI recommendations propose patient safety in mental health settings and reduced patient suicide rates in the UK. Their evidence is cited in national policies and clinical guidance and regulation in all UK countries (University of Manchester, 2019).

Many countries have policies and strategies to reduce suicide rates. However, approaches to reduce suicide rates require a plethora of interventions, a whole systems approach. Educating young children and preparing them for the challenges of life, working in partnership with families, resilience and coping, problem-solving skills, education initiatives local and nationally on suicide and self-harm. Evidence suggests that a greater number of suicides occur year on year in persons not known to mental health services in the UK (ONS, 2019). Therefore, we may provide better services to the persons known to health and social care services, but this does not address the needs of those whom are not known. National peer support networks from those who have been suicidal or attempted suicide may offer relatable support to those at risk. What is clear is that a broad range of stakeholder provisions is required, owned locally and networked nationally as each community may have specific issues operating.

Some evidence-based interventions may reduce the likelihood of suicide. However, for some organizations and groups, zero suicide is an aspiration and strengthening key evidence-based suicide prevention interventions (restricting access to means of suicide, responsible media reporting, working with young people on life skills, early identification, management, and follow-up; WHO, 2018) is required for this serious public health issue. Mental health services alone will have limited impact upon national figures in the UK, when comparing total suicide rates. This is important as persons who attempt or achieve suicide may have physical health conditions not solely mental health conditions, or both. Suicide therefore is not the sole domain of mental ill health.

Psychosocial perspective

It can be difficult to translate group-level statistical data into a form that has direct relevance to an individual contemplating self-harm or suicide or to the practitioners who may be working with them. Societal understanding of why an individual takes their own life is often one of disbelief or shock. Collating evidence within a chapter on suicide at best strives for a better understanding of the many challenges and uniquely individual circumstances operating. This evidence distances the reader from the individual. Ultimately the practitioner or reader should keep the unique individual and the context in which they exist in mind. Every effort should be made to resist reducing them to a technical label or a manifestation of group-level statistics.

Impairments in problem-solving abilities can make it more difficult to resolve challenges adaptively, resulting in the use of maladaptive responses which can include suicidal behaviour. Such impairments arise as a consequence of long-standing factors (e.g., related to intellectual functioning or stress management) or secondary to the adverse effects on cognitive processes of alcohol, illicit substances, or prescribed medication.

Substance misuse in mental health populations increases the risk of suicides (Østergaard et al., 2017).

Policy decisions regarding mental health have had to be reviewed in light of the pandemic as there have been continued calls for parity of esteem between mental and physical health. More work is required at a policy and funding level to maintain the momentum, as policy alone is not enough to generate change at an individual's level. Mental health is a global public health concern and the many consequences of lockdown that include fear, isolation, and limited mental health service provision have surely been compounded by COVID.

Approaches to reduce suicide rates require a plethora of interventions. Early in life these can be embedded in routine activities such as those in educational settings and may address issues such as resilience, coping, problem-solving skills, and dissemination of information about mental health and suicide and self-harm.

Care and intervention approaches must be joined up and meet local population needs. A public health approach throughout the life course has been advocated. Deprivation, debt, and inequality impact on suicide.

Media portrayal of suicide

Irresponsible and inappropriate reporting of suicide may contribute to negative attitudes towards suicide and self-harm and such attitudes may lead to a reluctance to seek help and individuals with self-harm or suicidal urges feeling ashamed. In India, for example, the shame and stigma of suicide upon the family can be considerable and this may be compounded by societal attitudes and media stereotypes. Suicide is often complex with no specific event or factor leading someone to end their life. It is usually a combination of different factors interacting with each other to increase likelihood.

The Samaritans have produced considered guidance on the reporting of suicides by the media https://www.samaritans.org/wales/about-samaritans/media-guidelines/

The Samaritans guidance places a spotlight on responsible reporting of suicides, and it is changing slowly. Guidance suggests the top 10 tips for reporting suicide.

Locality and area of residence

Statistically significant increases in male suicide rates have been seen in cities and towns (up 12.7% in England and Wales), and areas in the mid-range of deprivation (up 18.7% in England only; ONS, 2020). Housing policy, accommodation type, and deprivation areas warrant closer attention which is beyond the scope of this chapter.

Assessment

Structured approaches can help inform interventions. There are many widely available risk rating scales for suicide, hopelessness, and depression. It should be noted that they are somewhat mechanistic in style, but the questions give some insight into important psychosocial social determinants that may underpin suicidal behaviour.

These tools/scales below ask individuals to base replies on the past one to two weeks at the time of assessment.

Rating scales should inform clinical judgement and not replace it. They are tools to inform assessments and interventions. They also serve as discussion points to explore with individuals. Scores can change day by day and are influenced by life events, over reliance on the score either high or low requires careful holistic consideration.

Culture, religion, geographical location, and socioeconomic factors all impact on the attempt or completion of suicide. The reader is encouraged to reflect on this when exploring local, regional, and international influences on the person. Health and social care staff may not predict the attempt, but they could explore and improve processes beyond assessment, towards holistic intervention initiatives. This depends on skilled and supported interagency staff, multiagency joined up communication, and sufficient human resources.

> *Becks Hopelessness Scale (BHS)* – designed to measure an individual's attitudes about their long-term future and consists of 20 true/false items by endorsing a pessimistic statement or denying an optimistic statement. *BHS* acts as a powerful predictor of suicidal intent (Beck and Young, 1985).
>
> *Hospital Anxiety and Depression Scale (HADS)* – a valid and reliable self-rating scale that measures anxiety and depression in both hospital and community settings (Zigmond and Snaith, 1983).
>
> Peirce Suicide intent scale – suggests all suicide attempts should be taken seriously. This assessment intent scale is intended for use by professionals after an attempt (Pierce, 1977).
>
> *PHQ 9 and GAD 7* – for use in primary care to assess mood and anxiety (Spitzer et al., 1999).

Suicide prevention strategies

Suicide prevention programmes vary, but there are common factors present which include public education and awareness, at risk suicide screening measures, mental health treatment, restriction of lethal means, and responsible media reporting (Mann and Currier, 2011).

The National Suicide Prevention Strategy for England has identified several areas for action for suicide prevention. These include:

1 Reducing risk of suicide in high-risk groups (such as young men, people with a history of self-harm, people in contact with the criminal justice system)
2 Improving mental health for all and using tailored approaches to mental health support to help reach specific groups (such as children and young people, minority ethnic groups, the LGBT+ community, and people with chronic health conditions)
3 Reducing access to means of suicide
4 Providing better information and support for those bereaved or affected by suicide
5 Supporting the media in delivering sensitive approaches to suicide and suicidal behaviour
6 Supporting more research, data collection and monitoring

(NHS, 2018; HM Government, 2019)

Barriers exist and are multifactorial when assessing suicide

If a person presents to health services in a suicidal crisis (i.e., reporting or having acted on suicidal ideas), then in addition to assessing and offering treatment for physical health, consideration will need to be given to developing an understanding of their psychological and

> Several factors can impede the detection and prevention of suicide:
>
> - Stigma and secrecy
> - Failure to seek help
> - Lack of suicide knowledge and awareness amongst health professionalsSuicide is a rare event

psychiatric needs. The approach to management should include dealing with immediate safety issues as well as any interventions or support that might be indicated. It may be difficult to achieve an understanding of longer-term needs if the patient is currently in crisis (which may be the lingering causal context of, and/or the consequence, of the suicidal behaviour). If a diagnosable condition is identified, then steps should be taken to ensure the individual can access recommended support and treatment. This may involve input from different services (e.g., mental health and substance misuse services) which ideally should be coordinated and collaboratively delivered. Whatever the identified needs, critical in the assessment and intervention phases is the interpersonal approach of professionals. An emotionally validating and compassionate approach should be maintained.

There is a disparate evidence base for the effectiveness of certain interventions to reduce the likelihood of suicidal behaviour (Turecki and Brent, 2016). National suicide prevention strategies have been encouraged, but evaluation of their effectiveness is limited (Platt et al., 2019). Psychological interventions have been found to ameliorate psychological and psychiatric correlates of suicidal behaviour (e.g., Witt et al., 2019), and some studies have found an effect on suicidal behaviour itself. There is support for the effectiveness of cognitive behavioural therapy in reducing self-harm repetition amongst patients after self-harm (Hawton et al., 2016). There is also some evidence in favour of brief interventions for patients who have presented at emergency departments with suicidal behaviour (McCabe et al., 2018).

Legislation

This section introduces the reader to the Suicide Act. The Mental Capacity Act and Mental Health Act may be considered for use in suicide and self-harm behaviours and are addressed in other chapters.

Suicide act

Suicide is the act of a person intentionally ending their own life. Prior to the 1961 Suicide Act, it was unlawful to attempt to end one's life and if the person survived, they faced potential prosecution.

The Suicide Act of 1961 effectively decriminalised suicidal acts and removed criminal justice punishments. However, it did introduce legislation for the act of aiding or assisting a person to attempt suicide.

'A person who aids, abets, counsels or procures the suicide of another, or attempt by another to commit suicide shall be liable on conviction on indictment to imprisonment for a term not exceeding fourteen years' (Suicide Act, 1961).

Euthanasia debate

A landmark case best highlights the ethics and law interface and deeper levels of reflection, thought, and debate relating the autonomy and euthanasia. Euthanasia is a debate that has to be further held in the UK to establish legal parameters.

A human rights challenge (under article 2 of the Human Rights Act/Right to life) to the 1961 Suicide Act received much media attention in 2001 under the European Convention on Human Rights (ECHR) by Diane Pretty (*Pretty v Director of Public*

Prosecutions (2002) 1 AC 800) with the ECHR rejecting the application. With some sadness shortly after the case ruling Diane Pretty died by natural causes. Diane Pretty suffered from motor neurone disease, was effectively paralysed from the neck down, had little if any comprehensible speech, and received her nutrition and fluids via a feeding tube.

Knowing she had only a few weeks to live, she argued that she was frightened and distressed by the undignified death and suffering she was likely to encounter. She further argued she wanted her husband to provide assistance in ending her life when she felt unable go on. In the case she intended to perform the final act herself. However, because her husband was involved in the process, she feared he may face prosecution for assisting in her timely death. Dianne Pretty therefore challenged the Department of Public Prosecutions (DPP) which was asked to agree not to prosecute. When this agreement was refused, the case began. Whilst the ruling went against Dianne Pretty, she did secure guidelines issued by the Director of the DPP on what constitutes assisting in a death and by default what does not.

English law retains the position that dying is an inevitable consequence of life, the right to life under the ECHR convention implies the obligation to have nature follow its natural course.

Summary

Suicidal behaviour is not a unitary entity. It is a term that encompasses a range of behaviours from an act in which the intention to ends one's life is realised through to a non-fatal act of self-harm. This behaviour in its different forms is prevalent across the world. Suicidal behaviour has often been framed within a medical paradigm and thus may be seen as the result of a psychiatric condition for which treatment is necessary. However, empirical research has uncovered specific psychological correlates which allow more individualised formulations and interventions. Assessment may be supplemented by the use of standardised tools, but such tools should not replace holistic approaches to understanding the unique set of social and psychological contributory circumstances. Key to understanding the behaviour is to recognise the interaction between the individual and their environmental contexts. Adopting a wider lens also allows consideration of the latent social forces at play, such as those described by Durkheim. Approaches to reduce the likelihood of suicidal behaviour have been developed in the form of population or subpopulation prevention programmes.

Points to ponder

Providing up-to-date evidence-based recommendations when working with those who self-harm and/or attempt suicide, following NICE guidance.

Timely communication and liaison with other agencies is often reported as problematic following inquires in competed suicides in non-mental health and mental health populations.

Relationship building, openness, and listening skills assist people who self-harm and their carers' in making informed decisions.

Stigma and shame following the attempt to end their life may lower their mood and sense of failure further, shame and stigma are encountered by the individual and their wider social network, and this is not helpful.

Don't be afraid to ask those questions about harms, it does not raise risk but reduces it – allows reflection – but be prepared for replies if the individual states they intend to die.

Those working with individuals who are at risk do require regular practice supervision and support; no matter how experienced or senior you get in your careers we all should have lifelong practice/clinical supervision. This supervision is protective when working with individuals in distress and accompanying them in their recovery, sharing in their pain, and helps to reduce vicarious trauma in professionals.

Perhaps consider self-harm as a means of reaching out and communicating distress for whatever reason, and it can take many forms that are not always visible to the individual or their support network

Quiz

This is not so much about getting the answer right but exploring your knowledge and attitudes towards individuals who may often have complex psychosocial needs. Some of the true or false answers can be debated. More often than not there are two sides or perspectives that operate.

1. People who self-harm do so to seek attention – **False**. People who self-harm seek understanding and are communicating their pain or distress inwardly and perhaps to others
2. A self-harmer is at a greater risk of suicide – **True**. There is evidence for those who self-harm do onto complete suicide. The difficulty is establishing the percentage of the population that do so. This is why it is important to try to understand the motivations and intent behind the harms.
3. Asking and talking to someone about their suicidal ideas increases the risk – **False**. Asking and working with people about their suicidal ideas reduce the risk, encouraging reflection an exploring protective factor further reduces risk.
4. Self-harm is an attempt at committing suicide – **False**. Whilst it is false as self-harm and suicide can be separated conceptually, in society and practice it is more challenging as suicide and self-harm can co-exist
5. Self-harm is almost entirely a woman's problem – **False**. Evidence suggests that in many cultures (but not all) women occupy a greater percentage of total self-harm populations, whereas men have higher figures globally for competed suicides to women.
6. Self-harm is often seen as an effective coping strategy by the individual – **True**. Self-harm is often a complex behaviour and used as a way of coping with psychological pain, causes are multifactorial that underpin the behaviour.
7. When exploring individual's suicidal ideas, professional ask the person about their ideas, plans, and intent. Intent is the largest indicator of risk – **True**. Most people in society think about suicide at some stage in their lives, suicidal intent must always be taken seriously.
8. The use of risk indicators and measures to support professional judgements is good practice – **True**. The aim is for evidence-based practice and empirical rating scales support evidence-based practice.
9. Those who attempt suicide and successfully commit must have a mental health problem – **False**. Whilst some who attempt to end their lives or take their own life

have mental health problems, not all do. Many factors exist and are specific to that individual. The aim is to identify and work with the individual on those factors to reduce the risk. Factors can include financial, relationship, employment, offending, substance misuse, and a wide range of others. This is why it is imperative to explore an individual's wider psychosocial issues and problem solve with them. Those with mental health issues need continued psychological support, perhaps in combination with medication.

10 Self-harm is a complex subject encompassing many forms of behaviour. It is a means of coping with intense emotional distress or pain by inflicting harm on one's own body. It is not a failed suicide attempt –**True**. Needs no explanation.
11 Suicide is an impulsive act – **False**. Not always and can involve significant planning.
12 There is nothing that can be done for someone who is suicidal and wants to end their life – **False**. Might be following referral that support services are found, offering something to the person and time to reflect with another, problem-solving one area at a time.

Individual/group topic-related activities

- Self-harm does not often simply follow the wish to die. Those who self-harm may do so to communicate with others or influence them to secure help or care. They may self-harm to obtain relief from a particular emotional state or overwhelming situation. Explore your small group beliefs and perceptions of the type of person who self-harms, being mindful of stereotypes.
- In small groups list some of the issues or factors that may precede a harm attempt on a flip chart or other suitable media. Then group them under individual, family, and/or societal owned. It could be that some are interlinked.
- How might you or in small groups improve communication between healthcare professionals, people who self-harm/attempt and their careers.
- Explore what services are available to support the person once identified as at risk of harm, locally and nationally, this might provide a piece in the person support package. You may also discuss some potential barriers that the person or their family face when accessing services.
- **Debriefing of the group and class is suggested following all class exercises and is good for reflective and safer practice.**

Supplementary reading

Cutcliffe, J. and Santos, J.C. (2012). *Suicide and Self Harm: An Evidence Based Approach*. Quay Books.
Hawton, K. et al. (2016). Psychosocial Interventions Following Self-harm in Adults: A Systematic Review and Meta-analysis. *The Lancet Psychiatry*, 3(8), 740–750.
Jones, S., Krishna, M., Rajendra, R., and Keenan, P. (2015). Nurses Attitudes and Beliefs to Attempted Suicide in Southern India. *Journal of Mental Health*, 24(6), 423.
National Institute for Clinical Excellence (NICE, 2013). Self-Harm Quality Standard. Quality Standard 34. https://www.nice.org.uk/guidance/qs34/resources/selfharm-pdf-2098606243525 accessed on 24/2/21
University of Manchester (2019) National Confidential Inquiry into Suicides. https://sites.manchester.ac.uk/ncish/

Helpful topic-related websites

World Health Organization (2018). National suicide prevention strategies: progress, examples and indicators. World Health Organization, Geneva.

World Health Organization (2019). Suicide in the World; Global Health Estimates. WHO. Geneva.

Support service resource (third sector) useful resources

A wide range of resources are available for students, clinical staff and families from the national confidential inquiry into suicides team at the University of Manchester https://sites.manchester.ac.uk/ncish/

This list of some services below may provide help to individuals at risk and their families. The list highlights so many individual circumstances and combinations that may lead an individual to harm. When searching the sites review is they are 24/7 or not as suicidal thoughts' are not 9-5 Monday to Friday. But some services have resource limitations against increasing demands.

CALM. Is the Campaign against Living Miserably, for men aged 15–35: www.thecalmzone.net

Mind. Promotes the views and needs of people with mental health problems: www.mind.org.uk

PAPYRUS. Young suicide prevention society: www.papyrus-uk.org

Rethink Mental Illness. Support and advice for people living with mental illness: www.rethink.org

Support After Suicide Partnership. Strives to provide individuals who have been bereaved by suicide with appropriate and timely support: www.supportaftersuicide.org.uk/about/

Alzheimer's Society. Provides information on dementia, including factsheets and helplines: www.alzheimers.org.uk

References

American Psychiatric Association (2013). *Diagnostic and Statistical Manual of Mental Disorders*, 5th ed. Arlington, VA: American Psychiatric Association.

Beck, A.T. and Young, J.E. (1985). Depression. In D.H. Barlow (Ed.), *Clinical Handbook of Psychological Disorders: A Step-By-Step Treatment Manual* (pp. 206–244). New York: The Guilford Press.

Bertolote, J.M. and Fleischmann, A. (2002). Suicide and Psychiatric Diagnosis: A Worldwide Perspective. *World Psychiatry: Official Journal of the World Psychiatric Association (WPA)*, 1(3), 181–185.

Bille-Brahe, U. (2000). Sociology and Suicidal Behaviour. In K. Hawton and K. van Heeringen (Eds.), *The International Handbook of Suicide and Attempted Suicide* (pp. 193–207). Chichester: John Wiley & Sons, Ltd.

Dong, M. et al. (2019) Prevalence of Suicide Attempt in Individuals with Major Depressive Disorder: A Meta-Analysis of Observational Surveys. *Psychological Medicine*, 49(10), 1691–1704.

Durkheim, É., Spaulding, J.A., and Simpson, G. (2002). *Suicide : A Study in Sociology*. London: Routledge Classics, xi.

Hawton, K., Witt, K.G., Taylor Salisbury, T.L., Arensman, E., Gunnell, D., Hazell, P., Townsend, E., and van Heeringen, K. (2015) Pharmacological Interventions for Self-harm in Adults. *Cochrane Database of Systematic Reviews*, 7. Art. No.: CD011777.

Hawton, K. et al. (2016). Psychosocial Interventions Following Self-harm in Adults: A Systematic Review and Meta-analysis. *The Lancet Psychiatry*, 3(8), 740–750.

HM Government (2019). Preventing Suicide in England: Fourth Progress Report of the Cross-government Outcomes Strategy to Save Lives.

Johnson, B.D. (1965). Durkheim's One Cause of Suicide. *American Sociological Review*, 30(6), 875–886.

Jones, S., Krishna, M., Rajendra, R., and Keenan, P. (2015). Nurses Attitudes and Beliefs to Attempted Suicide in Southern India. *Journal of Mental Health*, 24(6), 423.

Kumar, N., Rajendra, R., Sumanth, M.M., Krishna, M., Keenan, P., and Jones, S. (2016). Attitudes of General Hospital Staff Towards Patients Who Self-harm in South India: A Cross-sectional Study. *Indian Journal of Psychological Medicine*, 38(6), 547–552.

Kutcher, S. and Chehill, S. (2007). *Suicide Risk Management: A Manual for Health Professionals*. Chichester: John Wiley and Sons.

Mann, J. and Currier, D. (2011). Evidence-Based Suicide Prevention Strategies: An Overview. In Pompili, M. and Taterelli, R. (eds.), *Evidence Based Practice in Suicidology*. Cambridge, MA: Hogrefe Publishing, 67–88.

McCabe, R. et al. (2018). Effectiveness of Brief Psychological Interventions for Suicidal Presentations: A Systematic Review. *BMC Psychiatry*, 18(1), 1–13.

Millard, C. (2013). *A History of Self-harm in Britain: A Genealogy of Cutting and Overdosing*. London: Palgrave Macmillan.

National Institute for Clinical Excellence (NICE, 2013). Self-Harm Quality Standard. Quality Standard 34. https://www.nice.org.uk/guidance/qs34/resources/selfharm-pdf-2098606243525 accessed on 24/2/21

National Records Service (NRS) (2020). Probable Suicides: Deaths Which Are the Result of Intentional Self-harm or Events of Undetermined Intent. https://www.nrscotland.gov.uk/statistics-and-data/statistics/statistics-by-theme/vital-events/deaths/suicides accessed 4/2/20

NHS (2018). Health A-Z: Self-Harm Overview. https://www.nhs.uk/conditions/self-harm/

Northern Ireland Statistics and Research Agency (NISRA, 2020). Suicide Deaths. https://www.nisra.gov.uk/statistics/cause-death/suicide-deaths accessed 4/2/20

O'Connor, R.C. and Kirtley, O.J. (2018). The Integrated Motivational-Volitional Model of Suicidal Behaviour. *Philosophical Transactions of the Royal Society B: Biological Sciences*, 373, 20170268. http://dx.doi.org/10.1098/rstb.2017.0268

Office of National Statistics (2019). Suicide Rates in the UK QMI; Quality and Methodology Information for Suicides in the UK, Detailing the Strengths and Limitations of the Data, Methods Used, and Data Uses and Users. https://www.ons.gov.uk/peoplepopulationandcommunity/birthsdeathsandmarriages/deaths/methodologies/suicideratesintheukqmi accessed 1/3/21

Office of National Statistics (2020). Recent Trends in Suicide: Death Occurrences in England and Wales between 2001 and 2018. www.ons.gov.uk/peoplepopulationandcommunity/birthsdeathsandmarriages/deaths/articles/recenttrendsinsuicidedeathoccurrencesinenglandandwalesbetween2001and2018/2020-12-08 accessed on 4/2/20

Østergaard, M.L.D., Nordentoft, M., and Hjorthøj, C. (2017) Associations Between Substance Use Disorders and Suicide or Suicide Attempts in People with Mental Illness: A Danish Nation-Wide, Prospective, Register-Based Study of Patients Diagnosed with Schizophrenia, Bipolar Disorder, Unipolar Depression or Personal. *Addiction*, 112, 1250–1259.

Pierce, D.W. (1977) Suicidal Intent in Self-injury. *British Journal of Psychiatry*, 130, 377–385.

Platt, S., Arensman, E., and Rezaeian, M. (2019). National Suicide Prevention Strategies – Progress and Challenges. *Pretty v Director of Public Prosecutions* (2002) 1 AC 800.

Scottish Public Health Observatory (2020). *Suicide Scottish Trends*. https://www.scotpho.org.uk/health-wellbeing-and-disease/suicide/data/scottish-trends/ accessed 4/2/20

Spitzer, R.L., Kroenke, K., and Williams. J.B.W. (1999). Patient Health Questionnaire Study Group. Validity and utility of a self-report version of PRIME-MD: the PHQ Primary Care Study. *JAMA*, 282, 1737–1744.

Stack, S. (2004). Emile Durkheim and Altruistic Suicide. *Archives of Suicide Research*, 8(1), 9–22.

Steggals, P., Graham, R., and Lawler, S. (2020) Self-injury in Social Context: An Emerging Sociology. *Social Theory & Health*, 18, 201–210.

Sudol, K. and Mann, J.J. (2017). Biomarkers of Suicide Attempt Behavior: Towards a Biological Model of Risk. *Current Psychiatry Reports*, 19(6), 31.

Suicide Act (1961). Section 2(1). https://www.legislation.gov.uk/ukpga/Eliz2/9-10/60/contents accessed on 4/3/21

Temes, C.M., Frankenburg, F.R., Fitzmaurice, G.M., and Zanarini, M.C. (2019, January 22). Deaths by Suicide and Other Causes among Patients with Borderline Personality Disorder and Personality-Disordered Comparison Subjects Over 24 Years of Prospective Follow-Up. *The Journal of Clinical Psychiatry*, 80(1), 18m12436.

Turecki, G. and Brent, D.A. (2016). Suicide and Suicidal Behaviour. *The Lancet* 387(10024), 1227–1239.

University of Manchester (2019). National Confidential Inquiry into Suicides. https://sites.manchester.ac.uk/ncish/ accessed on 4/2/20

Witt, K. et al. (2019). Effectiveness of Universal Programmes for the Prevention of Suicidal Ideation, Behaviour and Mental Ill Health in Medical Students: A Systematic Review and Meta-analysis. *Evidence-Based Mental Health*, 22(2), 84–90.

World Health Organization (2018). *National Suicide Prevention Strategies: Progress, Examples and Indicators*. Geneva: World Health Organization.

World Health Organization (2019). *Suicide in the World; Global Health Estimates*. Geneva: WHO.

Zigmond, A.S. and Snaith, R.P. (1983). The Hospital Anxiety and Depression Scale. *Acta Psychiatrica Scandinavica*, 67, 361–370.

12 Exploring Homelessness

Will Hay and Mike Taylor

Introduction

It is well known that the need for shelter and a roof over one's head is at the very pinnacle of Maslow's hierarchy of need and for good reason. As the homelessness charity, Crisis (2022) has noted, the average age of death for people experiencing street homelessness is 45 for men and 43 for women. People living on the street are almost 17 times more likely to be victims of violence whilst homeless and homeless people are over nine times more likely to take their own life than the general population. These three statistics, alone, paint a grim picture of the potential catastrophic consequences of people having to live without a roof over their head or a home they can legally call their own. Understanding and tackling homelessness is self-evidently of paramount importance. The chapter that is devoted to what for many may well consider the most serious social problem of all has several aims and objectives. Chief among them is the need to place homelessness in its moral, socio-economic, political and practice contexts. In terms of content, it seeks to define what is meant and understood by the term, before moving on to discuss prevalence, causation, consequences and effects, legislation and housing policy. The chapter perhaps differs from others in this volume by drawing upon three case studies as a way of integrating theoretical, conceptual, organisational and practice concerns.

BOX 12.1 SECTIONS IN THIS CHAPTER

- Defining Homelessness
- Perceptions of Homelessness
- Prevalence
- Causes
- Consequences and Effects
- Housing Policy
- Legislation
- Interventions
- Conclusion
- Sources and Links

Though this chapter is concerned with homelessness in the UK, homelessness is a world-wide phenomenon. Housing provides not just the obvious protection from the elements, but also security and control over one's environment and life. Homelessness affects people from diverse economic, social and cultural backgrounds, in both developed and developing countries, though clearly it affects disproportionately the lives of some much more than others. At the sharp end, we are all accustomed to seeing people 'living on the streets'. Such scenarios and encounters are vivid and we can easily picture them in our mind's eye. Homelessness, even without its attendant images, conjures up thoughts and feelings of absence, of something lacking and a sense of helplessness, even hopelessness. Perhaps above all, there can be a stigma attached to being homeless, accompanied with labelling and stereotyping. Living on the street has become matter of fact, thought of, albeit regrettably, as part of life. Sleeping rough, however, is but the most visible and high-profile aspect of this most acute of social problems. Homelessness is much broader than that. As we shall see, a good deal of homelessness is not only hidden from view but involves a much wider variety of people and situations than we might at first expect.

Defining Homelessness

BOX 12.2 WORLD HOMELESSNESS DAY

World Homeless Day is an annual event on **10 October**. In a variety of ways, the main aims are to highlight and change the lives of people experiencing homelessness in their local community.

Though definitions of homelessness exist for different purposes and with variations across the UK for legal and policy reasons (Office for National Statistics (ONS) 2020), we tend to look at homelessness in two main ways. The first is as a state of being; a type of existence and lived experience that is particular, highly situational and individual. The second is to look at people who are homeless as a group: as certain types of people ('the homeless') that have homelessness as a common, and defining, characteristic. Though we do not have too much to quibble about conceiving homelessness in terms of the former, there is a real danger when referring to the latter of falling into the trap of thinking about 'the homeless' as if such a homogenous group exists and is readily identifiable.

BOX 12.3 KEY TERMS

Sofa surfer – usually a single person staying in someone else's home, metaphorically or literally sleeping on their sofa. That person is able to stay only with the permission of someone else, whose home it is, and lives in a state of impermanence. They may have a roof over their head but they have no rights, control or certainty.

> **Temporary accommodation** – people are housed and have somewhere to stay but not actually settle. Such accommodation may be provided by a local council or charities, particularly to families, for whom there is more likely to be a legal duty to provide accommodation. A hostel is an example, but people are also 'placed' in shared houses, if single, or in family housing.
>
> **Rough sleepers** – people living on the streets and sleeping outside, whether in particular spots they have chosen or different ones each night. They are among the most marginalised and victimised of all vulnerable groups. People without a roof over their heads often live precarious lives are required to build lives without access to key facilities: toilets, showers of one's own through to kitchens and the ability to keep food and make meals.

However, this caveat only takes us so far. As the Economic and Social Council of the United Nations (2019) has noted, there is no single, universally agreed, definition of what is meant by homelessness. In many ways, this is surprising. After all, at one level, homelessness is relatively easy to define. A person or family is homeless when they do not have a home which they can call their own. Rough sleepers most clearly fit this category. However, homelessness is not confined to people who are 'street homeless', those living without walls around them and a roof above their heads. Homelessness, as Kemeny (1992) among others has noted, is not simply a 'bricks and mortar' problem. A person or family may not have a home of their own; they may well be accommodated in some way or other, just not in accommodation that is 'theirs'. This is often the case for people in various forms of temporary accommodation insofar as they are housed but do not have a home of their own in legal terms. Indeed, the vast majority of people who are homeless at any time do not sleep on the street but are in accommodation that is inadequate or is simply temporary. Though it is not common, even rough sleepers may have accommodation to which they can go but are unable or unwilling to do so.

Homelessness, therefore, does not necessarily mean being without somewhere to stay. Designation in such broad terms is, however, not without its problems. Including everyone who does not have a home to go to casts a very wide net that catches a large, broad and diverse group of people, all of whom live in unique circumstances. In countless ways, those sleeping and living rough have considerably different experiences from – say – those living in decent temporary accommodation, whilst waiting to be offered permanent housing. Yet both come under the term homeless. Though in some instances appropriate, it is useful to remember, when we encounter and engage with descriptions of the needs of homeless people or see statistics regarding this cohort, that they will usually be based on selected groups from within that wider population. For instance, often details given regarding health, life expectancy or other matters derive from research on people who are rough sleepers but are then, sometimes, misleadingly applied to people who are homeless in other or all circumstances. They will not necessarily apply to the group overall, purely a specific sub-section. For example, using the ONS (2020) as a source, it is often reported that the mean life expectancy of homeless people is in the mid-forties (46 for men and 43 for women). However, the ONS figure applies only to people sleeping rough or in emergency accommodation, not to the many people in other forms of temporary accommodation. Given that street homelessness is very different from most other forms, it is thus necessary to be specific in the terms we use in our definitions of homelessness if it is to be meaningful.

Perceptions of Homelessness

Research into attitudes towards homelessness is sparse. In the USA, Tsai et al. (2017) contended that there has been an increase in compassion and liberal attitudes towards homelessness in the past two decades. Knowledge of homelessness, however, proved to be both patchy and partial. When asked about the demographic composition of the homeless population, respondents tended to overestimate the proportions who were young and of a particular racial or ethnic background, whilst underestimating the proportions who were married or had mental health or substance abuse problems.

BOX 12.4 MYTHS

- People begging are street homeless – a BBC Freedom Of Information Request to the police in 2015 found that to be true of only 1 in 5 people begging.
- All homeless people sleep rough – the majority of people who are homeless in the UK sleep indoors, many in temporary accommodation (hostels and other provision)
- People who sleep rough just need to be given a home – people sleeping rough are shown to be likely to have mental health and/or substance use issues, many having experienced trauma; the help they need is usually more than accommodation
- Certain people can jump the queue for housing – there are systems that are used to determine who is prioritised for social housing, vulnerability being a key factor.

Much of what we make of homelessness is influenced by media coverage and the prominence, or otherwise, that it is given. From time to time, newspapers or television news bulletins present figures on homelessness such as those we provide below; the occasional documentary appears, and it might form the basis of a discussion on programmes that examine current affairs, typically responding to the release of the annual rough sleeper statistics. Just because homelessness is such a serious condition worthy of political attention, does not make it of automatic importance to the media, still less part of any campaigning agenda. It is, for example, notable that in the UK the media are significantly more interested in homelessness, and the plight of people who are homeless, in the run up to Christmas, the 'season of goodwill'. This seasonal interest, with its focus on family, kindness and the need to be indoors, somewhere safe and warm, is accompanied by an increase in public support, as evidenced by a rise in donations to charities.

Prevalence

When probing homelessness, we are often inclined to ask questions such as how common it is and what circumstances might typically lead to it. Before we begin to provide answers to these questions, it is as well to deal with two statistical caveats.

> **BOX 12.5 HOMELESSNESS IN WALES**
>
> - In November 2020, throughout Wales, 988 people presenting as homeless were placed into temporary accommodation, 347 fewer than in October 2020. 136 were dependent children aged under 16, an increase of 21 from October 2020.
> - At 30 November 2020, 4,855 individuals were in temporary accommodation, an increase of 120 from 31 October 2020. 1,258 were dependent children aged under 16, an increase of 98 from 31 October 2020.
> - At 30 November 2020, 96 individuals were sleeping rough throughout Wales, a decrease of 14% from the 112 individuals sleeping rough at 31 October 2020.
> - On 30 November 2020, local authorities Newport (24), Cardiff (15) Caerphilly (14) and Ceredigion (10) reported the highest numbers of individuals sleeping rough.
>
> Source: Wales.gov (2021)

First, homelessness and housing are devolved matters. Definitions of homelessness and, by extension, the gathering of statistics thus differ across the countries of the UK. Consequently, though some attempt at harmonisation is taking place, as it stands, data are not currently comparable. Second, though we know much in qualitative terms about the nature and experience of homelessness, the same cannot be said regarding the scale of the problem. Difficulties arise, for example, over the hidden nature of much homelessness, as well as who to include and count in the definition.

Drawing upon the resources of outreach workers, local charities and community groups, local authorities across England take an autumn snapshot of people seen or thought to be seen sleeping rough on a single date on a 'typical night' between 1 October and 30 November (Ministry of Housing, Communities and Local Government 2019). There is guidance over how to do it, with the option either to carry out a count (people going out in the night to scour the area) or an estimate (relevant parties identify people known to be out and estimate how many would be on the night in question). To enhance reliability, validity as well as consistency, the whole process includes definitions, rules and external checks to be followed. The snapshot thus seeks to provide as robust a picture as possible of the number of those bedded down in open air locations, tents or make-shift shelters on a single night, making it possible to compare statistics on rough sleeping for an area, region and the country as a whole on an annual basis.

What is more, from time to time, changes are made to the ways in which data are collected by local authorities on statutory homelessness, such as occurred with the introduction in England of the Homelessness Reduction Act (HRA) 2017. Whilst establishing levels and trends in terms of whether homelessness is rising or falling in any given year or era has always been a complex task, these changes have made comparing previous years and the rates of other countries in the UK even more difficult. This notwithstanding, there are several data sources upon which we can draw that can help illuminate the prevalence, incidence and distribution of current homelessness at local, regional and between the countries that make up the UK. Links to these are provided at the end of this chapter. At this point, beginning with rough sleepers, we confine ourselves to some of the headline data concerning the situation in England provided by the ONS (2021).

BOX 12.6 HOMELESSNESS IN SCOTLAND

- The scale of statutory homelessness in Scotland has been relatively flat for the past five years. In 2017/2018 Scottish local authorities logged 34,950 statutory homelessness assessments, of which 28,792 were assessed as homeless. Levels of rough sleeping have also remained relatively stable over the last three years at a national level, although there has been considerable variation between different localities.
- As of 31st March 2018 there were 10,933 households in temporary accommodation in Scotland. Whilst most of these placements are in ordinary social housing stock, there has been a 12% increase in bed and breakfast placements in the three years to 2018. Temporary accommodation placements involving family households increased by 25% over the same period revealing blockages in the system that are restricting people's ability to build a better life and move on from homelessness.

Source: FitzPatrick et al. (2019)

On a single night in autumn 2020, it was estimated that there were 2,688 people sleeping rough in England, with 44% of this number being in London and the South-East. This represents a fall of 37% from the year before, though there has been a 52% increase since 2010. The 2020 fall in numbers is undoubtedly positive but took place during the COVID-19 pandemic, a period when additional efforts were made – and money provided – to support rough sleepers and to keep them off the street. The previous year had also seen a fall in numbers, if less significant. Of those seen, 85% were male, 87% were aged 26 years plus and 72% were from the UK. On a sombre note, there were 597 deaths of homeless people in 2017, an increase of 24% over a five-year period, 84% of whom were men. Over half the deaths were due to drug poisoning, liver disease or suicide.

In England during 2019–2020, 288,470 people were legally entitled to assistance from their council to prevent or relieve homelessness. Households with children constituted nearly 70% of cases and single households 30%. The largest number of applicants were aged between 25 and 34. Approximately a third of applicants were registered unemployed, followed in percentage terms by applicants not working due to illness or disability, meaning that, when taken together, half of the applicants were unemployed.

There were some marked differences between different household groups along ethnicity lines. Of the people owed a prevention or relief duty in 2019, a disproportionate number were from a Black/African/Caribbean or Black British origin (10.7% of the total sample, whereas this ethnic group constitutes only 3.6% of the population of England). 18,100 Asian or Asian British were owed help by their council (a relief duty), though in this group's case proportionally this was less than the percentage breakdown by overall population (6.3% of the sample compared with 8.1% by overall population). Households in the mixed and multiple ethnic groups owed prevention or relief duty were also disproportionate to the English population overall (2.9% compared with 1.8%).

> **BOX 12.7 HOMELESSNESS IN NORTHERN IRELAND**
>
> - Of the 8,527 households who presented in October–March 2019, the most commonly quoted cause of homelessness was 'accommodation not reasonable' with 2,156 (25%), followed by sharing breakdown/family dispute with 1,832 (21%) and loss of rented accommodation with 1,270 (15%)
> - Of the 5,732 households accepted as statutory homeless, slightly more than a third were families, followed by single people (males and females) in the 26–59 age group and pensioner households.
>
> Source: Northern Ireland Homelessness Bulletin (2019)

As the ONS (2021) has noted, the reason for loss of last settled home is a good indication of the cause of homelessness for households assessed as being owed a housing duty. Of those known reasons, nearly 30% of households already homeless were owed help because family or friends were no longer able to accommodate them. This is followed by reasons due to a breakdown in the relationship because of violence, the end of privately rented tenancy and non-violent relationship breakdown, constituting roughly 10–15% of cases in each category. Eviction from supported housing and the end of a social rented tenancy closely follow.

Causes

We have no shortage of explanations as to the causes and effects of homelessness. Though there is considerable overlap between each of them, for conceptual and practical purposes, it is useful to divide these accounts into six distinct categories, none directly and inevitably causing homelessness but commonly associated with it. The first concerns the identification of forms of what might be deemed 'risky behaviour' that we know to be associated with homelessness, such as misuse of alcohol and other drugs, alongside criminal activity. The second concerns 'economic factors' such as housing shortage and unemployment. The third area of interest focuses upon 'life events', which may lead to homelessness, for example, leaving prison, care or the army. Fourth is the place that 'traumatic' experiences that many homeless people have lived through as children and which continue to dominate their lives, for example, sexual and physical abuse, parents addicted to alcohol and other drugs, absent parents, exploitation and bereavement. Fifth is the contention that 'structural factors' create the conditions that allow homelessness to increase. These include societal and economic issues such as the lack of affordable housing; the decline of the social sector; unfavourable housing conditions; and reduced welfare benefits. Finally, if there is a single variable that crops up time and time again within the debates over what causes homelessness, it is the role that 'poverty' plays in its genesis and continuation. Reviewing the literature on this relationship, Johnson and Watts (2014) concluded that although the prominence and place of poverty in accounts of homelessness causation have varied over time, it is now almost universally agreed that poverty is not only a key contributory factor, but also one shared by the vast majority of homeless people in the UK and elsewhere.

Some of these reasons are clearly informed by theories of 'individual' causality and (personal) responsibility, whereas others are rooted in 'structural' processes. Fitzpatrick

(2005) and Bramley and Fitzpatrick (2018) make the case 'that the balance of underlying causal factors may vary between different homeless groups, with structural causes more important in some cases and individual causes more important in others'. In this they are surely right, acknowledging that both societal policies and personal factors specific to the individual affect people becoming homeless. Meanwhile Somerville (2013) criticises approaches which reduce or deny the importance of agency for homeless people. Rather, we need to understand homelessness as multidimensional, in terms that do not diminish the humanity of people experiencing homelessness, and as 'storied' accounts that focus on the whole life of a homeless person, rather than selected episodes.

In essence, these two frameworks start from very different vantage points. Fitzpatrick (2005) and Bramley and Fitzpatrick (2018) adopt what might be termed an aerial view in which they survey the homelessness landscape as a whole, selecting what they consider to be the essential landmarks and asking what part each particular feature plays. Somerville is looking from the ground up, seeking to establish wider patterns from the detailed stories and narratives of individuals he says need to be established and critically examined.

BOX 12.8 PRISON AND HOMELESSNESS

One in seven people who left prison was homeless
One in five people serving less than 6 months was homeless
Two in five women left prison without settled accommodation
One in 20 women was sleeping rough
One of the five most predictive factors for violent reoffending among women is lack of accommodation

Source: HM Prison and Probation Service (2021)

This difference in approach aside, above all, what emerges from within the homelessness discourse is that the causes of homelessness are varied, invariably complex, and often inextricably linked to other social problems. This is illustrated by the fact that over half of all deaths of people defined as homeless in 2017 were due to drug poisoning, liver disease or suicide (ONS, 2020b). Whilst the causes vary for individuals and different subgroups, so do prevalence rates. Homelessness among ethnic minorities is a good case in point. Though figures for numbers and details of people presenting to councils as homeless need careful consideration, any interpretation or analysis of them needs to start with the complex cycle of deprivation to which many people are particularly vulnerable. For instance, if a particular ethnic group is disproportionately represented in seeking social housing, we might also ask if that group is also, as Gulliver (2016) found, disproportionately represented in lower income jobs, potentially reflecting on other societal issues of inclusion and opportunity.

The causes of homelessness cannot simply be put down to one or the other of personal vulnerabilities and behavioural patterns of individuals, nor to structural accounts of broader socio-economic conditions, housing policies and procedures discussed above, about which individuals who find themselves homeless have no control. The task of explaining homelessness, in any rounded or comprehensive sense, requires nuance, including any and sometimes all of these factors and potentially others.

Consequences and Effects

The life-changing, frequently tragic and considerable psychosocial and physical harms, together with the adverse impact of homelessness on health, finances, relationships, families and upon the wider community have all been well documented. It has become common to refer to people bound up in such situations as having multiple and complex needs. This is an acknowledgement that homelessness and other issues often occur together and may exacerbate each other. As we have established, homelessness refers to a wide variety of circumstances and to situations that vary in length and depth as well as in terms of impact. The circumstances and impact of the health and wellbeing of someone sleeping rough for months are very different from someone who has sofa-surfed for a few nights and will differ again markedly for a person staying briefly in temporary accommodation until they secure their own tenancy. At the same time, a person moving swiftly through a service to move into their own tenancy has a different experience from someone going into a hostel for a year or more, potentially with the risk of becoming institutionalised.

In terms of health, as Leng (2017) has noted, people who are homeless report much poorer health than the general population. It is frequently the case that homelessness results in ill health or exacerbates existing health conditions. Gunner et al. (2019) remind us that those who are homeless are known to be 40 times less likely to be registered with a mainstream general practice compared with the general population, have their health worsened by delayed diagnosis and treatment of illness and are up to 60 times more likely than the general population to attend an accident and emergency department. Himsworth, Paudyal and Sergeant (2020) have shown that the poorer health outcomes of homeless people, particularly the complex interplay of chronic physical illness, mental illness and alcohol and/or drug misuse within the homeless population are linked with a higher rate of unplanned hospital admissions compared with the non-homeless population. That being the case, it is worth posing the question as to whether unplanned hospital admissions are the result of homelessness or whether it is that people whose personal vulnerability, poor health and highly precarious circumstances are also more likely to be homeless. Either way, there are certainly implications and severe consequences and effects from the insecurity and instability that of homelessness engenders.

The links with children's health and well-being are particularly pronounced, often extending well beyond the period of homelessness itself. Children living in overcrowded conditions – whether they are deemed homeless or not – frequently miss school because of ill health. They are also shown to be at greater risk of infection and accidents in the home (Shelter, 2007). 'Homelessness in early life', notes Leng, 'can impact on life chances and the longer a person experiences homelessness the more likely their health and wellbeing will be at risk' (2017: 5). They are more likely, she points out, to experience stress and anxiety, resulting in depression and behavioural issues, have their school performance affected and be absent more often. Additionally, homelessness may 'single out' a child in a new school, increasing the likelihood of bullying and isolation (2017: 7).

Often the result of relationship breakdown, young people who find themselves homeless are extremely vulnerable to a wide range of adverse situations, not necessarily resulting from homelessness, but certainly not helped by it. Matters might even be made worse by the temporary nature of the accommodation they are likely to be provided with if presenting to their local authority. As Leng (2017) notes, young homeless people may lack relationship and independent living skills and formal support, and struggle to access services. They are more likely to: have experienced trauma, abuse and other adverse experiences; have been absent and/or excluded from school and not been in education, employment or training; experience mental health problems, self-harm, drug and alcohol use; be exploited, abused and trafficked; be involved in gang and/or criminal activity; pick up sexually transmitted infections; and have an unwanted pregnancy and more likely to come under pressure to exchange sex for food, shelter, drugs and money.

In addition to the serious toll on people's physical and mental health and sense of isolation, homelessness is linked with people being victims of violence, abuse or anti-social behaviour. This is especially true of rough sleepers. A survey by Crisis (2020) of 458 recent or current rough sleepers in England and Wales revealed that whilst street homeless, more than one in three have been deliberately hit or kicked. The same percentage had had things thrown at them. Nearly 10% had been urinated upon. Seven percent had been the victim of a sexual assault. Almost half had been intimidated or threatened with violence and nearly two-thirds had been verbally abused or harassed whilst homeless.

BOX 12.9 HUMAN RIGHTS

Having access to safe, stable and adequate housing is internationally recognised as a basic human right.
    Source: The Office of the High Commissioner for Human Rights (OHCHR)

The interplay of several social problems at once and the consequences of this interaction emphasises that establishing cause and effect is deeply complicated. As noted, homelessness might cause or exacerbate some issues and at other times be an effect or symptom of them. Though it is possible to discern highly regular patterns, identify key risk factors and establish the interplay between various other social problems, causes and effects are simultaneously experienced at an individual level. If there is one lesson to be learned in all of this, it is homelessness is disproportionately experienced by people with other social and health-related issues and conditions. Whether it is a cause or a symptom varies from case to case.

Housing Policy

If homelessness can be the result of many factors – personal and structural, financial and behavourial – then access to housing is only one issue and only one potential remedy. Nevertheless, access to accommodation is crucial and it is therefore vital to take government housing policy into account. Indeed, among the many components and aspects, that are instrumental in giving shape and meaning to housing policies on homelessness, it is possible to distinguish three that are of particular importance. Though inter-related and overlaid on each other, each of them plays a distinctive role in creating the structural conditions, doctrines, regulations and laws that govern housing policy.

BOX 12.10 ROUGH SLEEPERS INITIATIVE

Rough sleeping and the need to lessen the numbers of rough sleepers have been a recurrent theme within politics. Arguably, elected not simply to replace a tired and moribund government, but to create a fairer, more egalitarian society, the

> incoming Labour government of 1997 created what it called the Social Exclusion Unit, a vehicle which gave priority to key social issues and problems including rough sleeping. Central to this strategy was the creation of a Rough Sleepers Unit (RSU).
>
> In 2018, the administration (re)introduced a Rough Sleepers Initiative (RSI) of its own. £30 million was allocated to local authorities estimated to have the highest number of rough sleepers. The initiative has brought together specialist advisors from within local authorities and the not-for-profit and charitable sectors with the aim of reducing numbers and supporting people sleeping rough, and other vulnerable people, by improving access to accommodation and relevant support.

First, let us take the significance of culture. To own one's home has for some considerable time been thought of culturally, almost as an article of faith, as an unequivocal good in and of itself. More pragmatically, owning one's own home has, in financial terms, been shown to be a very safe bet long term. Home ownership is thus an important social norm; something to be valued, pursued and to which we should all aspire. It is, then, very much part of the British psyche. As a result, we now live in a society where the majority of people live or aspire to live in owner-occupied housing, only a minority of the population living in rented accommodation. It is therefore scarcely surprising that politicians responsible for forging housing policy, perhaps inevitably, focus on home ownership, rather than on creating and developing the kind of fair, healthy and robust rental market necessary for any strategy to reduce homelessness and ameliorate its worst effects. This emphasis is a very different scenario from the 'homes fit for heroes' approach following the two world wars in which other forms of housing, especially the necessity of building social housing, was much lauded.

The second dimension is thus the political and ideological orientations towards housing policy. So embedded and widespread is this norm of home ownership that no major political party in the UK would do anything other than reinforce it at every opportunity. It was this dynamic combination that underpinned its growth in the 1980s and 1990s under the 'Right to Buy' housing policy. This allowed tenants in social housing to purchase the home in which they were living at a large discount, which as Kemeny (1995) reminds us, resulted in one million council-owned houses being purchased. It is perhaps more than ironic that today so many 'ex-council' properties are now rented out privately, particularly in the London area, for 'market', rather than social, rents. It is notable that the Scottish government has now abandoned any notion of a 'right to buy' policy.

Third, if cultural and political processes emerge as starting points for forging housing policy, economics and planning are at least as vital. For whatever policy the minister for Housing and Communities thinks fit to pursue to tackle homelessness, its implementation is heavily, if not totally, dependent upon the approval of the Treasury and the amount the financial arm of government is willing to invest. At the same time, restrictive planning policy regularly limits vision. Together these directly affect all three of the main housing sectors, private ownership, private rental and social housing, with supply often not matching demand, particularly in some parts of the country.

The supply and demand for housing to rent overlap with issues of occupancy. Following their election in 2010, the government of the day took a proactive approach to addressing what it considered 'under-occupancy' in social housing. This involved charging tenants extra rent for unused bedrooms – such as occurs when a grown-up child leaves the family home – in what has become known as 'the bedroom tax'. It is generally agreed that the policy caused a great deal of uncertainty, worry and financial costs to occupiers. There were also unintended consequences for councils, many of them ending up using funds to prevent or end homelessness to help families to cover the extra costs in order to avoid being evicted.

There are two other senses in which economics is important for recent housing policy. The first concerns the programme of austerity put in place in 2010 to curb welfare expenditure, decrease investment and reduce the funding of local government. This has contributed to a shortage of affordable accommodation, an increase in unemployment, rising poverty levels, lower incomes and more debt-related issues; the net effect being that people having fewer resources to secure accommodation at a time there is more competition for it. The second concerns building capacity. There is widespread agreement that, for some considerable time, finance and policy have not followed the political call for more housing, especially affordable housing. As Crisis (2020a) has noted, decades of under-investment, coupled with the erosion of welfare benefits have seriously undermined the impact of homelessness protection and local government's ability to deliver it.

Legislation

BOX 12.11

Homelessness Reduction Act 2017

Duties upon English Local Authorities

The Main Duty

A duty to secure accommodation for households who are eligible, unintentionally homeless, and with a priority need (e.g., households with dependent children, pregnant women or are vulnerable due to one of a number of specified reasons).

Prevention Duty

A duty to work with people who are threatened with homelessness within 56 days to help prevent them from becoming homelessness.

Relief Duty

A duty that local authorities must take to ensure that reasonable steps are made to secure that suitable accommodation becomes available for occupation for at least six months.

As a key area of social policy, governments of various political persuasions have, it has to be said, introduced much legislation with which to govern homelessness, both directly and indirectly. The duties, powers and obligations on local authorities and other organisations towards people who are assessed as homeless or threatened with homelessness are, for example, set out in law. Indeed, there is a legal duty across all of the nations within the UK for the state to help people who are homeless or threatened with homelessness. Nonetheless, legislation and its implementation vary between each of the countries, with each country taking a slightly different approach. As Full Fact (2020) has noted, in England, Wales and Scotland, it is local authorities who have responsibility, whereas Northern Ireland has a single organisation responsible for housing. In England, councils only have a duty to house someone if they are in 'priority need', whereas this is not the case in Scotland, at least for people who haven't become homeless intentionally (optional for councils in Wales).

The most recent major piece of English legislation, the HRA 2017, introduced new statutory duties upon local authorities to tackle homelessness. In particular, councils are required to work more directly to prevent homelessness and to allocate a greater period of time (an increase from 28 to 56 days) in which they provide advice and support to people who present to them, either to prevent or resolve homelessness.

Interventions

What should be done about the problem? It is perhaps obvious at this point that there is no 'one size fits all' form of intervention that will effectively tackle all of the problems and issues associated with homelessness in one fell-swoop. It is a truism that prevention is always better than cure, as is early intervention, such as addressing childhood trauma. We can thus be assured that improvements to the health and social care system and its governance will contribute greatly to the prevention and resolution of homelessness, as would establishing better pathways to housing.

BOX 12.12 ACCOMMODATION-BASED INTERVENTIONS

Hostels

Often imposing strict rules on behaviour and time-keeping, hostels provide for short-term housing needs. Sleeping arrangements vary, historically some consisting of dormitories but mostly now with individual rooms or even bed-sit type flats. Services, such as kitchens, are frequently communal. The type of support and practical help provided also varies.

Shelters

Shelters provide overnight accommodation, usually in a shared space.* Very much seen as transitory, like hostels, strict rules are often applied. Often staffed by volunteers, shelters may also provide meals as well as support to help individuals connect to key health and social care organisations.

Supported housing

Supported housing combines housing need with other needs. Tailored to the needs of individuals it can be permanent or temporary; have a series of strict rules

> or be fairly liberal; may or may not have staff living on the premises; may or may not be community-based. The support offered can be wide-ranging, including help with mental health issues, drug and alcohol misuse, through to support to find employment, help in accessing services, and claiming benefit.

Equally, a blanket approach to address poverty needs to be complemented by a more targeted approach for those at most risk and much more emphasis placed upon preventative measures. Such measures necessitate addressing the multiple and complex needs to which we have referred above such as substance misuse, criminal activity, domestic violence and other social problems discussed in this volume, all of which would help reduce the numbers of people acutely vulnerable to becoming homeless. On cost grounds alone, to draw on Zaretzky et al. (2017), there is a significant economic argument to be made for government intervention to break the various cycles of deprivation linked to homelessness, especially those with diagnosed mental health disorders, drug related problems and long-term rough sleeping.

On a practical level, many areas of the UK will have soup runs and some day centres, providing food, advice and company to people, some homeless and almost all marginalised and poor. They are safety nets but also indications of need and gaps, reflecting people and parts of society now often described as 'left behind'. Some might therefore say that the need for such – often unfunded – services shows that the benefits system and other parts of the state simply don't work sufficiently well for many thousands of people at any time. Hence, there is need for change, for a system that is more accessible and more generous/practical.

Alongside poverty and access to care, the supply of affordable housing is an equal priority: the availability and accessibility of affordable housing have to increase significantly if the UK is to reduce homelessness and to do so longer term. The under-investment in housing and planning laws thus need to be addressed. That said, in a world in which an increasing number of people are working from home and town-centres under-used, there is at least an argument to be made that a review be undertaken as to the purpose and use of many of our existing buildings, with significant opportunities to re-purpose some commercial premises into housing.

That leads on to improving access to accommodation on a structural, rather than an individual, basis. As we have illustrated, there are various barriers people face in securing accommodation (deposits, rent in advance, references and more). For someone who has received notice to leave their long-term flat, the right support to address their homelessness may simply be financial help to secure another tenancy. Thus, it may be that a scheme to support people to secure rented accommodation may be sufficient, helping the person find a deposit or providing a deposit guarantee instead. Such schemes, where they exist, seek to minimise the duration, risk and impact of homelessness for people who primarily need support simply to be re-accommodated.

In addition, it would be helpful, as some charities and groups such as Crisis advocate, to have a register of landlords. Apart from anything else, such a move would fit the agenda of placing the role of landlord in a more professional, business-like context, with expectations around business planning and the setting of standards, as well as understanding of, and adherence to legislation, potentially improving standards and reducing the number of illegal evictions. Indeed, in Wales all landlords with privately rented property let out on a domestic tenancy have been legally required to join the register there since 2015.

What is fully apparent from what has been presented above is that some people who are homeless, particularly those who are sleeping rough, have multiple and complex needs, some relating to ill-health, others to behavioural difficulties of one sort or another, in some cases homelessness being a symptom and result of those rather than a cause of them in and of itself. Successful intervention to tackle homelessness thus needs not just to focus upon housing alone but to view homelessness much more in the round, including recognising, as Elsinga (2020) has noted, its moral dimension, which he considers to be just as important as its ideological basis. To draw on Somerville (2013), it involves more than just the provision of shelter; it involves tackling deprivation across a number of different dimensions, and above all a recognition of its multidimensional character including the need for creature comforts, satisfying relationships, a space of one's own, ontological security and sense of worth.

In operational terms, this requires joining up of support, potentially with the building of multi-organisational coalitions across the health and social care divide, with the establishment of necessary memoranda of understanding, linkages and active backing of commissioners in central and local government. Here, we are talking of the kinds of support and range of services that can be offered to those who find themselves homeless. There are encouraging signs that strategies, frameworks and commitments are being put into practice in all four countries in the UK, each having a strategy for preventing homelessness (England, 2019; Northern Ireland, 2017; Scottish Government, 2018; Welsh Government, 2019). More specifically, many of England's local authorities have their own homelessness and rough sleepers strategies and detailed action plans, as have many statutory organisations. Prison and probation providers, for example, for whom homelessness is a huge problem, are subject to a statutory 'duty to refer' to the local authorities anyone at the risk of homelessness (HM Prison and Probation Service, 2020).

We are also referring to the knowledge, values and interpersonal skills required by practitioners and the training that they need in models of face-to-face working that can be adopted in work with homeless people, such as can be found in the literature on ideas expressed by Miller and Rollnik (2013) on motivational interviewing, mental health awareness and safeguarding. It is now commonly accepted – indeed required by many potential funders of support for those sleeping rough in particular – that to engage with and support people who are street homeless, services must be based around building relationships between individual workers and service users.; In this regard, services require staff members who are able to listen to, advise and support their clients on a range of issues, whilst actively linking them with services such as those provided by mental health and substance use organisations.

One of the responses to homelessness that has caught a degree of attention in the UK since its introduction is Housing First, a scheme that began in the USA in the late 1980s which has been adopted by various countries, notably including Canada and Finland. In essence, the approach is based on the notion that what people who are long-term homeless most need is stable housing. Providing stable housing, with the support to maintain it, thus gives them the best chance to stop the revolving door of homelessness that many find themselves going through. What elevates this approach above common sense is that Housing First is aimed at people who often have significant mental health and/or addiction issues with which to contend, and for whom homelessness has exacerbated their struggle to tackle such problems. By providing stable accommodation at the outset, Housing First ensures the provision of stability as a secure foundation upon which to address the issues in question.

Housing First, it must be said, is not a panacea. It faces two main challenges before it can be scaled up for wider implementation: the availability and quality of affordable housing and the availability of sufficient and long-term funding for support services. These notwithstanding, Housing First is proving to be a vital addition to the menu of responses that can and should be provided. We can best substantiate the success of this and other interventions by way of concrete examples, made anonymous and necessarily summarised from actual practice.

Case 1

The first involves someone who had been homeless off and on for many years. The person concerned had problems with alcohol, a significant history of anti-social behaviour and a reputation that frightened off landlords. The homelessness organisation supporting him asked him what he wanted and took at face value his assertion that he wanted two main things: his own home and to turn his life around. The combination of that support and advocacy, with the man's own determination and access to Housing First, led to him setting up a tenancy, living in the community and caring about himself and his home. When someone in the community tried to exploit him, he told his support worker and the homelessness organisation and landlord worked together to make him safe in his home again.

Case 2

The second case involves a younger person with behavioural issues, poor mental health, an intravenous drug addiction and what might be described, in Care Act terms, as a tendency towards significant self-neglect. Even with provision of stable housing, support and drug treatment, he lost his housing, due to drug dealing, associated anti-social behaviour and distress caused to his neighbours.

For whatever reasons, what was provided did not prove sufficient at that time. However, in line with the Housing First principle of continued support, the homelessness organisation to which he had been referred steered through the transition out of the tenancy and arranged other accommodation, with even more support available. The aim remained to keep him accommodated and safe, providing the right response at the right time.

Case 3

The third case concerns a woman referred to a homelessness agency by probation. She was homeless and sofa-surfing with her mother after leaving her home city to make a better life for herself and her children. Her children were eventually taken into care due to substance misuse and offending behaviour. She suffers from severe anxiety and depression. The agency managed to place her in temporary accommodation, where she successfully maintained her room. She was then referred to a private rented access scheme which offered her a deposit guarantee to help her secure a tenancy. A flat was then found, and direct debits established in order to pay bills. She had a budget, to which she adhered to the best of her ability, never missing essential payments that would otherwise put her tenancy in jeopardy. The agency also successfully applied for a personal independence payment (PIP), which has maximised her income. Throughout she engaged well with probation worker and staff at the housing agency. She completed a course associated with her substance misuse and related addictive behaviours and worked on her personal development and her relationships with others. She regained contact with all of her children, working towards the goals of having the two youngest live with her.

These examples help point up the 'chicken and egg' type conundrum as to what comes first; whether homelessness causes other problems or whether other issues are the genesis of homelessness. Consider the case (again taken from practice) of someone with mental health issues who was housed in a flat but was at risk of becoming homeless. When she was referred to a homelessness service she was genuinely at risk of losing her accommodation and needed support and guidance. The referrer thought of it as a housing need, which in part was clearly the case. As such the person received the support she needed to enable her to keep her flat. But the issues that this person was facing were much broader and more pronounced, requiring advocacy and support. Though the help was social and health-related, the reason she was at risk was that she had come to believe that her neighbours were conspiring against her and wanted her evicted. The more she believed that, the more her behaviour confused and worried people, meaning that interactions were more strained. It was self-fulfilling. Arguably, this was a mental health issue (episode) that was likely going to lead to the woman losing her accommodation by walking away from it, which is what she was threatening to do, in her distress. But, in such circumstances, the issues intertwine, both needing to be addressed; and needing to be addressed together, through joined-up working.

These studies help illustrate the links between substance abuse, offending behaviour, mental health and homelessness. They very much uphold the tenet expressed by Somerville (2013) for the need to understand homelessness as multidimensional and storied. They also help confirm the need for solutions that provide stable accommodation, one-to-one support, positive development opportunities and the necessary joint working of relevant agencies.

Other examples are also easily cited. Take the case of a male who is alcohol dependent and drinks to the extent that his behaviour is often anti-social. Being unable to maintain accommodation, he may be homeless (on the streets or in and out of hostels) and have regular contact with homelessness services and the police. Possibly one or both have linked him with substance support, too. If organisations work well together, they may look jointly at the man's needs and work together to best try to meet them. If not, and historically, the question of whether the person is primarily homeless or a someone with an alcohol addiction can be crucial, determining from which services he receives support, potentially in isolation rather than collaboration. This parallels the common debate between substance use and mental health services, the so-called 'dual diagnosis' debate that has often seen people told by two services that their needs should be being met by the other.

If this were not complex enough, when this person gets older and potentially experiences dementia, the way forward becomes even more complicated. Services may (and do) argue that it is impossible to assess the dementia because of the alcohol use and may say that it is impossible to engage with someone concerning their alcohol use whilst they are homeless. Landlords may then say it is impossible to house them whilst their behaviour is as it is, whether the cause is alcohol or dementia. Such circular discussions or others very similar concerning different variables occur on a daily basis across the country.

Conclusion

When it comes down to it, homelessness, is many things. Homelessness can perhaps best be defined succinctly as a situational condition experienced by a person or persons, voluntarily or involuntarily, where they have no home of their own. Forms including sleeping outside or in makeshift shelters through to having somewhere to stay but no long-term legal right to do so.

For some, it relates to deprivation, sometimes trauma, mental health issues and marginalisation. For others, it is more a result of a lack of sufficient resources. To take the most obvious example, if people have money, they can afford to rent somewhere to live. People more often than not need a deposit, a month's rent in advance and to be able to show that they can pay the rent. If they can do that, homelessness is less likely. Equally, homelessness is much *more* likely if someone is unable to do those things. As Tunstall et al. (2013) have noted, poverty and material deprivation affect housing circumstances much more strongly than housing circumstances affect poverty. Addressing poverty must therefore be a vital element of any serious government commitment to addressing homelessness. That can include help to provide rent in advance and deposits but more broadly requires levels of income on which people can afford to plan, budget and live independently.

Homelessness is also a resource issue in a much wider sense. As we have established, there are close links between homelessness and the current lack of affordable housing. In most parts of Britain, people compete for housing, each hoping that they will be successful in what is heavily competitive market. Put simply, landlords do not need to scour the streets for people who will give them some money for living in their properties. Clearly, this process does not make things easy for those with fewest resources, with least to offer (money, references, guarantors): it pits them against people who are seen as safer bets.

Government could, of course, limit what landlords can ask for or can charge to secure and rent housing, as happened with ending letting agent fees for tenants under the Tenant Fees Act 2019. That could potentially make housing more accessible, both private rented and social. Regardless of who owns housing (a private individual, company, charity or other), government can to a great extent stipulate the way it is run and the rules under which it operates, if it is willing. Inevitably, what counts for many tenants is accessibility, affordability and maintenance.

BOX 12.13 SUMMARY

- Homelessness is a term used to cover a wide variety of experiences
- Commonly, definitions centre around the absence of a home a person has a legal right to occupy
- Rough sleeping is a particular and visible element of homelessness, those affected typically having a life expectancy in their forties

- There are many reasons people may face homelessness, including relationship breakdown or being given notice by an existing landlord, some primarily needing help to secure another tenancy
- With the circumstances and needs of people becoming homeless varying, so must responses and interventions
- Nevertheless, poverty and marginalisation are strongly associated with it
- It is worth considering homelessness both on a structural basis – in terms of society and government – and on an individual basis, a person's own circumstances: both directly affect people's circumstances
- Whilst no one intervention can meet the needs of all, experience in the UK shows that government can reduce homelessness by improving access to affordable housing, funding advice and support and ensuring provision of joined-up help on related issues.

The need for 'joined up thinking' and collaboration does not, however, make it easy to achieve. Of course, this is not to say that attempts should not be, and are not being, made to tackle such fault lines and for the various tensions to be reconciled in whatever ways they can; indeed, that should be a priority. We make these points simply to demonstrate that intervening to tackle homelessness is a major undertaking. Indeed, to do something about homelessness is not simply an option, one among many, but a socio-political, socio-economic and above all a categorically moral imperative.

Points to Ponder

Is it possible to define satisfactorily what is meant by homelessness?

What lessons can be learned concerning the portrayal of homelessness in the media?

Are the theoretical frameworks that have been used to explain the causes of homelessness of equal weight or are some more convincing than others?

Are current housing policies and legislation sufficient to ameliorate the worst consequences of homelessness?

Quiz

1. What is the life expectancy for a woman sleeping rough in England?
   - # 43
   - # 48
   - # 53
   - # 58
2. The number of people sleeping rough in England in 2020 was lower than the previous year. True or false?
3. Hostels are a form of what type of accommodation?
   - # private rented
   - # permanent
   - # temporary
4. What is the name of the scheme developed in the USA to address long-term homelessness among people with substance use and/or mental health issues?

5. What is the Initiative that has been established to reduce street homelessness in the UK?
6. What is the dominant form of housing tenure in the UK?
   # social rented
   # private rented
   # owner occupier
7. What government department in Westminster does homelessness predominantly sit under?
8. Which country in the UK no longer uses the concept of 'priority need' to determine whether someone is entitled to housing?
9. What is the duty that public bodies in England have if they find that someone they are engaging with is homeless?
10. Which two things will a landlord generally require for someone to take on a tenancy:
    # tenancy deposit
    # copies of the tenant's contents insurance
    # summary of the tenant's latest medical records
    # rent in advance payment

Quiz Answers

1. 43
2. True: Lower
3. Temporary (can also be described as supported)
4. Housing First
5. Rough Sleeper Initiative
6. Owner-occupier
7. Ministry of Housing, Communities and Local Government
8. Scotland
9. Duty to refer (to the person's local authority); it's part of the Homelessness Reduction Act
10. Tenancy deposit, rent in advance. (And often ID & guarantor.)

Key Questions for Discussion

1. Is the current definition of homelessness too wide to be meaningful?
2. To what degree is homelessness a housing issue?
3. To what extent has legislation and subsequent housing policy specifically aimed at reducing and alleviating the problems associated with homelessness been successful?
4. What might a government committed to reducing homelessness now prioritise?

Activity

Create three cases where people may find themselves homeless, identifying backgrounds and reasons and then consider for each what the person may do and what support they may need and receive.

Helpful Electronic Sources and Links
Office for National Statistics
https://www.ons.gov.uk/peoplepopulationandcommunity/householdcharacteristics
Ministry of Housing, Communities and Local Government
https://www.gov.uk/government/organisations/ministry-of-housing-communities-and-local-government

Third Sector, Charitable and Not for Profit, Campaigning Housing Organisations
Crisis
https://www.crisis.org.uk
Shelter
https://www.shelter.org.uk
Centrepoint
https://www.centrepoint.org.uk
St Mungos
https://www.mungos.org
Glassdoor
https://www.glassdoor.org.uk
Church Urban Fund
Web-of-Poverty_2014.pdf (cuf.org.uk)
Child Poverty Action Group
The effects of poverty | CPAG
Homelessness and Poverty
ENHRfullpaper_H_P.pdf (hw.ac.uk)
Youth Homelessness
https://www.homeless.org.uk/sites/default/files/site-attachments/Young%20and%20Homeless%202020.pdf

References

Bramley, G. & Fitzpatrick, S. (2018) Homelessness in the UK: Who Is Most at Risk?, *Housing Studies*, 33:1, 96–116, DOI: 10.1080/02673037.2017.1344957

Crisis (2020a) The Plan to End Homelessness, https://www.crisis.org.uk/ending-homelessness/the-plan-to-end-homelessness-full-version/background/chapter-2-public-policy-and-homelessness/

Crisis (2022) About Homelessness, https://www.crisis.org.uk/ending-homelessness/about-homelessness/

Economic and Social Council of the United Nations (2019) Affordable Housing and Social Protection Systems for All to Address Homelessness: Report of the Secretary-General.

Elsinga, M. (2020) About Housing Systems and Underlying Ideologies, *Housing, Theory and Society*, 37:5, 557–561.

Fitzpatrick, S. (2005) Explaining Homelessness: a Critical Realist Perspective, *Housing, Theory and Society*, 22:1, 1–17, DOI: 10.1080/14036090510034563

Fitzpatrick, S., Pawson, H., Bramley, G., Wilcox, S., Watts, B., Wood, J., Stephens, M., & Blenkinsopp, J. (2019) *The Homelessness Monitor: Scotland 2019*, London: Crisis.

Full Fact (2020) https://fullfact.org/economy/homelessness-england/

Gulliver, K. (2016) *Forty Years of Struggle: A Window on Race and Housing, Disadvantage and Exclusion*, The Human City Institute.

Gunner, E., Chandan, S., Warwick, S., Saunders, K., Burwood, S., Yahyouche, A., & Paudyal, V. (2019) Provision and Accessibility of Primary Healthcare Services for People Who Are Homeless, *British Journal of General Practice 2019*, DOI: 10.3399/bjgp19X704633

Himsworth, C., Priyamvada Paudyal, P., & Christopher Sargeant, C. (2020) Risk Factors for Unplanned Hospital Admission in a Specialist Homeless General Practice Population: Case–Control Study to Investigate the Relationship with Tri-morbidity, *British Journal of General Practice*, 70: 695, e406–e411, DOI: 10.3399/bjgp20X710141

HM Prison and Probation Service (2020) HMPPS Operational Accommodation Framework. Report published 8th July 2020; UK: HMPPS.

Kemeny, J. (1992) *Housing and Social Theory*, London: Routledge.

Kemeny, J. (1995) *From Public Housing to the Social Market. Rental Policy Strategies in Comparative Perspective*, London: Routledge, DOI: 10.1080/02815738408730045.

Leng, G. (2017) The Impact of Homelessness on Health: A Guide for Local Authorities, https://www.local.gov.uk/sites/default/files/documents/22.7%20HEALTH%20AND%20HOMELESSNESS_v08_WEB_0.PDF

Miller, W. & Rollnick, S. (2013) *Motivational Interviewing: Helping People Change* (3rd edition), NY: Guilford Press.

Ministry of Housing, Communities and Local Government (2019) *Homelessness: Causes of Homelessness and Rough Sleeping, Rapid Evidence Assessment*, Alma Economics.

Northern Ireland Homelessness Bulletin (2019) https://www.communities-ni.gov.uk/system/files/publications/communities/ni-homelessness-bulletin-oct-mar-2019.PDF

Office for National Statistics (2020) https://www.gov.uk/government/publications/rough-sleeping-snapshot-in-england-autumn-2019/rough-sleeping-snapshot-in-england-autumn-2019

Scottish Government (2018) Ending Homelessness Together, https://www.gov.scot/binaries/content/documents/govscot/publications/strategy-plan/2018/11/ending-homelessness-together-high-level-action-plan/documents/00543359-pdf/00543359-pdf/govscot%3Adocument/00543359.pdf

Shelter (2007) Homelessness Factsheet, https://england.shelter.org.uk/professional_resources/policy_and_research/policy_library/homelessness_factsheet

Somerville, P. (2013) Understanding Homelessness, *Housing, Theory and Society*, 30:4, 384–415, DOI: 10.1080/14036096.2012.756096

Tsai, J., Yun See Lee, C., Byrne, T., Pietrzak, R., & Southwick, S. (2017) Changes in Public Attitudes and Perceptions about Homelessness Between 1990 and 2016, *American Journal of Community Psychology*, 60: 3–4, 599–606.

Tunstall, R., Bevan, M., Bradshaw, J., Croucher, K., Duffy, S., Hunter, C., Jones, A., Rugg, J., Wallace, A., & Wilcox, S. (2013) The Links Between Housing and Poverty: An Evidence Review, *Joseph Rowntree Foundation: York*.

Welsh Government (2019) Strategy for Preventing and Ending Homelessness, https://gov.wales/sites/default/files/publications/2019-10/homelessness-strategy.pdf

Wales.gov (2021) https://gov.wales/homelessness

Zaretzky, K., Flatau, P., Spicer, B., Conroy, E., & Burns, L. (2017) What Drives the High Health Care Costs of the Homeless?, *Housing Studies*, 32: 7, 931–947, DOI: 10.1080/02673037.2017.1280777

13 Multicultural societies

Diversity, discrimination and social inclusion

Berkeley Wilde

The chapter explores the intersections of identity politics and the tensions causing contemporary "social problems" across the countries of the UK, including the so-called "culture wars", with an underpinning of global, social, economic and wider health and social inequalities.

It also examines the prejudices, racial biases and racial profiling which has permeated through organisations and institutions; through the police, the wider criminal justice system and other statutory and non-statutory organisations to create an environment of hostility towards Black, Asian and Minority Ethnic communities. As well as increasingly towards minority communities from a range of backgrounds, and other protected characteristics, such as disability and different aspects of identity.

The chapter concludes with the legal and social policy frameworks across the four nations of the UK, as well as practical guidance on creating and developing an organisational policy framework for advancing equality, diversity, equity and inclusion.

Introduction

Diversity and discrimination are at the forefront of news and social media and in conversations taking place across the countries of the UK. Not a day goes by without front-page headlines taunting often already highly marginalised individuals, communities and groups.

We have seen a shift in discourse from the silencing of "Stop being so PC" and "It's political correctness gone mad" to "It's just the woke generation"; as well as global awakenings through movements including Black Lives Matter, Trans Lives Matter and Black Trans Lives Matter. As well as advances in the rights of Disabled people and the rights of women and girls, including through social and political movements such as the #MeToo movement and Reclaim These Streets.

Case study: George Floyd

The murder of George Floyd, on 25 May 2020, sparked global outrage and protests across the world through the Black Lives Matter movement. Protests took place in over 2000 cities in 60 countries around the world, including the UK. The movement has called for an end to police violence and the mistreatment of Black communities by the police.

> In April 2021, Derek Chauvin was convicted of the murder of George Floyd. On 5 May 2021, Chauvin's legal team filed for a retrial. Justice, for the lives of Black people, is an ongoing battle being fought in court rooms, on the streets and in the institutions across society.

Discourse and dialogue, on themes of equality, diversity, equity and inclusion are often silenced or shut down by the media, mainly associated with the political right. High-profile national events including the EU Referendum and Brexit, in 2016, the victories of centrist and populist governments across Europe. As well as terror attacks including Manchester Arena, London Bridge, Westminster Bridge, Borough Market and the Finsbury Park Mosque, which all took place in 2017. Events which have seen already marginalised communities experiencing an increase in hate crime, hate incidents and discrimination, as well as increasing health and social inequalities. Health inequalities which have been further exacerbated by the global pandemic – COVID-19 – which is often compounded by poverty, health, housing, diet and a wide range of health and social inequalities. The experience, through the pandemic, has also seen a sharp increase in hate crimes and hate incidents directed at people from Chinese, East Asian and South Asian communities. There has also been a sharp increase in attacks against people from Muslim communities, in response to the terrorist attacks in the US on 11 September 2001. Muslim women, in the months immediately following the attacks, reported having their veils pulled off, as well as reports of being verbally abused and violently attacked (Spalek, 2002).

Terminology

The 1965 Race Relations Act defined racism as hatred on the grounds of colour, race, ethnic or national origins (UK Parliament, 1965). The Act was subsequently incorporated into the Equality Act 2010. Institutional racism – originally defined by Carmichael and Hamilton (Hamilton & Ture, 1992) and subsequently re-defined by Macpherson in the Macpherson Report (Macpherson, 1999) and the Stephen Lawrence Inquiry stated:

> *The collective failure of an organisation to provide an appropriate and professional service to people because of their colour, culture, or ethnic origin. It can be seen or detected in processes, attitudes and behaviour that amount to discrimination through prejudice, ignorance, thoughtlessness, and racist stereotyping which disadvantage minority ethnic people.*

> ### Case study: Bijan Ebrahimi
>
> Bijan Ebrahimi was an Iranian refugee who was killed in Bristol in 2013 by his neighbour Lee James. Bijan had made numerous complaints to the police, and local housing officers, about anti-social behaviour around his home, as well as racist incidents where Bijan was repeatedly targeted. Bijan would, on occasion, film anti-social behaviour happening around his neighbourhood. This led to accusations from his neighbours of Bijan being a paedophile, who had been filming children. An inquiry into the case found that the police and Local Authority were

found guilty of institutional racism and this led to the conviction of two police officers. Underlying this case is both unconscious bias and groupthink; Bijan was seen as *problematic* by those dealing with his case; he was considered a "problem". Work to address unconscious bias, within the police and local authority, has subsequently led to the police in Bristol making unconscious bias training mandatory (Safer Bristol Partnership, 2017).

Oppression is described as unjust treatment or the exercise of power. Which links to our understanding of privilege. Examples of privilege include male privilege and White privilege, the privileges of being born male and White in a culture or society that places a hierarchy on to these forms of identity.

Prejudice means to pre-judge and is based on a lack of experience rather than of actual experience. A lot of prejudice is instinctive and unconscious. We protect ourselves from the unknown by making up our mind in advance about something.

Stereotyping is a cousin to prejudice. It labels groups of people and says they all share the same characteristics. Stereotyping people also means clumping people or groups together in an arbitrary fashion. Stereotypes can be positive or negative. For example, stereotypes such as that all Black people can dance and are good at sports. Often stereotypes come from experiences of other people and groups.

Discrimination can manifest itself in many settings including in education, employment, housing, healthcare and in the provision of goods and services. In most of the nations of the UK, including England, Scotland and Wales, the Equality Act 2010 protects people from a range of protected characteristics from discrimination, harassment and victimisation. The equality legal and policy framework in Northern Ireland is different to Great Britain and is discussed later in the chapter.

BOX 13.1 DISCRIMINATION

Discrimination is defined in the Equality Act 2010 in six different ways including direct discrimination, indirect discrimination, discrimination by association, by perception, harassment and victimisation. These are defined in the Act as follows:

- Direct discrimination – someone with a protected characteristic is treated less favourably due to their protected characteristic
- Indirect discrimination – a policy, procedure or practice which unfairly disadvantages someone with a protected characteristic
- Association – someone is treated less favourable because they associate with someone with a protected characteristic
- Perception – someone is treated less favourably when they are perceived to have a protected characteristic
- Harassment – any unwanted conduct based on a protected characteristic which has the effect of belittling, intimidating, hostile or degrading environment. For example, sexual harassment
- Victimisation – when someone is treated less favourably, having made a complaint about discrimination, because of a protected characteristic.

Types of discrimination

Direct racial discrimination, refusing to employ someone or provide them with a service based on their ethnicity, isn't the only form of racial discrimination. There are many other forms of discrimination including indirect discrimination whereby someone is unfairly disadvantaged because they belong to a particular race or ethnic group or through institutional discrimination, including institutional racism whereby a system disadvantages individuals and groups or has the outcome of discrimination based on systemic failure to treat people fairly and appropriately because of their race or ethnicity, see Macpherson above. Discrimination can also occur because of bias, making assumptions about an individual or group, based on their race or ethnicity. Further, discrimination can take on subtle forms such as avoidance, for example in social or workplace settings. Psychological studies on avoidance are evidenced in in-group and out-group theories, whereby people favour people who are like them, who come from a similar background to them. In-group and out-group theories were tested in experiments carried out by Tajfel and Brown in 1979.

> This is known as in-group (us) and out-group (them). The central hypothesis of social identity theory is that group members of an in-group will seek to find negative aspects of an out-group, thus enhancing their own self-image.
>
> (Tajfel, 1979)

In earlier work Gordon Allport, a researcher and criminologist working in the US in the 1950s described how discrimination can escalate from low-level examples such as social avoidance, racial slurs or comments, escalating to acts of prejudice, discrimination (in housing, education, healthcare and employment) to physical attacks on property and on individuals, for example, hate crime and hate incidents, to murder and ultimately to genocide. The low-level verbal assaults create a hostile environment for victims. If left unchallenged these acts can and do escalate (Allport, 1954).

BOX 13.2 HATE CRIME AND HATE INCIDENT

The Criminal Justice Act (2003) defines a hate crime as:

Any criminal offence that is motivated by hostility or prejudice based upon the victim's race, disability, faith, religion or belief, gender reassignment or sexual orientation.

A hate incident is defined as *"any incident which is perceived to be discriminatory by the victim or by any other person"*. There may be no criminal offence and such incidents can be recognised as Anti-Social Behaviour (Crown Prosecution Service, 2020).

Hatred related to sexism and ageism, though increasingly recorded by the police, are not currently included in the Home Office definition of hate crimes as monitored strands (Crown Prosecution Service, 2020). The Law Commission has carried out a review of the hate crime strands, it is likely that the review will recommend inclusion of age (ageism) and sex (sexism and misogyny) motivated hate crimes. The law does not currently treat each characteristic equally. For example, someone who is assaulted because of their disability will not be treated the same as someone who is assaulted because of their race or ethnicity. It is also likely that people who are assaulted or targeted because they are homeless, street sex workers or because they look "different", such as alternative sub-cultures, will also be included in the review and recommendations (Law Commission, 2021).

BOX 13.3 DISABILITY DEFINITION

The Equality Acts (2010) defines disability as:

A physical or mental impairment which has a substantial and long-term adverse effect on your ability to carry out normal day-to-day activities.

Employers have to make reasonable adjustments to ensure that an employee with a disability, including mental ill health, can carry out their role or function. Reasonable adjustments can also be made during the recruitment and interview process to ensure that a disabled candidate is not disadvantaged and to make things easier for the candidate.

Discrimination arising from disability means that someone is treated less favourably because they are disabled. When there should be no reason or justification for the less favourable treatment. There are limited exceptions, for example on the grounds of health and safety. There is a duty on employers and service providers to make reasonable adjustments to ensure that disabled people can carry out their job role or access goods and services (Equality and Human Rights Commission, 2021).

BOX 13.4 REASONABLE ADJUSTMENTS

Employers must make reasonable adjustments to make sure workers with disabilities, or physical or mental health conditions, aren't substantially disadvantaged when doing their jobs.

- changing the recruitment process so a candidate can be considered for a job
- doing things another way, such as allowing someone with social anxiety disorder to have their own desk instead of hot-desking
- making physical changes to the workplace, like installing a ramp for a wheelchair user or an audio-visual fire alarm for a deaf person
- letting a disabled person work somewhere else, such as on the ground floor for a wheelchair user
- changing their equipment, for instance providing a special keyboard if they have arthritis
- allowing employees who become disabled to make a phased return to work, including flexible hours or part-time working
- offering employees training opportunities, recreation and refreshment facilities.

Workplace discrimination

Despite the legal reforms a report carried out in 2019 found that the UK has one of the highest levels of workplace discrimination in Europe. More than a third (38%) of respondents to a Europe-wide survey said they had been discriminated at work. The policy and legal framework whilst robust can leave workers experiencing workplace discrimination (ADP, 2019).

BOX 13.5 MYTHS AND FACTS

Myth 1: Diversity is just about race and sex
Fact: Diversity covers a range of characteristics which are referred to in the Equality Act as "protected characteristics" and include age, disability, gender reassignment, marriage and civil partnership, pregnancy and maternity, race, religion and belief, sex and sexual orientation. Diversity also encompasses factors such as socioeconomics, as well as autism and neurodiversity, and may include diversity of thought and opinion. Diversity is therefore about a much wider range of social, cultural, political and identity factors and differences. Diversity is about what makes us unique individuals.

Myth 2: Disabled people aren't discriminated against
Fact: There are many myths and stereotypes about disabled people including that disabled people are useless and are a drain on the economy; through to more serious and dangerous myths such as adults with learning disabilities being a risk to children. Disabled people can experience many forms of discrimination including in education, healthcare, employment and in accessing goods and services.

Myth 3: Black males are lazy
Fact: Myths about Black men stem from racism, and stereotypes of *the dangerous Black male*. The Black male is seen as a criminal, a drug dealer, a pimp and a gangster. These myths and stereotypes contribute to the likelihood of increased incarceration of Black men. For example, in the UK Black men are three times more likely to be arrested than White men (UK Government, 2020). Black men are 26% more likely to be remanded in custody than White men (Prison Reform Trust, 2021).

Myth 4: Girls prefer pink and boys prefer blue
Fact: From the moment children are born gender stereotyping begins. "Is it a boy" or "is it a girl" is often the first question people ask when a child is born. The use of gender stereotyping, girls prefer pink and boys prefer blue, places constraints and limitations around femininity and masculinity. Constraints placed on children as they grow up and are trying to make sense of the world. This can often lead to a lifetime of gender stereotyping.

Myth 5: Muslims are terrorists
Fact: Since the terror attacks in the US on 11 September 2001 there has been a rise in the number of hate crimes and hate incidents perpetrated towards Muslim communities, including attacks on people perceived to be Muslim (Spalek, 2002). Data from the Federal Bureau of Investigation (FBI) in the US shows that the number of attacks increased from 28 incidents of anti-Muslim hate crimes in the year 2000 and increased to 481 attacks in 2001.

Theoretical explanations and frameworks

The following theoretical models and frameworks underpin equality, diversity, equity and inclusion. These theoretical models and frameworks explain some of the impacts on the victims and survivors of discrimination as well as providing a call to action for social and political change.

The social model of disability

The social model of disability defines how disabled people are disabled by the environment in which they live, socialise, study or work. The social model places the responsibility for the experience of discrimination, or inequalities, on the environment in which disabled people live rather than on the individual disabled persons impairment being the cause of the discrimination or inequality. Many disabled people view the environment in which they live in as the "problem" rather than their impairment being the "problem". The disability is external, within the environment, rather than internal, within the individual. The social model of disability was developed by and for disabled people (Scope, 2021).

BOX 13.6 SOCIAL MODEL OF DISABILITY

The social model of disability is a way of viewing the world developed by disabled people.

The model says that people are disabled by barriers in society, not by their impairment or difference. Barriers can be physical, like buildings not having accessible toilets. Or they can be caused by people's attitudes to difference, like assuming disabled people can't do certain things. The social model helps recognise barriers that make life harder for disabled people Removing these barriers creates equality and offers disabled people more independence, choice and control (Scope, 2021).

The social construction of gender

Sex and gender can be distinguished as sex being about the physical attributes when sex is assigned at birth and include male, female and intersex conditions which can be chromosomal, hormonal or reproductive characteristics. Gender can be categorised as being the way in which someone identifies in relation to individual femininity or masculinity and will include people who feel their gender is different to the sex they were assigned at birth. For example, the experience of trans/transgender and non-binary people. Gender impacts on people's experiences of access to services such as health and reproductive rights. For example, women and girls often experience poorer health outcomes and higher inequalities than men and boys – across many cultures and societies. Geography also plays an important part in the experience based on the individual experience of their sex and gender. For example, the sex-based rights of women and girls in patriarchal societies including Iran, Iraq and Yemen.

Patriarchy and gender

Patriarchy is a system in which men hold power over women and children. This power can be in the home, in the workplace, in education, across systems, institutions and society. Patriarchal societies around the world exist where men hold all or most of the social, political, financial control and ownership of property. For example, in patriarchal societies male privilege extends to things such as access to education and the workplace leaving women and girls without access to basic education and employment opportunities. In some countries and states, girls are forced into arranged marriages and their access to education is taken away, leaving many girls and young women in some countries illiterate (World Economic Forum, 2013).

Intersectional theory

The term intersectionality was first coined by the Black American feminist academic Kimberlé Crenshaw in 1989 and explores the interconnected and interrelated experiences of race, sex and gender through the experiences of racism and sexism. More broadly the term includes the experiences of discrimination and oppression experienced by other groups including disabled people, people with mental ill health, as well as other marginalised communities and groups. Intersectionality explores the connections of the oppressions experienced, for example, a Black woman's experiences of racism and sexism and their impact (Crenshaw, 1989).

> ### BOX 13.7 INTERSECTIONALITY
>
> An intersectional approach to diversifying a workplace or institution acknowledges the interconnected nature of social categories such as race, ethnicity, class, gender, age, ability, sexual or religious orientation, etc. as they apply to an individual or group. These interconnected social categories create overlapping and interdependent systems of privilege and advantage or discrimination and disadvantage, which shift according to geographical location and historical, political and cultural context.
>
> Source: Crenshaw (1989)

The lived experience of many people with protected characteristics can be described as intersectional – the idea that everyone has multiple ways in which identity is made up including their age, sex, race, sexual orientation and having or not having a faith, religion or belief. For example, the lived experience of a Black Gay Man will be very different to the lived experience of a White Gay Man; the Black Gay Man will have a very different experience of racism to that of a White Gay Man. Whilst both men may share an experience of homophobia, the Black Gay Man will have an acute experience of racism, especially when growing up in a predominantly White and Western culture. The intersections of identity can be broken down further; for example, the experience of two Black Gay Men, one from an African Caribbean heritage and one from an African heritage may be as different and varied as the experience between a Black Gay Man and White Gay Man.

Lived experiences shape people's experiences of social issues. For example, a Black male is nine times more likely to be stopped and searched by the police than a White male (UK Government, 2021a). Black males are 26% more likely to be in custody than White males (Prison Reform Trust, 2021). Black males are more likely to be physically assaulted than White males. Black males are more likely to be involved in violent crime than White males (Ministry of Justice, 2018). Black males are less likely to reach a higher educational attainment level than White males and Black males being less likely to be afforded a place at a university than White males (Advance HE, 2017). There is also evidence that Black Americans experience of racism is also linked to increased blood pressure across the life span (Armstead et al., 1989).

Prejudice and discrimination

Prejudice and discrimination are widespread across society and across communities. Socioeconomic factors, such as class, wealth and privilege, underpin individual and group experiences of prejudice and discrimination.

Implications for people – individual, family and society

Year-on-year data, from the Crime Survey of England and Wales (Home Office, 2019), has recorded a drop in overall crime rates; yet the number of cases of hate crimes has increased each year since hate crime recording began in 2011. Prior to 2010–2011 the Home Office only recorded racist incidents. The Crime Survey of England and Wales, in 2015, found the lowest recorded crime rates in England and Wales since recording began in 1981. However, there has been an increase in recorded hate crimes; with crimes doubling since recording began in 2012 (UK Parliament, 2021). Whilst this can be partly attributed to improvements in recording by the police; events such as Brexit and the EU Referendum, as well as terrorist attacks in London and Manchester, have caused spikes in recorded hate crime numbers since 2016.

With over 105,000 recorded hate crimes in the year 2019 (Home Office, 2019) this impacts on the lives of individuals, families and communities across the country. In the context of hidden hate crimes, for example, data from Stonewall (Bachmann & Gooch, 2017) found there is robust evidence that the underreporting of hate crime, over 80% go unreported to the police, which means that we are only aware of the *tip of the iceberg*. The primary reasons given for victims not reporting hate crime is a fear of discrimination, when reporting, as well as not being believed, not being taken seriously, incidents not being considered serious enough and incidents taking place too often – sometimes as often as on a daily basis (Bachmann & Gooch, 2017).

Since the cuts to Legal Aid in 2013 employment discrimination cases have dropped significantly, with no cases of employment discrimination receiving Legal Aid funding between 2013 and 2018 (Equality and Human Rights Commission, 2019). Since cuts to Legal Aid were introduced; these changes have meant that most employment discrimination cases were no longer covered by Legal Aid. Many victims of discrimination are being denied justice – according to the discrimination watchdog the Equality & Human Rights Commission (Equality and Human Rights Commission, 2019). In a parliamentary question asked by the Labour MP Richard Burgon, in 2019, the Shadow Justice Secretary at the time, the UK Government confirmed that there has been a 50% reduction in the number of Law Centres, and not-for-profit legal advice services, in

England and Wales (Guardian, 2019; UK Parliament, 2019). This was compounded by a reduction in local authority funding through the austerity policies introduced by the coalition Government during the years 2010–2015.

Impact of COVID-19

Following a Freedom of Information Request to the Metropolitan Police on racist hate crimes experienced by those who were Chinese or East Asian, there was a five-fold increase in the number of hate crimes experienced by those who were "oriental" or perceived to be "oriental" between January 2020 and March 2020. There were 20 recorded hate crimes in January 2020 and 186 recorded hate crimes in March 2020. This was almost double the figures recorded in the previous year (Metropolitan Police, 2020).

Linkages with other social issues/problems

As this chapter explores there are often many links with other social problems and issues and these often compound the lived experience of those people with protected characteristics.

Domestic violence discrimination

> **BOX 13.8 DISCRIMINATION AND GENDER-BASED VIOLENCE**
>
> The United Nations Declaration on the Elimination of Violence against Women defines gender-based violence in the following way:
>
> *The definition of discrimination includes gender-based violence, that is, violence that is directed against a woman because she is a woman or that affects women disproportionately. It includes acts that inflict physical, mental or sexual harm or suffering, threats of such acts, coercion and other deprivations of liberty.*
>
> Source: United Nations (1993)

The Office for National Statistics (ONS) found that 7.3% of women (1.6 million) and 3.6% of men (757,000) were the victims of domestic abuse in the previous year (Office for National Statistics, 2020). The charity SafeLives report that women are more likely than men to experience severe domestic abuse, with 95% of cases going to Marac or accessing an IDVA service are women (SafeLives, 2014). Marac is a Multi-Agency Risk Assessment Conference which is called whenever a high-risk case of domestic violence is identified. The conference includes the police, health services, child protection, housing and an IDVA. IDVA is an Independent Domestic Violence Advocate which is a supporting role provided to high-risk victims of domestic violence and abuse.

Different forms of discrimination, in the context of domestic violence, can be demonstrated through the experience of male victims of domestic violence, as well as through the experience of many in same sex relationships and LGBT+ people's experiences, as well as the experiences of Black, Asian and Minority Ethnic victims. According to the charity SafeLives, only 4.4% of male victims are receiving support from domestic abuse services (SafeLives, 2014).

The experience of people in same-sex relationships is often compounded by homophobia, biphobia and transphobia, as well as the fear of discrimination when help-seeking. This leads to the increased likelihood of people in same-sex relationships fleeing or seeking help when in abusive relationships, help-seeking informally amongst friends and family instead (SafeLives, 2018).

The experience of a lack of funding for domestic violence and abuse support for victims from Black, Asian and Minority Ethnic communities has been highlighted by Women's Aid in their annual audit report (Women's Aid, 2021).

Mental health and discrimination

For decades mental health has been misunderstood within society. Many people with mental ill health were often unseen and their challenges were invisible. This led to ignorance about mental ill health and as a result discrimination against people with mental health challenges was significant. Since the Disability Discrimination Act (1995) became statutory, and more recently the Equality Act (2010), discrimination on the grounds of disability, including both physical impairment and mental impairment has been illegal in employment, in work or applying for jobs and in the provision of goods and services across the UK.

Whilst enforcement, through the law, exists this has not stopped the everyday discrimination people living with mental ill health experience; as well as being the target of bullying, harassment, hate crime and hate incidents. National charities, including Rethink Mental Illness and the Mental Health Foundation, campaign against discrimination experienced by people with mental ill health (Rethink Mental Illness, 2021). According to the Mental Health Foundation, nearly nine out of ten people with a mental health condition report that stigma and discrimination has a negative effect on their lives (Mental Health Foundation, 2021).

HIV and discrimination

Another area of public policy, which has witnessed some of the most difficult forms of stigma and discrimination in living memory, is the experience of HIV and AIDS, especially during the 1980s and into the 1990s. From the mass media campaigns of the mid 1980s including "AIDS: Don't Die of Ignorance", from the Department of Health in 1986, (National Archives, 2016), including a mailshot campaign distributed to 23-million homes; whilst at the time there was no treatment and little chance of living with and surviving HIV and AIDS. In the book Rejoice! Rejoice! Britain in the 1980s by author Alwyn W. Turner describes:

> *The first couple of years of the syndrome's progress in Britain were characterized by some hysterical reporting, with a particular emphasis on the fact that it was primarily gay men who were showing up as being infected. The expression "gay plague" became accepted media shorthand.*
> (Turner, 2013)

This led to the mass media hysteria of the "Gay plague" throughout the remainder of the 1980s; to the dramatic shift in Government policy in the mid-1980s, following the then

Secretary of State for Health and Social Services Sir Norman Fowler's visit to the AIDS wards in San Francisco, and his witnessing first-hand the impact of HIV and AIDS on a generation of gay and bisexual men in the US. Documented in the film After 82: The Untold Story of the AIDS Crisis by Ben Lord and Steve Keeble (After 82, 2017).

The shift then in the 1990s towards emerging treatments for people with HIV through the developments of combination therapies, moving from death and dying towards surviving and living with HIV. Yet the stigma and discrimination towards people living with HIV and AIDS is as acute today as it was in those earlier decades. Generations of young people have grown up and gone all the way through the education system with very little, if any, significant formal educational input on HIV and sexual health. Many young people today believe that the AIDS crisis is over and that they are somehow invincible, and that HIV and AIDS won't impact their lives. This has been amplified in the series made for Channel 4 television by Russell T Davis called "It's A Sin". The series follows the lives of a group of young people, including young gay and bisexual men and their friends over the years from 1981 to 1991. Following the airing on television in the UK, search engines saw dramatic percentage increases in keyword searches including 40% increase in "Can you get AIDS from kissing", 700% increase in "HIV vs AIDS", 2150% increase in the search "Can women get AIDS" and a 4300% increase in searches for "Does AIDS cause fits" (Terrence Higgins Trust, 2021).

People living with HIV continue to report experiences of stigma and discrimination despite the fact that education on HIV and AIDS has been available in schools in the UK since the 1990s. The National AIDS Trust report that people living with HIV experience a wide range of discrimination and stigma including direct discrimination, stigma in relation to physical and mental health, stigma in relation to accessing HIV treatments as well as in health promotion, prevention and education (National AIDS Trust, 2016).

Health, social inequalities and discrimination

The COVID-19 pandemic has highlighted the acute health and social inequalities across society. Inequalities that were already acute have been made more so by the pandemic. Inequalities including health, education, employment, poverty and housing have been brought into sharp focus. Whilst the UK Government made attempts to cushion some of the most vulnerable in society, through for example, the government furlough scheme, (UK Government, 2021b) from the direct impact of the pandemic, poverty has been amplified as a result of the pandemic. The use of food banks is at a record high with weekly averages reported by the Trussell Trust, a national charity which supports a UK-wide network of 1200 food banks predicted a 61% increase in the use of foodbanks in the autumn of 2020. With families with children being impacted the most (The Trussell Trust, 2020).

A study published in 2019 found that discrimination was directly related to other inequalities including poorer health, increased likelihood of depression and greater strain on relationships. The study also found links between experiences of discrimination and stress as well as poorer mental and physical health. Stress, from experience of discrimination, can cause long-term impacts on physical health and on mortality (Wofford et al., 2019).

Substance misuse and discrimination

People affected by substance misuse, including the misuse of alcohol, recreational and/or prescription drugs, experience everyday discrimination. In a report in 2012 the charity

Adfam, working with families of people affected by alcohol, drugs and/or gambling addictions found high levels of stigma experienced by both those experiencing addiction themselves and their families (Adfam, 2012).

Social class and discrimination

The Equality Act 2010 does not include socio-economic status, also referred to as social class, as a protected characteristic. In the Equality Act draft legislation, socio-economic status was included as a protected characteristic. This was removed by the coalition government by the Home Secretary, Teresa May, in 2010. Whilst public sector organisations do need to pay due regard to socio-economic status, in particular, when carrying out equality impact assessments through the Socio-Economic Duty, part of the (Section 1) Equality Act 2010 (The Equality Trust, 2021).

> *An authority to which this section applies must, when making decisions of a strategic nature about how to exercise its functions, have due regard to the desirability of exercising them in a way that is designed to reduce the inequalities of outcome which result from socio-economic disadvantage.*

Despite the existence of the Socio-Economic Duty, successive UK Governments have consistently refused to enshrine the socio-economic duty into law. Scotland, however, has taken measures towards enhancing the socio-economic duty through the Fairer Scotland Duty which was first published in April 2018. This places a duty on public bodies in Scotland to *"actively consider how they can reduce inequalities of outcome caused by socio-economic disadvantage, when making strategic decisions"* (Fairer Scotland Duty, 2018).

Social class underpins many inequalities and can be witnessed in the context of health inequalities, in housing, education, criminal justice and across systems and institutions.

UK, a pluralistic society

The debate between the UK as a pluralistic society, or as a multicultural society, raises the question of how diversity exists within a society with a complexity of inequalities. Many of the examples of discrimination included in this chapter have illustrated how complex issues including health, housing, socioeconomics, education and overall access to resources shape the way society is viewed and how we might explain inequalities. The experience of those from minority backgrounds, based on experiences of race, sex, disability and other protected characteristics reveal how it is important to have a sense of belonging to a society or a community in order to thrive.

Multiculturalism: migration and diversity

A sense of belonging to a society is an important factor particularly for newly arriving communities in the UK. Migration has brought challenges and has led to community tensions between the settled majority community and newly arriving communities. Refugee and asylum-seeking communities often fleeing from war or starvation can be welcomed or rejected by the majority. Notions of identity and of nationalism have been tested in the last decade through political debates including the EU Referendum in 2016 and the fallout from the referendum and all that has happened since through the process called Brexit.

BOX 13.9 ANTISEMITISM

The International Holocaust Remembrance Alliance (IHRA) working definition:

Antisemitism is a certain perception of Jews, which may be expressed as hatred toward Jews. Rhetorical and physical manifestations of antisemitism are directed toward Jewish or non-Jewish individuals and/or their property, toward Jewish community institutions and religious facilities.

Source: International Holocaust Remembrance Alliance (2016)

BOX 13.10 ISLAMOPHOBIA

Islamophobia is rooted in racism and is a type of racism that targets expressions of Muslimness or perceived Muslimness (Islamophobia Definitions, 2021). Islamophobia has been defined as:

Having unfounded hostility towards Islam which results in direct discrimination against Muslims and the exclusion of Muslims from mainstream political and social affairs.

Source: Conway (1997)

Equalities timeline

Since the first strides forward in equalities legislation in the UK took place in the 1960s and 1970s; including the Race Relations Act (1965) and the Sex Discrimination Act (1975), many individuals, communities and groups have seen advances in protection from discrimination impacting on a range of characteristics including age, faith, race and sex.

A further significant legal and political milestone occurred in 1995 with the advent of the Disability Discrimination Act. Despite the Disability Discrimination Act, known as the DDA, being statutory for over 25 years, there is still wide-spread discrimination against disabled people – in institutions including in education, health, housing, workplaces and accessing goods and services. Whilst reasonable adjustments can be made by employers and businesses to enable disabled people to participate, many disabled people experience a lack of accessibility and a lack of consideration and inclusion, especially in decision-making, which means discrimination on the grounds of disability continues.

Advances in rights for Lesbian, Gay, Bisexual and Trans (LGBT+) communities in the UK have been varied. During the Thatcher era Government, in the 1980s, legislation known as Section 28 of the Local Government Act (1988), was introduced which aimed to *"prevent Local Authorities from intentionally promoting homosexuality as a pretend family relationship"*. Whilst the legislation was never tested in court the impact, especially on schools, teachers and generations of school children and young people, meant that even talking about being Lesbian, Gay or Bisexual was prevented in schools; as was, for example, discussion about same-sex parenting, including adoption and fostering rights. Whilst at the same time homophobic, biphobic and transphobic bullying increased in schools (UK Government, 2018).

The rights of Lesbian, Gay, Bisexual and Trans people were protected in the UK from the early 2000s. In 2003 saw the implementation of Sexual Orientation Regulations, protecting Lesbian, Gay and Bisexual people from discrimination at work, in education and training and in the provision of goods and services. The Civil Partnership Act (2005), another significant legal milestone, which enabled people in same-sex relationships who entered into a civil partnership the same legal status as those in opposite-sex marriages. Marriage equality was achieved across the UK from 2013 with the introduction of the Marriage (Same-Sex Couples) Act in England and Wales, in Scotland in 2014 and in Northern Ireland in 2020.

Advances in the rights for Trans people in the UK have been varied and complex. From individual early cases taken to the European Court of Justice, in 2002, which led to the Blair Government implementing the Gender Recognition Act (2004), known as the GRA. The GRA enables Trans people the ability to apply to a Gender Recognition Panel for a Gender Recognition Certificate, which means the state is then required to treat the person in the gender in which they live. The principle of the Act enables Trans people to live freely in the gender identity in which they choose to live. However, differences between the Gender Recognition Act and the Equality Act exist. A scenario, outlined in the Equality Act, describes how a women-only counselling service could discriminate against trans women when delivering, for example, women-only counselling services (Equality Act, 2010). This is despite the 2004 GRA requiring the state, and its agents, to treat Trans people in the gender in which they live full-time and permanently. Another contention exists in the Marriage (Same-Sex Couples) Act (2013), whereby trans people are required to have the permission of their spouse to permit their gender transition, known as the *spousal veto*. This contention in the legislation causes many trans people undue stress, often leading to relationship breakdown and in some cases divorce (Barker, 2019).

A further, and increasingly heightening, contention exists between feminism, in particular areas of "gender critical" feminism and the rights of trans people; particularly the rights of trans women in access to women-only services and spaces. Whilst the Equality Act 2010 has meant, for over ten years, that trans people shouldn't be discriminated against when accessing goods and services, debates continue, in sometimes heated and hateful ways, between opposing groups. Many in the "gender critical" movement view allowing trans women into women-only spaces as putting other women at risk. Whilst the trans community, and allies, view this as discriminatory.

Policies and legislation

The following legal frameworks, including legislation and social policy, outline the legal contexts across the nations of the UK including England, Scotland, Wales and Northern Ireland.

Equality Act 2010

The key provisions of the Equality Act (2010) are to provide protection from discrimination, harassment and victimisation to nine protected characteristics including: age, disability, marriage and civil partnership, gender reassignment, pregnancy and maternity, race, religion and belief, sex and sexual orientation. The Act drew together over 116 pieces of legislation which were developed from the mid-1960s to 2010– into one single Act of Parliament. The purpose was to harmonise, strengthen and streamline the existing equalities legislation. The Act applies to the UK including England, Scotland and Wales (Equality Act, 2010).

Northern Ireland

The Northern Ireland Act (1988) established the devolved Northern Ireland Assembly. Anti-discrimination law is devolved to the Northern Ireland Assembly. Equality laws in Northern Ireland are different and are principally from Section 75 of the Northern Ireland Act (1988). Though Northern Ireland does incorporate most of the protected characteristics in the Equality Act, including age, disability, race, religion and belief, including political opinion, sex, gender reassignment, marriage and civil partnerships, pregnancy and maternity and sexual orientation. However, the differences between equality law and the laws in the rest of the UK include the lack of harmonisation and simplification of Northern Ireland equality law. Sections 73 and 74 of the Northern Ireland Act established the Equality Commission for Northern Ireland. The Commission has called for changes in equality law in the areas of age discrimination, disability legislation, sex and gender pay, as well as the provision of goods and services and strengthened positive action measures (Equality Commission for Northern Ireland, 2021). The UN Committee on the Convention for the Elimination of all forms or Racial Discrimination (CERD) has urged the UK Government to ensure that the Equality Act 2010 is also enshrined in law in Northern Ireland (Equality Commission for Northern Ireland, 2019). Under the Fair Employment and Treatment (Northern Ireland) Order (1988) political opinion is protected as a ground under which discrimination should not take place. Whilst in the rest of the UK political philosophies would be included within the protected characteristics of religion and belief (Carr, 2016).

Scotland

The Scotland Act (2015) was passed in the UK Parliament and devolved equality provisions to the Scottish Parliament. The Scottish Parliament has far-ranging devolved powers and duties including in the area of equal opportunities. This enables functions including employment tribunals and employment appeals tribunals. One further area of public policy, where Scotland differs, is in the provisions of the Public Sector Equality Duty. The socio-economic duty is applied in Scotland through the provision of the duty. This does have a considerable impact as the Scottish Government is responsible for public services including education, housing, local authorities and health. The Scottish Government has made equal opportunities a key issue and has established an Equality Unit to take forward equality and to promote equal opportunities (Carr, 2016).

Wales

Equality is a central aspect of devolution in Wales and is at the core of the Welsh Governments founding legislation. The Welsh Assembly has a duty to ensure equal opportunities and that there should be equality of opportunity for all. Wales also has the ability to determine how to apply the duties within the Public Sector Equality Duty. Key differences between England and Wales, in relation to the Public Sector Equality Duty, include the Welsh Government having an obligation to carry out Equality Impact Assessments and to assess gender pay differences. The socio-economic duty is also devolved to the Welsh Assembly (Carr, 2016).

Issues for reflection/points to ponder

How can we move from being non to anti (racist, sexist, ageist, disablist, transphobic, etc.)? By educating ourselves and each other, by bringing others along with us on the journey from being non to anti. By moving through education and awareness, to acting, to challenging and calling others out when we witness, or experience, discrimination – requires us all to act. By seeking out people who are different to by us, who think differently, who act differently and who come from different backgrounds to us. By spending time with individuals, communities and groups who share different values and experiences, who are different to us, we become better educated and informed.

Quiz

1. The Equality Act 2010 exists to eliminate and prevent _____, for a range of protected characteristics, in employment and when accessing _____.
   Answers: Eliminating and preventing discrimination, when accessing goods and services.
2. The _____ protected characteristics include: ____, sex, disability, sexual orientation, _____, religion and belief, _____, marriage and civil partnership, pregnancy and maternity.
   Answers: Nine protected characteristics including: race, disability and age (Figure 13.1)

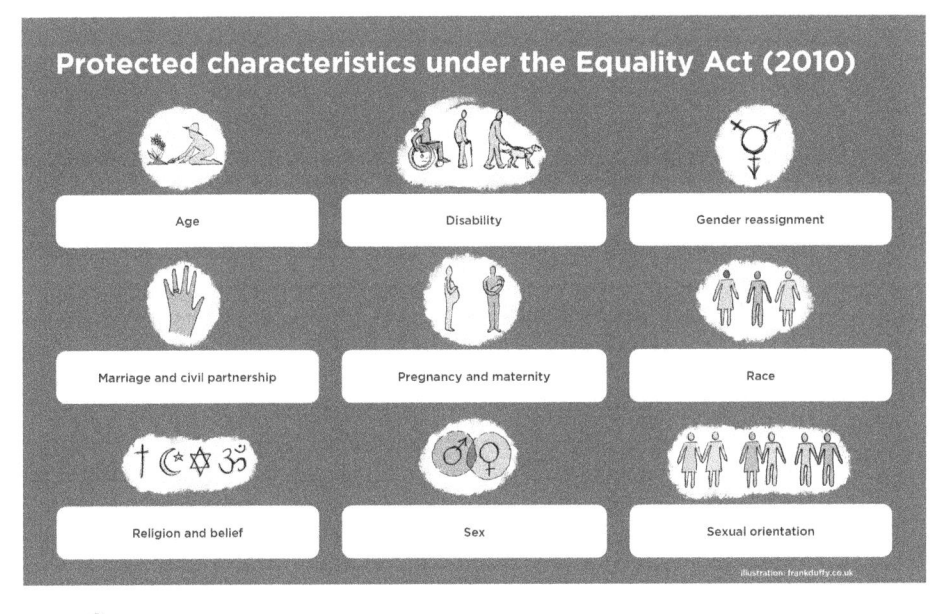

Figure 13.1 Protected characteristics under the Equality Act.

3 The Equality Act 2010 defines discrimination in how many different ways?

   Answer: The Equality Act defines discrimination in six different ways including: Direct discrimination, indirect discrimination, discrimination by association, discrimination by perception, harassment and victimisation. For the definitions of each form of discrimination please use the terminology section of the chapter.

4 It is legally possible to discriminate on the grounds of someone's age. True or false?

   Answer: True, but in limited ways. The Equality Act 2010 has limited exceptions on age-related discrimination. For example, students are not protected from age-related discrimination at school, the sale of alcohol is age restricted. The Equality Act 2010 includes an exception for paying workers of different ages at different rates, if the age bands are set within the national minimum wage.

   Employers might use what is referred to as a *proportionate means of achieving a legitimate aim*. For example, on the grounds of health and safety or for the requirements of the business, service or organisation. Age-related discrimination may apply as a proportionate means of achieving a legitimate aim. A proportionate means of achieving a legitimate means is defined as an objective justification. An example in the police service where the retirement age is set at age 60, the Home Office states this is objectively justified.

5 It is possible to appoint someone of a certain sex to work in a single-sex service, such as a women's refuge, domestic violence and abuse service, or a rape and sexual violence counselling service. True or false?

   Answer: True, this is known as an *occupational requirement* and is a form of positive discrimination. An occupational requirement can also apply to other protected characteristics, other than sex, including race, religion, disability or sexual orientation.

6 Reasonable adjustments apply to disabled people. True or false?

   Answer: True, a reasonable adjustment is a change of policy, procedure or practice; or a change to a workplace or service; to enable a disabled worker, service user or customer to be able to access their job or service. For example, making adaptations to a physical environment to ensure disabled people aren't disadvantaged at work.

7 Who might be unintentionally excluded from an event if it ran on a Friday lunch time?

   Answer: Running an event on a Friday lunchtime could unintentionally exclude people on the grounds of faith, religion or belief. For example, Muslims attending Friday prayers.

8 Discrimination on the grounds of paternity is unlawful. True or false?

   Answer: True, discrimination on the grounds of paternity is unlawful. In 2017 a claimant, Madasra Ali, went to an employment tribunal as his employer refused to give him more than 2-weeks paid leave to care for his child. Mr. Ali was treated differently to others in his workplace, for example, women were given 14-weeks paid leave, at full pay, whereas Mr. Ali was only given 2-weeks. The employment tribunal upheld his claim as discrimination on the grounds of paternity.

9 Positive discrimination in the UK is unlawful. True or false?

   Answer: True, positive discrimination in the UK is mostly unlawful. The UK does not adopt quotas or affirmative action as in other states. However, positive action is legitimate and lawful in the UK. Positive action can be applied when, for example, an organisation or service wants to address an imbalance in its workforce or amongst its clients. Setting up women-only services, offering crèche facilities, offering training and mentoring schemes are examples of positive action.

10 Where does the Equality Act 2010 apply? (multiple choice)

Public sector and functions
Education
Health
Housing
Employment
Premises
Workplaces
Transport
Private sector
Provision of goods and services
Clubs and associations

Answer: All of the above! The Equality Act 2010 applies in places which are legally constituted. For example, in the public and private sector, in education, health and housing; as well as in the provision of services, public functions, transport, clubs and associations; as well as in workplaces, in public buildings and premises.

Group activity – privilege exercise

For this activity, you will need a piece of paper and a pen. Divide the paper in half by drawing a line down the middle of the page to create a football pitch with two halves. Starting at the midline – as you work through each question you will either take one move forward, above the midline, if your answer to the question is "yes", stay in the same position, if you don't know the answer or it doesn't impact you, or move one step back if you answer with a "no" to the question. At the end of the activity share where you have ended up on the pitch, above or below the centre line.

1 If your parents worked nights and weekends to support your family, take one step back.
2 If you are able to move through the world without fear of sexual assault, take one step forward.
3 If you can show affection for your romantic partner in public without fear of ridicule or violence, take one step forward.
4 If you have ever been diagnosed as having a physical or mental illness/disability, take one step back.
5 If the primary language spoken in your household growing up was not English, take one step back.
6 If you came from a supportive family environment take one step forward.
7 If you have ever tried to change your speech or mannerisms to gain credibility, take one step back.
8 If you can go anywhere in the country and easily find the kinds of hair products you need and/or cosmetics that match your skin colour, take one step forward.

9 If you were embarrassed about your clothes or house whilst growing up, take one step back.
10 If you can make mistakes and not have people attribute your behaviour to flaws in your racial/gender group, take one step forward.
11 If you can legally marry the person you love, regardless of where you live, take one step forward.
12 If you were born in the United Kingdom, take one step forward.
13 If you or your parents have ever gone through a divorce, take one step back.
14 If you felt like you had adequate access to healthy food growing up, take one step forward
15 If you are reasonably sure you would be hired for a job based on your ability and qualifications, take one step forward.
16 If you would never think twice about calling the police when trouble occurs, take one step forward.
17 If you can see a doctor whenever you feel the need, take one step forward.
18 If you feel comfortable being emotionally expressive/open, take one step forward.
19 If you have ever been the only person of your race/gender/socio-economic status/sexual orientation in a classroom or workplace setting, please take one step back.
20 If you took out loans for your education take one step backward.
21 If you get time off for your religious holidays, take one step forward.
22 If you had a job during your high school and college years, take one step back.
23 If you feel comfortable walking home alone at night, take one step forward.
24 If you have ever travelled outside the United Kingdom, take one step forward.
25 If you have ever felt like there was not adequate or accurate representation of your racial group, sexual orientation group, gender group and/or disability group in the media, take one step back.
26 If you feel confident that your parents would be able to financially help/support you if you were going through a financial hardship, take one step forward.
27 If you have ever been bullied or made fun of based on something that you can't change, take one step back.
28 If there were more than 50 books in your house growing up, take one step forward.
29 If you studied the culture or the history of your ancestors in elementary school take one step forward.
30 If your parents or guardians attended college, take one step forward.
31 If you ever went on a family vacation, take one step forward.
32 If you can buy new clothes or go out to dinner when you want to, take one step forward.
33 If you were ever offered a job because of your association with a friend or family member, take one step forward.
34 If your family have ever worked for the police or fire service, take a step forward.
35 If one of your parents was ever laid off or unemployed not by choice, take one step back.
36 If you were ever uncomfortable about a joke or a statement you overheard related to your race, ethnicity, gender, appearance or sexual orientation but felt unsafe to confront the situation, take one step back.

(Adapted from McIntosh, 1988)

Supplementary reading

Akala. (2018). *Natives: Race & Class in the Ruins of Empire*. Two Roads.
Arday, J. (2018). *Dismantling Race in Higher Education*. Palgrave Macmillan.
DiAngelo, R. (2018). *White Fragility: Why It's So Hard for White People to Talk About Racism*. Penguin.
Eddo-Lodge, R. (2018). *Why I'm No Longer Talking to White People About Race*. Bloomsbury Publishing.
Holding, M. (2021). *Why We Kneel, How We Rise*. Simon & Schuster UK Ltd.
Kendi, I. X. (2019). *How to Be an Antiracist*. Bodley Head.
Saad, L. F. (2020). *Me and White Supremacy*. Quercus.

Useful websites

Citizen's Advice. (n.d.). Citizen's Advice. https://www.citizensadvice.org.uk
Disability Rights UK. (n.d.). Disability Rights UK. https://www.disabilityrightsuk.org
Diversity Trust CIC. (n.d.). Further Support. https://www.diversitytrust.org.uk/further-support/
Equality and Human Rights Commission. (n.d.). Equality and Human Rights Commission. https://www.equalityhumanrights.com/en
Fawcett Society. (n.d.). Fawcett: Equality. It's About Time. https://www.fawcettsociety.org.uk
Law Centres. (n.d.). Law Centres Network. https://www.lawcentres.org.uk
Mind Charity. (n.d.). Mind. https://www.mind.org.uk
Refugee Action. (n.d.). Refugee Action. https://www.refugee-action.org.uk
SARI Charity. (n.d.). Stand Against Racism & Inequality. https://www.sariweb.org.uk/
Stonewall UK. (n.d.). Stonewall. https://www.stonewall.org.uk
Stop Hate UK. (n.d.). Stop Hate UK. https://www.stophateuk.org
Terrence Higgins Trust (HIV/AIDS). (n.d.). Terrence Higgins Trust: Together We Can. https://www.tht.org.uk

References

Adfam. (2012). *Challenging Stigma: Tackling the Prejudice Experienced by the Families of Drug and Alcohol Users*. https://adfam.org.uk/files/docs/adfam_challenging_stigma.pdf
ADP. (2019). *The 2019 Workforce View in Europe Report*. https://uk.adp.com/resources/adp-articles-and-insights/articles/w/workforce-view-2019.aspx
Advance HE. (2017). *Degree Attainment Gaps*. https://www.advance-he.ac.uk/guidance/equality-diversity-and-inclusion/student-recruitment-retention-and-attainment/degree-attainment-gaps
After 82. (2017). *After 82: The Documentary*.
Allport, G. (1954). *The Nature of Prejudice*. Addison-Wesley.
Armstead, C. A., Lawler, K. A., Gorden, G., Cross, J., & Gibbons, J. (1989). Relationship of Racial Stressors to Blood Pressure Responses and Anger Expression in Black College Students. *Health Psychology*, 8, 541.
Bachmann, S. K., & Gooch, B. (2017). *LGBT in Britain. Hate Crime and Discrimination*. https://www.stonewall.org.uk/system/files/lgbt_in_britain_hate_crime.pdf
Barker, B. (2019). It's Time to Abolish the Spousal Veto over Gender Recognition for Married Trans People. *Politics Home*. https://www.politicshome.com/thehouse/article/its-time-to-abolish-the-spousal-veto-over-gender-recognition-for-married-trans-people
Carr, H. (2016). *Devolved Nations Equality Differences Briefing Paper*. Equality in Northern Ireland, Scotland and Wales. University and College Union.
Conway, G. (1997). *Islamophobia: A Challenge for Us All*. The Runnymede Trust.

Crenshaw, K. (1989) Demarginalizing the Intersection of Race and Sex: A Black Feminist Critique of Antidiscrimination Doctrine, Feminist Theory and Antiracist Politics. *University of Chicago Legal Forum*, 1, Article 8. http://chicagounbound.uchicago.edu/uclf/vol1989/iss1/8

Crown Prosecution Service. (2020). *Racist and Religious Hate Crime – Prosecution Guidance*. https://www.cps.gov.uk/legal-guidance/racist-and-religious-hate-crime-prosecution-guidance

Equality Act. (2010). *Balancing Rights in Single Sex Services*. https://publications.parliament.uk/pa/cm201719/cmselect/cmwomeq/1470/147010.htm

Equality Commission for Northern Ireland. (2019). *Committee on the Elimination of Discrimination against Women*. https://www.equalityni.org/ECNI/media/ECNI/Publications/Delivering%20Equality/CEDAW-ConcludingObservationsUK-Mar19.pdf

Equality Commission for Northern Ireland. (2021). *Gaps in Equality Law between GB& NI*. https://www.equalityni.org/Delivering-Equality/Addressing-inequality/Law-reform/Tabs/Gaps-in-equality-law

Equality and Human Rights Commission. (2019). *Access to Legal Aid for Discrimination Cases*. https://www.equalityhumanrights.com/sites/default/files/access-to-legal-aid-for-discrimination-cases-our-legal-aid-inquiry.pdf

Equality and Human Rights Commission. (2021). *Disability Discrimination*. https://www.equalityhumanrights.com/en/advice-and-guidance/disability-discrimination

The Equality Trust. (2021). *Socio-economic Duty*. https://www.equalitytrust.org.uk/socio-economic-duty

Fairer Scotland Duty. (2018). *Fairer Scotland Duty: Interim Guidance for Public Bodies*. https://www.gov.scot/publications/fairer-scotland-duty-interim-guidance-public-bodies/

Guardian. (2019). *Legal Advice Centres in England and Wales halved since 2013–14*. https://www.theguardian.com/law/2019/jul/15/legal-advice-centres-in-england-and-wales-halved-since-2013-14

Hamilton, C. & Ture, K. (1992). *Black Power: The Politics of Liberation in America*.

Home Office. (2019). *Hate Crime, England and Wales, 2018–19*. https://assets.publishing.service.gov.uk/government/uploads/system/uploads/attachment_data/file/839172/hate-crime-1819-hosb2419.pdf

International Holocaust Remembrance Alliance. (2016). *Working Definition of Antisemitism*. https://www.holocaustremembrance.com/resources/working-definitions-charters/working-definition-antisemitism

Islamophobia Definitions. (2021). *Islamophobia*. https://www.islamophobia-definition.com

Law Commission. (2021). *Hate Crime*. https://www.lawcom.gov.uk/project/hate-crime/

Macpherson, W. (1999). *The Stephen Lawrence Inquiry*. https://assets.publishing.service.gov.uk/government/uploads/system/uploads/attachment_data/file/277111/4262.pdf

Mental Health Foundation. (2021). *Stigma and Discrimination*. https://www.mentalhealth.org.uk/a-to-z/s/stigma-and-discrimination

Metropolitan Police. (2020). *Freedom of Information Request Reference No: 01.FOT.20.014027*. https://www.met.police.uk/SysSiteAssets/foi-media/metropolitan-police/disclosure_2020/may_2020/information-rights-unit---racist-hate-crimes-reported-where-the-victim-was-chinese-from-january-to-march-2018-to-2020

Ministry of Justice. (2018). *Statistics on Race and the Criminal Justice System 2018*. https://assets.publishing.service.gov.uk/government/uploads/system/uploads/attachment_data/file/849200/statistics-on-race-and-the-cjs-2018.pdf

National AIDS Trust. (2016). *Tackling HIV Stigma: What Works?* https://www.nat.org.uk/sites/default/files/publications/Jun_16_Tackling_HIV_Stigma.pdf

National Archives. (2016). *The AIDS Health Campaign*. https://blog.nationalarchives.gov.uk/aids-health-campaign/

Office for National Statistics. (2020). *Domestic Abuse Victim Characteristics, England and Wales: Year Ending March 2020*. https://www.ons.gov.uk/peoplepopulationandcommunity/crimeandjustice/articles/domesticabusevictimcharacteristicsenglandandwales/yearendingmarch2020

Prison Reform Trust. (2021). *Race*.
Rethink Mental Illness. (2021). *Discrimination and Mental Health*. https://www.rethink.org/advice-and-information/rights-restrictions/mental-health-laws/discrimination-and-mental-health/
SafeLives. (2014). *Getting It Right First Time*. https://safelives.org.uk/sites/default/files/resources/Getting%20it%20right%20first%20time%20-%20complete%20report.pdf
SafeLives. (2018). *Free To Be Safe: LGBT+ People Experiencing Domestic Abuse*. https://safelives.org.uk/sites/default/files/resources/Free%20to%20be%20safe%20web.pdf
Safer Bristol Partnership. (2017). *Multi-Agency Learning Review Following the Murder of Bijan Ebrahimi*. https://www.bristol.gov.uk/documents/20182/35136/Multi-agency+learning+review+following+the+murder+of+Bijan+Ebrahimi
Scope. (2021). *Social Model of Disability*. https://www.scope.org.uk/about-us/social-model-of-disability/
Spalek, B. (2002). *Hate Crimes against British Muslims in the Aftermath of September 11th*. Centre for Crime and Justice Studies. https://www.crimeandjustice.org.uk/sites/crimeandjustice.org.uk/files/09627250208553447.pdf
Tajfel, H. (1979). Individuals and Groups in Social Psychology. *British Journal of Social and Clinical Psychology*, 18, 183–190.
Terrence Higgins Trust. (2021). https://twitter.com/THTorguk
The Trussell Trust. (2020). *New Report Reveals How Coronavirus Has Affected Food Bank Use*. https://www.trusselltrust.org/2020/09/14/new-report-reveals-how-coronavirus-has-affected-food-bank-use/
Turner, A. W. (2013). *Rejoice! Rejoice! Britain in the 1980s*. Aurum Press Ltd.
UK Government. (2018). *National LGBT Survey: Summary Report*. https://www.gov.uk/government/publications/national-lgbt-survey-summary-report/national-lgbt-survey-summary-report
UK Government. (2020). *Arrests*. https://www.ethnicity-facts-figures.service.gov.uk/crime-justice-and-the-law/policing/number-of-arrests/latest
UK Government. (2021a). *Stop and Search*. https://www.ethnicity-facts-figures.service.gov.uk/crime-justice-and-the-law/policing/stop-and-search/latest
UK Government. (2021b). *Claim for Wages through the Coronavirus Job Retention Scheme*. https://www.gov.uk/guidance/claim-for-wages-through-the-coronavirus-job-retention-scheme
UK Parliament. (1965). *Race Relations Act*. https://www.parliament.uk/about/living-heritage/transformingsociety/private-lives/relationships/collections1/race-relations-act-1965/race-relations-act-1965/
UK Parliament. (2019). *Written Questions, Answers and Statements. Law Centres. Question for the Ministry of Justice*. https://questions-statements.parliament.uk/written-questions/detail/2019-07-04/273435
UK Parliament. (2021). House of Commons Library. *Hate Crime Statistics*. https://commonslibrary.parliament.uk/research-briefings/cbp-8537/
United Nations. (1993). *Declaration on the Elimination of Violence against Women*. https://www.ohchr.org/EN/ProfessionalInterest/Pages/ViolenceAgainstWomen.aspx
Wofford, N., Defever, A., & Chopik, W. J. (2019). The Vicarious Effects of Discrimination: How Partner Experiences of Discrimination Affect Individual Health. *Social Psychological and Personality Science*, 10(1), 121–130.
Women's Aid. (2021). *The Domestic Abuse Report 2021: The Annual Audit*. Bristol: Women's Aid.
World Economic Forum. (2013). *The Global Gender Gay Report*. http://www3.weforum.org/docs/WEF_GenderGap_Report_2013.pdf

Index

Note: **Bold** page numbers refer to tables and *italic* page numbers refer to figures.

abortion: history of 105; legalised abortions in UK 102; psychological trauma and morbidities 108; teenage 108, 109
Abouchaar, A. 69
absolute poverty 6, 38
abuse: alcohol 72, 156, 169, 174; child (*see* child abuse); domestic (*see* domestic abuse); economic 83; physical 106, 125, 126, 130, 132, 184, 239; sexual 58, 106–107, 127–128, 136, 140, 183–184; substance 91, 107, 125, 153, 178, 249
addiction: cycle 11, 170; drug (*see* drug misuse); and offending 135
addictive personality theory 21, 176
adolescence 21, 22, 72, 102, 106, 150, 152, 157, 184
adolescent pregnancy *see* teenage pregnancy
Adoption and Children Act 2002 138
adulthood 21, 40, 70–73, 102, 108, 153, 183, 184
adverse childhood experiences (ACEs) 153
agency 18–19
age of criminal responsibility 130, 147, 148
Agrawal, A. 20
Ainsworth, Mary 63
Alcohol and Families Alliance (AFA) 187
alcohol: and intimate partner violence 184; and mental health 182–183
alcohol consumption: conceptual causal model 173; explanatory frameworks 174; familial influences 174; during lockdown 172; low-risk drinking guidelines *171*; and mental health 182–183; and older people 185; patterns across UK 171–172; peer influences 174; psychological perspectives (*see* psychological perspectives on alcohol consumption); and religion 173–174; socio-cultural influences 172–173; sociological perspectives (*see* sociological perspectives on alcohol consumption); in young people 184
alcoholism 168–170, 174–176; genetic transmission 175
alcohol misuse: addiction cycle 170, *170*; alcohol-related harm 179–180; biological bases 175; celebrity alcohol-related deaths 168; neurobiology 175–176
alcohol policy: England 187–188; evidence-based policy *187*; Government's Alcohol Strategy 185–186; 'Health First' alcohol strategy (2013) 186; Northern Ireland 188; recommendations of Alcohol and Families Alliance, UK (2018) 187; Scotland 188; Wales 188
alcohol-related deaths 168, 181
alcohol-related harm 11, 173; Commission on Alcohol Harm (2020) recommendations 189; excessive alcohol consumption *179*, 179–180; harm to others 181–182; impacts on range of priorities *181*; overall cost of 180
alcohol-related hospitalisations 181
alcohol strategy 185, 186, 189
Alexander, J. 23
Alliance for Useful Evidence 186
Allport, G. 258
Ally, A.K. 173
altruistic suicide 218
Amato, P. R. 73
amelioration 1, 21, 26, 41
American Psychiatric Association 203
Andrews, D. A. 154
anti domestic violence movement 87
antisemitism 268

anti-social behaviour 154, 158, 186, 242, 248, 256, 258
attachment theory 61–64, 90–91, 133
attitudes: to alcohol use 174; cause of poverty 41; cognitive dimension 22; cultural 23; knowledge and 12; negative 224; positive 188; societal 12; towards abortion 108
austerity 47, 48, 244, 264
automatic process theories (APT) 207

Bandura, A. 62, 177
battered woman syndrome 10, 90, 92, 93
batterer intervention standards 90
Becks Hopelessness Scale (BHS) 225
'the bedroom tax' 244
behavioural models 177, 212
Bell, G. 157
Benson, H. 64, 75
Bernardi, F. 69
Berrington, A. 67
Beveridge, William 4, 42
Big Society 47, 50
Bijan Ebrahimi, case study 256–257
biological bases of alcohol consumption 175
biological theory (BT) 196
biology 19, 20, 175
bio-psychosocial model 178
black and minority ethnic (BME) communities 86–87
Blumer, H. 16
Boertien, D. 69
Bonta, J. 154
Booth, Charles 35, 36
Bottoms, A. 24, 25
Bowlby, John 21, 63, 133
Brain, Russell 210
Bramley, G. 240
Brewer, M. 69
Brexit 267; description 7; and impact on people with disabilities 8, **8**; and impact on women 8, **8**; minority ethnic people 8–9, **9**
British System 210
Broken Britain 47, 48
Bronfenbrenner, U. 133
Buchanan, T. M. 58
Buller, Francis 84
Burgon, Richard 263

causation 10, 17–18, 25, 176, 202–204, 233, 239
censure 25
Chandra-Mouli, V. 113

Chicago School 16
Chief Probation Officers 93
child abuse 123; categories of 125; children in need 124; child sexual exploitation 128; child trafficking 128–129; community/environmental factors 135; emotional abuse 126; family risk factors 135; historical context 124–125; INSPIRE 136; legislative framework 137; myths and misconceptions 131, 132; parent/caregiver factors 134; physical abuse 126–127; prevalence of 129–130; protective factors 135; right to fair and public hearing 137–138; risk factors 134–136; sexual abuse 127–128; 'significant harm' 123–124; as social issue 130; in UK 129–130; 'wicked' problem 130
Child Assessment Order 138
Child Criminal Exploitation (CCE) 150, 155
child, defined 123
childhood: abuse (*see* child abuse); development of moral reasoning 21; poverty in 34–35; sexual abuses in 106–107
child neglect: making child protection plans 125; manifestations of 125–126
child protection: in Northern Ireland (NI) 138–140; in Scotland 140–141; theoretical frameworks 132–134
Child Protection Plan (CPP) 126
Children Act 1989 138
children's hearings 11, 140–141
children in need 124
child sexual exploitation (CSE) 128
child trafficking 128–129
choice theory 176
claims-making 3
Clark, J. 40
Clarkson, T. 7
classical conditioning 177
Cochrane, A. 40
Commission on Alcohol Harm 189
contraception 104, 112, 113
co-offending 150, 151, 153, 154
county lines 125, 129, 130, 150, 155, 157, 159, 160
county lines 150
Cowie, H. 157
Crenshaw, K. 262
crimes: economic costs 149–150; hate 258; honour 86; knife 149, 155, 157; violent 149
criminal justice 27, 34, 84, 135, 151, 153, 155, 180, 188, 201, 202, 204, 210, 211, 267
cultural identity theory 178

culture 10–11, 18, 22, 65, 86, 108, 115, 130, 154, 173, 174, 177, 243, 257, 259; of poverty 44; social problems 23
culture wars 255
cycle of deprivation 44, 115, 240

Daly, M. 64
Davis, Russell T. 266
day centres 246
dependence/dependency 11, 17, 19–20, 42, 169–170, 175, 201–203, 205–206, 210–212; culture 44, 48; economic 48, 109
deposit guarantee 246, 249
depressants 197, 198, 201
deprivation: of liberty 88; social 11, 104–107, 155–156
Desforges, C. 69
deviance 15
deviant group 153–155
disability: defined 259; social model 261
Disability Discrimination Act (DDA) 268
discrimination: direct racial discrimination 258; from disability 259–260; domestic violence discrimination 264–265; equalities timeline 268–269; Equality Act 269–270, *271*; and gender-based violence 264; hate crime and hate incident 258; health and social inequalities 267; and HIV 265–266; impact of COVID-19 264; implications for people, individual, family and society 264; indirect discrimination 258; institutional discrimination 258; intersectional theory 262–263; linkages with social issues/problems 264; and mental health 265; multiculturalism, migration and diversity 267; myths and facts 260; Northern Ireland Act (1988) 270; patriarchy and gender 262; policies and legislation 269; and prejudice 263; reasonable adjustments 259; Scotland Act (2015) 270; and social class 267; social construction of gender 261; and substance misuse 266–267; theoretical explanations and frameworks 261; UK, pluralistic society 267; in Wales 270–271; workplace discrimination 260
disease model of alcoholism 176
divorce: act, influence of 65–66; family breakdown 65–66
domestic abuse: causes of family breakdown 67; defined 83, 91; failure of socialisation and emotional development 22; victims of 82, 85–87, 264

Domestic Abuse Bill 10, 82–84, 91, 94
domestic violence (DV): attachment theory 90–91; battered woman syndrome 92, 93; BME communities 86–87; and children 84, 92; COVID-19 pandemic 82; cycles of violence 92; defined 82, 83; Domestic Abuse Bill (2020) 82, 84, 94; economic abuse 83; facts and statistics 84; feminist approach 89–90; GBV (*see* gender-based violence (GBV)); IPV (*see* intimate partner violence (IPV)); legislation 93–94; and minority ethnic groups 86–87; myths and misconceptions 85–86; signs and indicators 93; social-ecological perspective 90; structural model 88; structural violence 89; and substance abuse 91; theoretical understandings 87–88; in UK 83, 84, 85
Donne, John 18
Drink-Drive Legal Limits 180
Drinking Guidelines 170, 171
drive theory (DT) 207
drug legislation: contemporary policies 210–211; historical overview 209–210
drug misuse: automatic process theories 207; biological theory 196; depressants, positive/negative factors **198**; drive theory 207; drug addiction 201, 206–207; drug dealers 196; drug strategies in UK **211**; in England *197*; financial cost 202–203; hallucinogens, positive/negative factors **198**; harm reduction model 205; impact on children 205–206; implications for people, psychosocial perspective 200–202; legal classification in UK **199**; links with other social issues 205; Medical, Psychological, and Social Model 206–207; NHS Wales 196, *197*; in Northern Ireland 196; polysubstance use 202; prevalence and magnitude 196–197; Process of Change Theories 207; in Scotland 196; Social Contagion Theory 209; social context of 199–200; Social Network Theories 208–209; stages of change *208*; stimulants, positive/negative factors **198**; substance misuse and mental health issues 203–204; terminology 197–199; theoretical and operational frameworks 206–209; Transtheoretical Model 207–208; UK criminal justice system 204
drug policy 205, 209–211
drug use 196; on children and young people 205–206; illegal 201; illicit 198, 202; recreational 202

dual diagnosis 203, 204, 249
Duck, S. 61, 62
Duck's dissolution model: dyadic stage 61; grave-dressing stage 61; intrapsychic stage 61; resurrection stage 62; social stage 61
Duncan Smith, Iain 48, 72
Durkheim, E´. 12, 25, 40, 218–219, 227
Durrant, R. 19
duty to refer 247

economic abuse 83
economic inequality 39, 52, 204
economics 5, 10, 24, 199, 208, 243, 244
educational attainment 104, 105, 263
egoistic 218
Elsinga, M. 247
emotional abuse 126
Equality Act 2010 256, 257; defines disability as 259; as protected characteristics 260
Equality and Human Rights Commission (EHRC) 147
Erikson, Erik 21
Ersche, K. 19
expectancy theory 176

familial homicide 94
familial influences on alcohol consumption 174
family: COVID-19 pandemic and its impact in UK 60; defined 58; modern family 58–59; non-traditional family 58; traditional family 58
family breakdown: changing faces of divorce laws 65–66; consequences of 68–69; divorce act, influence of 65–66; and domestic violence 67; implications for individuals 58; incidences of homelessness 72–73; increased dysfunction 73; individualism, influence of 64–65; juvenile behaviour 72; key factors *64*; legal reforms 74; and lifecycle *68*; limited economic resources 69–70; parental conflict 70–71; reduced quality in parent–child relationships 69; relocation 71–72; social reforms 75; societal-related harm 72; structural modifications and changes 66–67; and substance misuse 68; taxpayer costs 73–74; theories explaining 60–64
family structures, in UK 59, *59*
family systems 82, 86, 178
feminist 10, 82, 86, 88, 89, 262
Fisher, H. 69
Fitzpatrick, S. 239, 240
Five Giants 4

food banks 50–51, 266
Fowler, Norman 266
Freud, Sigmund 21

GAD 7 225
gang membership 151–154
gateway theory 184
gender-based violence (GBV) 88–89, 264
Gender Recognition Act (GRA) (2004) 269
genes 20, 23, 239, 249
geopolitics 10
George Floyd (case study) 255–256
Gillingham, P. 133
globalisation 5–6
Goldstein, P. J. 91
Goodwin, D. W. 175
Gordon, D. 48
Gravningen, K. 67
Gross Domestic Product (GDP) 52
Groupthink 257
Gulliver, K. 240
Gunner, E. 241

Hadley, A. 113
Hagenbuch, W. 5
hallucinogens 197, 198
harassment and victimisation 257
harmful use 169, 180
harm reduction 11, 187, 188, 200, 201, 205, 206, 208, 211
hate crime 258
hate incident 258
Haynie, D. L. 72
Hay, Will 202
hazardous use 169
health: 'Health First' alcohol strategy (2013) 186; inequalities 266; mental 182–183; and social inequalities 266
Hearing Scottish Children's Reporter Administration 140
Henry VII 65
Himsworth, C. 241
Hoftede, G. 65
homelessness: causes 239–240; consequences and effects 241–242; defined 234; Homelessness Reduction Act 2017 244; housing policy 242–244; human rights 242; interventions 245–250; legislation 244–245; perceptions of 236; prevalence 236–239; rough sleepers 235; rough sleepers initiative 242–243; Sofa surfer 234; temporary accommodation 235; World Homelessness Day 234

Homelessness Reduction Act 237, 244
homelessness service 249
honour-based violence 130
honour crimes 86
Hospital Anxiety and Depression Scale (HADS) 225
Households below average income (HBAI) 37
Housing First 247, 248
housing policy 12, 224, 233, 242–244
Howe, D. 63
humanitarian principles 4

ideology 41–43, 45, 48, 50
individualism 64–65, 101, 218
individualist model 82
inequalities: economic 39, 52, 204; social 266
Ingham, R. 113
ingroup 3
institutional racism 256–257, 258
interdependence 62, 65
intergenerational 11, 102, 104, 108, 112, 115, 136
international trade 200, 209
intersectionality 262, 263
intimate partner violence (IPV) 82, 83, 85–87, 91
Islamophobia 268

Jellinek, E. M. 176
Jewkes, J. 22
Judge Thumb 84
juvenile delinquency 147
juvenile deviance: gang and group offending interventions 154; models of interventions 154–155; psychological risk factors 152–153; social risk factors 152; theoretical explanations frameworks 153–154
juvenile offenders 147

Kahneman, D. 18
Karriker-Jaffe, K. J. 181
Keeble, Steve 266
Kemeny, J. 235, 243
Keynes, John Maynard 42
Kituse, J.I. 3
knife crimes 149, 155, 157
knob-stick marriage/shotgun wedding 101
Koehler, J. A. 155
Kohlberg, L. 22
Krystal, H. 176

Lampard, R. 66
learning by association 177

Lebow, J. L. 60
Leeds, J. 22
Lee, E. J. 108
left behind 246
legal reforms 74, 260
legislation: domestic violence 93–94; homelessness 244–245; policies and 269; suicide 226
Leng, Gill 241
Levitas, R. 46
life chances 24, 34, 70, 104, 105, 109, 110, 112, 241
life expectancy 24, 34, 205, 235, 250
Lister, R. 46
lived experience 10, 33, 52, 90, 204, 234, 263, 264
Local Government Association (LGA) 114
Lord, Ben 26
Lowe, G. 168
Low, H. 69

Macvarish, J. 112
Mahoney, J. 2
Maio, G. 22
marriage: arranged 130; breakdown (*see* divorce); and cohabitation 67; forced 86, 125; idea of "no-fault" 66; impact of pandemic 60; knob-stick marriage 101; unhappy 66
Marx, Karl 39, 209
May, Teresa 267
McClelland, D. C. 62
McConnell, A. R. 58
McKay, S. 75
McKeganey, N. 202
median income 37
mental disorder & offending 151–153, 156, 159
mental health: and alcohol consumption 182–183; and discrimination 265–266; issues 203–204
Millard, C. 219
Miller, W. 247
Mills, C. 15
minimum age of criminal responsibility (MACR) 147–148
minimum unit pricing 186
minority ethnic 8, 9, 86–87, 106, 112, 255, 264, 265
misogyny 258
models of interventions 154–155
moral reasoning 21, 22
Morgenstern, J. 22
motherhood 35, 101, 104, 106, 108, 111, 112

multi agency risk assessment conference (MARAC) 264
Multi-Country Study on Women's Health and Domestic Violence 89
multiple and complex needs 241, 246, 247
Munro, E. 132, 133
Murray, Charles 44
Myers, C. A. 157

Nandi, A. 69
National Association for People Abused in Childhood (NAPAC) 143
National Crime Agency (2019) 150
National Drug Treatment Monitoring System (NDTMS) 196
neurobiology and alcohol consumption 175–176
neurology 19, 153, 177, 206
neurotransmitters 175
New Psychoactive Substances (NPS) 198
New Strategic Direction for Alcohol and Drugs (NSD) 188
norms 1, 16, 22, 23, 25, 26, 28, 36, 43, 58, 88, 104, 106, 136, 172, 177
Northern Ireland Statistics and Research Agency (NISRA) 103, 221
Nutt, Peter 199

occupational requirement 40, 272
offending behaviour 11, 25, 150, 151, 156, 158–159, 248, 249
O'Neil, Dennis 131
operant conditioning 177
opiates 19, 175, 197, 202
opium 209, 210
oppression 3, 41, 257, 262
outgroup 3

parental alcohol misuse (PAM) 11, *183*; implications for children 183; inconsistent and unpredictable parenting 183–184; social cognitive model 184
parent-child relationships 61, 69–71, 133, 136
parenthood: early 34, 105–106; lone 59, 66–67, 70; single 66; teenage 34, 104–105, 111, 113; in young people strategy 2016–2026 115
parenting: abusive 136; bad 17, 70, 108; capacity of individuals 68; fathers in 136; 'good enough parenting' 205; non-abusive 136; same-sex 269; skills 135; stress and families 127, 134
Parrillo, V. N. 2

Pasqualini, M. 72
patriarchal privilege 89
patriarchy 10, 89, 90, 262
Patterson, S. E. 73
Paudyal, Priyamvada P. 241
pauperism 35
peer influences on alcohol consumption 174
Peirce Suicide intent scale 225
perpetrator: of crime 160; of domestic abuse 91; of IPV 89; male 22; and victim 83–84, 90, 149, 156, 184
PHQ 9 225
physical abuse 126–127
Piaget, Jean 21
Pickett, K. 24, 178
Pilnick, A. 20
place 24–25
policing 135, 157, 186, 202
Poor Law 4, 35, 42
positive action 270, 273
positive discrimination 272
post-structuralist 82
poverty: absolute or relative 36; agentic explanations 41; austerity 47–48; Big Society and charitable responses 50; and 'Broken Britain' 48; in childhood 34–35; cultural representations 46–47; defined 36–37; Foodbanks 50; impact of COVID-19 pandemic 33; income poverty 38–39; measurement 37, 38; median income 37; myths 48–49; neo-liberal ideology 41; and neo-liberalism 42–43; New Labour's approach 45; 'othering' of the poor 46; psychological explanations 40; in recent policy 47; social construction of 43–44; and social democracy 42; social democratic ideology 41; and social exclusion 45–46; as social problem 35–36, 45; social security 42; social structural explanations 40–41; solutions to tackle poverty 51–52; statistics 33, 37–38; stigma and shame of 51; third way ideology 45; traditional sociological theories 39–40; Trussell Trust emergency *51*; in UK 34, 35; and underclass 44; universal basic income scheme 52; welfare state 41–42; work and worklessness 49–50
Poverty and Social Exclusion (PSE) Survey 39
poverty line 35, 36, 38, 53
poverty porn 47
the precariat 49
prejudice 138, 255, 257–258, 263

prevention: and social policy 159; suicide 225–226; youth offending 158–159
principle of less eligibility 49
private rented 248, 250
Process of Change Theories (PCT) 207
protected characteristics 255, 257, 260, 262, 264, 267, 269–271
protective factors 11, 65, 133–136, 151, 153, 157, 221
psychological perspectives on alcohol consumption: Addictive Personality theory 176; behavioural models 177; choice theory 176; disease model 176; expectancy theory 176–177; social learning theory 177
psychology 18, 20–22, 207
Public Health England (PHE) 114
Public Health Scotland (PHS) 103
public issue 15

racism 9, 26, 41, 86, 89, 155, 256, 257, 258, 260, 262, 263
reasonable adjustment 259, 268
redistribution of wealth 42
Regulation 40B of the Defence of the Realm Act 1914 (DORA) 210
relapse 170
relationship: between abuser and abused 83; between biology and human society 19; familial 108, 110; heterosexual and same-sex 90–91, 264–265; marital 67, 101–102, 106, 111; parent–child relationships 61–62, 69, 71; violent 89–90, 95, 239
relative poverty 36, 38, 89
religion and alcohol 173–174
Restorative Justice 157
Right to Buy housing policy 243
risk factors: child abuse 134–136; family 135; juvenile deviance 152–153; psychological 152–153; social 152
Risk, Need, Responsivity (RNR) model 154
risky behaviour 21, 64, 239
Rivett, M. 60
Rollnik, S. 247
rough sleeping 38, 237, 238, 242, 243, 246, 250
Rowntree, Seebohm 35, 36

safeguarding 11, 113, 123–141
Sargeant, Christopher C. 241
Savage, M. 60
Scharp, K. M. 61, 62; distancing theory 62
Scheiwe, K. 64
Seidman, S. 23

Seifman R. 60
self-harm, defined 222–223
sexism 41, 258, 262
sexual abuse 127–128
sexual behaviour 68, 106, 107, 112
Shildrick, T. 48
Skog, O. J. R. 176
slave trade, abolition of 7
social change 4, 6–9, 82, 91
social constructionism 3, 43
social construction theory 177
Social Democratic Consensus 42, 43
social ecological 82, 86, 90
social exclusion: cause and consequence of 104; and poverty 45–46; for teenage mothers 107–108, 112
Social Exclusion Unit (SEU) 243; teenage pregnancy 112–114
social housing 111, 236, 238, 240, 243
social inequalities 266
social investment state 45
socialisation 22, 41, 63, 89, 157
social issues 1, 9, 33, 34, 108, 111, 115, 155–156, 172, 205, 243, 264–265
social justice 5, 41, 43, 45, 48, 66, 75, 89, 91
social learning theory 61–63, 71, 177
social model of disability 261
social movements 6–9
social network theory 178
social policy 4–5, 115
social problems 16; amelioration 26–27; biology and behaviour 19–20; causation 17–18; censoriousness 25; culture 23; development of 3–4; emergence of Welfare State 4–5; external factors 23; features associated with 1–3; framing of 18; geopolitical environment 24; and globalisation 5–6; knowledge and understanding 27–28; moral philosophy 25; moral sensibilities 26; and political forces 7–9; psychological factors 20–22; the Self, and Agency 18–19; social scientific study of 15–17; socio-economics 24; use of time and space 25; values 26
social reforms 75
social security 5, 42
socio economics 24
sociological perspectives on alcohol consumption: bio-psychosocial model 178; cultural identity theory 178; family systems theory 178; integrated perspective 178–179; social construction theory 177; social network theory 178; structural-functional paradigm 178

sociology 1, 9, 23, 39, 168
Somerville, P. 240, 247, 249
South, S.J. 72
Spector, M. 3
spousal veto 269
stereotyping 111, 234, 257, 260
stigma 34, 50–51, 61, 110, 111, 187, 222, 224, 266–267
stimulants 197, 198
structural-functional paradigm 178
structure: family 58, 59, 63, 66, 68, 69; social 90, 111
submerged social stratum 44
substance misuse 2, 9, 11–12, 20, 22, 68; and discrimination 266–267; and mental health issues 203–204
Suffragettes 7
suicide: assessment 224–225; conceptualising suicide 217, 219, 228 definition 222; Durkheim's contribution 218–219; in England and Wales 220–221; Euthanasia debate 226–227; explanatory models of suicidal behaviour 217–218; legislation 226; locality and area of residence 224; media portrayal 224; Northern Ireland Statistics and Research Agency report 221; prevention strategies 225–226; psychosocial perspective 223–224; rates, gender, and age 221; for Scotland 221; and self-harm 219–220; statistics in context 220; suicide act 226

teenage mothers: social exclusion for 107–108, 112; supporting 114–115
teenage pregnancy: adverse health outcomes 109; causes of 104–105; consequences of 107–108; defined 101; education and socioeconomic impact 109–110; and ethnicity 106; a global problem 102–106; issue of 114, *114*; knob-stick marriage/shotgun wedding 101; misconceptions and stigma 110–111; Northern Ireland Statistics and Research Agency 103; policies and strategies of intervention 112; *Pregnancy and Parenthood in Young People Strategy 2016-2026* 115; Public Health Scotland 103; rates of 103, *103*; and sexual abuse 106–107; and sexual misuse 107; social and sexual changes 101–102; and social deprivation 105–106; Social Exclusion Unit (1999) 112–114; social problem or public health issue 111–112; teenage abortions 108; teenage mothers and young fathers 114–115; *Teenage Pregnancy Prevention Framework* 115; in UK 102, 104; Women's Liberation Movement 102
temporary accommodation 235–238, 241, 248
Tiebout, H. 176
time 25, 268–269
Todd, J.E. 174
tolerance 170, 173, 176, 185
Tomlinson, M. 180
Townsend, P. 36
Toynbee, P. 51
troubled families programme (TFP) 75
Tsai, J. 236
Tunstall, R. 250
Turner, A.W. 265

unconscious bias 257
UN Declaration 88
underclass 44, 45, 47
universal basic income (UBI) scheme 10, 52
universal credit 49
universality, of social problems 5
unplanned pregnancy 121

values 20, 22, 23, 25–26, 43, 65, 95, 125, 130, 218, 271
victimisation 107, 151, 153, 257, 269
victims: of domestic abuse 82, 85–87, 264; and perpetrator 83–84, 90, 149, 156, 184
violence: cycles of 90, 92; domestic (*see* domestic violence (DV)); gender-based (*see* gender-based violence (GBV)); intimate partner (*see* intimate partner violence (IPV))
violence against women 93
Violence Against Women and Girls Strategy 84

Walker, R. 51
Weber, Max 39, 40
welfare 5, 11, 24, 48, 72, 110
welfare benefits 3, 42, 43, 45–47, 49, 50, 69, 70, 83, 111, 239, 244
welfare state 4, 41–43, 45, 50
Welshman, J. 44
wicked problem 130
Wikstrom, P.-O. 17
Wiles, P. 24, 25
Wilkinson, R. 24, 178
Wilson, S. 52
withdrawal 7, 8, 170, 175–177, 204
Womens Aid 85, 86, 94, 265
work and worklessness 49–50
Wurmser, Leon 176

young offenders 147; statistics 148
Young, S. 147
Youth Justice Board (YJB) report 148
youth offending (YO): age of criminal responsibility 148; behaviour programmes and strategies 158–159; child first principle 158; co-offending 150; county lines and child criminal exploitation 150; current policy and responses 156–157; defined 147–148; economic costs of crime 149–150; gang membership 151–152; MACR 147–148; to mental disorders and substance use 156; prevention and reduction 158–159; and racialised identity 155; and social deprivation 155–156; social policy and prevention 159; UNICEF recommendations 148; violent crimes 149; Youth Justice Statistics 148–149
Youth Offending Services 157, 158
youth offending teams (YOTs) 158–159

Zaretzky, Kaylene 246

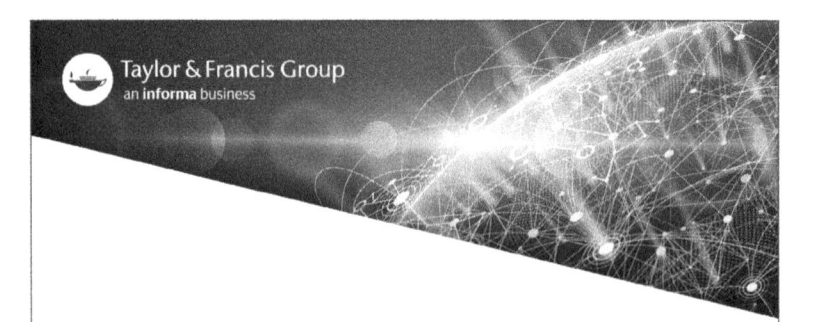

Taylor & Francis eBooks

www.taylorfrancis.com

A single destination for eBooks from Taylor & Francis with increased functionality and an improved user experience to meet the needs of our customers.

90,000+ eBooks of award-winning academic content in Humanities, Social Science, Science, Technology, Engineering, and Medical written by a global network of editors and authors.

TAYLOR & FRANCIS EBOOKS OFFERS:

- A streamlined experience for our library customers
- A single point of discovery for all of our eBook content
- Improved search and discovery of content at both book and chapter level

REQUEST A FREE TRIAL
support@taylorfrancis.com

Routledge
Taylor & Francis Group

CRC Press
Taylor & Francis Group

Milton Keynes UK
Ingram Content Group UK Ltd.
UKHW032250211223
434815UK00010B/108